FREE Study Skills Videos/DVD Offer

Dear Customer,

Thank you for your purchase from Mometrix! We consider it an honor and a privilege that you have purchased our product and we want to ensure your satisfaction.

As part of our ongoing effort to meet the needs of test takers, we have developed a set of Study Skills Videos that we would like to give you for <u>FREE</u>. These videos cover our *best practices* for getting ready for your exam, from how to use our study materials to how to best prepare for the day of the test.

All that we ask is that you email us with feedback that would describe your experience so far with our product. Good, bad, or indifferent, we want to know what you think!

To get your FREE Study Skills Videos, you can use the **QR code** below, or send us an **email** at studyvideos@mometrix.com with *FREE VIDEOS* in the subject line and the following information in the body of the email:

- The name of the product you purchased.
- Your product rating on a scale of 1-5, with 5 being the highest rating.
- Your feedback. It can be long, short, or anything in between. We just want to know your impressions and experience so far with our product. (Good feedback might include how our study material met your needs and ways we might be able to make it even better. You could highlight features that you found helpful or features that you think we should add.)

If you have any questions or concerns, please don't hesitate to contact me directly.

Thanks again!

Sincerely,

Jay Willis
Vice President
jay.willis@mometrix.com
1-800-673-8175

CSP

Comprehensive Practice Exam Secrets Study Guide

CSP Test Review for the
Certified Safety Professional Exam

Copyright © 2024 by Mometrix Media LLC

All rights reserved. This product, or parts thereof, may not be reproduced, stored in a retrieval system, or transmitted in any form or by any means—electronic, mechanical, photocopy, recording, scanning, or other—except for brief quotations in critical reviews or articles, without the prior written permission of the publisher.

Written and edited by Mometrix Test Prep

Printed in the United States of America

This paper meets the requirements of ANSI/NISO Z39.48-1992 (Permanence of Paper).

Mometrix offers volume discount pricing to institutions. For more information or a price quote, please contact our sales department at sales@mometrix.com or 888-248-1219.

Mometrix Media LLC is not affiliated with or endorsed by any official testing organization. All organizational and test names are trademarks of their respective owners.

Paperback
ISBN 13: 978-1-60971-581-6
ISBN 10: 1-6097-1581-0

DEAR FUTURE EXAM SUCCESS STORY

First of all, **THANK YOU** for purchasing Mometrix study materials!

Second, congratulations! You are one of the few determined test-takers who are committed to doing whatever it takes to excel on your exam. **You have come to the right place.** We developed these study materials with one goal in mind: to deliver you the information you need in a format that's concise and easy to use.

In addition to optimizing your guide for the content of the test, we've outlined our recommended steps for breaking down the preparation process into small, attainable goals so you can make sure you stay on track.

We've also analyzed the entire test-taking process, identifying the most common pitfalls and showing how you can overcome them and be ready for any curveball the test throws you.

Standardized testing is one of the biggest obstacles on your road to success, which only increases the importance of doing well in the high-pressure, high-stakes environment of test day. Your results on this test could have a significant impact on your future, and this guide provides the information and practical advice to help you achieve your full potential on test day.

Your success is our success

We would love to hear from you! If you would like to share the story of your exam success or if you have any questions or comments in regard to our products, please contact us at **800-673-8175** or **support@mometrix.com**.

Thanks again for your business and we wish you continued success!

Sincerely,
The Mometrix Test Preparation Team

Need more help? Check out our flashcards at:
http://mometrixflashcards.com/CSP

TABLE OF CONTENTS

INTRODUCTION _____ 1

SECRET KEY #1 – PLAN BIG, STUDY SMALL _____ 2

SECRET KEY #2 – MAKE YOUR STUDYING COUNT _____ 3

SECRET KEY #3 – PRACTICE THE RIGHT WAY _____ 4

SECRET KEY #4 – PACE YOURSELF _____ 6

SECRET KEY #5 – HAVE A PLAN FOR GUESSING _____ 7

TEST-TAKING STRATEGIES _____ 10

SIX-WEEK CSP STUDY PLAN _____ 14
  WEEK 1: ADVANCED SCIENCES AND MATH _____ 14
  WEEK 2: MANAGEMENT SYSTEMS & RISK MANAGEMENT _____ 15
  WEEK 3: ADVANCED APPLICATION OF KEY SAFETY CONCEPTS & EMERGENCY PREPAREDNESS, FIRE
  PREVENTION, AND SECURITY _____ 16
  WEEK 4: OCCUPATIONAL HEALTH AND ERGONOMICS & ENVIRONMENTAL MANAGEMENT SYSTEMS 17
  WEEK 5: TRAINING AND EDUCATION & LAW AND ETHICS _____ 18
  WEEK 6: PRACTICE TESTS _____ 19

ADVANCED SCIENCES AND MATH _____ 20
  ANATOMY AND PHYSIOLOGY _____ 20
  CHEMISTRY _____ 29
  PHYSICS _____ 46
  MATHEMATICS _____ 51
  STATISTICS FOR INTERPRETING DATA _____ 112
  RESEARCH METHODOLOGY _____ 118
  MICROBIOLOGY _____ 120
  CHAPTER QUIZ _____ 121

MANAGEMENT SYSTEMS _____ 122
  BENCHMARKS AND PERFORMANCE STANDARDS _____ 122
  ORGANIZATIONAL CULTURE _____ 123
  INCIDENT INVESTIGATION _____ 124
  MANAGEMENT OF CHANGE _____ 125
  SYSTEM SAFETY ANALYSIS _____ 125
  BUSINESS CONTINUITY AND CONTINGENCY PLANS _____ 126
  LEADING AND LAGGING SAFETY, HEALTH, ENVIRONMENTAL, AND SECURITY PERFORMANCE INDICATORS
  _____ 127
  SAFETY, HEALTH, AND ENVIRONMENTAL MANAGEMENT AND AUDIT SYSTEMS _____ 128
  APPLICABLE REQUIREMENTS FOR PLANS, SYSTEMS, AND POLICIES _____ 130
  DOCUMENT RETENTION _____ 131
  MANAGEMENT LEADERSHIP _____ 132
  PROJECT MANAGEMENT _____ 137
  CHAPTER QUIZ _____ 139

RISK MANAGEMENT _____ 140

HAZARD IDENTIFICATION AND ANALYSIS METHODS _____ 140

RISK ANALYSIS _____ 142

RISK EVALUATION _____ 143

THE RISK MANAGEMENT PROCESS _____ 144

THE COSTS AND BENEFITS OF RISK ASSESSMENT PROCESS _____ 145

INSURANCE AND RISK TRANSFER PRINCIPLES _____ 146

CHAPTER QUIZ _____ 147

ADVANCED APPLICATION OF KEY SAFETY CONCEPTS _____ 148

SAFETY THROUGH DESIGN _____ 148

ENGINEERING CONTROLS _____ 149

ADMINISTRATIVE CONTROLS _____ 150

PERSONAL PROTECTIVE EQUIPMENT _____ 151

CHEMICAL PROCESS SAFETY MANAGEMENT _____ 152

REDUNDANCY SYSTEMS _____ 153

COMMON WORKPLACE HAZARDS _____ 154

FACILITY LIFE SAFETY FEATURES _____ 163

FLEET SAFETY _____ 163

TRANSPORTATION SAFETY _____ 165

MATERIALS HANDLING _____ 166

FOREIGN MATERIAL EXCLUSION (FME) AND FOREIGN OBJECT DAMAGE (FOD) _____ 172

HAZARDOUS MATERIALS MANAGEMENT _____ 172

MULTI-EMPLOYER WORKSITE ISSUES _____ 178

SOURCES OF INFORMATION ON HAZARD AND RISK MANAGEMENT OPTIONS _____ 180

SAFETY DESIGN CRITERIA FOR WORKPLACE FACILITIES, MACHINES, AND PRACTICES _____ 180

TOOLS, MACHINES, PRACTICES, AND EQUIPMENT SAFETY _____ 181

WORKPLACE HAZARDS _____ 184

HUMAN PERFORMANCE _____ 186

CHAPTER QUIZ _____ 187

EMERGENCY PREPAREDNESS, FIRE PREVENTION, AND SECURITY _____ 188

EMERGENCY RESPONSE PLANNING AND BUSINESS CONTINUITY _____ 188

FIRE PREVENTION, PROTECTION, AND SUPPRESSION SYSTEMS _____ 195

TRANSPORTATION AND SECURITY OF HAZARDOUS MATERIALS _____ 203

WORKPLACE VIOLENCE AND PREVENTION _____ 205

CHAPTER QUIZ _____ 205

OCCUPATIONAL HEALTH AND ERGONOMICS _____ 206

TOXICOLOGY _____ 206

CARCINOGENS _____ 207

ERGONOMICS AND HUMAN FACTORS _____ 208

RECOGNIZING, EVALUATING, AND CONTROLLING OCCUPATIONAL EXPOSURES _____ 210

EMPLOYEE SUBSTANCE ABUSE _____ 211

EPIDEMIOLOGY _____ 212

OCCUPATIONAL EXPOSURE LIMITS _____ 212

CHAPTER QUIZ _____ 214

ENVIRONMENTAL MANAGEMENT SYSTEMS _____ 215

ENVIRONMENTAL PROTECTION AND POLLUTION PREVENTION _____ 215

HAZARDOUS MATERIAL MIGRATION _____ 216

SUSTAINABILITY _____ 216

WASTE WATER TREATMENT _____ 217
CHAPTER QUIZ _____ 218

TRAINING AND EDUCATION _____ 219
TRAINING, QUALIFICATION, AND COMPETENCY REQUIREMENTS _____ 220
DETERMINING THE EFFECTIVENESS OF TRAINING PROGRAMS _____ 222
EFFECTIVE PRESENTATION TECHNIQUES _____ 222
CHAPTER QUIZ _____ 225

LAW AND ETHICS _____ 226
LEGAL ISSUES _____ 226
PROTECTION OF CONFIDENTIAL INFORMATION _____ 227
STANDARDS DEVELOPMENT PROCESSES _____ 228
ETHICAL PROFESSIONAL PRACTICE _____ 228
RELATIONSHIP BETWEEN LABOR AND MANAGEMENT _____ 229
BCSP CODE OF ETHICS _____ 230
WORKERS' COMPENSATION _____ 231
CHAPTER QUIZ _____ 232

CSP PRACTICE TEST #1 _____ 233

ANSWER KEY AND EXPLANATIONS FOR TEST #1 _____ 269

CSP PRACTICE TEST #2 _____ 298

HOW TO OVERCOME TEST ANXIETY _____ 299

ADDITIONAL BONUS MATERIAL _____ 305

Introduction

Thank you for purchasing this resource! You have made the choice to prepare yourself for a test that could have a huge impact on your future, and this guide is designed to help you be fully ready for test day. Obviously, it's important to have a solid understanding of the test material, but you also need to be prepared for the unique environment and stressors of the test, so that you can perform to the best of your abilities.

For this purpose, the first section that appears in this guide is the **Secret Keys**. We've devoted countless hours to meticulously researching what works and what doesn't, and we've boiled down our findings to the five most impactful steps you can take to improve your performance on the test. We start at the beginning with study planning and move through the preparation process, all the way to the testing strategies that will help you get the most out of what you know when you're finally sitting in front of the test.

We recommend that you start preparing for your test as far in advance as possible. However, if you've bought this guide as a last-minute study resource and only have a few days before your test, we recommend that you skip over the first two Secret Keys since they address a long-term study plan.

If you struggle with **test anxiety**, we strongly encourage you to check out our recommendations for how you can overcome it. Test anxiety is a formidable foe, but it can be beaten, and we want to make sure you have the tools you need to defeat it.

Copyright © Mometrix Media. You have been licensed one copy of this document for personal use only. Any other reproduction or redistribution is strictly prohibited. All rights reserved. This content is provided for test preparation purposes only and does not imply an endorsement by Mometrix of any particular political, scientific, or religious point of view.

Secret Key #1 – Plan Big, Study Small

There's a lot riding on your performance. If you want to ace this test, you're going to need to keep your skills sharp and the material fresh in your mind. You need a plan that lets you review everything you need to know while still fitting in your schedule. We'll break this strategy down into three categories.

Information Organization

Start with the information you already have: the official test outline. From this, you can make a complete list of all the concepts you need to cover before the test. Organize these concepts into groups that can be studied together, and create a list of any related vocabulary you need to learn so you can brush up on any difficult terms. You'll want to keep this vocabulary list handy once you actually start studying since you may need to add to it along the way.

Time Management

Once you have your set of study concepts, decide how to spread them out over the time you have left before the test. Break your study plan into small, clear goals so you have a manageable task for each day and know exactly what you're doing. Then just focus on one small step at a time. When you manage your time this way, you don't need to spend hours at a time studying. Studying a small block of content for a short period each day helps you retain information better and avoid stressing over how much you have left to do. You can relax knowing that you have a plan to cover everything in time. In order for this strategy to be effective though, you have to start studying early and stick to your schedule. Avoid the exhaustion and futility that comes from last-minute cramming!

Study Environment

The environment you study in has a big impact on your learning. Studying in a coffee shop, while probably more enjoyable, is not likely to be as fruitful as studying in a quiet room. It's important to keep distractions to a minimum. You're only planning to study for a short block of time, so make the most of it. Don't pause to check your phone or get up to find a snack. It's also important to **avoid multitasking**. Research has consistently shown that multitasking will make your studying dramatically less effective. Your study area should also be comfortable and well-lit so you don't have the distraction of straining your eyes or sitting on an uncomfortable chair.

 The time of day you study is also important. You want to be rested and alert. Don't wait until just before bedtime. Study when you'll be most likely to comprehend and remember. Even better, if you know what time of day your test will be, set that time aside for study. That way your brain will be used to working on that subject at that specific time and you'll have a better chance of recalling information.

Finally, it can be helpful to team up with others who are studying for the same test. Your actual studying should be done in as isolated an environment as possible, but the work of organizing the information and setting up the study plan can be divided up. In between study sessions, you can discuss with your teammates the concepts that you're all studying and quiz each other on the details. Just be sure that your teammates are as serious about the test as you are. If you find that your study time is being replaced with social time, you might need to find a new team.

Copyright © Mometrix Media. You have been licensed one copy of this document for personal use only. Any other reproduction or redistribution is strictly prohibited. All rights reserved. This content is provided for test preparation purposes only and does not imply an endorsement by Mometrix of any particular political, scientific, or religious point of view.

Secret Key #2 – Make Your Studying Count

You're devoting a lot of time and effort to preparing for this test, so you want to be absolutely certain it will pay off. This means doing more than just reading the content and hoping you can remember it on test day. It's important to make every minute of study count. There are two main areas you can focus on to make your studying count.

Retention

It doesn't matter how much time you study if you can't remember the material. You need to make sure you are retaining the concepts. To check your retention of the information you're learning, try recalling it at later times with minimal prompting. Try carrying around flashcards and glance at one or two from time to time or ask a friend who's also studying for the test to quiz you.

To enhance your retention, look for ways to put the information into practice so that you can apply it rather than simply recalling it. If you're using the information in practical ways, it will be much easier to remember. Similarly, it helps to solidify a concept in your mind if you're not only reading it to yourself but also explaining it to someone else. Ask a friend to let you teach them about a concept you're a little shaky on (or speak aloud to an imaginary audience if necessary). As you try to summarize, define, give examples, and answer your friend's questions, you'll understand the concepts better and they will stay with you longer. Finally, step back for a big picture view and ask yourself how each piece of information fits with the whole subject. When you link the different concepts together and see them working together as a whole, it's easier to remember the individual components.

Finally, practice showing your work on any multi-step problems, even if you're just studying. Writing out each step you take to solve a problem will help solidify the process in your mind, and you'll be more likely to remember it during the test.

Modality

Modality simply refers to the means or method by which you study. Choosing a study modality that fits your own individual learning style is crucial. No two people learn best in exactly the same way, so it's important to know your strengths and use them to your advantage.

For example, if you learn best by visualization, focus on visualizing a concept in your mind and draw an image or a diagram. Try color-coding your notes, illustrating them, or creating symbols that will trigger your mind to recall a learned concept. If you learn best by hearing or discussing information, find a study partner who learns the same way or read aloud to yourself. Think about how to put the information in your own words. Imagine that you are giving a lecture on the topic and record yourself so you can listen to it later.

For any learning style, flashcards can be helpful. Organize the information so you can take advantage of spare moments to review. Underline key words or phrases. Use different colors for different categories. Mnemonic devices (such as creating a short list in which every item starts with the same letter) can also help with retention. Find what works best for you and use it to store the information in your mind most effectively and easily.

3

Copyright © Mometrix Media. You have been licensed one copy of this document for personal use only. Any other reproduction or redistribution is strictly prohibited. All rights reserved. This content is provided for test preparation purposes only and does not imply an endorsement by Mometrix of any particular political, scientific, or religious point of view.

Secret Key #3 – Practice the Right Way

Your success on test day depends not only on how many hours you put into preparing, but also on whether you prepared the right way. It's good to check along the way to see if your studying is paying off. One of the most effective ways to do this is by taking practice tests to evaluate your progress. Practice tests are useful because they show exactly where you need to improve. Every time you take a practice test, pay special attention to these three groups of questions:

- The questions you got wrong
- The questions you had to guess on, even if you guessed right
- The questions you found difficult or slow to work through

This will show you exactly what your weak areas are, and where you need to devote more study time. Ask yourself why each of these questions gave you trouble. Was it because you didn't understand the material? Was it because you didn't remember the vocabulary? Do you need more repetitions on this type of question to build speed and confidence? Dig into those questions and figure out how you can strengthen your weak areas as you go back to review the material.

 Additionally, many practice tests have a section explaining the answer choices. It can be tempting to read the explanation and think that you now have a good understanding of the concept. However, an explanation likely only covers part of the question's broader context. Even if the explanation makes perfect sense, **go back and investigate** every concept related to the question until you're positive you have a thorough understanding.

As you go along, keep in mind that the practice test is just that: practice. Memorizing these questions and answers will not be very helpful on the actual test because it is unlikely to have any of the same exact questions. If you only know the right answers to the sample questions, you won't be prepared for the real thing. **Study the concepts** until you understand them fully, and then you'll be able to answer any question that shows up on the test.

It's important to wait on the practice tests until you're ready. If you take a test on your first day of study, you may be overwhelmed by the amount of material covered and how much you need to learn. Work up to it gradually.

On test day, you'll need to be prepared for answering questions, managing your time, and using the test-taking strategies you've learned. It's a lot to balance, like a mental marathon that will have a big impact on your future. Like training for a marathon, you'll need to start slowly and work your way up. When test day arrives, you'll be ready.

Start with the strategies you've read in the first two Secret Keys—plan your course and study in the way that works best for you. If you have time, consider using multiple study resources to get different approaches to the same concepts. It can be helpful to see difficult concepts from more than one angle. Then find a good source for practice tests. Many times, the test website will suggest potential study resources or provide sample tests.

Copyright © Mometrix Media. You have been licensed one copy of this document for personal use only. Any other reproduction or redistribution is strictly prohibited. All rights reserved.
This content is provided for test preparation purposes only and does not imply an endorsement by Mometrix of any particular political, scientific, or religious point of view.

Practice Test Strategy

If you're able to find at least three practice tests, we recommend this strategy:

Untimed and Open-Book Practice

Take the first test with no time constraints and with your notes and study guide handy. Take your time and focus on applying the strategies you've learned.

Timed and Open-Book Practice

Take the second practice test open-book as well, but set a timer and practice pacing yourself to finish in time.

Timed and Closed-Book Practice

Take any other practice tests as if it were test day. Set a timer and put away your study materials. Sit at a table or desk in a quiet room, imagine yourself at the testing center, and answer questions as quickly and accurately as possible.

Keep repeating timed and closed-book tests on a regular basis until you run out of practice tests or it's time for the actual test. Your mind will be ready for the schedule and stress of test day, and you'll be able to focus on recalling the material you've learned.

Copyright © Mometrix Media. You have been licensed one copy of this document for personal use only. Any other reproduction or redistribution is strictly prohibited. All rights reserved.
This content is provided for test preparation purposes only and does not imply an endorsement by Mometrix of any particular political, scientific, or religious point of view.

Secret Key #4 – Pace Yourself

Once you're fully prepared for the material on the test, your biggest challenge on test day will be managing your time. Just knowing that the clock is ticking can make you panic even if you have plenty of time left. Work on pacing yourself so you can build confidence against the time constraints of the exam. Pacing is a difficult skill to master, especially in a high-pressure environment, so **practice is vital**.

Set time expectations for your pace based on how much time is available. For example, if a section has 60 questions and the time limit is 30 minutes, you know you have to average 30 seconds or less per question in order to answer them all. Although 30 seconds is the hard limit, set 25 seconds per question as your goal, so you reserve extra time to spend on harder questions. When you budget extra time for the harder questions, you no longer have any reason to stress when those questions take longer to answer.

Don't let this time expectation distract you from working through the test at a calm, steady pace, but keep it in mind so you don't spend too much time on any one question. Recognize that taking extra time on one question you don't understand may keep you from answering two that you do understand later in the test. If your time limit for a question is up and you're still not sure of the answer, mark it and move on, and come back to it later if the time and the test format allow. If the testing format doesn't allow you to return to earlier questions, just make an educated guess; then put it out of your mind and move on.

On the easier questions, be careful not to rush. It may seem wise to hurry through them so you have more time for the challenging ones, but it's not worth missing one if you know the concept and just didn't take the time to read the question fully. Work efficiently but make sure you understand the question and have looked at all of the answer choices, since more than one may seem right at first.

Even if you're paying attention to the time, you may find yourself a little behind at some point. You should speed up to get back on track, but do so wisely. Don't panic; just take a few seconds less on each question until you're caught up. Don't guess without thinking, but do look through the answer choices and eliminate any you know are wrong. If you can get down to two choices, it is often worthwhile to guess from those. Once you've chosen an answer, move on and don't dwell on any that you skipped or had to hurry through. If a question was taking too long, chances are it was one of the harder ones, so you weren't as likely to get it right anyway.

On the other hand, if you find yourself getting ahead of schedule, it may be beneficial to slow down a little. The more quickly you work, the more likely you are to make a careless mistake that will affect your score. You've budgeted time for each question, so don't be afraid to spend that time. Practice an efficient but careful pace to get the most out of the time you have.

Copyright © Mometrix Media. You have been licensed one copy of this document for personal use only. Any other reproduction or redistribution is strictly prohibited. All rights reserved.
This content is provided for test preparation purposes only and does not imply an endorsement by Mometrix of any particular political, scientific, or religious point of view.

Secret Key #5 – Have a Plan for Guessing

When you're taking the test, you may find yourself stuck on a question. Some of the answer choices seem better than others, but you don't see the one answer choice that is obviously correct. What do you do?

The scenario described above is very common, yet most test takers have not effectively prepared for it. Developing and practicing a plan for guessing may be one of the single most effective uses of your time as you get ready for the exam.

In developing your plan for guessing, there are three questions to address:

- When should you start the guessing process?
- How should you narrow down the choices?
- Which answer should you choose?

When to Start the Guessing Process

Unless your plan for guessing is to select C every time (which, despite its merits, is not what we recommend), you need to leave yourself enough time to apply your answer elimination strategies. Since you have a limited amount of time for each question, that means that if you're going to give yourself the best shot at guessing correctly, you have to decide quickly whether or not you will guess.

Of course, the best-case scenario is that you don't have to guess at all, so first, see if you can answer the question based on your knowledge of the subject and basic reasoning skills. Focus on the key words in the question and try to jog your memory of related topics. Give yourself a chance to bring the knowledge to mind, but once you realize that you don't have (or you can't access) the knowledge you need to answer the question, it's time to start the guessing process.

It's almost always better to start the guessing process too early than too late. It only takes a few seconds to remember something and answer the question from knowledge. Carefully eliminating wrong answer choices takes longer. Plus, going through the process of eliminating answer choices can actually help jog your memory.

Summary: Start the guessing process as soon as you decide that you can't answer the question based on your knowledge.

Copyright © Mometrix Media. You have been licensed one copy of this document for personal use only. Any other reproduction or redistribution is strictly prohibited. All rights reserved.
This content is provided for test preparation purposes only and does not imply an endorsement by Mometrix of any particular political, scientific, or religious point of view.

How to Narrow Down the Choices

The next chapter in this book (**Test-Taking Strategies**) includes a wide range of strategies for how to approach questions and how to look for answer choices to eliminate. You will definitely want to read those carefully, practice them, and figure out which ones work best for you. Here though, we're going to address a mindset rather than a particular strategy.

Your odds of guessing an answer correctly depend on how many options you are choosing from.

Number of options left	5	4	3	2	1
Odds of guessing correctly	20%	25%	33%	50%	100%

You can see from this chart just how valuable it is to be able to eliminate incorrect answers and make an educated guess, but there are two things that many test takers do that cause them to miss out on the benefits of guessing:

- Accidentally eliminating the correct answer
- Selecting an answer based on an impression

We'll look at the first one here, and the second one in the next section.

To avoid accidentally eliminating the correct answer, we recommend a thought exercise called **the $5 challenge**. In this challenge, you only eliminate an answer choice from contention if you are willing to bet $5 on it being wrong. Why $5? Five dollars is a small but not insignificant amount of money. It's an amount you could afford to lose but wouldn't want to throw away. And while losing $5 once might not hurt too much, doing it twenty times will set you back $100. In the same way, each small decision you make—eliminating a choice here, guessing on a question there—won't by itself impact your score very much, but when you put them all together, they can make a big difference. By holding each answer choice elimination decision to a higher standard, you can reduce the risk of accidentally eliminating the correct answer.

The $5 challenge can also be applied in a positive sense: If you are willing to bet $5 that an answer choice *is* correct, go ahead and mark it as correct.

Summary: Only eliminate an answer choice if you are willing to bet $5 that it is wrong.

Copyright © Mometrix Media. You have been licensed one copy of this document for personal use only. Any other reproduction or redistribution is strictly prohibited. All rights reserved.
This content is provided for test preparation purposes only and does not imply an endorsement by Mometrix of any particular political, scientific, or religious point of view.

Which Answer to Choose

You're taking the test. You've run into a hard question and decided you'll have to guess. You've eliminated all the answer choices you're willing to bet $5 on. Now you have to pick an answer. Why do we even need to talk about this? Why can't you just pick whichever one you feel like when the time comes?

The answer to these questions is that if you don't come into the test with a plan, you'll rely on your impression to select an answer choice, and if you do that, you risk falling into a trap. The test writers know that everyone who takes their test will be guessing on some of the questions, so they intentionally write wrong answer choices to seem plausible. You still have to pick an answer though, and if the wrong answer choices are designed to look right, how can you ever be sure that you're not falling for their trap? The best solution we've found to this dilemma is to take the decision out of your hands entirely. Here is the process we recommend:

Once you've eliminated any choices that you are confident (willing to bet $5) are wrong, select the first remaining choice as your answer.

Whether you choose to select the first remaining choice, the second, or the last, the important thing is that you use some preselected standard. Using this approach guarantees that you will not be enticed into selecting an answer choice that looks right, because you are not basing your decision on how the answer choices look.

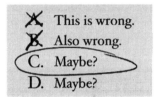

This is not meant to make you question your knowledge. Instead, it is to help you recognize the difference between your knowledge and your impressions. There's a huge difference between thinking an answer is right because of what you know, and thinking an answer is right because it looks or sounds like it should be right.

Summary: To ensure that your selection is appropriately random, make a predetermined selection from among all answer choices you have not eliminated.

Copyright © Mometrix Media. You have been licensed one copy of this document for personal use only. Any other reproduction or redistribution is strictly prohibited. All rights reserved.
This content is provided for test preparation purposes only and does not imply an endorsement by Mometrix of any particular political, scientific, or religious point of view.

Test-Taking Strategies

This section contains a list of test-taking strategies that you may find helpful as you work through the test. By taking what you know and applying logical thought, you can maximize your chances of answering any question correctly!

It is very important to realize that every question is different and every person is different: no single strategy will work on every question, and no single strategy will work for every person. That's why we've included all of them here, so you can try them out and determine which ones work best for different types of questions and which ones work best for you.

Question Strategies

☑ READ CAREFULLY

Read the question and the answer choices carefully. Don't miss the question because you misread the terms. You have plenty of time to read each question thoroughly and make sure you understand what is being asked. Yet a happy medium must be attained, so don't waste too much time. You must read carefully and efficiently.

☑ CONTEXTUAL CLUES

Look for contextual clues. If the question includes a word you are not familiar with, look at the immediate context for some indication of what the word might mean. Contextual clues can often give you all the information you need to decipher the meaning of an unfamiliar word. Even if you can't determine the meaning, you may be able to narrow down the possibilities enough to make a solid guess at the answer to the question.

☑ PREFIXES

If you're having trouble with a word in the question or answer choices, try dissecting it. Take advantage of every clue that the word might include. Prefixes can be a huge help. Usually, they allow you to determine a basic meaning. *Pre-* means before, *post-* means after, *pro-* is positive, *de-* is negative. From prefixes, you can get an idea of the general meaning of the word and try to put it into context.

☑ HEDGE WORDS

Watch out for critical hedge words, such as *likely, may, can, sometimes, often, almost, mostly, usually, generally, rarely,* and *sometimes.* Question writers insert these hedge phrases to cover every possibility. Often an answer choice will be wrong simply because it leaves no room for exception. Be on guard for answer choices that have definitive words such as *exactly* and *always.*

☑ SWITCHBACK WORDS

Stay alert for *switchbacks.* These are the words and phrases frequently used to alert you to shifts in thought. The most common switchback words are *but, although,* and *however.* Others include *nevertheless, on the other hand, even though, while, in spite of, despite,* and *regardless of.* Switchback words are important to catch because they can change the direction of the question or an answer choice.

☑ FACE VALUE

When in doubt, use common sense. Accept the situation in the problem at face value. Don't read too much into it. These problems will not require you to make wild assumptions. If you have to go beyond creativity and warp time or space in order to have an answer choice fit the question, then you should move on and consider the other answer choices. These are normal problems rooted in reality. The applicable relationship or explanation may not be readily apparent, but it is there for you to figure out. Use your common sense to interpret anything that isn't clear.

Copyright © Mometrix Media. You have been licensed one copy of this document for personal use only. Any other reproduction or redistribution is strictly prohibited. All rights reserved.
This content is provided for test preparation purposes only and does not imply an endorsement by Mometrix of any particular political, scientific, or religious point of view.

Answer Choice Strategies

⊘ Answer Selection

The most thorough way to pick an answer choice is to identify and eliminate wrong answers until only one is left, then confirm it is the correct answer. Sometimes an answer choice may immediately seem right, but be careful. The test writers will usually put more than one reasonable answer choice on each question, so take a second to read all of them and make sure that the other choices are not equally obvious. As long as you have time left, it is better to read every answer choice than to pick the first one that looks right without checking the others.

⊘ Answer Choice Families

An answer choice family consists of two (in rare cases, three) answer choices that are very similar in construction and cannot all be true at the same time. If you see two answer choices that are direct opposites or parallels, one of them is usually the correct answer. For instance, if one answer choice says that quantity x increases and another either says that quantity x decreases (opposite) or says that quantity y increases (parallel), then those answer choices would fall into the same family. An answer choice that doesn't match the construction of the answer choice family is more likely to be incorrect. Most questions will not have answer choice families, but when they do appear, you should be prepared to recognize them.

⊘ Eliminate Answers

Eliminate answer choices as soon as you realize they are wrong, but make sure you consider all possibilities. If you are eliminating answer choices and realize that the last one you are left with is also wrong, don't panic. Start over and consider each choice again. There may be something you missed the first time that you will realize on the second pass.

⊘ Avoid Fact Traps

Don't be distracted by an answer choice that is factually true but doesn't answer the question. You are looking for the choice that answers the question. Stay focused on what the question is asking for so you don't accidentally pick an answer that is true but incorrect. Always go back to the question and make sure the answer choice you've selected actually answers the question and is not merely a true statement.

⊘ Extreme Statements

In general, you should avoid answers that put forth extreme actions as standard practice or proclaim controversial ideas as established fact. An answer choice that states the "process should be used in certain situations, if..." is much more likely to be correct than one that states the "process should be discontinued completely." The first is a calm rational statement and doesn't even make a definitive, uncompromising stance, using a hedge word *if* to provide wiggle room, whereas the second choice is far more extreme.

⊘ Benchmark

As you read through the answer choices and you come across one that seems to answer the question well, mentally select that answer choice. This is not your final answer, but it's the one that will help you evaluate the other answer choices. The one that you selected is your benchmark or standard for judging each of the other answer choices. Every other answer choice must be compared to your benchmark. That choice is correct until proven otherwise by another answer choice beating it. If you find a better answer, then that one becomes your new benchmark. Once you've decided that no other choice answers the question as well as your benchmark, you have your final answer.

Copyright © Mometrix Media. You have been licensed one copy of this document for personal use only. Any other reproduction or redistribution is strictly prohibited. All rights reserved.
This content is provided for test preparation purposes only and does not imply an endorsement by Mometrix of any particular political, scientific, or religious point of view.

⏱ PREDICT THE ANSWER

Before you even start looking at the answer choices, it is often best to try to predict the answer. When you come up with the answer on your own, it is easier to avoid distractions and traps because you will know exactly what to look for. The right answer choice is unlikely to be word-for-word what you came up with, but it should be a close match. Even if you are confident that you have the right answer, you should still take the time to read each option before moving on.

General Strategies

⏱ TOUGH QUESTIONS

If you are stumped on a problem or it appears too hard or too difficult, don't waste time. Move on! Remember though, if you can quickly check for obviously incorrect answer choices, your chances of guessing correctly are greatly improved. Before you completely give up, at least try to knock out a couple of possible answers. Eliminate what you can and then guess at the remaining answer choices before moving on.

⏱ CHECK YOUR WORK

Since you will probably not know every term listed and the answer to every question, it is important that you get credit for the ones that you do know. Don't miss any questions through careless mistakes. If at all possible, try to take a second to look back over your answer selection and make sure you've selected the correct answer choice and haven't made a costly careless mistake (such as marking an answer choice that you didn't mean to mark). This quick double check should more than pay for itself in caught mistakes for the time it costs.

⏱ PACE YOURSELF

It's easy to be overwhelmed when you're looking at a page full of questions; your mind is confused and full of random thoughts, and the clock is ticking down faster than you would like. Calm down and maintain the pace that you have set for yourself. Especially as you get down to the last few minutes of the test, don't let the small numbers on the clock make you panic. As long as you are on track by monitoring your pace, you are guaranteed to have time for each question.

⏱ DON'T RUSH

It is very easy to make errors when you are in a hurry. Maintaining a fast pace in answering questions is pointless if it makes you miss questions that you would have gotten right otherwise. Test writers like to include distracting information and wrong answers that seem right. Taking a little extra time to avoid careless mistakes can make all the difference in your test score. Find a pace that allows you to be confident in the answers that you select.

⏱ KEEP MOVING

Panicking will not help you pass the test, so do your best to stay calm and keep moving. Taking deep breaths and going through the answer elimination steps you practiced can help to break through a stress barrier and keep your pace.

Copyright © Mometrix Media. You have been licensed one copy of this document for personal use only. Any other reproduction or redistribution is strictly prohibited. All rights reserved.
This content is provided for test preparation purposes only and does not imply an endorsement by Mometrix of any particular political, scientific, or religious point of view.

Final Notes

The combination of a solid foundation of content knowledge and the confidence that comes from practicing your plan for applying that knowledge is the key to maximizing your performance on test day. As your foundation of content knowledge is built up and strengthened, you'll find that the strategies included in this chapter become more and more effective in helping you quickly sift through the distractions and traps of the test to isolate the correct answer.

Now that you're preparing to move forward into the test content chapters of this book, be sure to keep your goal in mind. As you read, think about how you will be able to apply this information on the test. If you've already seen sample questions for the test and you have an idea of the question format and style, try to come up with questions of your own that you can answer based on what you're reading. This will give you valuable practice applying your knowledge in the same ways you can expect to on test day.

Good luck and good studying!

Copyright © Mometrix Media. You have been licensed one copy of this document for personal use only. Any other reproduction or redistribution is strictly prohibited. All rights reserved. This content is provided for test preparation purposes only and does not imply an endorsement by Mometrix of any particular political, scientific, or religious point of view.

Six-Week CSP Study Plan

On the next few pages, we've provided an optional study plan to help you use this study guide to its fullest potential over the course of six weeks. If you have twelve weeks available and want to spread it out more, spend two weeks on each section of the plan.

Below is a quick summary of the subjects covered in each week of the plan.

- Week 1: Advanced Sciences and Math
- Week 2: Management Systems & Risk Management
- Week 3: Advanced Application of Key Safety Concepts & Emergency Preparedness, Fire Prevention, and Security
- Week 4: Occupational Health and Ergonomics & Environmental Management Systems
- Week 5: Training and Education & Law and Ethics
- Week 6: Practice Tests

Please note that not all subjects will take the same amount of time to work through.

Two full-length practice tests are included in this study guide. We recommend saving any additional practice tests until after you've completed the study plan. Take these practice tests without any reference materials a day or two before the real thing as practice runs to get you in the mode of answering questions at a good pace.

Week 1: Advanced Sciences and Math

INSTRUCTIONAL CONTENT

First, read carefully through the Advanced Sciences and Math chapter in this book, checking off your progress as you go:

- ❏ Anatomy and Physiology
- ❏ Chemistry
- ❏ Physics
- ❏ Mathematics
- ❏ Statistics for Interpreting Data
- ❏ Research Methodology
- ❏ Microbiology

As you read, do the following:

- Highlight any sections, terms, or concepts you think are important
- Draw an asterisk (*) next to any areas you are struggling with
- Work through any practice problems at the end of each section
- Watch the review videos to gain more understanding of a particular topic
- Take notes in your notebook or in the margins of this book

After you've read through everything, go back and review any sections that you highlighted or that you drew an asterisk next to, referencing your notes along the way.

14

Copyright © Mometrix Media. You have been licensed one copy of this document for personal use only. Any other reproduction or redistribution is strictly prohibited. All rights reserved.
This content is provided for test preparation purposes only and does not imply an endorsement by Mometrix of any particular political, scientific, or religious point of view.

Week 2: Management Systems & Risk Management

INSTRUCTIONAL CONTENT

First, read carefully through the Management Systems & Risk Management chapters in this book, checking off your progress as you go:

- ❏ Benchmarks and Performance Standards
- ❏ Organizational Culture
- ❏ Incident Investigation
- ❏ Management of Change
- ❏ System Safety Analysis
- ❏ Business Continuity and Contingency Plans
- ❏ Leading and Lagging Safety, Health, Environmental, and Security Performance Indicators
- ❏ Safety, Health, and Environmental Management and Audit Systems
- ❏ Applicable Requirements for Plans, Systems, and Policies
- ❏ Document Retention
- ❏ Management Leadership
- ❏ Project Management
- ❏ Hazard Identification and Analysis Methods
- ❏ Risk Analysis
- ❏ Risk Evaluation
- ❏ The Risk Management Process
- ❏ The Costs and Benefits of Risk Assessment Process
- ❏ Insurance and Risk Transfer Principles

As you read, do the following:

- Highlight any sections, terms, or concepts you think are important
- Draw an asterisk (*) next to any areas you are struggling with
- Take notes in your notebook or in the margins of this book

After you've read through everything, go back and review any sections that you highlighted or that you drew an asterisk next to, referencing your notes along the way.

Copyright © Mometrix Media. You have been licensed one copy of this document for personal use only. Any other reproduction or redistribution is strictly prohibited. All rights reserved.
This content is provided for test preparation purposes only and does not imply an endorsement by Mometrix of any particular political, scientific, or religious point of view.

Week 3: Advanced Application of Key Safety Concepts & Emergency Preparedness, Fire Prevention, and Security

INSTRUCTIONAL CONTENT

First, read carefully through the Advanced Application of Key Safety Concepts & Emergency Preparedness, Fire Prevention, and Security chapters in this book, checking off your progress as you go:

- ❏ Safety Through Design
- ❏ Engineering Controls
- ❏ Administrative Controls
- ❏ Personal Protective Equipment
- ❏ Chemical Process Safety Management
- ❏ Redundancy Systems
- ❏ Common Workplace Hazards
- ❏ Facility Life Safety Features
- ❏ Fleet Safety
- ❏ Transportation Safety
- ❏ Materials Handling
- ❏ Foreign Material Exclusion (FME) and Foreign Object Damage (FOD)
- ❏ Hazardous Materials Management
- ❏ Multi-Employer Worksite Issues
- ❏ Sources of Information on Hazard and Risk Management Options
- ❏ Safety Design Criteria for Workplace Facilities, Machines, and Practices
- ❏ Tools, Machines, Practices, and Equipment Safety
- ❏ Workplace Hazards
- ❏ Human Performance
- ❏ Emergency Response Planning and Business Continuity
- ❏ Fire Prevention, Protection, and Suppression Systems
- ❏ Transportation and Security of Hazardous Materials
- ❏ Workplace Violence and Prevention

As you read, do the following:

- Highlight any sections, terms, or concepts you think are important
- Draw an asterisk (*) next to any areas you are struggling with
- Take notes in your notebook or in the margins of this book

After you've read through everything, go back and review any sections that you highlighted or that you drew an asterisk next to, referencing your notes along the way.

Copyright © Mometrix Media. You have been licensed one copy of this document for personal use only. Any other reproduction or redistribution is strictly prohibited. All rights reserved.
This content is provided for test preparation purposes only and does not imply an endorsement by Mometrix of any particular political, scientific, or religious point of view.

Week 4: Occupational Health and Ergonomics & Environmental Management Systems

INSTRUCTIONAL CONTENT

First, read carefully through the Occupational Health and Ergonomics & Environmental Management Systems chapters in this book, checking off your progress as you go:

- ❏ Toxicology
- ❏ Carcinogens
- ❏ Ergonomics and Human Factors
- ❏ Recognizing, Evaluating, and Controlling Occupational Exposures
- ❏ Employee Substance Abuse
- ❏ Epidemiology
- ❏ Occupational Exposure Limits
- ❏ Environmental Protection and Pollution Prevention
- ❏ Hazardous Material Migration
- ❏ Sustainability
- ❏ Waste Water Treatment

As you read, do the following:

- Highlight any sections, terms, or concepts you think are important
- Draw an asterisk (*) next to any areas you are struggling with
- Take notes in your notebook or in the margins of this book

After you've read through everything, go back and review any sections that you highlighted or that you drew an asterisk next to, referencing your notes along the way.

Copyright © Mometrix Media. You have been licensed one copy of this document for personal use only. Any other reproduction or redistribution is strictly prohibited. All rights reserved.
This content is provided for test preparation purposes only and does not imply an endorsement by Mometrix of any particular political, scientific, or religious point of view.

Week 5: Training and Education & Law and Ethics

INSTRUCTIONAL CONTENT

First, read carefully through the Training and Education & Law and Ethics chapters in this book, checking off your progress as you go:

- ❏ Training, Qualification, and Competency Requirements
- ❏ Determining the Effectiveness of Training Programs
- ❏ Effective Presentation Techniques
- ❏ Legal Issues
- ❏ Protection of Confidential Information
- ❏ Standards Development Processes
- ❏ Ethical Professional Practice
- ❏ Relationship Between Labor and Management
- ❏ BCSP Code of Ethics
- ❏ Worders' Compensation

As you read, do the following:

- Highlight any sections, terms, or concepts you think are important
- Draw an asterisk (*) next to any areas you are struggling with
- Take notes in your notebook or in the margins of this book

After you've read through everything, go back and review any sections that you highlighted or that you drew an asterisk next to, referencing your notes along the way.

Copyright © Mometrix Media. You have been licensed one copy of this document for personal use only. Any other reproduction or redistribution is strictly prohibited. All rights reserved.
This content is provided for test preparation purposes only and does not imply an endorsement by Mometrix of any particular political, scientific, or religious point of view.

Week 6: Practice Tests

Your success on test day depends not only on how many hours you put into preparing, but also on whether you prepared the right way. It's good to check along the way to see if your studying is paying off. One of the most effective ways to do this is by taking practice tests to evaluate your progress. Practice tests are useful because they show exactly where you need to improve. Every time you take a practice test, pay special attention to these three groups of questions:

- The questions you got wrong
- The questions you had to guess on, even if you guessed right
- The questions you found difficult or slow to work through

This will show you exactly what your weak areas are, and where you need to devote more study time. Ask yourself why each of these questions gave you trouble. Was it because you didn't understand the material? Was it because you didn't remember the vocabulary? Do you need more repetitions on this type of question to build speed and confidence? Dig into those questions and figure out how you can strengthen your weak areas as you go back to review the material.

PRACTICE TEST #1

Now that you've read over the instructional content, it's time to take a practice test. Complete Practice Test #1. Take this test with **no time constraints**, and feel free to reference the applicable sections of this guide as you go. Once you've finished, check your answers against the provided answer key. For any questions you answered incorrectly, review the answer rationale, and then **go back and review** the applicable sections of the book. The goal in this stage is to understand why you answered the question incorrectly, and make sure that the next time you see a similar question, you will get it right.

PRACTICE TEST #2

Next, complete Practice Test #2. This time, give yourself **5.5 hours** to complete all of the questions. You should again feel free to reference the guide and your notes, but be mindful of the clock. If you run out of time before you finish all of the questions, mark where you were when time expired, but go ahead and finish taking the practice test. Once you've finished, check your answers against the provided answer key, and as before, review the answer rationale for any that you answered incorrectly and then go back and review the associated instructional content. Your goal is still to increase understanding of the content but also to get used to the time constraints you will face on the test.

As you go along, keep in mind that the practice test is just that: practice. Memorizing these questions and answers will not be very helpful on the actual test because it is unlikely to have any of the same exact questions. If you only know the right answers to the sample questions, you won't be prepared for the real thing. **Study the concepts** until you understand them fully, and then you'll be able to answer any question that shows up on the test.

Copyright © Mometrix Media. You have been licensed one copy of this document for personal use only. Any other reproduction or redistribution is strictly prohibited. All rights reserved.
This content is provided for test preparation purposes only and does not imply an endorsement by Mometrix of any particular political, scientific, or religious point of view.

Advanced Sciences and Math

Transform passive reading into active learning! After immersing yourself in this chapter, put your comprehension to the test by taking a quiz. The insights you gained will stay with you longer this way. Scan the QR code to go directly to the chapter quiz interface for this study guide. If you're using a computer, simply visit the bonus page at **mometrix.com/bonus948/csp** and click the Chapter Quizzes link.

Anatomy and Physiology

INTEGUMENTARY SYSTEM

The integumentary system, which consists of the skin including the sebaceous glands, sweat glands, hair, and nails, serves a variety of functions associated with protection, secretion, and communication. In the functions associated with protection, the integumentary system protects the body from **pathogens** including bacteria, viruses, and chemicals. In the functions associated with secretion, **sebaceous glands** secrete **sebum** (oil) that waterproofs the skin, and **sweat glands** assist with **thermoregulation**. Sweat glands also serve as excretory organs and help rid the body of metabolic waste. In the functions associated with communication, **sensory receptors** distributed throughout the skin send information to the brain regarding pain, touch, pressure, and temperature. In addition to protection, secretion, and communication, the skin manufactures **vitamin D** with the help of ultraviolet light and can absorb certain chemicals, such as specific medications.

MUSCULAR SYSTEM

There are three types of muscle tissue: **skeletal**, **cardiac**, and **smooth**. There are more than 600 muscles in the human body. All muscles have these three properties in common:

- **Excitability**: All muscle tissues have an electric gradient that can reverse when stimulated.
- **Contraction**: All muscle tissues have the ability to contract, or shorten.
- **Elongate**: All muscle tissues share the capacity to elongate, or relax.

TYPES OF MUSCULAR TISSUE

Smooth muscle tissues are involuntary muscles that are found in the walls of internal organs such as the stomach, intestines, and blood vessels. Smooth muscle tissues, or **visceral tissue,** is nonstriated. Smooth muscle cells are shorter and wider than skeletal muscle fibers. Smooth muscle tissue is also found in sphincters or valves that control the movement of material through openings throughout the body.

Cardiac muscle tissue is involuntary muscle that is found only in the heart. Like skeletal muscle cells, cardiac muscle cells are also striated.

Skeletal muscles are voluntary muscles that work in pairs to move parts of the skeleton. Skeletal muscles are composed of **muscle fibers** (cells) that are bound together in parallel **bundles**. Skeletal muscles are also known as **striated muscle** due to their striped histological appearance under a microscope.

Only skeletal muscle interacts with the skeleton to move the body. When they contract, the muscles transmit **force** to the attached bones. Working together, the muscles and bones act as a system of levers that move around the joints.

20

Copyright © Mometrix Media. You have been licensed one copy of this document for personal use only. Any other reproduction or redistribution is strictly prohibited. All rights reserved.
This content is provided for test preparation purposes only and does not imply an endorsement by Mometrix of any particular political, scientific, or religious point of view.

SKELETAL SYSTEM

The human skeletal system, which consists of 206 bones along with numerous tendons, ligaments, and cartilage, is divided into the axial skeleton and the appendicular skeleton.

The **axial skeleton** consists of 80 bones and includes the vertebral column, rib cage, sternum, skull, and hyoid bone. The **vertebral column** consists of 33 vertebrae classified as cervical vertebrae, thoracic vertebrae, lumbar vertebrae, and sacral vertebrae. The **rib cage** includes 12 paired ribs, 10 pairs of true ribs and two pairs of floating ribs, and the **sternum**, which consists of the manubrium, corpus sterni, and xiphoid process. The **skull** includes the cranium and facial bones. The **ossicles** are bones in the middle ear. The **hyoid bone** provides an attachment point for the tongue muscles. The axial skeleton protects vital organs including the brain, heart, and lungs.

The **appendicular skeleton** consists of 126 bones including the pectoral girdle, pelvic girdle, and appendages. The **pectoral girdle** consists of the scapulae (shoulder blades) and clavicles (collarbones). The **pelvic girdle** attaches to the sacrum at the sacroiliac joint. The upper appendages (arms) include the humerus, radius, ulna, carpals, metacarpals, and phalanges. The lower appendages (legs) include the femur, patella, fibula, tibia, tarsals, metatarsals, and phalanges.

> **Review Video: Skeletal System**
> Visit mometrix.com/academy and enter code: 256447

NERVOUS SYSTEM

The human nervous system senses, interprets, and issues commands as a response to conditions in the body's environment. This process is made possible by a complex communication system of cells called **neurons**.

Messages are sent across the plasma membrane of neurons through a process called **action potential**. These messages occur when a neuron is stimulated past a necessary threshold. These stimulations occur in a sequence from the stimulation point of one neuron to its contact with another neuron. At the point of contact, called a **chemical synapse**, a substance is released that stimulates or inhibits the action of the adjoining cell. A network of nerves composed of neurons fans out across the body and forms the framework for the nervous system. The direction the information flows depends on the specific organizations of nerve circuits and pathways.

> **Review Video: What is the Function of the Nervous System**
> Visit mometrix.com/academy and enter code: 708428

CENTRAL NERVOUS SYSTEM (CNS)

SPINAL CORD

The **central nervous system (CNS)** is made of the brain and the spinal cord. The **spinal cord** is encased in the bony **vertebral column** (composed of vertebrae), which protects and supports it. Its nervous tissue functions with respect to both voluntary and involuntary activity. Nerve bundles ascend and descend from the brain to all tissues in the body through the spinal cord.

BRAIN: FOREBRAIN

The brain consists of the hindbrain, midbrain, and forebrain. The **forebrain** includes the **cerebrum, thalamus,** and **hypothalamus**. The **cerebral cortex** is the outer layer of the cerebrum, and it is made of grey matter. The cerebrum is divided into two hemispheres, with each responsible for multiple functions. Each cerebral hemisphere is divided into four main **lobes**: the frontal lobe, the parietal lobe, the occipital lobe, and the temporal lobes. The **frontal lobe,** located in the front of the brain, is responsible for short-term and working memory and information processing as well as decision-making, planning, and judgment. The **parietal lobe** is located slightly toward the back of the brain and the top of the head and is responsible for sensory input as well as spatial positioning of the body. The **occipital lobe** is located at the back of the head just above the brain

21

Copyright © Mometrix Media. You have been licensed one copy of this document for personal use only. Any other reproduction or redistribution is strictly prohibited. All rights reserved.
This content is provided for test preparation purposes only and does not imply an endorsement by Mometrix of any particular political, scientific, or religious point of view.

stem. This lobe is responsible for visual input, processing, and output; specifically nerves from the eyes enter directly into this lobe. Finally, the **temporal lobes** are located at the left and right sides of the brain. These lobes are responsible for all auditory input, processing, and output.

The **thalamus** relays sensory signals and regulates sleep and consciousness. The **hypothalamus** is part of the thalamus and receives information from the autonomic nervous system and instructs the pituitary gland to regulate hormones.

BRAIN: MIDBRAIN AND HINDBRAIN

The **midbrain** integrates sensory signals and orchestrates responses to these signals. It lies above the pons and the medulla oblongata. The parts of the midbrain include the **tectum**, the **tegmentum**, and the **ventral tegmentum**. The midbrain is an important part of vision and hearing.

The **hindbrain** includes the **medulla oblongata**, **cerebellum**, and **pons**. Key functions of the **cerebellum**, found beneath the occipital lobes at the back of the brain and considered part of the hindbrain, include coordinating and smoothing motion and maintaining balance and posture. It allows for rapid and repetitive movements, such as playing a musical instrument or riding a bicycle. Cerebellar dysfunction will result in poor control of muscles, awkward, uncoordinated movement, speech problems, and intention tremors. The **pons** is between the midbrain and the medulla oblongata; it has many autonomic and sensory functions. The **medulla oblongata** (or medulla) is beneath the midbrain and the pons. The medulla oblongata plays a vital role in the autonomic nervous system as a regulator of the circulatory and respiratory systems.

The posterior area of the brain that is connected to the spinal cord is known as the **brain stem**. The **midbrain**, the **pons**, and the **medulla oblongata** are the three parts of the brain stem, which relays information between the body and the cerebral cortex.

PERIPHERAL NERVOUS SYSTEM (PNS)

The **peripheral nervous system** consists of the nerves and ganglia throughout the body that control both voluntary movement and involuntary functions. Involuntary functions are managed by **sympathetic nerves,** which trigger the "fight or flight" response, and **parasympathetic nerves,** which control basic "rest and digest" body functions.

RESPIRATORY SYSTEM

The main function of the respiratory system is to supply the body with **oxygen** and rid the body of **carbon dioxide**. This exchange of gases occurs in millions of tiny **alveoli**, which are surrounded by blood capillaries. The respiratory system also filters air. Air is warmed, moistened, and filtered as it passes through the nasal passages before it reaches the lungs. The respiratory system also allows for speech. As air passes through the throat, it moves through the **larynx** (voice box), which vibrates and produces sound, before it enters the **trachea** (windpipe). Cough production allows foreign particles which have entered the nasal passages or airways to be expelled from the respiratory system. The respiratory system functions in the sense of smell using **chemoreceptors** that are located in the nasal cavity and respond to airborne chemicals. The respiratory system also helps the body maintain acid-base **homeostasis**. Hyperventilation can increase blood pH during **acidosis** (low pH). Slowing breathing during **alkalosis** (high pH) helps lower blood pH.

UPPER AND LOWER RESPIRATORY SYSTEM

The respiratory system can be divided into the upper and lower respiratory system. The **upper respiratory system** includes the nose, nasal cavity, mouth, pharynx, and larynx. The **lower respiratory system** includes the trachea, lungs, and bronchial tree. Alternatively, the components of the respiratory system can be categorized as part of the airway, the lungs, or the respiratory muscles. The **airway** includes the nose, nasal cavity, mouth, pharynx (throat), larynx (voice box), trachea (windpipe), bronchi, and bronchial network. The airway is lined with **cilia** that trap microbes and debris and sweep them back toward the mouth. The **lungs** are structures that house the **bronchi** and bronchial network, which extend into the lungs and terminate in

Copyright © Mometrix Media. You have been licensed one copy of this document for personal use only. Any other reproduction or redistribution is strictly prohibited. All rights reserved.
This content is provided for test preparation purposes only and does not imply an endorsement by Mometrix of any particular political, scientific, or religious point of view.

millions of **alveoli** (air sacs). The walls of the alveoli are only one cell thick, allowing for the exchange of gases with the blood capillaries that surround them. The right lung has three lobes. The left lung has only two lobes, leaving room for the heart on the left side of the body. The lungs are surrounded by a **pleural membrane**, which reduces friction between the lungs and walls of the thoracic cavity when breathing. The respiratory muscles include the **diaphragm** and the **intercostal muscles**. The diaphragm is a dome-shaped muscle that separates the thoracic and abdominal cavities; as it contracts, it expands the thoracic cavity which draws air into the lungs. The intercostal muscles are located between the ribs.

CIRCULATORY SYSTEM

The **circulatory system** is responsible for the internal transport of substances to and from the cells. The circulatory system consists of the following parts:

- **Blood**: Blood is composed of water, solutes, and other elements in a fluid connective tissue.
- **Blood vessels**: Vessels are tubules of different sizes that transport blood in a closed system to tissues throughout the body.
- **Heart**: The heart is a muscular pump providing the pressure necessary to keep blood flowing throughout the circulatory system.

As the blood moves through the system from larger tubules through smaller ones, the rate slows. The flow of blood in the **capillary beds**, the smallest tubules, is quite slow.

A supplementary system, the **lymph vascular system**, cleans excess fluids and proteins and returns them to the circulatory system.

> **Review Video: Functions of the Circulatory System**
> Visit mometrix.com/academy and enter code: 376581

HUMAN HEART

The **heart** is a muscular pump made of cardiac muscle tissue. Heart chamber contraction and relaxation is coordinated by electrical signals from the self-exciting **sinoatrial node** and the **atrioventricular node**. **Atrial contraction** fills the ventricles and **ventricular contraction** forces blood into arteries leaving the heart. This sequence is called the **cardiac cycle**. Valves keep blood moving through the heart in a single direction and prevent any backwash as it flows through its four chambers.

Deoxygenated blood from the body flows through the heart in this order:

1. The **superior vena cava** brings blood from the upper body; the **inferior vena cava** brings blood from the lower body.
2. Right atrium
3. Tricuspid valve (right atrioventricular [AV] valve)
4. Right ventricle
5. Pulmonary valve
6. Left and right pulmonary artery (note: these arteries carry deoxygenated blood)
7. Lungs (where gas exchange occurs)

Oxygenated blood returns to the body through:

8. Left and right pulmonary veins (note: these veins carry oxygenated blood)
9. Left atrium
10. Mitral valve (left atrioventricular [AV] valve)
11. Left ventricle
12. Aortic valve
13. Aortic arch

Copyright © Mometrix Media. You have been licensed one copy of this document for personal use only. Any other reproduction or redistribution is strictly prohibited. All rights reserved. This content is provided for test preparation purposes only and does not imply an endorsement by Mometrix of any particular political, scientific, or religious point of view.

14. Aorta

The left and right sides of the heart are separated by the septum. The heart has its own circulatory system with its own **coronary arteries**.

BLOOD

Blood helps maintain a healthy internal environment in animals by carrying raw materials to cells and removing waste products. It helps stabilize internal pH and hosts cells of the immune system.

An adult human has about five quarts of blood. Blood is composed of **red blood cells, white blood cells, platelets**, and **plasma**. Plasma constitutes more than half of the blood volume. It is mostly water and serves as a solvent. Plasma contains plasma proteins, ions, glucose, amino acids, hormones, and dissolved gases. **Platelets** are fragments of stem cells and serve an important function in blood clotting.

Red blood cells transport **oxygen** to cells. Red blood cells form in the bone marrow and can live for about four months. These cells are constantly being replaced by fresh ones, keeping the total number relatively stable. They lack a nucleus.

Part of the immune system, white blood cells defend the body against **infection** and remove wastes. The types of white blood cells include lymphocytes, neutrophils, monocytes, eosinophils, and basophils.

LYMPHATIC SYSTEM

The lymphatic system serves as a filter for the body's interstitial fluid. The interstitial fluid, white blood cells (leukocytes), and foreign microbes and particles within the fluid are absorbed into the lymphatic system's network of lymphatic vessels, at which point it is called lymphatic fluid, or lymph. From there, it circulates into lymph nodes, which contain macrophages and other immune cells to eliminate foreign matter from the lymph. The lymph vessels contain valves and circulate lymph by means of smooth muscle contractions and by influx of more fluid to the lymph vessels. Lymph is then returned to the blood through the lymphatic ducts.

IMMUNE SYSTEM

The immune system protects the body against invading **pathogens** including bacteria, viruses, fungi, and protists. The immune system includes the **lymphatic system** (lymph, lymph capillaries, lymph vessel, and lymph nodes) as well as the **red bone marrow** and numerous **leukocytes**, or white blood cells. Tissue fluid enters the **lymph capillaries**, which combine to form **lymph vessels**. Skeletal muscle contractions move the lymph one way through the lymphatic system to lymphatic ducts, which dump back into the venous blood supply and the **lymph nodes**, which are situated along the lymph vessels, and filter the lymph of pathogens and other matter. The lymph nodes are concentrated in the neck, armpits, and groin areas. Outside the lymphatic vessel system lies the **lymphatic tissue,** including the tonsils, adenoids, thymus, spleen, and Peyer's patches. The **tonsils,** located in the pharynx, protect against pathogens entering the body through the mouth and throat. The **thymus** serves as a maturation chamber for immature T cells that are formed in the bone marrow. The **spleen** cleans the blood of dead cells and pathogens. **Peyer's patches**, which are located in the small intestine, protect the digestive system from pathogens.

> **Review Video: Immune System**
> Visit mometrix.com/academy and enter code: 622899

Copyright © Mometrix Media. You have been licensed one copy of this document for personal use only. Any other reproduction or redistribution is strictly prohibited. All rights reserved.
This content is provided for test preparation purposes only and does not imply an endorsement by Mometrix of any particular political, scientific, or religious point of view.

DIGESTIVE SYSTEM

The digestive system uses the following processes to convert protein, fats, and carbohydrates into usable energy for the body:

- **Movement**: Movement mixes and passes nutrients through the system and eliminates waste.
- **Secretion**: Enzymes, hormones, and other substances necessary for digestion are secreted into the digestive tract.
- **Digestion**: Digestion includes the chemical breakdown of nutrients into smaller units that enter the internal environment.
- **Absorption**: Nutrients pass through plasma membranes into the blood or lymph and then to the body.

PRE-GASTRIC

The mouth is the beginning of the digestive system. **Mastication**, the process of chewing, increases the surface area of food in the process of physical digestion to expedite chemical digestion. Amylase (an enzyme that breaks down simple carbohydrates) and lingual lipase (a salivary enzyme that starts to break down lipids) begin the process of chemical digestion.

Through the process of swallowing, food moves from the mouth to the **esophagus**. The **epiglottis** prevents food from entering the larynx and trachea. The esophagus serves to transport food to the stomach; the **lower esophageal sphincter (LES)**, located at the bottom of the esophagus, prevents stomach acid from entering the esophagus.

STOMACH

The **stomach** physically and chemically digests food further, and it stores food and allows for its slow release into the small intestine's duodenum. Smooth stomach muscles contract to grind and mix ingesta, and gastric acid (with a pH between 1.5 and 3.5) and proteases (enzymes that break down proteins) chemically digest ingesta.

The **pyloric sphincter** allows for the slow release of **chyme** (ingesta after gastric digestion) into the duodenum of the small intestine.

INTESTINES

The **small intestine** has three sections: the duodenum, the jejunum, and ileum. The **duodenum** continues chemical digestion and begins the process of **absorption**, which is the transfer of the simple nutrient molecules from the lumen of the intestine to the bloodstream for use by the body. The **jejunum** and the **ileum** both continue to absorb the products of digestion.

The **large intestine** is much shorter than the small intestine and absorbs water from its contents before they are excreted.

LIVER

The liver is the largest solid organ of the body. It is also the largest gland. It weighs about three pounds in an adult and is located below the diaphragm on the right side of the abdomen. The liver is made up of four **lobes**: right, left, quadrate, and caudate lobes. The liver is secured to the diaphragm and abdominal walls by five **ligaments**. They are called the falciform (which forms a membrane-like barrier between the right and left lobes), coronary, right triangular, left triangular, and round ligaments.

The liver processes blood once it has received nutrients from the intestines via the **hepatic portal vein**. The **hepatic artery** supplies oxygen-rich blood from the abdominal aorta so that the organ can function. Blood leaves the liver through the **hepatic veins**. The liver's functional units are called **lobules** (made up of layers of liver cells). Blood enters the lobules through branches of the portal vein and hepatic artery. The blood then flows through small channels called **sinusoids**.

Copyright © Mometrix Media. You have been licensed one copy of this document for personal use only. Any other reproduction or redistribution is strictly prohibited. All rights reserved. This content is provided for test preparation purposes only and does not imply an endorsement by Mometrix of any particular political, scientific, or religious point of view.

FUNCTIONS

The liver is responsible for performing many vital functions in the body including the following:

- Production of **bile**
- Production of certain **blood plasma proteins**
- Production of **cholesterol** (and certain proteins needed to carry fats)
- Storage of excess glucose in the form of **glycogen** (that can be converted back to glucose when needed)
- Regulation of **amino acids**
- Processing of **hemoglobin** (to store iron)
- Conversion of ammonia (that is poisonous to the body) to **urea** (a waste product excreted in urine)
- **Purification** of the blood (clearing out drugs and other toxins)
- Regulation of **blood clotting**
- Controlling infections by boosting **immune factors** and removing bacteria.
- The nutrients (and drugs) that pass through the liver are converted into forms that are appropriate for the body to use.

PANCREAS

The pancreas is six to ten inches long in an adult and located at the back of the abdomen behind the stomach. It is a long, tapered organ. The wider (right) side is called the **head,** and the narrower (left) side is called the **tail**. The head lies near the **duodenum** (the first section of the small intestine), and the tail ends near the **spleen**. The body of the pancreas lies between the head and the tail. The pancreas is made up of exocrine and endocrine tissues. The **exocrine tissue** secretes digestive enzymes from a series of ducts that collectively form the main pancreatic duct (that runs the length of the pancreas). The **main pancreatic duct** connects to the common bile duct near the duodenum. The **endocrine tissue** secretes hormones (such as insulin) into the bloodstream. Blood is supplied to the pancreas from the splenic artery, gastroduodenal artery, and superior mesenteric artery.

GALLBLADDER

The gallbladder is a small sac-like organ located below the liver. Together with the liver and bile ducts, it makes the biliary tract. The main functions of the gallbladder are to store and concentrate bile. Bile is a fluid containing amphipathic acids called bile salts, which are produced by the liver, to aid in absorbing and digesting lipids (fats). The bile is concentrated in the gallbladder by removal of water and is released through the common bile duct into the duodenum, where it encounters chyme from the stomach and pancreatic secretions and eventually is mostly reabsorbed through the ileum at the end of the small intestine.

ENDOCRINE SYSTEM

The endocrine system is responsible for secreting **hormones** and other molecules that help regulate the entire body in both the short and long term. There is a close working relationship between the endocrine and nervous systems. The **hypothalamus** and the **pituitary gland** coordinate to serve as a **neuroendocrine control center**.

Hormone secretion is triggered by a variety of signals, including hormonal signs, chemical reactions, and environmental cues. Only cells with particular **receptors** can benefit from hormonal influence. This is the "key in the lock" model for hormonal action. **Steroid hormones** trigger gene activation and protein synthesis in some target cells. **Protein hormones** change the activity of existing enzymes in target cells. Hormones such as **insulin** work quickly when the body signals an urgent need. Slower-acting hormones afford longer, gradual, and sometimes permanent changes in the body.

Copyright © Mometrix Media. You have been licensed one copy of this document for personal use only. Any other reproduction or redistribution is strictly prohibited. All rights reserved.
This content is provided for test preparation purposes only and does not imply an endorsement by Mometrix of any particular political, scientific, or religious point of view.

MAJOR ENDOCRINE GLANDS

Endocrine glands are intimately involved in a myriad of reactions, functions, and secretions that are crucial to the well-being of the body. The eight major endocrine glands and their functions include the following:

- **Adrenal cortex**: Monitors blood sugar level; helps in lipid and protein metabolism
- **Adrenal medulla**: Controls cardiac function; raises blood sugar and controls the size of blood vessels
- **Thyroid gland**: Helps regulate metabolism and functions in growth and development
- **Parathyroid**: Regulates calcium levels in the blood
- **Pancreas islets**: Raises and lowers blood sugar; active in carbohydrate metabolism
- **Thymus gland**: Plays a role in immune responses
- **Pineal gland**: Has an influence on daily biorhythms and sexual activity
- **Pituitary gland**: Plays an important role in growth and development

> **Review Video: Endocrine System**
> Visit mometrix.com/academy and enter code: 678939

RENAL SYSTEM

The renal system produces and eliminates fluid waste from the body, while maintaining the fluid and pH balance needed for the body to function. It consists mainly of the kidneys, ureters, bladder, and urethra.

KIDNEYS

The kidneys are bean-shaped organs that are located at the back of the abdominal cavity just under the diaphragm. Each **kidney** (the labeled diagram on the left) consists of the renal cortex (outer layer), renal medulla (inner layer), and renal pelvis, which collects waste products from the nephrons and funnels them to the ureter.

The **renal cortex** (1) is composed of approximately one million **nephrons** (6; magnified as the labeled diagram on the right), which are the tiny, individual filters of the kidneys. Each nephron contains a cluster of capillaries called a **glomerulus** (8) surrounded by the cup-shaped **Bowman's capsule** (9), which leads to a **tubule** (10).

The kidneys receive blood from the **renal arteries (3)**, which branch off the aorta. In general, the kidneys filter the blood (F), reabsorb needed materials (R), and secrete (S) and excrete (E) wastes and excess water in the urine. More specifically, blood flows from the renal arteries into **arterioles** (7) into the glomerulus, where it is filtered. The **glomerular filtrate** enters the **proximal convoluted tubule,** where water, glucose, ions, and other organic molecules are reabsorbed back into the bloodstream through the **renal vein** (4). Reabsorption and secretion occur between the tubules and the **peritubular capillaries** (12).

Additional substances such as urea and drugs are removed from the blood in the **distal convoluted tubule.** Also, the pH of the blood can be adjusted in the distal convoluted tubule by the secretion of **hydrogen ions.** Finally, the unabsorbed materials flow out from the collecting tubules located in the **renal medulla** (2) to the

Copyright © Mometrix Media. You have been licensed one copy of this document for personal use only. Any other reproduction or redistribution is strictly prohibited. All rights reserved.
This content is provided for test preparation purposes only and does not imply an endorsement by Mometrix of any particular political, scientific, or religious point of view.

renal pelvis as urine. Urine is drained from the kidneys through the **ureters** (5) to the **urinary bladder**, where it is stored until expulsion from the body through the **urethra**.

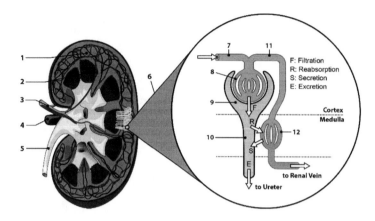

MALE REPRODUCTIVE SYSTEM

The functions of the male reproductive system are to produce, maintain, and transfer **sperm** and **semen** into the female reproductive tract and to produce and secrete **male hormones**.

The external structure includes the penis, scrotum, and testes. The **penis**, which contains the **urethra**, can fill with blood and become erect, enabling the deposition of semen and sperm into the female reproductive tract during sexual intercourse. The **scrotum** is a sack of skin and smooth muscle that houses the testes and keeps the testes outside the body wall at a cooler, proper temperature for **spermatogenesis**. The **testes**, or testicles, are the male gonads, which produce sperm and testosterone.

The internal structure includes the epididymis, vas deferens, ejaculatory ducts, urethra, seminal vesicles, prostate gland, and bulbourethral glands. The **epididymis** stores the sperm as it matures. Mature sperm moves from the epididymis through the **vas deferens** to the **ejaculatory duct**. The **seminal vesicles** secrete alkaline fluids with proteins and mucus into the ejaculatory duct also. The **prostate gland** secretes a milky white fluid with proteins and enzymes as part of the semen. The **bulbourethral**, or Cowper's glands, secrete a fluid into the urethra to neutralize the acidity in the urethra, which would damage sperm.

Additionally, the hormones associated with the male reproductive system include **follicle-stimulating hormone (FSH)**, which stimulates spermatogenesis; **luteinizing hormone (LH)**, which stimulates testosterone production; and **testosterone**, which is responsible for the male sex characteristics. FSH and LH are gonadotropins, which stimulate the gonads (male testes and female ovaries).

FEMALE REPRODUCTIVE SYSTEM

The functions of the female reproductive system are to produce **ova** (oocytes or egg cells), transfer the ova to the **fallopian tubes** for fertilization, receive the sperm from the male, and provide a protective, nourishing environment for the developing **embryo**.

The external portion of the female reproductive system includes the labia majora, labia minora, Bartholin's glands, and clitoris. The **labia majora** and the **labia minora** enclose and protect the vagina. The **Bartholin's glands** secrete a lubricating fluid. The **clitoris** contains erectile tissue and nerve endings for sensual pleasure.

The internal portion of the female reproductive system includes the ovaries, fallopian tubes, uterus, and vagina. The **ovaries**, which are the female gonads, produce the ova and secrete **estrogen** and **progesterone**. The **fallopian tubes** carry the mature egg toward the uterus. Fertilization typically occurs in the fallopian tubes. If fertilized, the egg travels to the **uterus**, where it implants in the uterine wall. The uterus protects and

Copyright © Mometrix Media. You have been licensed one copy of this document for personal use only. Any other reproduction or redistribution is strictly prohibited. All rights reserved.
This content is provided for test preparation purposes only and does not imply an endorsement by Mometrix of any particular political, scientific, or religious point of view.

nourishes the developing embryo until birth. The **vagina** is a muscular tube that extends from the **cervix** of the uterus to the outside of the body. The vagina receives the semen and sperm during sexual intercourse and provides a birth canal when needed.

Chemistry

GENERAL CHEMISTRY CONCEPTS

NOMENCLATURE

Nomenclature refers to the manner in which chemical compounds are named.

BINARY MOLECULAR COMPOUNDS

The names of binary molecular compounds follow this pattern: [prefix + first element name] [prefix + root of second element name + -ide].

If a prefix ends with *a* or *o* and the element name begins with *a* or *o*, the first *a* or *o* of the prefix is dropped. For example, N_2O_5 is named dinitrogen pentoxide. The prefix *mono-* is usually dropped unless more than one binary compound may be formed from the two elements involved.

Binary Molecular Compounds

#	Prefix	#	Prefix
1	mono-	6	hexa-
2	di-	7	hepta-
3	tri-	8	octa-
4	tetra-	9	nona-
5	penta-	10	deca-

BINARY IONIC COMPOUNDS

The names of binary ionic compounds follow this pattern: [cation name] [anion name].

The name of simple cations is usually the element name. For example, the K^+ cation is named potassium. Some cations exist in more than one form. In those cases, the charge of the ion follows the element as a Roman numeral in parentheses. For example, the Cu^+ ion is named copper(I) and the Cu^{2+} ion is named copper(II). Simple anions are named with the root of the element name followed by the suffix *-ide*. For example, the O^{2-} anion is named oxide, and the F^- ion is named fluoride. The following are some examples of names of binary ionic compounds: KI is named potassium iodide, and FeO is named iron(II) oxide.

Examples:

N_2O_4

This is a binary molecular compound. Using the prefixes *di-* for 2 and *tetra-* for 4, this compound is named dinitrogen tetroxide. Note that the entire element name is retained for the cation, but the root plus *-ide* is used for the anion name.

S_2F_{10}

This is a binary molecular compound. Using the prefixes *di-* for 2 and *deca-* for 10, this compound is named disulfur decafluoride. Note that the entire element name is retained for the cation, but the root plus *-ide* is used for the anion name.

Copyright © Mometrix Media. You have been licensed one copy of this document for personal use only. Any other reproduction or redistribution is strictly prohibited. All rights reserved.
This content is provided for test preparation purposes only and does not imply an endorsement by Mometrix of any particular political, scientific, or religious point of view.

Fe₂O₃

This is a binary ionic compound. Iron forms two types of cations Fe^{2+} and Fe^{3+}, but because the anion is O^{2-}, this must be the Fe^{3+} ion in order to balance the charges. This compound is named iron(III) oxide.

CuCl₂

This is a binary ionic compound. Copper forms two types of cations Cu^+ and Cu^{2+}, but because the anion is Cl^-, this must be the Cu^{2+} ion in order to balance the charges. This compound is named copper(II) chloride.

ACIDS

Acids are generally categorized as binary acids or oxyacids. Binary acids are named by the pattern: [*hydro-* + root of element + *-ic*] acid. For example, HI is named hydroiodic acid, and HCl is named hydrochloric acid. One exception is that in hydrosulfuric acid (H_2S), the entire element name sulfur is used. The names of oxyacids depend on the endings of their polyatomic anions. If the polyatomic anions end in *-ate*, then the acid names end in *-ic*. If the anions end in *-ite*, the acid names end in *-ous*. The naming pattern for an oxyacid is as follows: [anion root + ending] acid. For example, H_2CO_3 is named carbonic acid because the carbonate ion ends in *-ate*, and H_2SO_3 is named sulfurous acid because the sulfite ion ends in *-ite*.

HYDRATES

Hydrates form from salts (ionic compounds) that attract water. Hydrates are named from their salt (ionic compound) name and the number of water molecules involved in the following pattern:

[salt name] [prefix + hydrate].

For example, the name of $CuSO_4 \cdot 5H_2O$ is copper(II) sulfate pentahydrate, and the name of $CoCl_2 \cdot 6H_2O$ is cobalt(II) chloride hexahydrate.

Binary Molecular Compounds

#	Prefix	#	Prefix
1	mono-	6	hexa-
2	di-	7	hepta-
3	tri-	8	octa-
4	tetra-	9	nona-
5	penta-	10	deca-

SALTS

Salts are ionic compounds with any cation except H^+ from an aqueous base and any anion except OH^- from an aqueous acid. Salts are named like regular ionic compounds with the name of the cation followed by the name of the anion. Examples of salts include sodium chloride (NaCl), potassium fluoride (KF), magnesium iodide (MgI_2), sodium acetate ($NaC_2H_3O_2$), and ammonium carbonate ((NH_4)$_2CO_3$).

BASES

Bases are typically ionic compounds with a hydroxide anion and are named following the conventions of naming ionic compounds. For example, NaOH is named sodium hydroxide and $Mg(OH)_2$ is named magnesium hydroxide.

BALANCING A CHEMICAL EQUATION

According to the law of conservation of mass, the mass of the products must always equal the mass of the reactants in a chemical reaction. Because mass is conserved, the number of each type of atom in the products must equal the number of each type of atom in the reactants. The key to **balancing a chemical reaction** is in balancing the number of each type of atom on both sides of the equation. Only the coefficients in front of the

Copyright © Mometrix Media. You have been licensed one copy of this document for personal use only. Any other reproduction or redistribution is strictly prohibited. All rights reserved.
This content is provided for test preparation purposes only and does not imply an endorsement by Mometrix of any particular political, scientific, or religious point of view.

reactants and products may be changed to accomplish this, not the subscripts in the molecules themselves. Try balancing the largest number of a type of atom first. Also, check if any odd numbers need to be changed to even. Always leave the uncombined elements to balance until the end.

Below is an unbalanced example of the chemical reaction that occurs when propane gas is burned in air.

$$C_3H_8 \ (g) + O_2(g) \rightarrow CO_2 \ (g) + H_2O \ (g) + heat$$

To balance the equation, first determine the types and numbers of each type of atom on each side of the equation:

	Reactants	Products
C	3	1
H	8	2
O	2	3

Since hydrogen has the largest number of atoms, balance it first. Adding a coefficient of 4 to the H_2O on the right side makes the number of hydrogen atoms the same on both sides.

$$C_3H_8 \ (g) + O_2(g) \rightarrow CO_2 \ (g) + 4H_2O \ (g) + heat$$

Oxygen has the next-highest number of atoms to balance, but because it is uncombined with other elements on the left side, it is better to balance carbon first. Adding a coefficient of 3 to the CO_2 on the right side makes the number of carbon atoms the same on both sides.

$$C_3H_8 \ (g) + O_2(g) \rightarrow 3CO_2 \ (g) + 4H_2O \ (g) + heat$$

All that's left now are the oxygen atoms. Adding a coefficient of 5 to the O_2 on the left side completes the balancing process, leaving the correct equation:

$$C_3H_8 \ (g) + 5O_2(g) \rightarrow 3CO_2 \ (g) + 4H_2O \ (g) + heat$$

CHEMICAL REACTIONS
BASIC MECHANISMS

Chemical reactions normally occur when electrons are transferred from one atom or molecule to another. Reactions and reactivity depend on the **octet rule**, which describes the tendency of atoms to gain or lose electrons until their outer energy levels contain eight. The changes in a reaction may be in **composition** or **configuration** of a compound or substance, and result in one or more products being generated which were not present in isolation before the reaction occurred. For instance, when oxygen reacts with methane (CH_4), water and carbon dioxide are the products; one set of substances ($CH_4 + O$) was transformed into a new set of substances ($CO_2 + H_2O$).

Reactions depend on the presence of a **reactant**, or substance undergoing change, a **reagent**, or partner in the reaction less transformed than the reactant (such as a catalyst), and **products**, or the final result of the reaction. **Reaction conditions**, or environmental factors, are also important components in reactions. These include conditions such as temperature, pressure, concentration, whether the reaction occurs in solution, the type of solution, and presence or absence of catalysts. Chemical reactions are usually written in the following format: Reactants → Products.

COMBINATION REACTIONS

Combination reactions: In a combination reaction, two or more reactants combine to make one product. This can be seen in the equation A + B → AB. These reactions are also known as synthesis or addition reactions. An example is burning hydrogen in air to produce water. The equation is $2H_2 \ (g) + O_2 \ (g) \rightarrow 2H_2O \ (l)$. Another example is when water and sulfur trioxide react to form sulfuric acid. The equation is $H_2O + SO_3 \rightarrow H_2SO_4$.

Copyright © Mometrix Media. You have been licensed one copy of this document for personal use only. Any other reproduction or redistribution is strictly prohibited. All rights reserved. This content is provided for test preparation purposes only and does not imply an endorsement by Mometrix of any particular political, scientific, or religious point of view.

DECOMPOSITION REACTIONS

Decomposition (or *desynthesis, decombination, or deconstruction*) reactions are considered chemical reactions whereby a reactant is broken down into two or more products. This can be seen in the equation AB → A + B. These reactions are also called analysis reactions. When a compound or substance separates into these simpler substances, the byproducts are often substances that are different from the original. Decomposition can be viewed as the *opposite* of combination reactions. These reactions are also called analysis reactions. Most decomposition reactions are **endothermic**. Heat needs to be added for the chemical reaction to occur. **Thermal decomposition** is caused by heat. **Electrolytic decomposition** is due to electricity. An example of this type of reaction is the decomposition of water into hydrogen and oxygen gas. The equation is $2H_2O → 2H_2 + O_2$. Separation processes can be **mechanical** or **chemical**, and usually involve reorganizing a mixture of substances without changing their chemical nature. The separated products may differ from the original mixture in terms of chemical or physical properties. Types of separation processes include **filtration**, **crystallization**, **distillation**, and **chromatography**. Basically, decomposition *breaks down* one compound into two or more compounds or substances that are different from the original; separation *sorts* the substances from the original mixture into like substances.

SINGLE REPLACEMENT REACTIONS

Single substitution, displacement, or replacement reactions occur when one reactant is displaced by another to form the final product (A + BC → B + AC). Single substitution reactions can be **cationic** or **anionic**. When a piece of copper (Cu) is placed into a solution of silver nitrate ($AgNO_3$), the solution turns blue. The copper appears to be replaced with a silvery-white material. The equation is $2AgNO_3 + Cu → Cu(NO_3)_2 + 2Ag$. When this reaction takes place, the copper dissolves and the silver in the silver nitrate solution precipitates (becomes a solid), thus resulting in copper nitrate and silver. Copper and silver have switched places in the nitrate.

> **Review Video: What is a Single-Replacement Reaction?**
> Visit mometrix.com/academy and enter code: 442975

DOUBLE REPLACEMENT REACTIONS

Double displacement, double replacement, substitution, metathesis, or ion exchange reactions occur when ions or bonds are exchanged by two compounds to form different compounds (AC + BD → AD + BC). An example of this is that silver nitrate and sodium chloride form two different products (silver chloride and sodium nitrate) when they react. The formula for this reaction is $AgNO_3 + NaCl → AgCl + NaNO_3$.

Double replacement reactions are **metathesis reactions**. In a double replacement reaction, the chemical reactants exchange ions but the oxidation state stays the same. One of the indicators of this is the formation of a **solid precipitate**. In acid/base reactions, an **acid** is a compound that can donate a proton, while a **base** is a compound that can accept a proton. In these types of reactions, the acid and base react to form a salt and water. When the proton is donated, the base becomes **water** and the remaining ions form a **salt**. One method

Copyright © Mometrix Media. You have been licensed one copy of this document for personal use only. Any other reproduction or redistribution is strictly prohibited. All rights reserved.
This content is provided for test preparation purposes only and does not imply an endorsement by Mometrix of any particular political, scientific, or religious point of view.

of determining whether a reaction is an oxidation/reduction or a metathesis reaction is that the oxidation number of atoms does not change during a metathesis reaction.

Types of Chemical Reactions

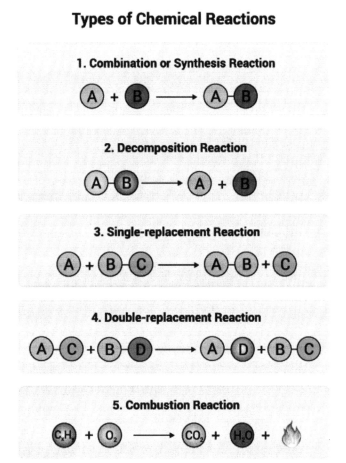

COMBUSTION REACTIONS

Combustion, or burning, is a sequence of chemical reactions involving **fuel** and an **oxidant** that produces heat and sometimes light. There are many types of combustion, such as rapid, slow, complete, turbulent, microgravity, and incomplete. Fuels and oxidants determine the **compounds** formed by a combustion reaction. For example, when rocket fuel consisting of hydrogen and oxygen combusts, it results in the formation of water vapor. When air and wood burn, resulting compounds include nitrogen, unburned carbon, and carbon compounds. Combustion is an **exothermic** process, meaning it releases energy. Exothermic energy is commonly released as heat, but can take other forms, such as light, electricity, or sound.

> **Review Video: Combustion**
> Visit mometrix.com/academy and enter code: 592219

CATALYSTS

Catalysts, substances that help *change the rate of reaction* without changing their form, can increase reaction rate by decreasing the number of steps it takes to form products. The **mass** of the catalyst should be the same at the beginning of the reaction as it is at the end. The **activation energy** is the minimum amount required to get a reaction started. Activation energy causes particles to collide with sufficient energy to start the reaction. A **catalyst** enables more particles to react, which lowers the activation energy. Examples of catalysts in

Copyright © Mometrix Media. You have been licensed one copy of this document for personal use only. Any other reproduction or redistribution is strictly prohibited. All rights reserved.
This content is provided for test preparation purposes only and does not imply an endorsement by Mometrix of any particular political, scientific, or religious point of view.

reactions are manganese oxide (MnO_2) in the decomposition of hydrogen peroxide, iron in the manufacture of ammonia using the Haber process, and concentrate of sulfuric acid in the nitration of benzene.

Review Video: Catalysts
Visit mometrix.com/academy and enter code: 288189

IDEAL GAS LAW

An ideal gas is a hypothetical or theoretical gas. Ideal gases are assumed to be a set of randomly moving point particles that do not interact with each other. The collisions of ideal gases are assumed to be completely elastic, and the intermolecular forces are assumed to be zero. Real gases show more complex behaviors. The ideal gas laws tend to fail at low temperatures and high pressures when the effects of the particle size and intermolecular forces are more apparent. Also, the ideal gas assumptions do not account for phase transitions.

The ideal gas law combines Boyle's law, Charles's law, and Avogadro's law. According to Boyle's law, $V \propto \frac{1}{P}$. According to Charles's law, $V \propto T$. According to Avogadro's law, $V \propto n$. Combining these three relationships into one relationship yields $V \propto \frac{nT}{P}$. Multiplying through by P yields $PV \propto nT$, or $PV = nRT$, where R is the ideal gas constant of 0.0821 L·atm/(K·mol), P is the pressure in atm, V is the volume in L, n is the number of moles in mol, and T is the temperature in K.

Example:

Consider a vehicle in a 22° C garage. Its tires are inflated with 3.2 moles of air at 33 psi. Calculate the volume of air in its tires.

Using the ideal gas law,

$$°K = °C + 273 = 22 + 273 = 295 \text{ K}$$

$$P = 33 \text{ psi} \times \frac{1 \text{ atm}}{14.696 \text{ psi}} = 2.25 \text{ atm}$$

$$V = \frac{nRT}{P} = \frac{3.2 \text{ mol} \times 0.082 \frac{\text{L} \cdot \text{atm}}{\text{K} \cdot \text{mol}} \times 295 \text{ K}}{2.25 \text{ atm}} = 34.48 \text{ L}$$

PH

The **potential of hydrogen** (pH) is a measurement of the *concentration of hydrogen ions* in a substance in terms of the number of moles of H^+ per liter of solution. All substances fall between 0 and 14 on the pH scale. A lower pH indicates a higher H^+ concentration, while a higher pH indicates a lower H^+ concentration.

Pure water has a **neutral pH**, which is 7. Anything with a pH lower than pure water (<7) is considered **acidic**. Anything with a pH higher than pure water (>7) is a **base**. Drain cleaner, soap, baking soda, ammonia, egg whites, and sea water are common bases. Urine, stomach acid, citric acid, vinegar, hydrochloric acid, and battery acid are acids. A **pH indicator** is a substance that acts as a detector of hydrogen or hydronium ions. It is **halochromic**, meaning it changes color to indicate that hydrogen or hydronium ions have been detected.

Review Video: Overview of pH Levels
Visit mometrix.com/academy and enter code: 187395

Copyright © Mometrix Media. You have been licensed one copy of this document for personal use only. Any other reproduction or redistribution is strictly prohibited. All rights reserved.
This content is provided for test preparation purposes only and does not imply an endorsement by Mometrix of any particular political, scientific, or religious point of view.

BIOCHEMISTRY CONCEPTS
CHEMICAL STRUCTURES AND PROPERTIES OF BIOLOGICALLY IMPORTANT MOLECULES
CHEMICAL BONDING PROPERTIES OF CARBON

Carbon is considered to be the central atom of organic compounds. Carbon atoms each have four valence electrons and require four more electrons to have a stable outer shell. Due to the repulsion between the valence electrons, the bond sites are all equidistant from each other. This enables carbon to form longs chains and rings. Carbon atoms can form four single covalent bonds with other atoms. For example, methane (CH_4) consists of one carbon atom singly bonded to four separate hydrogen atoms. Carbon atoms can also form double or triple covalent bonds. For example, an oxygen atom can form a double bond with a carbon atom, and a nitrogen atom can form a triple bond with a carbon atom.

ORGANIC AND INORGANIC MOLECULES

Organic molecules contain carbon and hydrogen. Because carbon can form four covalent bonds, organic molecules can be very complex structures. Organic molecules can have carbon backbones that form long chains, branched chains, or even rings. Organic compounds tend to be less soluble in water than inorganic compounds. Organic compounds include four classes: carbohydrates, lipids, proteins, and nucleic acids. Specific examples of organic compounds include sucrose, cholesterol, insulin, and DNA. **Inorganic molecules** do not contain carbon and hydrogen that are bonded together. Inorganic compounds include salts and metals. Specific examples of inorganic molecules include sodium chloride, oxygen, and carbon dioxide.

CHEMICAL BONDS

Chemical bonds are the attractive forces that bind atoms together to form molecules. Chemical bonds include covalent bonds, ionic bonds, and metallic bonds. **Covalent bonds** are formed from the sharing of electron pairs between two atoms in a molecule. In organic molecules, carbon atoms form single, double, or triple covalent bonds. Organic compounds including proteins, carbohydrates, lipids, and nucleic acids are molecular compounds formed by covalent bonds.

> **Review Video: Basics of Organic Acids**
> Visit mometrix.com/academy and enter code: 238132

INTERMOLECULAR FORCES

Intermolecular forces are the attractive forces between molecules. Intermolecular forces include hydrogen bonds, London or dispersion forces, and dipole-dipole forces. **Hydrogen bonds** are the attractive forces between molecules containing hydrogen atoms covalently bonded to oxygen, fluorine, or nitrogen. Hydrogen bonds bind the two strands of a DNA molecule to each other. Two hydrogen bonds join each adenosine and thymine, and three hydrogen bonds join each cytosine and guanine.

ATP

Adenosine triphosphate (ATP) is the energy source for most cellular functions. Each ATP molecule is a nucleotide consisting of a central ribose sugar flanked by a purine base and a chain of three phosphate groups. The purine base is adenine, and when adenine is joined to ribose, an adenosine is formed, explaining the name

Copyright © Mometrix Media. You have been licensed one copy of this document for personal use only. Any other reproduction or redistribution is strictly prohibited. All rights reserved.
This content is provided for test preparation purposes only and does not imply an endorsement by Mometrix of any particular political, scientific, or religious point of view.

adenosine triphosphate. If one phosphate is removed from the end of the molecule, adenosine diphosphate (ADP) is formed.

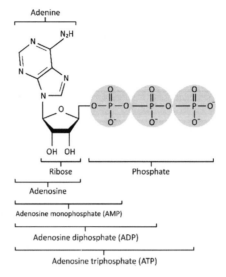

PROPERTIES OF WATER

Water exhibits numerous properties. Water has a high surface tension due to the cohesion between water molecules from the hydrogen bonds between the molecules. The capillary action of water is also due to this cohesion, and the adhesion of water is due to its polarity. Water is an excellent solvent due to its polarity and is considered the universal solvent. Water exists naturally as a solid, liquid, and gas. The density of water decreases as ice freezes and forms crystals in the solid phase. Water is most dense at 4°C. Water can act as an acid or base in chemical reactions. Pure water is an insulator because it has virtually no ions. Water has a high specific heat capacity due to its low molecular mass and bent molecular shape.

> **Review Video: Properties of Water**
> Visit mometrix.com/academy and enter code: 279526

BIOLOGICAL MACROMOLECULES

Macromolecules are large molecules made up of smaller organic molecules. Four classes of macromolecules include carbohydrates, nucleic acids, proteins, and lipids. Carbohydrates, proteins, and nucleic acids are polymers that are formed when the monomers are joined together in a dehydration process. In this dehydration process, the monomers are joined by a covalent bond and a water molecule is released. The monomers in carbohydrates are simple sugars such as glucose, while polysaccharides are polymers of carbohydrates. The monomers in proteins are amino acids. The amino acids form polypeptide chains, which are folded into proteins. The monomers in nucleic acids are nucleotides. Lipids are not actually considered to be polymers. Lipids typically are classified as fats, phospholipids, or steroids.

> **Review Video: Macromolecules**
> Visit mometrix.com/academy and enter code: 220156

BIOLOGICAL PROCESSES DEPENDENT ON CHEMICAL PRINCIPLES

BIOCHEMICAL PATHWAYS

Autotrophs that use light to produce energy use **photosynthesis** as a biochemical pathway. In eukaryotic autotrophs photosynthesis takes place in chloroplasts. Prokaryotic autotrophs that use inorganic chemical reactions to produce energy use **chemosynthesis** as a biochemical pathway. Heterotrophs require food and use **cellular respiration** to release energy from chemical bonds in the food. All organisms use cellular

Copyright © Mometrix Media. You have been licensed one copy of this document for personal use only. Any other reproduction or redistribution is strictly prohibited. All rights reserved.
This content is provided for test preparation purposes only and does not imply an endorsement by Mometrix of any particular political, scientific, or religious point of view.

respiration to release energy from stored food. Cellular respiration can be aerobic or anaerobic. Most eukaryotes use cellular respiration that takes place in the mitochondria.

PHOTOSYNTHESIS

Photosynthesis is a food-making process that occurs in three processes: light-capturing events, light-dependent reactions, and light-independent reactions. In light-capturing events, the thylakoids of the chloroplasts, which contain chlorophyll and accessory pigments, absorb light energy and produce excited electrons. Thylakoids also contain enzymes and electron-transport molecules. Molecules involved in this process are arranged in groups called photosystems. In light-dependent reactions, the excited electrons from the light-capturing events are moved by electron transport in a series of steps in which they are used to split water into hydrogen and oxygen ions. The oxygen is released, and the $NADP^+$ bonds with the hydrogen atoms and forms NADPH. ATP is produced from the excited electrons. The light-independent reactions use this ATP, NADPH, and carbon dioxide to produce sugars.

> **Review Video: Photosynthesis**
> Visit mometrix.com/academy and enter code: 227035

C_3 AND C_4 PHOTOSYNTHESIS

Plants undergo an additional process during photosynthesis that is known as photorespiration. Photorespiration is a wasteful process that uses energy and decreases sugar synthesis. This process occurs when the enzyme rubisco binds to oxygen rather than atmospheric carbon dioxide. There are three different processes that plants use to fix carbon during photosynthesis and these include C_3, C_4, and crassulacean acid metabolism (CAM). Some plants, such as C_4 and CAM plants, can decrease photorespiration and therefore minimize energy lost, while C_3 plants, which make up more than 85% of plants, have no special adaptations to stop photorespiration from occurring. C_3 and C_4 plants are named for the type of carbon molecule (three-carbon or four-carbon) that is made during the first step of the reaction. The first step of the C_3 process involves the formation of two three-carbon molecules (3-phosphoglycerate; 3-PGA) from carbon dioxide being fixed by the enzyme. The first step of C_4 photosynthesis is carbon dioxide being fixed by the enzyme PEP carboxylase, which unlike rubisco does not have the ability to bind to oxygen. This fixation forms a four-carbon molecule (oxaloaceate) and these initial steps occur in the mesophyll cell. Next, oxaloacetate is converted into a malate, a molecule that can enter the bundle sheath cells, and then is broken down to release carbon dioxide. From there, the carbon dioxide is fixed by rubisco as it undergoes the Calvin cycle seen in C_3 photosynthesis. Because C_4 plants undergo an initial step that allows carbon dioxide to be more readily available (via the use of malate), photorespiration is minimized.

CRASSULACEAN ACID METABOLISM

Crassulacean acid metabolism (CAM) is a form of photosynthesis adapted to dry environments. While C_4 plants separate the Calvin cycle via space, or by having different cells for different functions and processes, CAM plants separate the processes by time of day. During the night, pores of the plant leaves, called stomata, open to receive carbon dioxide, which combines with PEP carboxylase to form oxaloacetate. Oxaloacetate is eventually converted into malate, which is stored in vacuoles until the next day. During the following day, the stomata are closed and the malate is transported to chloroplasts, where malate is broken down into pyruvate (three-carbon molecule) and carbon dioxide. The carbon dioxide released from malate is used in photosynthesis during the daytime. One advantage of the CAM cycle is that it minimizes loss of water through the stomata during the daytime. A second advantage is that concentrating carbon dioxide in the chloroplasts in this manner increases the efficiency of the enzyme rubisco to fix carbon dioxide and complete the Calvin cycle.

AEROBIC RESPIRATION

Aerobic cellular respiration is a series of enzyme-controlled chemical reactions in which oxygen reacts with glucose to produce carbon dioxide and water, releasing energy in the form of adenosine triphosphate (ATP).

Copyright © Mometrix Media. You have been licensed one copy of this document for personal use only. Any other reproduction or redistribution is strictly prohibited. All rights reserved. This content is provided for test preparation purposes only and does not imply an endorsement by Mometrix of any particular political, scientific, or religious point of view.

Cellular respiration occurs in a series of three processes: glycolysis, the Krebs cycle, and the electron-transport system.

Review Video: **Aerobic Respiration**
Visit mometrix.com/academy and enter code: 770290

GLYCOLYSIS

Glycolysis is a series of enzyme-controlled chemical reactions that occur in the cell's cytoplasm. Each glucose molecule is split in half to produce two pyruvic acid molecules, four ATP molecules, and two NADH molecules. Because two ATP molecules are used to split the glucose molecule, the net ATP yield for glycolysis is two ATP molecules.

Review Video: **Glycolysis**
Visit mometrix.com/academy and enter code: 466815

KREBS CYCLE

The **Krebs cycle** is also called the citric acid cycle or the tricarboxylic acid cycle (TCA). It is a **catabolic pathway** in which the bonds of glucose, and occasionally fats or lipids, are broken down and reformed into ATP. It is a respiration process that uses oxygen and produces carbon dioxide, water, and ATP. Cells require energy from ATP to synthesize proteins from amino acids and replicate DNA. The cycle is acetyl CoA, citric acid, isocitric acid, ketoglutaric acid (products are amino acids and CO_2), succinyl CoA, succinic acid, fumaric acid, malic acid, and oxaloacetic acid. One of the products of the Krebs cycle is NADH, which is then used in the electron transport chain system to manufacture ATP. From glycolysis, pyruvate is oxidized in a step linking to the Krebs cycle. After the Krebs cycle, NADH and succinate are oxidized in the electron transport chain.

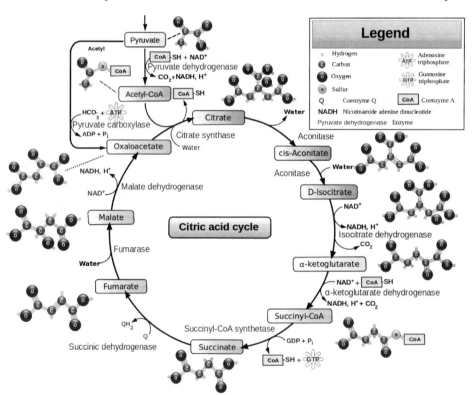

ELECTRON TRANSPORT CHAIN

The **electron transport chain** is part of phosphorylation, whereby electrons are transported from enzyme to enzyme until they reach a final acceptor. The electron transport chain includes a series of oxidizing and

Copyright © Mometrix Media. You have been licensed one copy of this document for personal use only. Any other reproduction or redistribution is strictly prohibited. All rights reserved. This content is provided for test preparation purposes only and does not imply an endorsement by Mometrix of any particular political, scientific, or religious point of view.

reducing molecules involved in the release of energy. In **redox reactions**, otherwise known as oxidation-reduction reactions, electrons and H^+ (protons) are either removed from or added to a substrate (reacts with a reagent to generate a product). During a reduction reaction, a substrate will gain electrons and protons or conversely lose them in an oxidation reaction. For example, when glucose is oxidized, electrons are lost and energy is released. These electrons will then be carried across enzymes along the membrane of mitochondria by a co-enzyme. Protons are also released to the other side of the membrane. For example, FAD and $FADH_2$ are used in oxidative phosphorylation. FAD is reduced to $FADH_2$. Electrons are stored there and then sent onward, and the $FADH_2$ becomes FAD again. In aerobic respiration, the final electron acceptor is O_2. In anaerobic respiration, it is something other than O_2.

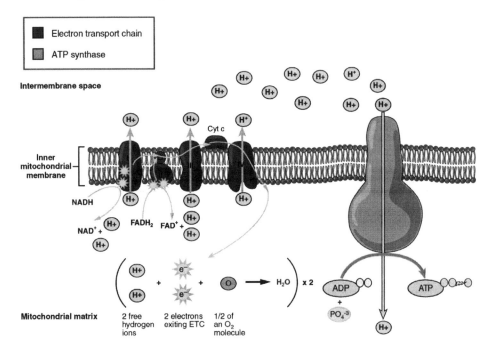

FERMENTATION

Fermentation is an anaerobic reaction in which glucose is only partially broken down. It releases energy through the oxidation of sugars or other types of organic molecules. Oxygen is sometimes involved, but not always. It is different from respiration in that it uses neither the Krebs cycle nor the electron transport chain, and the final electron acceptor is an organic molecule. It uses **substrate-level phosphorylation** to form ATP. NAD^+ is reduced to NADH and NADH further reduces pyruvic acid to various end products. Fermentation can lead to excess waste products and is less efficient than aerobic respiration. **Homolactic fermentation** refers to lactic acid fermentation in which the sugars are converted to lactic acid only (there is only one end product). In **heterolactic fermentation**, the sugars are converted to a range of products.

EXAMPLES OF FERMENTATION

Lactic acid fermentation is the breakdown of glucose and six-carbon sugars into lactic acid to release energy. It is an anaerobic process, meaning that it does not require oxygen. It can occur in muscle cells and is also performed by streptococcus and lactobacillus bacteria. It can also be used to make yogurt and other food products.

Alcohol fermentation is the breakdown of glucose and six-carbon sugars into ethanol and carbon dioxide to release energy. It is also an anaerobic process. It is performed by yeast and used in the production of alcoholic beverages.

Copyright © Mometrix Media. You have been licensed one copy of this document for personal use only. Any other reproduction or redistribution is strictly prohibited. All rights reserved.
This content is provided for test preparation purposes only and does not imply an endorsement by Mometrix of any particular political, scientific, or religious point of view.

CHEMOSYNTHESIS

Chemosynthesis is the food-making process of chemoautotrophs in extreme environments such as deep-sea vents, or hydrothermal vents. Unlike photosynthesis, chemosynthesis does not require light. In general, chemosynthesis involves the oxidation of inorganic substances to make a sugar, but there are several species that use different pathways or processes. For example, sulfur bacteria live near or in deep-sea vents and oxidize hydrogen sulfide released from those vents to make a sugar. Instead of sunlight, chemosynthesis uses the energy stored in the chemical bonds of chemicals such as hydrogen sulfide to produce food. During chemosynthesis, the electrons that are removed from the inorganic molecules are combined with carbon dioxide and oxygen to produce sugar, sulfur, and water. Some bacteria use metal ions such as iron and magnesium to obtain the needed electrons. For example, methanobacteria, such as those found in human intestines, combine carbon dioxide and hydrogen gas and release methane as a waste product. Nitrogen bacteria such as nitrogen-fixing bacteria in the nodules of legumes convert atmospheric nitrogen into nitrates.

STRUCTURE AND FUNCTION OF ENZYMES

ACTIVE SITE STRUCTURE AND SUBSTRATE BINDING

Each enzyme has a complex three-dimensional shape that is specifically designed to fit to a particular reactant, which is called the **substrate**. The enzyme and the substrate join temporarily forming the enzyme-substrate complex. This complex is unstable, and the chemical bonds are likely to be altered to produce a new molecule or molecules. Each enzyme can only combine with specific substrates because of this "lock-and-key" fit. Each enzyme has a designated binding site on the surface that binds to the substrate. Often, the binding site and the active site are at the same location. The enzyme and the substrate are specifically designed for each other, and as the substrate binds to the active site of the enzyme, that active site can bend and fold to form around the substrate. This concept of the active site slightly altering its shape is the **induced fit hypothesis**. The active site of the enzyme will return to its original shape after the products are released.

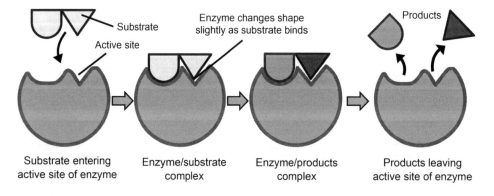

| Substrate entering active site of enzyme | Enzyme/substrate complex | Enzyme/products complex | Products leaving active site of enzyme |

EFFECTS OF TEMPERATURE, PH, AND INHIBITORS ON ENZYME ACTIVITY

The rate of an enzyme-controlled reaction is affected by factors such as temperature, pH, and inhibitors. According to kinetic-molecular theory, increasing the temperature increases the rate of molecular motion. Typically, increasing the temperature increases the rate of these reactions. The optimum temperature is the temperature at which the rate is the fastest and the most product is formed. Increasing the temperature above the optimum temperature actually decreases the reaction rate due to changes on the enzyme's structure that affect substrate binding. The pH also affects enzyme activity due to hydrogen ions binding to the enzyme's surface and changing the enzyme's surface shape. Because enzymes must have a specific shape for their specific substrate, enzymes have a certain pH range in which they can function. Inhibitors are molecules that attach to the enzymes and interfere with substrate binding which decreases or even halts enzyme-controlled reactions.

REGULATION OF ENZYMES BY FEEDBACK INHIBITION

Enzyme-controlled reactions can be regulated by feedback inhibition, or negative feedback. **Feedback inhibition** can be illustrated by a furnace and a thermostat. The inhibitor in this system is the heat. When the

Copyright © Mometrix Media. You have been licensed one copy of this document for personal use only. Any other reproduction or redistribution is strictly prohibited. All rights reserved.
This content is provided for test preparation purposes only and does not imply an endorsement by Mometrix of any particular political, scientific, or religious point of view.

furnace runs, the temperature increases. When the temperature reaches a specific level, the thermostat switches the furnace off. When the temperature decreases below a specific level, the thermostat switches the furnace back on, and the cycle begins again. In enzyme-controlled reactions, the end products of a metabolic pathway bind to the enzymes that initiate the metabolic pathway. This causes the reaction rate to decrease. The more product there is, the less product is produced. The less product there is, the more product is produced. This process of feedback inhibition enables a stable range of concentrations that are necessary for homeostasis.

> **Review Video: Enzymes**
> Visit mometrix.com/academy and enter code: 656995

BIOCHEMICAL PROCESSES WITHIN AN ORGANISM
CONCENTRATION GRADIENTS

Concentration gradients, also called diffusion gradients, are differences in the concentration or the number of molecules of solutes in a solution between two regions. A gradient can also result from an unequal distribution of ions across a cell membrane. Solutes move along a concentration gradient by random motion from the region of high concentration toward the region of low concentration in a process called **diffusion**. Diffusion is the movement of molecules or ions down a concentration gradient. Diffusion is the method by which oxygen, carbon dioxide, and other nonpolar molecules cross a cell membrane. The steepness of the concentration gradient affects the rate of diffusion. **Passive transport** makes use of concentration gradients as well as electric gradients to move substances across the cell membrane, while **active transport** can move a substance against its concentration gradient.

LAWS OF THERMODYNAMICS AND GIBBS FREE ENERGY

The **first law of thermodynamics** states that energy can neither be created nor destroyed. Energy may change forms, but the energy in a closed system is constant. The **second law of thermodynamics** states that systems tend toward a state of lower energy and greater disorder. This disorder is called **entropy**. According to the second law of thermodynamics, entropy is increasing. **Gibbs free energy** is the energy in a system that is available or "free" to be released to perform work at a constant temperature. Organisms must be able to use energy to survive and biological processes such as the chemical reactions involved in metabolism are governed by these laws.

ANABOLIC AND CATABOLIC REACTIONS

Anabolism and catabolism are metabolic processes. **Anabolism** is essentially the synthesis of large molecules from monomers, whereas **catabolism** is the decomposition of large molecules into their component monomers. Anabolism uses energy, whereas catabolism produces energy. Anabolism typically builds and repair tissues, and catabolism typically burns stored food to produce energy. Protein synthesis, which is the polymerization of amino acids to form proteins, is an anabolic reaction. Another anabolic process is the mineralization of bones. An example of a catabolic reaction is hydrolysis, which is the decomposition of polymers into monomers that releases a water molecule and energy. Cellular respiration is a catabolic process in which typically glucose combines with oxygen to release energy in the form of adenosine triphosphate (ATP).

OXIDATION-REDUCTION REACTIONS

Oxidation-reduction reactions, or redox reactions, involve the transfer of electrons from one substance to another. Reduction occurs in the substance that gains the electrons. Oxidation occurs in the substance that loses the electrons. Cellular respiration and photosynthesis are examples of redox reactions. During cellular respiration, glucose molecules are oxidized and oxygen molecules are reduced. Because electrons lose energy when being transferred to oxygen, the electrons are usually first transferred to the coenzyme NAD^+, which is reduced to NADH. The NADH then releases the energy to oxygen. During photosynthesis, water molecules are split and oxidized, and carbon dioxide molecules are reduced. When the water molecules are split, electrons are transferred with the hydrogen ions to the carbon dioxide molecules.

41

Copyright © Mometrix Media. You have been licensed one copy of this document for personal use only. Any other reproduction or redistribution is strictly prohibited. All rights reserved. This content is provided for test preparation purposes only and does not imply an endorsement by Mometrix of any particular political, scientific, or religious point of view.

ORGANIC CHEMISTRY CONCEPTS

NOMENCLATURE FOR ORGANIC COMPOUNDS

ALKANES, ALKENES, AND ALKYNES

Alkanes, alkenes, and alkynes are organic compounds called **hydrocarbons**, which consist only of carbon and hydrogen. **Alkanes** have only single bonds between their carbon atoms. Alkanes are saturated hydrocarbons because they contain as many hydrogen atoms as possible due to their single bonds. Alkanes include methane (CH_4), ethane (C_2H_8), propane (C_3H_8), and butane (C_4H_{10}).

Alkenes have at least one double bond between two of their carbon atoms. Alkenes are unsaturated hydrocarbons. Alkenes include ethene or ethylene (C_2H_4), propene (C_3H_6), 1-butene (C_4H_8), and 1-pentene (C_5H_{10}).

Alkynes have at least one triple bond between two of their carbon atoms. Like alkenes, alkynes are unsaturated hydrocarbons. Alkynes include ethyne or acetylene (C_2H_2), 1-propyne (C_3H_4), 1-butyne (C_4H_6), and 1-pentyne (C_5H_8).

NAMING ALKANES, ALKENES, AND ALKYNES

The prefixes of alkanes, alkenes, and alkynes are based on the number of carbon atoms. These prefixes are given by the table below. For example, an alkane with one carbon atom is named methane. An alkane with two carbon atoms would be named ethane. An alkene with two carbon atoms is named ethene. An alkene with five carbon atoms is named pentene. An alkyne with four carbon atoms is named butyne. An alkyne with eight carbon atoms is named octyne.

Hydrocarbons

#	Prefix	#	Prefix
1	meth-	6	hexa-
2	eth-	7	hepta-
3	prop-	8	octa-
4	but-	9	nona-
5	penta-	10	deca-

Review Video: Basics of Alkenes
Visit mometrix.com/academy and enter code: 916284

Review Video: Basics of Alkynes
Visit mometrix.com/academy and enter code: 963837

Review Video: Rules for Naming Alkanes, Alkenes, and Alkynes
Visit mometrix.com/academy and enter code: 441567

Copyright © Mometrix Media. You have been licensed one copy of this document for personal use only. Any other reproduction or redistribution is strictly prohibited. All rights reserved.
This content is provided for test preparation purposes only and does not imply an endorsement by Mometrix of any particular political, scientific, or religious point of view.

ALCOHOL

An **alcohol** is a substituted hydrocarbon compound with a hydroxyl group (-OH) bound to a saturated carbon. To name an alcohol, drop the *-e* from the name of the hydrocarbon and add *-ol*. For example, when the functional group for an alcohol replaces one hydrogen in methane, then the name is changed to methanol (left). Likewise, ethane becomes ethanol (right).

Review Video: Naming of Alcohols
Visit mometrix.com/academy and enter code: 737321

ETHER

An **ether** is a substituted hydrocarbon compound containing an oxygen molecule linking two hydrocarbon groups. Ethers are named for the two hydrocarbons that flank the functional group. The root of the shorter of the two chains is named first. This is followed by *-oxy-*, which is then followed by the name of the longer chain. For example, $CH_3OCH_2CH_3$ (below) is named methoxyethane (also commonly expressed C_3H_8O or ethyl methyl ether).

ALDEHYDE

An **aldehyde** is a substituted hydrocarbon compound with an oxygen molecule that is double-bound to the CH group at an end of a hydrocarbon chain. To name an aldehyde, drop the *-e* from the name of the hydrocarbon and add *-al*. For example, when the functional group for an aldehyde is substituted into methane, the aldehyde name would be methanal, also known as formaldehyde (below).

KETONE

A **ketone** is a substituted hydrocarbon compound containing an oxygen that is double-bound to a carbon atom somewhere within the hydrocarbon chain. The difference between a ketone and an aldehyde is that in an aldehyde the =O will be at one or both ends of the hydrocarbon molecule, whereas in a ketone the =O will be somewhere other than the end of the hydrocarbon molecule. To name a ketone, drop *-e* from the name of the hydrocarbon and add *-one*. For example, when the functional group for a ketone is inserted into propane, the name is changed to propanone, which is commonly known as acetone (below).

Copyright © Mometrix Media. You have been licensed one copy of this document for personal use only. Any other reproduction or redistribution is strictly prohibited. All rights reserved. This content is provided for test preparation purposes only and does not imply an endorsement by Mometrix of any particular political, scientific, or religious point of view.

CARBOXYLIC ACIDS

Carboxylic acids are organic compounds that contain a carboxyl functional group that consists of a carbon atom double-bonded to an oxygen and single-bonded to a hydroxyl (–OH). For example, the simplest carboxylic acid is formic acid, HCO_2H (left). Acetic acid or ethanoic acid, CH_3CO_2H or $HC_2H_3O_2$ (right), is commonly known as vinegar. Fatty acids and amino acids are also examples of carboxylic acids.

BENZENE

Benzene is an organic compound that is an aromatic hydrocarbon. Benzene has a molecular formula of C_6H_6, where the six carbon atoms are arranged in a "ring" shaped like a hexagon. Each carbon is single-bonded to two other carbons and single-bonded to one hydrogen. The remaining valence electrons from the six carbon atoms are delocalized electrons that are shared among all the carbons in the molecule and are typically represented with alternating double bonds.

Derivatives of benzene include phenol, which is used in producing carbonates; toluene, which is used as a solvent and an octane booster in gasoline; and aniline, which is used in the production of polyurethane.

AMINE

An **amine** is a compound with a nitrogen atom that contains a lone pair of electrons and is bound to one or more hydrocarbon groups. Amines may be named in more than one way. The two most common ways are either with the prefix *amino-* or the suffix *-amine.* Two simple amines are methylamine (CH_3NH_2) and ethylamine ($CH_3CH_2NH_2$).

BIOCHEMICAL COMPOUNDS

BIOCHEMICAL COMPOUNDS

The four major classes of biochemical compounds are carbohydrates, lipids, proteins, and nucleic acids. Examples of **carbohydrates** include monosaccharides such as glucose, fructose, and ribose; disaccharides such as sucrose and lactose; and polysaccharides such as starch, cellulose, and glycogen. Examples of **lipids** include fatty acids, triglycerides, oils, lard, fat-soluble vitamins, waxes, and steroids such as cholesterol. Examples of **proteins** include enzymes, collagen, hemoglobin, histones, many hormones, and antibodies. Examples of **nucleic acids** include deoxyribonucleic acid (DNA) and ribonucleic acid (RNA).

Copyright © Mometrix Media. You have been licensed one copy of this document for personal use only. Any other reproduction or redistribution is strictly prohibited. All rights reserved.
This content is provided for test preparation purposes only and does not imply an endorsement by Mometrix of any particular political, scientific, or religious point of view.

CARBOHYDRATES

Carbohydrates are organic compounds that produce energy. The empirical formula for most carbohydrates is CH_2O, which indicates that the ratio of carbon, hydrogen, and oxygen is always 1:2:1. The structure generally consists of aldehydes and ketones containing many hydroxyl groups. In general, carbohydrates are sugars and starches. Carbohydrates can be grouped as simple sugars or complex carbohydrates. The simple sugars include monosaccharides such as glucose and ribose and disaccharides such as sucrose and lactose. Complex carbohydrates are polymers of monosaccharides and include the polysaccharides such as cellulose, starch, and glycogen.

Review Video: Carbohydrates
Visit mometrix.com/academy and enter code: 601714

MONOSACCHARIDES, DISACCHARIDES, AND POLYSACCHARIDES

Monosaccharides, disaccharides, and polysaccharides are special types of organic compounds called carbohydrates, which are compounds composed of carbon, hydrogen, and oxygen. **Monosaccharides** and **disaccharides** are sugars. Monosaccharides are the simplest carbohydrates. Examples of monosaccharides are glucose, fructose (fruit sugar), ribose, and galactose. Disaccharides consist of two monosaccharides joined together. Examples of disaccharides include sucrose (table sugar), which is a compound of glucose and fructose, and lactose (milk sugar), which is a compound of glucose and galactose. **Polysaccharides** are polymers of monosaccharides. Examples of polysaccharides include cellulose, starch, and glycogen.

LIPIDS

Lipids have many functions. The main function of lipids is storing energy. One type of lipid is **triglycerides**, which include fats and oils. Lipids known as **phospholipids** also form the cell membranes of all plant and animal cells. Lipids can relay messages among cells in the nervous system and in the immune system. Some lipids are **steroids**, which serve many functions. For example, cholesterol helps make cell membranes pliable, and some steroids make up hormones such as testosterone and estrogen. Fat-soluble vitamins are also steroids.

Review Video: Lipids
Visit mometrix.com/academy and enter code: 269746

PROTEINS

Proteins are polymers of **amino acids**. The amino acids are joined together by peptide bonds. The two major groups of proteins are fibrous proteins and globular proteins. **Fibrous proteins** provide structure in cells, bone tissue, connective tissue and line cartilage, tendons, and epidermal tissue. Examples of fibrous proteins include collagen, elastin, and keratin. **Globular proteins** are folded molecules that include enzymes, hemoglobin, and some hormones. Antibodies are globular proteins that help defend the body from antigens. Some proteins, such as actin and myosin, are involved in muscle contraction. Some proteins act as storage containers for amino acids. Other proteins, such as hemoglobin, help transport materials throughout the body.

DNA

DNA, or deoxyribonucleic acid, is a two-stranded molecule in the shape of a double helix. DNA nucleotides consist of a deoxyribose (sugar), a phosphate, and a base. The bases are guanine, thymine, cytosine and adenine. Guanine always pairs with cytosine, and thymine always pairs with adenine. If the double helix is compared to a twisted ladder, the legs of the ladder are the sugars and phosphates, and the rungs of the ladder consist of the bases. The bases that make up the rungs of the ladder are bound together with hydrogen bonds.

DNA VS. RNA

Deoxyribonucleic acid (DNA) and ribonucleic acid (RNA) are both nucleic acids composed of **nucleotides**, which have three of their four bases in common: guanine, adenine, and cytosine. The sugar in DNA nucleotides is deoxyribose, whereas the sugar in RNA nucleotides is ribose. DNA contains the base thymine, but RNA

45

Copyright © Mometrix Media. You have been licensed one copy of this document for personal use only. Any other reproduction or redistribution is strictly prohibited. All rights reserved.
This content is provided for test preparation purposes only and does not imply an endorsement by Mometrix of any particular political, scientific, or religious point of view.

replaces thymine with uracil. DNA is double-stranded, and RNA is single-stranded. DNA has the shape of a double helix, whereas RNA is complexly folded. DNA stores the genetic information of the cell, while RNA has several forms. For example, mRNA, or messenger RNA, is a working copy of DNA, and tRNA, or transfer RNA, collects the needed amino acids for the ribosomes during the assembling of proteins.

NET EQUATION FOR PHOTOSYNTHESIS

Photosynthesis is the food-making process in green plants. Photosynthesis occurs in the chloroplasts of cells in the presence of light and chlorophyll. The reactants are **carbon dioxide** and **water**. The energy from the sunlight is absorbed and stored in the glucose molecules. The net equation for photosynthesis can be represented by the following equations:

$$\text{carbon dioxide} + \text{water} + \text{light} \xrightarrow{\text{chlorophyll}} \text{glucose} + \text{oxygen}$$

$$6CO_2 + 6H_2O + \text{light} \xrightarrow{\text{chlorophyll}} C_6H_{12}O_6 + 6O_2.$$

The products of photosynthesis are glucose and oxygen gas. Glucose is a simple carbohydrate or sugar, which is a six-carbon monosaccharide.

RESPIRATION

Cellular respiration is the process in which energy is released from glucose in the form of adenosine triphosphate (ATP). **Cellular respiration** is the reverse process of photosynthesis. In cellular respiration, glucose is burned or combined with oxygen as shown in the following equations:

$$\text{glucose} + \text{oxygen} \rightarrow \text{carbon dioxide} + \text{water} + \text{ATP}$$

$$C_6H_{12}O_6 + 6O_2 \rightarrow 6CO_2 + 6H_2O$$

The products of cellular respiration are carbon dioxide and water. Energy is released from glucose in the form of ATP.

ORGANIC COMPOUNDS

Organic compounds are compounds that contain carbon and hydrogen. **Carbon** has only four valence electrons and will form four covalent bonds with hydrogen and other atoms or groups of atoms in order to satisfy the octet rule. Carbon can form single, double, and triple bonds with other atoms. Carbon can form long chains, branched chains, and rings in organic compounds. **Hydrocarbons** are organic compounds that contain only carbon and hydrogen. **Substituted hydrocarbons** are hydrocarbons that still have the carbon backbone, but one or more of the hydrogen atoms have been substituted with a different atom or group of atoms called a functional group. **Functional groups** may be single atoms such as in the halocarbons, where a halogen such as chlorine or fluorine is substituted for a hydrogen atom. Some functional groups consist of more than one atom such as the alcohols, which have the hydroxyl (–OH) functional group.

Physics

NEWTON'S LAWS
NEWTON'S FIRST LAW

Before Newton formulated his laws of mechanics, it was generally assumed that some force had to act on an object continuously in order to make the object move at a constant velocity. Newton, however, determined that unless some other force acted on the object (most notably friction or air resistance), it would continue in the direction it was pushed at the same velocity forever. In this light, a body at rest and a body in motion are not all that different, and Newton's first law makes little distinction. It states that a body at rest will tend to remain at rest, while a body in motion will tend to remain in motion. This phenomenon is commonly referred to as inertia, the tendency of a body to remain in its present state of motion. In order for the body's state of motion

Copyright © Mometrix Media. You have been licensed one copy of this document for personal use only. Any other reproduction or redistribution is strictly prohibited. All rights reserved.
This content is provided for test preparation purposes only and does not imply an endorsement by Mometrix of any particular political, scientific, or religious point of view.

to change, it must be acted on by a non-zero net force. Net force is the vector sum of all forces acting on a body. If this vector sum is zero, then there is no unbalanced force, and the body will remain in its present state of motion. It is important to remember that this law only holds in inertial reference frames.

> **Review Video: Newton's First Law of Motion**
> Visit mometrix.com/academy and enter code: 590367

NEWTON'S SECOND LAW

Newton's second law states that an object's acceleration is directly proportional to the net force acting on the object, and inversely proportional to the object's mass. It is generally written in equation form **F** = m**a**, where **F** is the net force acting on a body, m is the mass of the body, and **a** is its acceleration. It is important to note from this equation that since the mass is always a positive quantity, the acceleration vector is always pointed in the same direction as the net force vector. Of course, in order to apply this equation correctly, one must clearly identify the body to which it is being applied. Once this is done, we may say that **F** is the vector sum of all forces acting on that body, or the net force. This measure includes only those forces that are external to the body; any internal forces, in which one part of the body exerts force on another, are discounted. Newton's second law somewhat encapsulates his first, because it includes the principle that if no net force is acting on a body, the body will not accelerate. As was the case with his first law, Newton's second law may only be applied in inertial reference frames.

> **Review Video: Newton's Second Law of Motion**
> Visit mometrix.com/academy and enter code: 737975

NEWTON'S THIRD LAW

Newton's third law of motion is quite simple: for every force, there is an equal and opposite force. When a hammer strikes a nail, the nail hits the hammer just as hard. If we consider two objects, A and B, then we may express any contact between these two bodies with the equation $F_{AB} = -F_{BA}$. It is important to note in this kind of equation that the order of the subscripts denotes which body is exerting the force. Although the two forces are often referred to as the *action* and *reaction* forces, in physics there is really no such thing. There is no implication of cause and effect in the equation for Newton's third law. At first glance, this law might seem to forbid any movement at all. We must remember, however, that these equal, opposite forces are exerted on different bodies with different masses, so they will not cancel each other out.

> **Review Video: Newton's Third Law of Motion**
> Visit mometrix.com/academy and enter code: 838401

ACCELERATION, VELOCITY, MOMENTUM

There are two types of velocity that are commonly considered in physics: average velocity and instantaneous velocity, although only the former is in the scope of this review. **Average velocity** is based on two variables: the displacement of the object, or the distance it has traveled, and the time it took to cover the distance. To calculate average velocity, use the following equation:

$$v_{avg} = \frac{(x_f - x_i)}{(t_f - t_i)}$$

where the subscripts i and f denote the initial and final values of the position and time. In other words, the average velocity is equal to the change in position divided by the change in time. This calculation will indicate the average distance that was covered per unit of time. Average velocity is a vector and will always point in the same direction as the displacement vector (since time is a scalar and always positive).

Copyright © Mometrix Media. You have been licensed one copy of this document for personal use only. Any other reproduction or redistribution is strictly prohibited. All rights reserved.
This content is provided for test preparation purposes only and does not imply an endorsement by Mometrix of any particular political, scientific, or religious point of view.

For example, if a man completes a 3.1-mile race in 18 minutes, his average velocity is:

$$v_{avg} = \frac{(3.1 \text{ miles} - 0 \text{ miles})}{\left(\left(18 \text{ min.} \times \frac{1 \text{ hour}}{60 \text{ min.}}\right) - 0\right)} = 10.33 \text{ mph}$$

Acceleration is the change in the velocity of an object. Like velocity, acceleration may be computed as an average or an instantaneous quantity. To calculate average acceleration, use the following equation:

$$a_{avg} = \frac{(v_f - v_i)}{(t_f - t_i)}$$

where the subscripts i and f denote the initial and final values of the velocity and time. The so-called instantaneous acceleration of an object can be found by reducing the time component to an instant, or almost zero. Acceleration is expressed in units of distance divided by time squared, such as feet per second squared.

For example, suppose a vehicle is traveling down the highway at 75 miles per hour, then enters a town and slows down to 40 miles per hour. If it takes the vehicle 10 seconds to slow down, its average acceleration in feet per second squared is:

$$(40 - 75 \text{ mph}) \times \frac{5280 \text{ feet}}{1 \text{ mile}} \times \frac{1 \text{ hour}}{3600 \text{ seconds}} = -51.33 \text{ ft/s}$$

$$a_{avg} = \frac{-51.33 \text{ ft/s}}{(10 \text{ seconds} - 0 \text{ seconds})} = -5.13 \text{ ft/s}^2$$

In physics, **linear momentum** can be found by multiplying the mass and velocity of a particle:

$$p = mv$$

Momentum has units of foot-pounds per second. Like velocity, momentum is a vector quantity and will always have the same direction as the velocity. Newton's second law describes momentum, stating that the rate of change of momentum is proportional to the force exerted, and is in the direction of the force.

For example, if a 54,000-pound fuel truck is driving at 30 mph, its momentum is:

$$30 \text{ mph} \times \frac{5280 \text{ ft}}{1 \text{ mile}} \times \frac{1 \text{ hour}}{3600 \text{ seconds}} = 44 \text{ ft/s}$$

$$p = 54,000 \text{ lb} \times 44 \text{ ft/s} = 2.77 \times 10^6 \text{ ft} \cdot \text{lb/s}$$

FRICTION

Friction is the resistance to motion of one object moving relative to another. Imagine a book resting on a table. As it sits there, the force of its weight (W) is equal and opposite to the normal force (N). If, however, a force (F) were to be exerted on one side of the book, a frictional force (f) would arise, equal and opposite to the pushing force. This kind of frictional force is known as **static frictional force**. As the force on the book is increased, however, it will eventually accelerate in the direction it is being pushed. At this point, the frictional force opposing the pushing force will be known as **kinetic frictional force**. For the most part, kinetic frictional force is lower than static frictional force, and so the amount of force needed to maintain the movement of the book will be less than that needed to initiate movement. Static frictional force has a maximum value, however, which is expressed as

$$f_{s_{max}} = \mu_s N$$

Copyright © Mometrix Media. You have been licensed one copy of this document for personal use only. Any other reproduction or redistribution is strictly prohibited. All rights reserved. This content is provided for test preparation purposes only and does not imply an endorsement by Mometrix of any particular political, scientific, or religious point of view.

where μ_s is the coefficient of static friction, and N is the magnitude of the normal force. If the magnitude of F should exceed the maximum value of static friction, the body will begin to move. Once the body has begun to slide, the frictional force will generally decrease. The value to which the frictional force will diminish is expressed as

$$f_k = \mu_k N$$

where μ_k is the coefficient of kinetic friction. For example, consider a shipping crate resting on a 30 degree slope. If the crate weighs 100 lb and the coefficient of static friction between the crate and the ramp is 0.3, the maximum static friction force must be:

$$N = 100 \times \cos(30°) = 86.6 \text{ lb}$$

$$f_{s_{max}=} 0.3 \times 86.6 = 26 \text{ lb}$$

KINETIC AND POTENTIAL ENERGY

The kinetic energy of an object is the quantity of its motion related to the amount of work performed on the object. **Kinetic energy** can be defined as

$$KE = \frac{1}{2} mv^2$$

in which m is the mass of an object and v is the magnitude of its velocity. Kinetic energy cannot be negative, since it depends on the square of velocity. Units for kinetic energy are the same as those for work: joules or foot-pounds.

Potential energy is the amount of energy that can be ascribed to a body or bodies based on configuration. Gravitational potential energy is the energy associated with the separation of bodies that are attracted to one another gravitationally. Any time an object is lifted, its gravitational potential energy is increased. Gravitational potential energy can be found by the equation

$$PE = mgh$$

where m is the mass of an object, g is the gravitational acceleration, and h is its height above a reference point, usually the ground. Another type of potential energy is elastic potential energy, which is associated with the compression or expansion of an elastic, or spring like, object.

Forces that change the state of a system by changing kinetic energy into potential energy, or vice versa, are called **conservative forces**. This name arises because these forces conserve the total amount of kinetic and potential energy. One example of a conservative force is *gravity*. Consider the path of a ball thrown straight up into the air. Right when it is thrown, all the energy is kinetic. At the peak of the throw, all the energy is potential. Since there is the same amount of energy in the system at all times, the kinetic energy when the ball is thrown is equal to the potential energy when it is highest in the air.

For example, if a high diver jumps off a diving board and enters the water at a speed of 50 mph, the height of the diving board can be calculated by equating his kinetic energy upon entering the water with his potential energy right before jumping.

$$50 \text{ mph} \times \frac{5280 \text{ ft}}{1 \text{ mile}} \times \frac{1 \text{ hour}}{3600 \text{ sec}} = 73.33 \text{ ft/s}$$

$$h = \frac{\frac{1}{2} v^2}{g} = \frac{\frac{1}{2} (73.33)^2}{32.17 \text{ ft/s}^2} = 83.6 \text{ ft}$$

Copyright © Mometrix Media. You have been licensed one copy of this document for personal use only. Any other reproduction or redistribution is strictly prohibited. All rights reserved.
This content is provided for test preparation purposes only and does not imply an endorsement by Mometrix of any particular political, scientific, or religious point of view.

EQUILIBRIUM EQUATIONS

If an object is not moving, all the forces on it must be **balanced**. They are not necessarily equal, but the sum of all the forces acting on the object is zero. This knowledge can be used to calculate missing forces in static situations. For example, if a block rests on the floor without motion, it is at **equilibrium**. Because the object has some force due to gravity pulling it down, the floor must be opposing the block with an equal, but opposite, force. Two-dimensional force equilibrium says that the sum of all forces in the x- and y-direction is zero, and the sum of all moments is zero:

$$\begin{cases} \sum F_x = 0 \\ \sum F_y = 0 \\ \sum M = 0 \end{cases}$$

STRESS AND STRAIN

In mechanics, stress is a quantity of force per unit area in or on an object. **Tensile** or **compressive stress** acts normal to the area of stress and is calculated with the following equation:

$$\sigma = \frac{F_n}{A}$$

where

σ is the compressive or tensile stress

F_n is the normal component force

A is the area

For example, if a reinforcement rod is pounded into the ground, it experiences compressive stress. If the rod is half an inch in diameter and is hit by a sledgehammer bearing 100 pounds of force, the stress can be calculated as

$$\sigma_{rod} = \frac{100 \text{ lb}}{\pi \times (0.25 \text{ in})^2} = 509.4 \text{ psi}$$

Strain is the deformation of an object due to stress and is expressed by the following equation:

$$\varepsilon = \frac{\Delta l}{l_0}$$

where

ε is the unitless measure of strain

Δl is the change in length

l_0 is the initial length

Suppose a 6-foot-long lead pipe has a tensile force applied to it and stretches to 6 ft $\frac{1}{32}$ in. The strain can be calculated as

Copyright © Mometrix Media. You have been licensed one copy of this document for personal use only. Any other reproduction or redistribution is strictly prohibited. All rights reserved.
This content is provided for test preparation purposes only and does not imply an endorsement by Mometrix of any particular political, scientific, or religious point of view.

$$\varepsilon_p = \frac{\frac{1}{32}\,\text{in} \times \frac{1\,\text{ft}}{12\,\text{in}}}{6\,\text{ft}} = 4.34 \times 10^{-4}$$

Hooke's law states that stress and strain are directly proportional, and equal to the modulus of elasticity:

$$E = \frac{\sigma}{\varepsilon}$$

where

    E is the modulus of elasticity (psi)

    σ is the stress

    ε is the strain

Using this information with regard to the lead pipe example, the stress on the pipe can be calculated given that the modulus of elasticity for lead is 2×10^6 psi:

$$\sigma_p = 2 \times 10^6 \times 4.34 \times 10^{-4} = 868 \text{ psi}$$

Mathematics

GEOMETRY
POINTS AND LINES

A **point** is a fixed location in space, has no size or dimensions, and is commonly represented by a dot. A **line** is a set of points that extends infinitely in two opposite directions. It has length, but no width or depth. A line can be defined by any two distinct points that it contains. A **line segment** is a portion of a line that has definite endpoints. A **ray** is a portion of a line that extends from a single point on that line in one direction along the line. It has a definite beginning, but no ending.

Point   Line   Segment   Ray

INTERACTIONS BETWEEN LINES

Intersecting lines are lines that have exactly one point in common. **Concurrent lines** are multiple lines that intersect at a single point. **Perpendicular lines** are lines that intersect at right angles. They are represented by the symbol ⊥. The shortest distance from a line to a point not on the line is a perpendicular segment from the point to the line. **Parallel lines** are lines in the same plane that have no points in common and never meet. It is possible for lines to be in different planes, have no points in common, and never meet, but they are not parallel because they are in different planes.

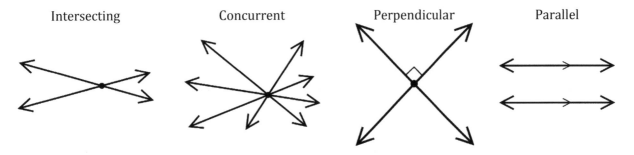

Intersecting   Concurrent   Perpendicular   Parallel

Copyright © Mometrix Media. You have been licensed one copy of this document for personal use only. Any other reproduction or redistribution is strictly prohibited. All rights reserved.
This content is provided for test preparation purposes only and does not imply an endorsement by Mometrix of any particular political, scientific, or religious point of view.

A **transversal** is a line that intersects at least two other lines, which may or may not be parallel to one another. A transversal that intersects parallel lines is a common occurrence in geometry. A **bisector** is a line or line segment that divides another line segment into two equal lengths. A **perpendicular bisector** of a line segment is composed of points that are equidistant from the endpoints of the segment it is dividing.

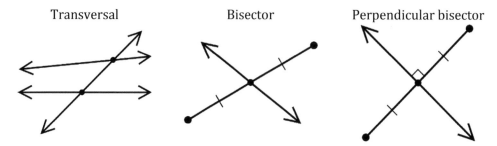

The **projection of a point on a line** is the point at which a perpendicular line drawn from the given point to the given line intersects the line. This is also the shortest distance from the given point to the line. The **projection of a segment on a line** is a segment whose endpoints are the points formed when perpendicular lines are drawn from the endpoints of the given segment to the given line. This is similar to the length a diagonal line appears to be when viewed from above.

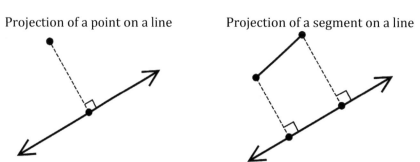

PLANES

A **plane** is a two-dimensional flat surface defined by three non-collinear points. A plane extends an infinite distance in all directions in those two dimensions. It contains an infinite number of points, parallel lines and segments, intersecting lines and segments, as well as parallel or intersecting rays. A plane will never contain a three-dimensional figure or skew lines, lines that don't intersect and are not parallel. Two given planes are either parallel or they intersect at a line. A plane may intersect a circular conic surface to form **conic sections**, such as a parabola, hyperbola, circle or ellipse.

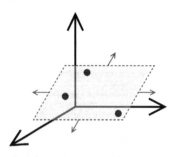

Review Video: <u>Lines and Planes</u>
Visit mometrix.com/academy and enter code: 554267

Copyright © Mometrix Media. You have been licensed one copy of this document for personal use only. Any other reproduction or redistribution is strictly prohibited. All rights reserved.
This content is provided for test preparation purposes only and does not imply an endorsement by Mometrix of any particular political, scientific, or religious point of view.

Angles and Vertices

An **angle** is formed when two lines or line segments meet at a common point. It may be a common starting point for a pair of segments or rays, or it may be the intersection of lines. Angles are represented by the symbol ∠.

The **vertex** is the point at which two segments or rays meet to form an angle. If the angle is formed by intersecting rays, lines, and/or line segments, the vertex is the point at which four angles are formed. The pairs of angles opposite one another are called vertical angles, and their measures are equal.

- An **acute** angle is an angle with a degree measure less than 90°.
- A **right** angle is an angle with a degree measure of exactly 90°.
- An **obtuse** angle is an angle with a degree measure greater than 90° but less than 180°.
- A **straight angle** is an angle with a degree measure of exactly 180°. This is also a semicircle.
- A **reflex angle** is an angle with a degree measure greater than 180° but less than 360°.

A **full angle** is an angle with a degree measure of exactly 360°. This is also a circle.

Relationships between Angles

Two angles whose sum is exactly 90° are said to be **complementary**. The two angles may or may not be adjacent. In a right triangle, the two acute angles are complementary.

Two angles whose sum is exactly 180° are said to be **supplementary**. The two angles may or may not be adjacent. Two intersecting lines always form two pairs of supplementary angles. Adjacent supplementary angles will always form a straight line.

Two angles that have the same vertex and share a side are said to be **adjacent**. Vertical angles are not adjacent because they share a vertex but no common side.

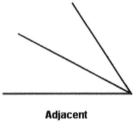

Adjacent
Share vertex and side

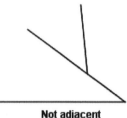

Not adjacent
Share part of side, but not vertex

When two parallel lines are cut by a transversal, the angles that are between the two parallel lines are **interior angles**. In the diagram below, angles 3, 4, 5, and 6 are interior angles.

When two parallel lines are cut by a transversal, the angles that are outside the parallel lines are **exterior angles**. In the diagram below, angles 1, 2, 7, and 8 are exterior angles.

When two parallel lines are cut by a transversal, the angles that are in the same position relative to the transversal and a parallel line are **corresponding angles**. The diagram below has four pairs of corresponding angles: angles 1 and 5, angles 2 and 6, angles 3 and 7, and angles 4 and 8. Corresponding angles formed by parallel lines are congruent.

When two parallel lines are cut by a transversal, the two interior angles that are on opposite sides of the transversal are called **alternate interior angles**. In the diagram below, there are two pairs of alternate interior angles: angles 3 and 6, and angles 4 and 5. Alternate interior angles formed by parallel lines are congruent.

Copyright © Mometrix Media. You have been licensed one copy of this document for personal use only. Any other reproduction or redistribution is strictly prohibited. All rights reserved. This content is provided for test preparation purposes only and does not imply an endorsement by Mometrix of any particular political, scientific, or religious point of view.

When two parallel lines are cut by a transversal, the two exterior angles that are on opposite sides of the transversal are called **alternate exterior angles**.

Review Video: Angles
Visit mometrix.com/academy and enter code: 264624

In the diagram below, there are two pairs of alternate exterior angles: angles 1 and 8, and angles 2 and 7. Alternate exterior angles formed by parallel lines are congruent.

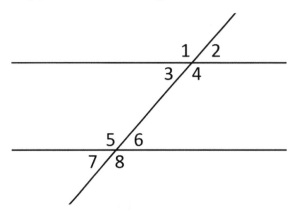

When two lines intersect, four angles are formed. The non-adjacent angles at this vertex are called vertical angles. Vertical angles are congruent. In the diagram, $\angle ABD \cong \angle CBE$ and $\angle ABC \cong \angle DBE$.

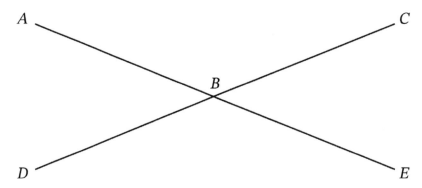

Copyright © Mometrix Media. You have been licensed one copy of this document for personal use only. Any other reproduction or redistribution is strictly prohibited. All rights reserved.
This content is provided for test preparation purposes only and does not imply an endorsement by Mometrix of any particular political, scientific, or religious point of view.

PRACTICE

P1. Find the measure of angles **(a)**, **(b)**, and **(c)** based on the figure with two parallel lines, two perpendicular lines and one transversal:

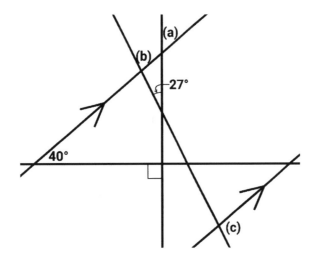

PRACTICE SOLUTIONS

P1. (a) The vertical angle paired with (a) is part of a right triangle with the 40° angle. Thus, the measure can be found:

$$90° = 40° + a$$
$$a = 50°$$

(b) The triangle formed by the supplementary angle to (b) is part of a triangle with the vertical angle paired with (a) and the given angle of 27°. Since $a = 50°$:

$$180° = (180° - b) + 50° + 27°$$
$$103° = 180° - b$$
$$-77° = -b$$
$$77° = b$$

(c) As they are part of a transversal crossing parallel lines, angles (b) and (c) are supplementary. Thus $c = 103°$.

POLYGONS

A **polygon** is a closed, two-dimensional figure with three or more straight line segments called **sides**. The point at which two sides of a polygon intersect is called the **vertex**. In a polygon, the number of sides is always equal to the number of vertices. A polygon with all sides congruent and all angles equal is called a **regular polygon**. Common polygons are:

$$\text{Triangle} = 3 \text{ sides}$$
$$\text{Quadrilateral} = 4 \text{ sides}$$
$$\text{Pentagon} = 5 \text{ sides}$$
$$\text{Hexagon} = 6 \text{ sides}$$
$$\text{Heptagon} = 7 \text{ sides}$$
$$\text{Octagon} = 8 \text{ sides}$$
$$\text{Nonagon} = 9 \text{ sides}$$
$$\text{Decagon} = 10 \text{ sides}$$
$$\text{Dodecagon} = 12 \text{ sides}$$

Copyright © Mometrix Media. You have been licensed one copy of this document for personal use only. Any other reproduction or redistribution is strictly prohibited. All rights reserved. This content is provided for test preparation purposes only and does not imply an endorsement by Mometrix of any particular political, scientific, or religious point of view.

More generally, an *n*-gon is a polygon that has *n* angles and *n* sides.

The sum of the interior angles of an *n*-sided polygon is $(n - 2) \times 180°$. For example, in a triangle $n = 3$. So the sum of the interior angles is $(3 - 2) \times 180° = 180°$. In a quadrilateral, $n = 4$, and the sum of the angles is $(4 - 2) \times 180° = 360°$.

Review Video: Intro to Polygons
Visit mometrix.com/academy and enter code: 271869

Review Video: Sum of Interior Angles
Visit mometrix.com/academy and enter code: 984991

APOTHEM AND RADIUS

A line segment from the center of a polygon that is perpendicular to a side of the polygon is called the **apothem**. A line segment from the center of a polygon to a vertex of the polygon is called a **radius**. In a regular polygon, the apothem can be used to find the area of the polygon using the formula $A = \frac{1}{2}ap$, where *a* is the apothem, and *p* is the perimeter.

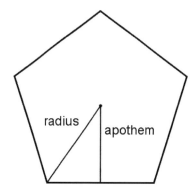

A **diagonal** is a line segment that joins two non-adjacent vertices of a polygon. The number of diagonals a polygon has can be found by using the formula:

$$\text{number of diagonals} = \frac{n(n - 3)}{2}$$

Note that *n* is the number of sides in the polygon. This formula works for all polygons, not just regular polygons.

Review Video: Diagonals of Parallelograms, Rectangles, and Rhombi
Visit mometrix.com/academy and enter code: 320040

CONVEX AND CONCAVE POLYGONS

A **convex polygon** is a polygon whose diagonals all lie within the interior of the polygon. A **concave polygon** is a polygon with a least one diagonal that is outside the polygon. In the diagram below, quadrilateral *ABCD* is

Copyright © Mometrix Media. You have been licensed one copy of this document for personal use only. Any other reproduction or redistribution is strictly prohibited. All rights reserved.
This content is provided for test preparation purposes only and does not imply an endorsement by Mometrix of any particular political, scientific, or religious point of view.

concave because diagonal $\overline{AC}$ lies outside the polygon and quadrilateral *EFGH* is convex because both diagonals lie inside the polygon

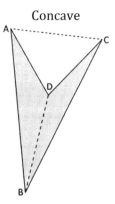

Concave

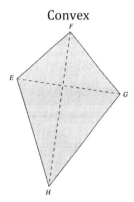

Convex

CONGRUENCE AND SIMILARITY

Congruent figures are geometric figures that have the same size and shape. All corresponding angles are equal, and all corresponding sides are equal. Congruence is indicated by the symbol ≅.

Congruent polygons

Similar figures are geometric figures that have the same shape, but do not necessarily have the same size. All corresponding angles are equal, and all corresponding sides are proportional, but they do not have to be equal. It is indicated by the symbol ∼.

 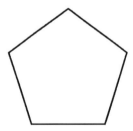

Similar polygons

Note that all congruent figures are also similar, but not all similar figures are congruent.

Copyright © Mometrix Media. You have been licensed one copy of this document for personal use only. Any other reproduction or redistribution is strictly prohibited. All rights reserved.
This content is provided for test preparation purposes only and does not imply an endorsement by Mometrix of any particular political, scientific, or religious point of view.

LINE OF SYMMETRY

A line that divides a figure or object into congruent parts is called a **line of symmetry**. An object may have no lines of symmetry, one line of symmetry, or multiple (i.e., more than one) lines of symmetry.

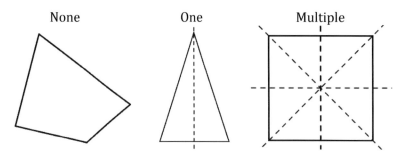

None   One   Multiple

Review Video: Symmetry
Visit mometrix.com/academy and enter code: 528106

TRIANGLES

A triangle is a three-sided figure with the sum of its interior angles being 180° The **perimeter of any triangle** is found by summing the three side lengths; $P = a + b + c$. For an equilateral triangle, this is the same as $P = 3a$, where a is any side length, since all three sides are the same length.

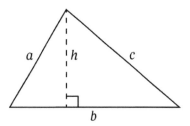

The **area of any triangle** can be found by taking half the product of one side length, referred to as the base and often given the variable b, and the perpendicular distance from that side to the opposite vertex, called the altitude or height and given the variable h. In equation form that is $A = \frac{1}{2}bh$. Another formula that works for any triangle is $A = \sqrt{s(s-a)(s-b)(s-c)}$, where s is the semiperimeter: $\frac{a+b+c}{2}$, and a, b, and c are the lengths of the three sides. Special cases include isosceles triangles: $A = \frac{1}{2}b\sqrt{a^2 - \frac{b^2}{4}}$, where b is the unique side and a is the length of one of the two congruent sides, and equilateral triangles: $A = \frac{\sqrt{3}}{4}a^2$, where a is the length of a side.

Review Video: Area and Perimeter of a Triangle
Visit mometrix.com/academy and enter code: 853779

PARTS OF A TRIANGLE

An **altitude** of a triangle is a line segment drawn from one vertex perpendicular to the opposite side. In the diagram below, $\overline{BE}$, $\overline{AD}$, and $\overline{CF}$ are altitudes. The length of an altitude is also called the height of the triangle. The three altitudes in a triangle are always concurrent. The point of concurrency of the altitudes of a triangle, O, is called the **orthocenter**. Note that in an obtuse triangle, the orthocenter will be outside the triangle, and in a right triangle, the orthocenter is the vertex of the right angle.

Copyright © Mometrix Media. You have been licensed one copy of this document for personal use only. Any other reproduction or redistribution is strictly prohibited. All rights reserved.
This content is provided for test preparation purposes only and does not imply an endorsement by Mometrix of any particular political, scientific, or religious point of view.

A **median** of a triangle is a line segment drawn from one vertex to the midpoint of the opposite side. In the diagram below, $\overline{BH}$, $\overline{AG}$, and $\overline{CI}$ are medians. This is not the same as the altitude, except the altitude to the base of an isosceles triangle and all three altitudes of an equilateral triangle. The point of concurrency of the medians of a triangle, T, is called the **centroid**. This is the same point as the orthocenter only in an equilateral triangle. Unlike the orthocenter, the centroid is always inside the triangle. The centroid can also be considered the exact center of the triangle. Any shape triangle can be perfectly balanced on a tip placed at the centroid. The centroid is also the point that is two-thirds the distance from the vertex to the opposite side.

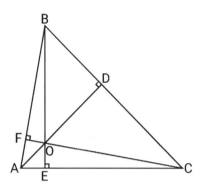 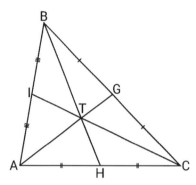

Review Video: Incenter, Circumcenter, Orthocenter, and Centroid
Visit mometrix.com/academy and enter code: 598260

QUADRILATERALS

A **quadrilateral** is a closed two-dimensional geometric figure that has four straight sides. The sum of the interior angles of any quadrilateral is 360°.

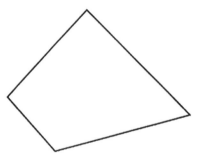

KITE

A **kite** is a quadrilateral with two pairs of adjacent sides that are congruent. A result of this is perpendicular diagonals. A kite can be concave or convex and has one line of symmetry.

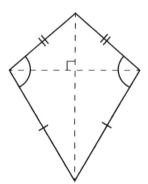 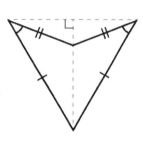

Copyright © Mometrix Media. You have been licensed one copy of this document for personal use only. Any other reproduction or redistribution is strictly prohibited. All rights reserved.
This content is provided for test preparation purposes only and does not imply an endorsement by Mometrix of any particular political, scientific, or religious point of view.

TRAPEZOID

Trapezoid: A trapezoid is defined as a quadrilateral that has at least one pair of parallel sides. There are no rules for the second pair of sides. So there are no rules for the diagonals and no lines of symmetry for a trapezoid.

The **area of a trapezoid** is found by the formula $A = \frac{1}{2}h(b_1 + b_2)$, where h is the height (segment joining and perpendicular to the parallel bases), and b_1 and b_2 are the two parallel sides (bases). Do not use one of the other two sides as the height unless that side is also perpendicular to the parallel bases.

The **perimeter of a trapezoid** is found by the formula $P = a + b_1 + c + b_2$, where a, b_1, c, and b_2 are the four sides of the trapezoid.

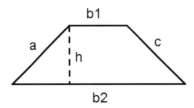

Review Video: **Area and Perimeter of a Trapezoid**
Visit mometrix.com/academy and enter code: 587523

Isosceles trapezoid: A trapezoid with equal base angles. This gives rise to other properties including: the two nonparallel sides have the same length, the two non-base angles are also equal, and there is one line of symmetry through the midpoints of the parallel sides.

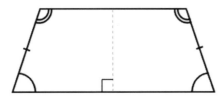

60

Copyright © Mometrix Media. You have been licensed one copy of this document for personal use only. Any other reproduction or redistribution is strictly prohibited. All rights reserved.
This content is provided for test preparation purposes only and does not imply an endorsement by Mometrix of any particular political, scientific, or religious point of view.

PARALLELOGRAM

Parallelogram: A quadrilateral that has two pairs of opposite parallel sides. As such it is a special type of trapezoid. The sides that are parallel are also congruent. The opposite interior angles are always congruent, and the consecutive interior angles are supplementary. The diagonals of a parallelogram divide each other. Each diagonal divides the parallelogram into two congruent triangles. A parallelogram has no line of symmetry, but does have 180-degree rotational symmetry about the midpoint.

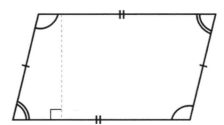

The **area of a parallelogram** is found by the formula $A = bh$, where b is the length of the base, and h is the height. Note that the base and height correspond to the length and width in a rectangle, so this formula would apply to rectangles as well. Do not confuse the height of a parallelogram with the length of the second side. The two are only the same measure in the case of a rectangle.

The **perimeter of a parallelogram** is found by the formula $P = 2a + 2b$ or $P = 2(a + b)$, where a and b are the lengths of the two sides.

> **Review Video: Area and Perimeter of a Parallelogram**
> Visit mometrix.com/academy and enter code: 718313

RECTANGLE

Rectangle: A quadrilateral with four right angles. All rectangles are parallelograms and trapezoids, but not all parallelograms or trapezoids are rectangles. The diagonals of a rectangle are congruent. Rectangles have 2 lines of symmetry (through each pair of opposing midpoints) and 180-degree rotational symmetry about the midpoint.

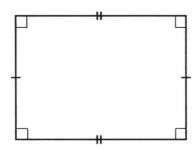

The **area of a rectangle** is found by the formula $A = lw$, where A is the area of the rectangle, l is the length (usually considered to be the longer side) and w is the width (usually considered to be the shorter side). The numbers for l and w are interchangeable.

The **perimeter of a rectangle** is found by the formula $P = 2l + 2w$ or $P = 2(l + w)$, where l is the length, and w is the width. It may be easier to add the length and width first and then double the result, as in the second formula.

Copyright © Mometrix Media. You have been licensed one copy of this document for personal use only. Any other reproduction or redistribution is strictly prohibited. All rights reserved.
This content is provided for test preparation purposes only and does not imply an endorsement by Mometrix of any particular political, scientific, or religious point of view.

RHOMBUS

Rhombus: A quadrilateral with four congruent sides. All rhombuses are parallelograms and kites; thus, they inherit all the properties of both types of quadrilaterals. The diagonals of a rhombus are perpendicular to each other. Rhombi have 2 lines of symmetry (along each of the diagonals) and 180-degree rotational symmetry. The **area of a rhombus** is half the product of the diagonals: $A = \frac{d_1 d_2}{2}$ and the perimeter of a rhombus is: $P = 2\sqrt{(d_1)^2 + (d_2)^2}$

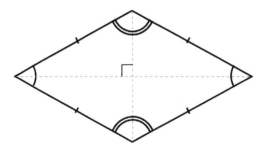

SQUARE

Square: A quadrilateral with four right angles and four congruent sides. Squares satisfy the criteria of all other types of quadrilaterals. The diagonals of a square are congruent and perpendicular to each other. Squares have 4 lines of symmetry (through each pair of opposing midpoints and along each of the diagonals) as well as 90-degree rotational symmetry about the midpoint.

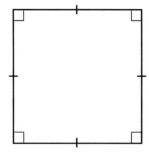

The **area of a square** is found by using the formula $A = s^2$, where s is the length of one side. The **perimeter of a square** is found by using the formula $P = 4s$, where s is the length of one side. Because all four sides are equal in a square, it is faster to multiply the length of one side by 4 than to add the same number four times. You could use the formulas for rectangles and get the same answer.

CIRCLES

The **center** of a circle is the single point from which every point on the circle is **equidistant**. The **radius** is a line segment that joins the center of the circle and any one point on the circle. All radii of a circle are equal. Circles that have the same center, but not the same length of radii are **concentric**. The **diameter** is a line segment that passes through the center of the circle and has both endpoints on the circle. The length of the

Copyright © Mometrix Media. You have been licensed one copy of this document for personal use only. Any other reproduction or redistribution is strictly prohibited. All rights reserved.
This content is provided for test preparation purposes only and does not imply an endorsement by Mometrix of any particular political, scientific, or religious point of view.

diameter is exactly twice the length of the radius. Point O in the diagram below is the center of the circle, segments $\overline{OX}$, $\overline{OY}$, and $\overline{OZ}$ are radii, and segment $\overline{XZ}$ is a diameter.

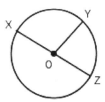

Review Video: <u>Points of a Circle</u>
Visit mometrix.com/academy and enter code: 420746
Review Video: <u>The Diameter, Radius, and Circumference of Circles</u>
Visit mometrix.com/academy and enter code: 448988

The **area of a circle** is found by the formula $A = \pi r^2$, where r is the length of the radius. If the diameter of the circle is given, remember to divide it in half to get the length of the radius before proceeding.

The **circumference** of a circle is found by the formula $C = 2\pi r$, where r is the radius. Again, remember to convert the diameter if you are given that measure rather than the radius.

Review Video: <u>Area and Circumference of a Circle</u>
Visit mometrix.com/academy and enter code: 243015

PRACTICE

P1. Find the area and perimeter of the following quadrilaterals:

   (a) A square with side length 2.5 cm.

   (b) A parallelogram with height 3 m, base 4 m, and other side 6 m.

   (c) A rhombus with diagonals 15 in and 20 in.

P2. Calculate the area of a triangle with side lengths of 7 ft, 8 ft, and 9 ft.

PRACTICE SOLUTIONS

P1. (a) $A = s^2 = (2.5 \text{ cm})^2 = 6.25 \text{ cm}^2$; $P = 4s = 4 \times 2.5 \text{ cm} = 10 \text{ cm}$

   (b) $A = bh = (3 \text{ m})(4 \text{ m}) = 12 \text{ m}^2$; $P = 2a + 2b = 2 \times 6 \text{ m} + 2 \times 4 \text{ m} = 20 \text{ m}$

   (c) $A = \frac{d_1 d_2}{2} = \frac{(15 \text{ in})(20 \text{ in})}{2} = 150 \text{ in}^2$;
   $P = 2\sqrt{(d_1)^2 + (d_2)^2} = 2\sqrt{(15 \text{ in})^2 + (20 \text{ in})^2} = 2\sqrt{625 \text{ in}^2} = 50 \text{ in}$

P2. Given only side lengths, we can use the semi perimeter to the find the area based on the formula, $A = \sqrt{s(s-a)(s-b)(s-c)}$, where s is the semiperimeter, $\frac{a+b+c}{2} = \frac{7+8+9}{2} = 12$ ft:

$$A = \sqrt{12(12-7)(12-8)(12-9)}$$
$$= \sqrt{(12)(5)(4)(3)}$$
$$= 12\sqrt{5} \text{ ft}^2$$

Copyright © Mometrix Media. You have been licensed one copy of this document for personal use only. Any other reproduction or redistribution is strictly prohibited. All rights reserved.
This content is provided for test preparation purposes only and does not imply an endorsement by Mometrix of any particular political, scientific, or religious point of view.

SOLIDS

The **surface area of a solid object** is the area of all sides or exterior surfaces. For objects such as prisms and pyramids, a further distinction is made between base surface area (B) and lateral surface area (LA). For a prism, the total surface area (SA) is $SA = LA + 2B$. For a pyramid or cone, the total surface area is $SA = LA + B$.

> **Review Video: How to Calculate the Volume of 3D Objects**
> Visit mometrix.com/academy and enter code: 163343

The **surface area of a sphere** can be found by the formula $A = 4\pi r^2$, where r is the radius. The volume is given by the formula $V = \frac{4}{3}\pi r^3$, where r is the radius. Both quantities are generally given in terms of π.

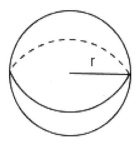

The **volume of any prism** is found by the formula $V = Bh$, where B is the area of the base, and h is the height (perpendicular distance between the bases). The surface area of any prism is the sum of the areas of both bases and all sides. It can be calculated as $SA = 2B + Ph$, where P is the perimeter of the base.

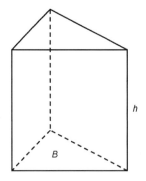

> **Review Video: Volume and Surface Area of a Prism**
> Visit mometrix.com/academy and enter code: 420158

Copyright © Mometrix Media. You have been licensed one copy of this document for personal use only. Any other reproduction or redistribution is strictly prohibited. All rights reserved.
This content is provided for test preparation purposes only and does not imply an endorsement by Mometrix of any particular political, scientific, or religious point of view.

For a **rectangular prism**, the volume can be found by the formula $V = lwh$, where V is the volume, l is the length, w is the width, and h is the height. The surface area can be calculated as $SA = 2lw + 2hl + 2wh$ or $SA = 2(lw + hl + wh)$.

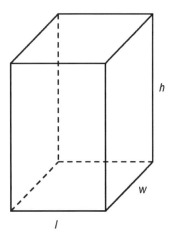

Review Video: Volume and Surface Area of a Rectangular Prism
Visit mometrix.com/academy and enter code: 282814

The **volume of a cube** can be found by the formula $V = s^3$, where s is the length of a side. The surface area of a cube is calculated as $SA = 6s^2$, where SA is the total surface area and s is the length of a side. These formulas are the same as the ones used for the volume and surface area of a rectangular prism, but simplified since all three quantities (length, width, and height) are the same.

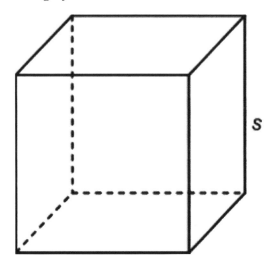

Review Video: Volume and Surface Area of a Cube
Visit mometrix.com/academy and enter code: 664455

Copyright © Mometrix Media. You have been licensed one copy of this document for personal use only. Any other reproduction or redistribution is strictly prohibited. All rights reserved.
This content is provided for test preparation purposes only and does not imply an endorsement by Mometrix of any particular political, scientific, or religious point of view.

The **volume of a cylinder** can be calculated by the formula $V = \pi r^2 h$, where r is the radius, and h is the height. The surface area of a cylinder can be found by the formula $SA = 2\pi r^2 + 2\pi rh$. The first term is the base area multiplied by two, and the second term is the perimeter of the base multiplied by the height.

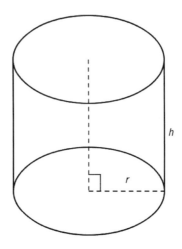

Review Video: <u>Finding the Volume and Surface Area of a Right Circular Cylinder</u>
Visit mometrix.com/academy and enter code: 226463

The **volume of a pyramid** is found by the formula $V = \frac{1}{3}Bh$, where B is the area of the base, and h is the height (perpendicular distance from the vertex to the base). Notice this formula is the same as $\frac{1}{3}$ times the volume of a prism. Like a prism, the base of a pyramid can be any shape.

Finding the **surface area of a pyramid** is not as simple as the other shapes we've looked at thus far. If the pyramid is a right pyramid, meaning the base is a regular polygon and the vertex is directly over the center of that polygon, the surface area can be calculated as $SA = B + \frac{1}{2}Ph_s$, where P is the perimeter of the base, and h_s is the slant height (distance from the vertex to the midpoint of one side of the base). If the pyramid is irregular, the area of each triangle side must be calculated individually and then summed, along with the base.

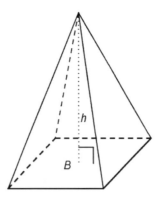

Review Video: <u>Finding the Volume and Surface Area of a Pyramid</u>
Visit mometrix.com/academy and enter code: 621932

The **volume of a cone** is found by the formula $V = \frac{1}{3}\pi r^2 h$, where r is the radius, and h is the height. Notice this is the same as $\frac{1}{3}$ times the volume of a cylinder. The surface area can be calculated as $SA = \pi r^2 + \pi rs$, where s

Copyright © Mometrix Media. You have been licensed one copy of this document for personal use only. Any other reproduction or redistribution is strictly prohibited. All rights reserved.
This content is provided for test preparation purposes only and does not imply an endorsement by Mometrix of any particular political, scientific, or religious point of view.

is the slant height. The slant height can be calculated using the Pythagorean theorem to be $\sqrt{r^2 + h^2}$, so the surface area formula can also be written as $SA = \pi r^2 + \pi r \sqrt{r^2 + h^2}$.

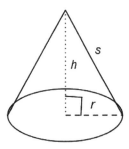

Review Video: Volume and Surface Area of a Right Circular Cone
Visit mometrix.com/academy and enter code: 573574

PRACTICE

P1. Find the surface area and volume of the following solids:

(a) A cylinder with radius 5 m and height 0.5 m.

(b) A trapezoidal prism with base area of 254 mm^2, base perimeter 74 mm, and height 10 mm.

(c) A half sphere (radius 5 yds) on the base of an inverted cone with the same radius and a height of 7 yds.

PRACTICE SOLUTIONS

P1. (a) $SA = 2\pi r^2 + 2\pi rh = 2\pi(5\text{ m})^2 + 2\pi(5\text{ m})(0.5\text{ m}) = 55\pi\text{ m}^2 \cong 172.79\text{ m}^2$;
$V = \pi r^2 h = \pi(5\text{ m})^2(0.5\text{ m}) = 12.5\pi\text{ m}^3 \cong 39.27\text{ m}^3$

(b) $SA = 2B + Ph = 2(254\text{ mm}^2) + (74\text{ mm})(10\text{ mm}) = 1248\text{ mm}^2$;
$V = Bh = (254\text{ mm}^2)(10\text{ mm}) = 2540\text{ mm}^3$

(c) We can find s, the slant height using the Pythagorean theorem, and since this solid is made of parts of simple solids, we can combine the formulas to find surface area and volume:

$$s = \sqrt{r^2 + h^2} = \sqrt{(5\text{ yd})^2 + (7\text{ yd})^2} = \sqrt{74}\text{ yd}$$

$$SA_{Total} = (SA_{sphere})/2 + SA_{cone} - SA_{base}$$
$$= \frac{4\pi r^2}{2} + (\pi rs + \pi r^2) - \pi r^2$$
$$= 2\pi(5\text{ yd})^2 + \pi(5\text{ yd})(\sqrt{74}\text{ yd})$$
$$= 5\pi(10 + \sqrt{74})\text{ yd}^2$$
$$\cong 292.20\text{ yd}^2$$

$$V_{Total} = (V_{sphere})/2 + V_{cone}$$
$$= \frac{\frac{4}{3}\pi r^3}{2} + \frac{1}{3}\pi r^2 h$$
$$= \frac{2}{3}\pi(5\text{ yd})^3 + \frac{1}{3}\pi(5\text{ yd})^2(7\text{ yd})$$
$$= \frac{5^2 \times \pi}{3}(10 + 7)\text{ yd}^3$$
$$\cong 445.06\text{ yd}^3$$

CLASSIFICATIONS OF TRIANGLES

A **scalene triangle** is a triangle with no congruent sides. A scalene triangle will also have three angles of different measures. The angle with the largest measure is opposite the longest side, and the angle with the smallest measure is opposite the shortest side. An **acute triangle** is a triangle whose three angles are all less than 90°. If two of the angles are equal, the acute triangle is also an **isosceles triangle**. An isosceles triangle will also have two congruent angles opposite the two congruent sides. If the three angles are all equal, the acute triangle is also an **equilateral triangle**. An equilateral triangle will also have three congruent angles,

Copyright © Mometrix Media. You have been licensed one copy of this document for personal use only. Any other reproduction or redistribution is strictly prohibited. All rights reserved.
This content is provided for test preparation purposes only and does not imply an endorsement by Mometrix of any particular political, scientific, or religious point of view.

each 60°. All equilateral triangles are also acute triangles. An **obtuse triangle** is a triangle with exactly one angle greater than 90°. The other two angles may or may not be equal. If the two remaining angles are equal, the obtuse triangle is also an isosceles triangle. A **right triangle** is a triangle with exactly one angle equal to 90°. All right triangles follow the Pythagorean theorem. A right triangle can never be acute or obtuse.

The table below illustrates how each descriptor places a different restriction on the triangle:

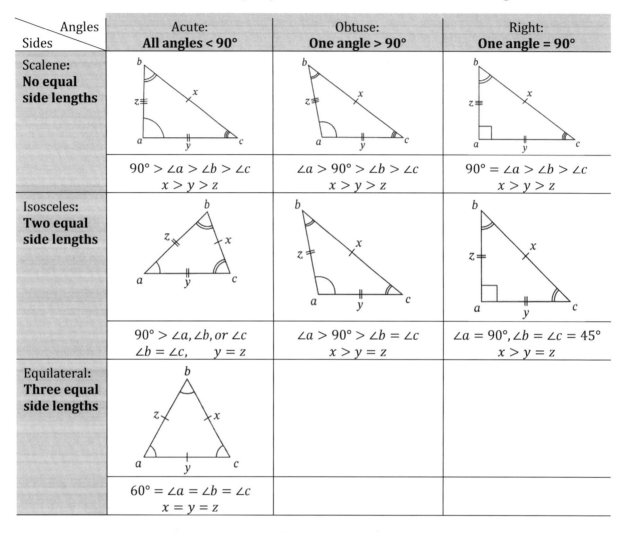

Angles / Sides	Acute: **All angles < 90°**	Obtuse: **One angle > 90°**	Right: **One angle = 90°**
Scalene: **No equal side lengths**	$90° > \angle a > \angle b > \angle c$ $x > y > z$	$\angle a > 90° > \angle b > \angle c$ $x > y > z$	$90° = \angle a > \angle b > \angle c$ $x > y > z$
Isosceles: **Two equal side lengths**	$90° > \angle a, \angle b, or \angle c$ $\angle b = \angle c, \quad y = z$	$\angle a > 90° > \angle b = \angle c$ $x > y = z$	$\angle a = 90°, \angle b = \angle c = 45°$ $x > y = z$
Equilateral: **Three equal side lengths**	$60° = \angle a = \angle b = \angle c$ $x = y = z$		

Review Video: Introduction to Types of Triangles
Visit mometrix.com/academy and enter code: 511711

SIMILARITY AND CONGRUENCE RULES

Similar triangles are triangles whose corresponding angles are equal and whose corresponding sides are proportional. Represented by AAA. Similar triangles whose corresponding sides are congruent are also congruent triangles.

Triangles can be shown to be **congruent** in 5 ways:

- **SSS**: Three sides of one triangle are congruent to the three corresponding sides of the second triangle.
- **SAS**: Two sides and the included angle (the angle formed by those two sides) of one triangle are congruent to the corresponding two sides and included angle of the second triangle.

Copyright © Mometrix Media. You have been licensed one copy of this document for personal use only. Any other reproduction or redistribution is strictly prohibited. All rights reserved.
This content is provided for test preparation purposes only and does not imply an endorsement by Mometrix of any particular political, scientific, or religious point of view.

- **ASA**: Two angles and the included side (the side that joins the two angles) of one triangle are congruent to the corresponding two angles and included side of the second triangle.
- **AAS**: Two angles and a non-included side of one triangle are congruent to the corresponding two angles and non-included side of the second triangle.
- **HL**: The hypotenuse and leg of one right triangle are congruent to the corresponding hypotenuse and leg of the second right triangle.

> **Review Video: Similar Triangles**
> Visit mometrix.com/academy and enter code: 398538

GENERAL RULES FOR TRIANGLES

The **triangle inequality theorem** states that the sum of the measures of any two sides of a triangle is always greater than the measure of the third side. If the sum of the measures of two sides were equal to the third side, a triangle would be impossible because the two sides would lie flat across the third side and there would be no vertex. If the sum of the measures of two of the sides was less than the third side, a closed figure would be impossible because the two shortest sides would never meet. In other words, for a triangle with sides lengths A, B, and C: $A + B > C$, $B + C > A$, and $A + C > B$

The sum of the measures of the interior angles of a triangle is always 180°. Therefore, a triangle can never have more than one angle greater than or equal to 90°.

In any triangle, the angles opposite congruent sides are congruent, and the sides opposite congruent angles are congruent. The largest angle is always opposite the longest side, and the smallest angle is always opposite the shortest side.

The line segment that joins the midpoints of any two sides of a triangle is always parallel to the third side and exactly half the length of the third side.

> **Review Video: General Rules (Triangle Inequality Theorem)**
> Visit mometrix.com/academy and enter code: 166488

PYTHAGOREAN THEOREM

The side of a triangle opposite the right angle is called the **hypotenuse**. The other two sides are called the legs. The Pythagorean theorem states a relationship among the legs and hypotenuse of a right triangle: $a^2 + b^2 = c^2$, where a and b are the lengths of the legs of a right triangle, and c is the length of the hypotenuse. Note that this formula will only work with right triangles.

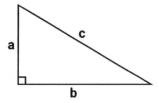

69

Copyright © Mometrix Media. You have been licensed one copy of this document for personal use only. Any other reproduction or redistribution is strictly prohibited. All rights reserved.
This content is provided for test preparation purposes only and does not imply an endorsement by Mometrix of any particular political, scientific, or religious point of view.

PRACTICE

P1. Given the following pairs of triangles, determine whether they are similar, congruent, or neither (note that the figures are not drawn to scale):

(a).

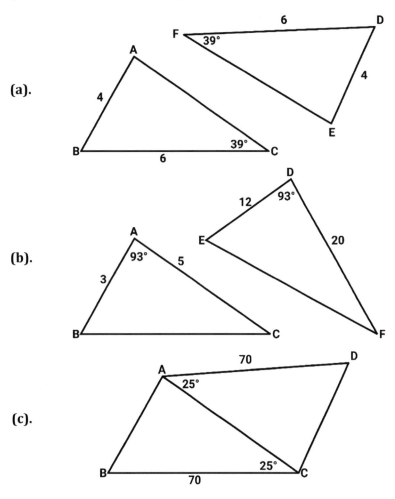

(b).

(c).

Copyright © Mometrix Media. You have been licensed one copy of this document for personal use only. Any other reproduction or redistribution is strictly prohibited. All rights reserved.
This content is provided for test preparation purposes only and does not imply an endorsement by Mometrix of any particular political, scientific, or religious point of view.

P2. Calculate the length of $\overline{\text{MO}}$ based on triangle MNO:

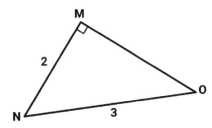

PRACTICE SOLUTIONS

P1. (a). Neither: We are given that two sides lengths and an angle are equal, however, the angle given is not between the given side lengths. That means there are two possible triangles that could satisfy the given measurements. Thus, we cannot be certain of congruence:

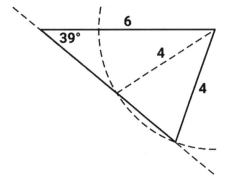

(b) Similar: Since we are given a side-angle-side of each triangle and the side lengths given are scaled evenly $\left(\frac{3}{5} \times \frac{4}{4} = \frac{12}{20}\right)$ and the angles are equal. Thus, $\triangle ABC \sim \triangle DEF$. If the side lengths were equal, then they would be congruent.

(c) Congruent: Even though we aren't given a measurement for the shared side of the figure, since it is shared it is equal. So, this is a case of SAS. Thus, $\triangle ABC \cong \triangle CDA$

P2. Since triangle MNO is a right triangle, we can use the simple form of the Pythagorean theorem to find the missing side length:

$$\left(\overline{\text{MO}}\right)^2 + 2^2 = 3^2$$
$$\left(\overline{\text{MO}}\right)^2 = 9 - 4$$
$$\overline{\text{MO}} = \sqrt{5}$$

ALGEBRA

TERMS AND COEFFICIENTS

Mathematical expressions consist of a combination of one or more values arranged in terms that are added together. As such, an expression could be just a single number, including zero. A **variable term** is the product of a real number, also called a **coefficient**, and one or more variables, each of which may be raised to an exponent. Expressions may also include numbers without a variable, called **constants** or **constant terms**. The expression $6s^2$, for example, is a single term where the coefficient is the real number 6 and the variable term is s^2. Note that if a term is written as simply a variable to some exponent, like t^2, then the coefficient is 1, because $t^2 = 1t^2$.

71

Copyright © Mometrix Media. You have been licensed one copy of this document for personal use only. Any other reproduction or redistribution is strictly prohibited. All rights reserved.
This content is provided for test preparation purposes only and does not imply an endorsement by Mometrix of any particular political, scientific, or religious point of view.

LINEAR EXPRESSIONS

A **single variable linear expression** is the sum of a single variable term, where the variable has no exponent, and a constant, which may be zero. For instance, the expression $2w + 7$ has $2w$ as the variable term and 7 as the constant term. It is important to realize that terms are separated by addition or subtraction. Since an expression is a sum of terms, expressions such as $5x - 3$ can be written as $5x + (-3)$ to emphasize that the constant term is negative. A real-world example of a single variable linear expression is the perimeter of a square, four times the side length, often expressed: $4s$.

In general, a **linear expression** is the sum of any number of variable terms so long as none of the variables have an exponent. For example, $3m + 8n - \frac{1}{4}p + 5.5q - 1$ is a linear expression, but $3y^3$ is not. In the same way, the expression for the perimeter of a general triangle, the sum of the side lengths: $a + b + c$, is considered to be linear, but the expression for the area of a square, the side length squared: s^2, is not.

LINEAR EQUATIONS

Equations that can be written as $ax + b = 0$, where $a \neq 0$, are referred to as **one variable linear equations**. A solution to such an equation is called a **root**. In the case where we have the equation $5x + 10 = 0$, if we solve for x we get a solution of $x = -2$. In other words, the root of the equation is -2. This is found by first subtracting 10 from both sides, which gives $5x = -10$. Next, simply divide both sides by the coefficient of the variable, in this case 5, to get $x = -2$. This can be checked by plugging -2 back into the original equation $(5)(-2) + 10 = -10 + 10 = 0$.

Review Video: Linear Equations Basics
Visit mometrix.com/academy and enter code: 793005

The **solution set** is the set of all solutions of an equation. In our example, the solution set would simply be -2. If there were more solutions (there usually are in multivariable equations), then they would also be included in the solution set. When an equation has no true solutions, this is referred to as an **empty set**. Equations with identical solution sets are **equivalent equations**. An **identity** is a term whose value or determinant is equal to 1.

Linear equations can be written many ways. Below is a list of some forms linear equations can take:

- **Standard Form**: $Ax + By = C$; the slope is $\frac{-A}{B}$ and the y-intercept is $\frac{C}{B}$
- **Slope Intercept Form**: $y = mx + b$, where m is the slope and b is the y-intercept
- **Point-Slope Form**: $y - y_1 = m(x - x_1)$, where m is the slope and (x_1, y_1) is a point on the line
- **Two-Point Form**: $\frac{y - y_1}{x - x_1} = \frac{y_2 - y_1}{x_2 - x_1}$, where (x_1, y_1) and (x_2, y_2) are two points on the given line
- **Intercept Form**: $\frac{x}{x_1} + \frac{y}{y_1} = 1$, where $(x_1, 0)$ is the point at which a line intersects the x-axis, and $(0, y_1)$ is the point at which the same line intersects the y-axis

---

Review Video: Slope-Intercept and Point-Slope Forms
Visit mometrix.com/academy and enter code: 113216

SOLVING ONE-VARIABLE LINEAR EQUATIONS

Multiply all terms by the lowest common denominator to eliminate any fractions. Look for addition or subtraction to undo so the variable can be isolated on one side of the equal sign. Divide both sides by the coefficient of the variable. When you have a value for the variable, substitute this value into the original equation to make sure you have a true equation. Consider the following example:

Copyright © Mometrix Media. You have been licensed one copy of this document for personal use only. Any other reproduction or redistribution is strictly prohibited. All rights reserved.
This content is provided for test preparation purposes only and does not imply an endorsement by Mometrix of any particular political, scientific, or religious point of view.

Kim's savings are represented by the table below. Represent her savings, using an equation.

X (Months)	Y (Total Savings)
2	$1300
5	$2050
9	$3050
11	$3550
16	$4800

The table shows a function with a constant rate of change, or slope, of 250. Given the points on the table, the slopes can be calculated as $(2050 - 1300)/(5 - 2)$, $(3050 - 2050)/(9 - 5)$, $(3550 - 3050)/(11 - 9)$, and $(4800 - 3550)/(16 - 11)$, each of which equals 250. Thus, the table shows a constant rate of change, indicating a linear function. The slope-intercept form of a linear equation is written as $y = mx + b$, where m represents the slope and b represents the y-intercept. Substituting the slope into this form gives $y = 250x + b$. Substituting corresponding x- and y-values from any point into this equation will give the y-intercept, or b. Using the point, (2, 1300), gives $1300 = 250(2) + b$, which simplifies as b = 800. Thus, her savings may be represented by the equation, $y = 250x + 800$.

RULES FOR MANIPULATING EQUATIONS
LIKE TERMS

Like terms are terms in an equation that have the same variable, regardless of whether or not they also have the same coefficient. This includes terms that *lack* a variable; all constants (i.e., numbers without variables) are considered like terms. If the equation involves terms with a variable raised to different powers, the like terms are those that have the variable raised to the same power.

For example, consider the equation $x^2 + 3x + 2 = 2x^2 + x - 7 + 2x$. In this equation, 2 and –7 are like terms; they are both constants. $3x$, x, and $2x$ are like terms; they all include the variable x raised to the first power. x^2 and $2x^2$ are like terms; they both include the variable x, raised to the second power. $2x$ and $2x^2$ are not like terms; although they both involve the variable x, the variable is not raised to the same power in both terms. The fact that they have the same coefficient, 2, is not relevant.

CARRYING OUT THE SAME OPERATION ON BOTH SIDES OF AN EQUATION

When solving an equation, the general procedure is to carry out a series of operations on both sides of an equation, choosing operations that will tend to simplify the equation when doing so. The reason why the same operation must be carried out on both sides of the equation is because that leaves the meaning of the equation unchanged, and yields a result that is equivalent to the original equation. This would not be the case if we carried out an operation on one side of an equation and not the other. Consider what an equation means; it is a statement that two values or expressions are equal. If we carry out the same operation on both sides of the equation—add 3 to both sides, for example—then the two sides of the equation are changed in the same way, and so remain equal. If we do that to only one side of the equation—add 3 to one side but not the other—then that wouldn't be true; if we change one side of the equation but not the other, then the two sides are no longer equal.

ADVANTAGE OF COMBINING LIKE TERMS

Combining like terms refers to adding or subtracting like terms—terms with the same variable—and therefore reducing sets of like terms to a single term. The main advantage of doing this is that it simplifies the equation. Often, combining like terms can be done as the first step in solving an equation, though it can also be done later, such as after distributing terms in a product.

For example, consider the equation $2(x + 3) + 3(2 + x + 3) = -4$. The 2 and the 3 in the second set of parentheses are like terms, and we can combine them, yielding $2(x + 3) + 3(x + 5) = -4$. Now, we can carry out the multiplications implied by the parentheses, distributing the outer 2 and 3 accordingly: $2x + 6 + 3x + 15 = -4$. The $2x$ and the $3x$ are like terms, and we can add them together: $5x + 6 + 15 = -4$. Now, the

73
Copyright © Mometrix Media. You have been licensed one copy of this document for personal use only. Any other reproduction or redistribution is strictly prohibited. All rights reserved. This content is provided for test preparation purposes only and does not imply an endorsement by Mometrix of any particular political, scientific, or religious point of view.

constants 6, 15, and −4 are also like terms, and we can combine them as well: subtracting 6 and 15 from both sides of the equation, we get $5x = -4 - 6 - 15$, or $5x = -25$, which simplifies further to $x = -5$.

Review Video: <u>Simplifying Equations by Combining Like Terms</u>

Visit mometrix.com/academy and enter code: 668506

CANCELING TERMS ON OPPOSITE SIDES OF AN EQUATION

Two terms on opposite sides of an equation can be canceled if and only if they *exactly* match each other. They must have the same variable raised to the same power and the same coefficient. For example, in the equation $3x + 2x^2 + 6 = 2x^2 - 6$, $2x^2$ appears on both sides of the equation, and can be canceled, leaving $3x + 6 = -6$. The 6 on each side of the equation can*not* be canceled, because it is added on one side of the equation and subtracted on the other. While they cannot be canceled, however, the 6 and −6 are like terms and can be combined, yielding $3x = -12$, which simplifies further to $x = -4$.

It's also important to note that the terms to be canceled must be independent terms and cannot be part of a larger term. For example, consider the equation $2(x + 6) = 3(x + 4) + 1$. We cannot cancel the xs, because even though they match each other they are part of the larger terms $2(x + 6)$ and $3(x + 4)$. We must first distribute the 2 and 3, yielding $2x + 12 = 3x + 12 + 1$. Now we see that the terms with the x's do not match, but the 12's do, and can be canceled, leaving $2x = 3x + 1$, which simplifies to $x = -1$.

PROCESS FOR MANIPULATING EQUATIONS

ISOLATING VARIABLES

To **isolate a variable** means to manipulate the equation so that the variable appears by itself on one side of the equation, and does not appear at all on the other side. Generally, an equation or inequality is considered to be solved once the variable is isolated and the other side of the equation or inequality is simplified as much as possible. In the case of a two-variable equation or inequality, only one variable needs to be isolated; it will not usually be possible to simultaneously isolate both variables.

Review Video: <u>Rules for Manipulating Equations</u>

Visit mometrix.com/academy and enter code: 838871

For a linear equation—an equation in which the variable only appears raised to the first power—isolating a variable can be done by first moving all the terms with the variable to one side of the equation and all other terms to the other side. (*Moving* a term really means adding the inverse of the term to both sides; when a term is *moved* to the other side of the equation its sign is flipped.) Then combine like terms on each side. Finally, divide both sides by the coefficient of the variable, if applicable. The steps need not necessarily be done in this order, but this order will always work.

Review Video: <u>Solving Equations with Variables on Both Sides</u>

Visit mometrix.com/academy and enter code: 402497

EQUATIONS WITH MORE THAN ONE SOLUTION

Some types of non-linear equations, such as equations involving squares of variables, may have more than one solution. For example, the equation $x^2 = 4$ has two solutions: 2 and −2. Equations with absolute values can also have multiple solutions: $|x| = 1$ has the solutions $x = 1$ and $x = -1$.

It is also possible for a linear equation to have more than one solution, but only if the equation is true regardless of the value of the variable. In this case, the equation is considered to have infinitely many solutions, because any possible value of the variable is a solution. We know a linear equation has infinitely many solutions if, when we combine like terms, the variables cancel, leaving a true statement. For example, consider the equation $2(3x + 5) = x + 5(x + 2)$. Distributing, we get $6x + 10 = x + 5x + 10$; combining like terms gives $6x + 10 = 6x + 10$, and the $6x$ terms cancel to leave $10 = 10$. This is clearly true, so the original equation

Copyright © Mometrix Media. You have been licensed one copy of this document for personal use only. Any other reproduction or redistribution is strictly prohibited. All rights reserved.
This content is provided for test preparation purposes only and does not imply an endorsement by Mometrix of any particular political, scientific, or religious point of view.

is true for any value of x. We could also have canceled the 10s leaving $0 = 0$, but again this is clearly true—in general, if both sides of the equation match exactly, it has infinitely many solutions.

EQUATIONS WITH NO SOLUTION

Some types of non-linear equations, such as equations involving squares of variables, may have no solution. For example, the equation $x^2 = -2$ has no solutions in the real numbers, because the square of any real number must be positive. Similarly, $|x| = -1$ has no solution, because the absolute value of a number is always positive.

It is also possible for an equation to have no solution, even if does not involve any powers greater than one, absolute values, or other special functions. For example, the equation $2(x + 3) + x = 3x$ has no solution. We can see that if we try to solve it: first we distribute, leaving $2x + 6 + x = 3x$. But now if we try to combine all the terms with the variable, we find that they cancel: we have $3x$ on the left and $3x$ on the right, canceling to leave us with $6 = 0$. This is clearly false. In general, whenever the variable terms in an equation cancel leaving different constants on both sides, it means that the equation has no solution. (If we are left with the *same* constant on both sides, the equation has infinitely many solutions instead.)

FEATURES OF EQUATIONS THAT REQUIRE SPECIAL TREATMENT

LINEAR EQUATIONS

A linear equation is an equation in which variables only appear by themselves: not multiplied together, not with exponents other than one, and not inside absolute value signs or any other functions. For example, the equation $x + 1 - 3x = 5 - x$ is a linear equation: while x appears multiple times, it never appears with an exponent other than one, or inside any function. The two-variable equation $2x - 3y = 5 + 2x$ is also a linear equation. In contrast, the equation $x^2 - 5 = 3x$ is *not* a linear equation, because it involves the term x^2. $\sqrt{x} = 5$ is not a linear equation, because it involves a square root. $(x - 1)^2 = 4$ is not a linear equation because even though there's no exponent on the x directly, it appears as part of an expression that is squared. The two-variable equation $x + xy - y = 5$ is not a linear equation because it includes the term xy, where two variables are multiplied together.

Linear equations can always be solved (or shown to have no solution) by combining like terms and performing simple operations on both sides of the equation. Some non-linear equations can also be solved by similar methods, but others may require more advanced methods of solution, if they can be solved analytically at all.

SOLVING EQUATIONS INVOLVING ROOTS

In an equation involving roots, the first step is to isolate the term with the root, if possible, and then raise both sides of the equation to the appropriate power to eliminate it. Consider an example equation, $2\sqrt{x + 1} - 1 = 3$. In this case, begin by adding 1 to both sides, yielding $2\sqrt{x + 1} = 4$, and then dividing both sides by 2, yielding $\sqrt{x + 1} = 2$. Now square both sides, yielding $x + 1 = 4$. Finally, subtracting 1 from both sides yields $x = 3$.

Squaring both sides of an equation may, however, yield a spurious solution—a solution to the squared equation that is *not* a solution of the original equation. It's therefore necessary to plug the solution back into the original equation to make sure it works. In this case, it does: $2\sqrt{3 + 1} - 1 = 2\sqrt{4} - 1 = 2(2) - 1 = 4 - 1 = 3$.

The same procedure applies for roots other than square roots. For example, given the equation $3 + \sqrt[3]{2x} = 5$, we can first subtract 3 from both sides, yielding $\sqrt[3]{2x} = 2$ and isolating the root. Raising both sides to the third power yields $2x = 2^3$, or $2x = 8$. We can now divide both sides by 2 to get $x = 4$.

> **Review Video: Solving Equations Involving Roots**
> Visit mometrix.com/academy and enter code: 297670

Copyright © Mometrix Media. You have been licensed one copy of this document for personal use only. Any other reproduction or redistribution is strictly prohibited. All rights reserved. This content is provided for test preparation purposes only and does not imply an endorsement by Mometrix of any particular political, scientific, or religious point of view.

SOLVING EQUATIONS WITH EXPONENTS

To solve an equation involving an exponent, the first step is to isolate the variable with the exponent. We can then take the appropriate root of both sides to eliminate the exponent. For instance, for the equation $2x^3 + 17 = 5x^3 - 7$, we can subtract $5x^3$ from both sides to get $-3x^3 + 17 = -7$, and then subtract 17 from both sides to get $-3x^3 = -24$. Finally, we can divide both sides by –3 to get $x^3 = 8$. Finally, we can take the cube root of both sides to get $x = \sqrt[3]{8} = 2$.

One important but often overlooked point is that equations with an exponent greater than 1 may have more than one answer. The solution to $x^2 = 9$ isn't simply $x = 3$; it's $x = \pm 3$: that is, $x = 3$ or $x = -3$. For a slightly more complicated example, consider the equation $(x - 1)^2 - 1 = 3$. Adding one to both sides yields $(x - 1)^2 = 4$; taking the square root of both sides yields $x - 1 = 2$. We can then add 1 to both sides to get $x = 3$. However, there's a second solution: we also have the possibility that $x - 1 = -2$, in which case $x = -1$. Both $x = 3$ and $x = -1$ are valid solutions, as can be verified by substituting them both into the original equation.

> **Review Video: Solving Equations with Exponents**
> Visit mometrix.com/academy and enter code: 514557

SOLVING EQUATIONS WITH ABSOLUTE VALUES

When solving an equation with an absolute value, the first step is to isolate the absolute value term. We then consider the two possibilities: when the expression inside the absolute value is positive or when it is negative. In the former case, the expression in the absolute value equals the expression on the other side of the equation; in the latter, it equals the additive inverse of that expression—the expression times negative one. We consider each case separately, and finally check for spurious solutions.

> **Review Video: Absolute Value**
> Visit mometrix.com/academy and enter code: 314669

For instance, consider solving $|2x - 1| + x = 5$ for x. We can first isolate the absolute value by moving the x to the other side: $|2x - 1| = -x + 5$. Now, we have two possibilities. First, that $2x - 1$ is positive, and hence $2x - 1 = -x + 5$. Rearranging and combining like terms yields $3x = 6$, and hence $x = 2$. The other possibility is that $2x - 1$ is negative, and hence $2x - 1 = -(-x + 5) = x - 5$. In this case, rearranging and combining like terms yields $x = -4$. Substituting $x = 2$ and $x = -4$ back into the original equation, we see that they are both valid solutions.

Note that the absolute value of a sum or difference applies to the sum or difference as a whole, not to the individual terms: in general, $|2x - 1|$ is not equal to $|2x + 1|$ or to $|2x| - 1$.

SPURIOUS SOLUTIONS

A **spurious solution** may arise when we square both sides of an equation as a step in solving it, or under certain other operations on the equation. It is a solution to the squared or otherwise modified equation that is *not* a solution of the original equation. To identify a spurious solution, it's useful when you solve an equation involving roots or absolute values to plug the solution back into the original equation to make sure it's valid.

CHOOSING WHICH VARIABLE TO ISOLATE IN TWO-VARIABLE EQUATIONS

Similar to methods for a one-variable equation, solving a two-variable equation involves isolating a variable: manipulating the equation so that a variable appears by itself on one side of the equation, and not at all on the other side. However, in a two-variable equation, you will usually only be able to isolate one of the variables; the other variable may appear on the other side along with constant terms, or with exponents or other functions.

Often one variable will be much more easily isolated than the other, and therefore that's the variable you should choose. If one variable appears with various exponents, and the other is only raised to the first power, the latter variable is the one to isolate: given the equation $a^2 + 2b = a^3 + b + 3$, the b only appears to the first

Copyright © Mometrix Media. You have been licensed one copy of this document for personal use only. Any other reproduction or redistribution is strictly prohibited. All rights reserved.
This content is provided for test preparation purposes only and does not imply an endorsement by Mometrix of any particular political, scientific, or religious point of view.

power, whereas a appears squared and cubed, so b is the variable that can be solved for: combining like terms and isolating the b on the left side of the equation, we get $b = a^3 - a^2 + 3$. If both variables are equally easy to isolate, then it's best to isolate the dependent variable, if one is defined; if the two variables are x and y, the convention is that y is the dependent variable.

PRACTICE

P1. Seeing the equation $2x + 4 = 4x + 7$, a student divides the first terms on each side by 2, yielding $x + 4 = 2x + 7$, and then combines like terms to get $x = -3$. However, this is incorrect, as can be seen by substituting –3 into the original equation. Explain what is wrong with the student's reasoning.

P2. Describe the steps necessary to solve the equation $2x + 1 - x = 4 + 3x + 7$.

P3. Describe the steps necessary to solve the equation $2(x + 5) = 7(4 - x)$.

P4. Find all real solutions to the equation $1 - \sqrt{x} = 2$.

P5. Find all real solutions to the equation $|x + 1| = 2x + 5$.

P6. Solve for x: $-x + 2\sqrt{x + 5} + 1 = 3$.

P7. Ray earns $10 an hour at his job. Write an equation for his earnings as a function of time spent working. Determine how long Ray has to work in order to earn $360.

P8. Simplify the following: $3x + 2 + 2y = 5y - 7 + |2x - 1|$

PRACTICE SOLUTIONS

P1. As stated, it's easy to verify that the student's solution is incorrect: $2(-3) + 4 = -2$ and $4(-3) + 7 = -5$; clearly $-2 \neq -5$. The mistake was in the first step, which illustrates a common type of error in solving equations. The student tried to simplify the two variable terms by dividing them by 2. However, it's not valid to multiply or divide only one term on each side of an equation by a number; when multiplying or dividing, the operation must be applied to *every* term in the equation. So, dividing by 2 would yield not $x + 4 = 2x + 7$, but $x + 2 = 2x + \frac{7}{2}$. While this is now valid, that fraction is inconvenient to work with, so this may not be the best first step in solving the equation. Rather, it may have been better to first combine like terms. Subtracting $4x$ from both sides yields $-2x + 4 = 7$; subtracting 4 from both sides yields $-2x = 3$; *now* we can divide both sides by –2 to get $x = -\frac{3}{2}$.

P2. Our ultimate goal is to isolate the variable, x. To that end, we first move all the terms containing x to the left side of the equation and all the constant terms to the right side. Note that when we move a term to the other side of the equation its sign changes. We are therefore now left with $2x - x - 3x = 4 + 7 - 1$.

Next, we combine the like terms on each side of the equation, adding and subtracting the terms as appropriate. This leaves us with $-2x = 10$.

At this point, we're almost done; all that remains is to divide both sides by -2 to leave the x by itself. We now have our solution, $x = -5$. We can verify that this is a correct solution by substituting it back into the original equation.

P3. Generally, in equations that have a sum or difference of terms multiplied by another value or expression, the first step is to multiply those terms, distributing as necessary: $2(x + 5) = 2(x) + 2(5) = 2x + 10$, and $7(4 - x) = 7(4) - 7(x) = 28 - 7x$. So, the equation becomes $2x + 10 = 28 - 7x$. We can now add $7x$ to both sides to eliminate the variable from the right-hand side: $9x + 10 = 28$. Similarly, we can subtract 10 from both sides to move all the constants to the right: $9x = 18$. Finally, we can divide both sides by 9, yielding the final answer, $x = 2$.

Copyright © Mometrix Media. You have been licensed one copy of this document for personal use only. Any other reproduction or redistribution is strictly prohibited. All rights reserved.
This content is provided for test preparation purposes only and does not imply an endorsement by Mometrix of any particular political, scientific, or religious point of view.

P4. It's not hard to isolate the root: subtract one from both sides, yielding $-\sqrt{x} = 1$. Finally, multiply both sides by –1, yielding $\sqrt{x} = -1$. Squaring both sides of the equation yields $x = 1$. However, if we plug this back into the original equation, we get $1 - \sqrt{1} = 2$, which is false. Therefore $x = 1$ is a spurious solution, and the equation has no real solutions.

P5. This equation has two possibilities: $x + 1 = 2x + 5$, which simplifies to $x = -4$; or $x + 1 = -(2x + 5) = -2x - 5$, which simplifies to $x = -2$. However, if we try substituting both values back into the original equation, we see that only $x = -2$ yields a true statement. $x = -4$ is a spurious solution; $x = -2$ is the only valid solution to the equation.

P6. Start by isolating the term with the root. We can do that by moving the $-x$ and the 1 to the other side, yielding $2\sqrt{x + 5} = 3 + x - 1$, or $2\sqrt{x + 5} = x + 2$. Dividing both sides of the equation by 2 would give us a fractional term that could be messy to deal with, so we won't do that for now. Instead, we square both sides of the equation; note that on the left-hand side the 2 is outside the square root sign, so we have to square it. As a result, we get $4(x + 5) = (x + 2)^2$. Expanding both sides gives us $4x + 20 = x^2 + 4x + 4$. In this case, we see that we have $4x$ on both sides, so we can cancel the $4x$ (which is what allows us to solve this equation despite the different powers of x). We now have $20 = x^2 + 4$, or $x^2 = 16$. Since the variable is raised to an even power, we need to take the positive and negative roots, so $x = \pm 4$: that is, $x = 4$ or $x = -4$. Substituting both values into the original equation, we see that $x = 4$ satisfies the equation but $x = -4$ does not; hence $x = -4$ is a spurious solution, and the only solution to the equation is $x = 4$.

P7. The number of dollars that Ray earns is dependent on the number of hours he works, so earnings will be represented by the dependent variable y and hours worked will be represented by the independent variable x. He earns 10 dollars per hour worked, so his earnings can be calculated as $y = 10x$. To calculate the number of hours Ray must work in order to earn \$360, plug in 360 for y and solve for x:

$$360 = 10x$$
$$x = \frac{360}{10} = 36$$

P8. To simplify this equation, we must isolate one of its variables on one side of the equation. In this case, the x appears under an absolute value sign, which makes it difficult to isolate. The y, on the other hand, only appears without an exponent—the equation is linear in y. We will therefore choose to isolate the y. The first step, then, is to move all the terms with y to the left side of the equation, which we can do by subtracting $5y$ from both sides:

$$3x + 2 - 3y = -7 + |2x - 1|$$

We can then move all the terms that do *not* include y to the right side of the equation, by subtracting $3x$ and 2 from both sides of the equation:

$$-3y = -3x - 9 + |2x - 1|$$

Finally, we can isolate the y by dividing both sides by –3.

$$y = x + 3 - \frac{1}{3}|2x - 1|$$

This is as far as we can simplify the equation; we cannot combine the terms inside and outside the absolute value sign. We can therefore consider the equation to be solved.

INEQUALITIES

Commonly in algebra and other upper-level fields of math you find yourself working with mathematical expressions that do not equal each other. The statement comparing such expressions with symbols such as <

Copyright © Mometrix Media. You have been licensed one copy of this document for personal use only. Any other reproduction or redistribution is strictly prohibited. All rights reserved.
This content is provided for test preparation purposes only and does not imply an endorsement by Mometrix of any particular political, scientific, or religious point of view.

(less than) or > (greater than) is called an *inequality*. An example of an inequality is $7x > 5$. To solve for x, simply divide both sides by 7 and the solution is shown to be $x > \frac{5}{7}$. Graphs of the solution set of inequalities are represented on a number line. Open circles are used to show that an expression approaches a number but is never quite equal to that number.

> **Review Video: Solving Multi-Step Inequalities**
> Visit mometrix.com/academy and enter code: 347842

Conditional inequalities are those with certain values for the variable that will make the condition true and other values for the variable where the condition will be false. **Absolute inequalities** can have any real number as the value for the variable to make the condition true, while there is no real number value for the variable that will make the condition false. Solving inequalities is done by following the same rules for solving equations with the exception that when multiplying or dividing by a negative number the direction of the inequality sign must be flipped or reversed. **Double inequalities** are situations where two inequality statements apply to the same variable expression. An example of this is $-c < ax + b < c$.

> **Review Video: Conditional and Absolute Inequalities**
> Visit mometrix.com/academy and enter code: 980164

DETERMINING SOLUTIONS TO INEQUALITIES

To determine whether a coordinate is a solution of an inequality, you can substitute the values of the coordinate into the inequality, simplify, and check whether the resulting statement holds true. For instance, to determine whether $(-2, 4)$ is a solution of the inequality $y \geq -2x + 3$, substitute the values into the inequality, $4 \geq -2(-2) + 3$. Simplify the right side of the inequality and the result is $4 \geq 7$, which is a false statement. Therefore, the coordinate is not a solution of the inequality. You can also use this method to determine which part of the graph of an inequality is shaded. The graph of $y \geq -2x + 3$ includes the solid line $y = -2x + 3$ and, since it excludes the point $(-2, 4)$ to the left of the line, it is shaded to the right of the line.

FLIPPING INEQUALITY SIGNS

When given an inequality, we can always turn the entire inequality around, swapping the two sides of the inequality and changing the inequality sign. For instance, $x + 2 > 2x - 3$ is equivalent to $2x - 3 < x + 2$. Aside from that, normally the inequality does not change if we carry out the same operation on both sides of the inequality. There is, however, one principal exception: if we *multiply* or *divide* both sides of the inequality by a *negative number*, the inequality is flipped. For example, if we take the inequality $-2x < 6$ and divide both sides by -2, the inequality flips and we are left with $x > -3$. This *only* applies to multiplication and division, and only with negative numbers. Multiplying or dividing both sides by a positive number, or adding or subtracting any number regardless of sign, does not flip the inequality. Another special case that flips the inequality sign is when reciprocals are used. For instance, $3 > 2$ but the relation of the reciprocals is $\frac{1}{2} < \frac{1}{3}$.

COMPOUND INEQUALITIES

A **compound inequality** is an equality that consists of two inequalities combined with *and* or *or*. The two components of a proper compound inequality must be of opposite type: that is, one must be greater than (or greater than or equal to), the other less than (or less than or equal to). For instance, "$x + 1 < 2$ or $x + 1 > 3$" is a compound inequality, as is "$2x \geq 4$ and $2x \leq 6$." An *and* inequality can be written more compactly by having one inequality on each side of the common part: "$2x \geq 1$ and $2x \leq 6$," can also be written as $1 \leq 2x \leq 6$.

In order for the compound inequality to be meaningful, the two parts of an *and* inequality must overlap; otherwise, no numbers satisfy the inequality. On the other hand, if the two parts of an *or* inequality overlap, then *all* numbers satisfy the inequality and as such is usually not meaningful.

Copyright © Mometrix Media. You have been licensed one copy of this document for personal use only. Any other reproduction or redistribution is strictly prohibited. All rights reserved.
This content is provided for test preparation purposes only and does not imply an endorsement by Mometrix of any particular political, scientific, or religious point of view.

Solving a compound inequality requires solving each part separately. For example, given the compound inequality "$x + 1 < 2$ or $x + 1 > 3$," the first inequality, $x + 1 < 2$, reduces to $x < 1$, and the second part, $x + 1 > 3$, reduces to $x > 2$, so the whole compound inequality can be written as "$x < 1$ or $x > 2$." Similarly, $1 \leq 2x \leq 6$ can be solved by dividing each term by 2, yielding $\frac{1}{2} \leq x \leq 3$.

> **Review Video: Compound Inequalities**
> Visit mometrix.com/academy and enter code: 786318

SOLVING INEQUALITIES INVOLVING ABSOLUTE VALUES

To solve an inequality involving an absolute value, first isolate the term with the absolute value. Then proceed to treat the two cases separately as with an absolute value equation, but flipping the inequality in the case where the expression in the absolute value is negative (since that essentially involves multiplying both sides by -1.) The two cases are then combined into a compound inequality; if the absolute value is on the greater side of the inequality, then it is an *or* compound inequality, if on the lesser side, then it's an *and*.

Consider the inequality $2 + |x - 1| \geq 3$. We can isolate the absolute value term by subtracting 2 from both sides: $|x - 1| \geq 1$. Now, we're left with the two cases $x - 1 \geq 1$ or $x - 1 \leq -1$: note that in the latter, negative case, the inequality is flipped. $x - 1 \geq 1$ reduces to $x \geq 2$, and $x - 1 \leq -1$ reduces to $x \leq 0$. Since in the inequality $|x - 1| \geq 1$ the absolute value is on the greater side, the two cases combine into an *or* compound inequality, so the final, solved inequality is "$x \leq 0$ or $x \geq 2$."

> **Review Video: Solving Absolute Value Inequalities**
> Visit mometrix.com/academy and enter code: 997008

SOLVING INEQUALITIES INVOLVING SQUARE ROOTS

Solving an inequality with a square root involves two parts. First, we solve the inequality as if it were an equation, isolating the square root and then squaring both sides of the equation. Second, we restrict the solution to the set of values of x for which the value inside the square root sign is non-negative.

For example, in the inequality, $\sqrt{x - 2} + 1 < 5$, we can isolate the square root by subtracting 1 from both sides, yielding $\sqrt{x - 2} < 4$. Squaring both sides of the inequality yields $x - 2 < 16$, so $x < 18$. Since we can't take the square root of a negative number, we also require the part inside the square root to be non-negative. In this case, that means $x - 2 \geq 0$. Adding 2 to both sides of the inequality yields $x \geq 2$. Our final answer is a compound inequality combining the two simple inequalities: $x \geq 2$ and $x < 18$, or $2 \leq x < 18$.

Note that we only get a compound inequality if the two simple inequalities are in opposite directions; otherwise, we take the one that is more restrictive.

The same technique can be used for other even roots, such as fourth roots. It is *not*, however, used for cube roots or other odd roots—negative numbers *do* have cube roots, so the condition that the quantity inside the root sign cannot be negative does not apply.

> **Review Video: Solving Inequalities Involving Square Roots**
> Visit mometrix.com/academy and enter code: 800288

SPECIAL CIRCUMSTANCES

Sometimes an inequality involving an absolute value or an even exponent is true for all values of x, and we don't need to do any further work to solve it. This is true if the inequality, once the absolute value or exponent term is isolated, says that term is greater than a negative number (or greater than or equal to zero). Since an absolute value or a number raised to an even exponent is *always* non-negative, this inequality is always true.

Copyright © Mometrix Media. You have been licensed one copy of this document for personal use only. Any other reproduction or redistribution is strictly prohibited. All rights reserved.
This content is provided for test preparation purposes only and does not imply an endorsement by Mometrix of any particular political, scientific, or religious point of view.

GRAPHICAL SOLUTIONS TO EQUATIONS AND INEQUALITIES

When equations are shown graphically, they are usually shown on a **Cartesian coordinate plane**. The Cartesian coordinate plane consists of two number lines placed perpendicular to each other and intersecting at the zero point, also known as the origin. The horizontal number line is known as the x-axis, with positive values to the right of the origin, and negative values to the left of the origin. The vertical number line is known as the y-axis, with positive values above the origin, and negative values below the origin. Any point on the plane can be identified by an ordered pair in the form (x, y), called coordinates. The x-value of the coordinate is called the abscissa, and the y-value of the coordinate is called the ordinate. The two number lines divide the plane into **four quadrants**: I, II, III, and IV.

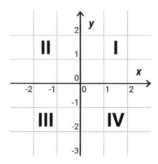

Note that in quadrant I $x > 0$ and $y > 0$, in quadrant II $x < 0$ and $y > 0$, in quadrant III $x < 0$ and $y < 0$, and in quadrant IV $x > 0$ and $y < 0$.

Recall that if the value of the slope of a line is positive, the line slopes upward from left to right. If the value of the slope is negative, the line slopes downward from left to right. If the y-coordinates are the same for two points on a line, the slope is 0 and the line is a **horizontal line**. If the x-coordinates are the same for two points on a line, there is no slope and the line is a **vertical line**. Two or more lines that have equivalent slopes are **parallel lines**. **Perpendicular lines** have slopes that are negative reciprocals of each other, such as $\frac{a}{b}$ and $\frac{-b}{a}$.

GRAPHING SIMPLE INEQUALITIES

To graph a simple inequality, we first mark on the number line the value that signifies the end point of the inequality. If the inequality is strict (involves a less than or greater than), we use a hollow circle; if it is not strict (less than or equal to or greater than or equal to), we use a solid circle. We then fill in the part of the number line that satisfies the inequality: to the left of the marked point for less than (or less than or equal to), to the right for greater than (or greater than or equal to).

For example, we would graph the inequality $x < 5$ by putting a hollow circle at 5 and filling in the part of the line to the left:

GRAPHING COMPOUND INEQUALITIES

To graph a compound inequality, we fill in both parts of the inequality for an *or* inequality, or the overlap between them for an *and* inequality. More specifically, we start by plotting the endpoints of each inequality on the number line. For an *or* inequality, we then fill in the appropriate side of the line for each inequality. Typically, the two component inequalities do not overlap, which means the shaded part is *outside* the two points. For an *and* inequality, we instead fill in the part of the line that meets both inequalities.

Copyright © Mometrix Media. You have been licensed one copy of this document for personal use only. Any other reproduction or redistribution is strictly prohibited. All rights reserved.
This content is provided for test preparation purposes only and does not imply an endorsement by Mometrix of any particular political, scientific, or religious point of view.

For the inequality "$x \leq -3$ or $x > 4$," we first put a solid circle at –3 and a hollow circle at 4. We then fill the parts of the line *outside* these circles:

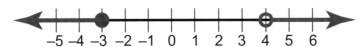

GRAPHING INEQUALITIES INCLUDING ABSOLUTE VALUES

An inequality with an absolute value can be converted to a compound inequality. To graph the inequality, first convert it to a compound inequality, and then graph that normally. If the absolute value is on the greater side of the inequality, we end up with an *or* inequality; we plot the endpoints of the inequality on the number line and fill in the part of the line *outside* those points. If the absolute value is on the smaller side of the inequality, we end up with an *and* inequality; we plot the endpoints of the inequality on the number line and fill in the part of the line *between* those points.

For example, the inequality $|x + 1| \geq 4$ can be rewritten as $x \geq 3$ or $x \leq -5$. We place solid circles at the points 3 and -5 and fill in the part of the line *outside* them:

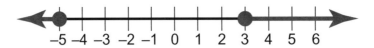

GRAPHING EQUATIONS IN TWO VARIABLES

One way of graphing an equation in two variables is to plot enough points to get an idea for its shape, and then draw the appropriate curve through those points. A point can be plotted by substituting in a value for one variable and solving for the other. If the equation is linear, we only need two points, and can then draw a straight line between them.

For example, consider the equation $y = 2x - 1$. This is a linear equation—both variables only appear raised to the first power—so we only need two points. When $x = 0$, $y = 2(0) - 1 = -1$. When $x = 2$, $y = 2(2) - 1 = 3$. We can therefore choose the points $(0, -1)$ and $(2, 3)$, and draw a line between them:

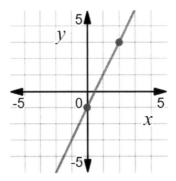

Review Video: Graphing Linear Functions
Visit mometrix.com/academy and enter code: 699478

PRACTICE

P1. Analyze the following inequalities:

    (a) $2 - |x + 1| < 3$
    (b) $2(x - 1)^2 + 7 \leq 1$

82

Copyright © Mometrix Media. You have been licensed one copy of this document for personal use only. Any other reproduction or redistribution is strictly prohibited. All rights reserved.
This content is provided for test preparation purposes only and does not imply an endorsement by Mometrix of any particular political, scientific, or religious point of view.

P2. Graph the following on a number line:

(a) $x \geq 3$
(b) $-2 \leq x \leq 6$
(c) $|x| < 2$

PRACTICE SOLUTIONS

P1. (a) Subtracting 2 from both sides yields $-|x + 1| < 1$; multiplying by -1 (and flipping the inequality, since we're multiplying by a negative number) yields $|x + 1| > -1$. But since the absolute value cannot be negative, it's *always* greater than –1, so this inequality is true for all values of x.

(b) Subtracting 7 from both sides yields $2(x - 1)^2 \leq -6$; dividing by 2 yields $(x - 1)^2 \leq -3$. But $(x - 1)^2$ must be nonnegative, and hence cannot be less than or equal to –3; this inequality has no solution.

P2. (a) We would graph the inequality $x \geq 3$ by putting a solid circle at 3 and filling in the part of the line to the right:

(b) The inequality $-2 \leq x \leq 6$ is equivalent to "$x \geq -2$ and $x \leq 6$." To plot this compound inequality, we first put solid circles at –2 and 6, and then fill in the part of the line *between* these circles:

(c) The inequality $|x| < 2$ can be rewritten as "$x > -2$ and $x < 2$." We place hollow circles at the points –2 and 2 and fill in the part of the line between them:

BASIC FUNCTIONS

When expressing functional relationships, the **variables** x and y are typically used. These values are often written as the **coordinates** (x, y). The x-value is the independent variable and the y-value is the dependent variable. A **relation** is a set of data in which there is not a unique y-value for each x-value in the dataset. This means that there can be two of the same x-values assigned to different y-values. A relation is simply a relationship between the x and y-values in each coordinate but does not apply to the relationship between the values of x and y in the data set. A **function** is a relation where one quantity depends on the other. For example, the amount of money that you make depends on the number of hours that you work. In a function, each x-value in the data set has one unique y-value because the y-value depends on the x-value.

> **Review Video: Definition of a Function**
> Visit mometrix.com/academy and enter code: 784611

A function has exactly one value of **output variable** (dependent variable) for each value of the **input variable** (independent variable). The set of all values for the input variable (here assumed to be x) is the domain of the function, and the set of all corresponding values of output variable (here assumed to be y) is the range of the function. When looking at a graph of an equation, the easiest way to determine if the equation is a function or not is to conduct the vertical line test. If a vertical line drawn through any value of x crosses the graph in more than one place, the equation is not a function.

Copyright © Mometrix Media. You have been licensed one copy of this document for personal use only. Any other reproduction or redistribution is strictly prohibited. All rights reserved.
This content is provided for test preparation purposes only and does not imply an endorsement by Mometrix of any particular political, scientific, or religious point of view.

FINDING THE DOMAIN AND RANGE OF A FUNCTION

The **domain** of a function $f(x)$ is the set of all input values for which the function is defined. The **range** of a function $f(x)$ is the set of all possible output values of the function—that is, of every possible value of $f(x)$, for any value of x in the function's domain. For a function expressed in a table, every input-output pair is given explicitly. To find the domain, we just list all the x values and to find the range, we just list all the values of $f(x)$. Consider the following example:

x	-1	4	2	1	0	3	8	6
$f(x)$	3	0	3	−1	−1	2	4	6

In this case, the domain would be {-1, 4, 2, 1, 0, 3, 8, 6}, or, putting them in ascending order, {-1, 0, 1, 2, 3, 4, 6, 8}. (Putting the values in ascending order isn't strictly necessary, but generally makes the set easier to read.) The range would be {3, 0, 3, −1, −1, 2, 4, 6}. Note that some of these values appear more than once. This is entirely permissible for a function; while each value of x must be matched to a unique value of $f(x)$, the converse is not true. We don't need to list each value more than once, so eliminating duplicates, the range is {3, 0, −1, 2, 4, 6}, or, putting them in ascending order, {−1, 0, 2, 3, 4, 6}.

Note that by definition of a function, no input value can be matched to more than one output value. It is good to double check to make sure that the data given follows this and is therefore actually a function.

> **Review Video: How to Find Domain and Range**
> Visit mometrix.com/academy and enter code: 778133

DETERMINING A FUNCTION

You can determine whether an equation is a **function** by substituting different values into the equation for x. You can display and organize these numbers in a data table. A **data table** contains the values for x and y, which you can also list as coordinates. In order for a function to exist, the table cannot contain any repeating x-values that correspond with different y-values. If each x-coordinate has a unique y-coordinate, the table contains a function. However, there can be repeating y-values that correspond with different x-values. An example of this is when the function contains an exponent. For example, if $x^2 = y$, $2^2 = 4$, and $(−2)^2 = 4$.

WRITING A FUNCTION RULE USING A TABLE

If given a set of data, place the corresponding x and y-values into a table and analyze the relationship between them. Consider what you can do to each x-value to obtain the corresponding y-value. Try adding or subtracting different numbers to and from x and then try multiplying or dividing different numbers to and from x. If none of these **operations** give you the y-value, try combining the operations. Once you find a rule that works for one pair, make sure to try it with each additional set of ordered pairs in the table. If the same operation or combination of operations satisfies each set of coordinates, then the table contains a function. The rule is then used to write the equation of the function in "$y = f(x)$" form.

DIRECT AND INVERSE VARIATIONS OF VARIABLES

Variables that vary directly are those that either both increase at the same rate or both decrease at the same rate. For example, in the functions $y = kx$ or $y = kx^n$, where k and n are positive, the value of y increases as the value of x increases and decreases as the value of x decreases.

Variables that vary inversely are those where one increases while the other decreases. For example, in the functions $y = \frac{k}{x}$ or $y = \frac{k}{x^n}$ where k and n are positive, the value of y increases as the value of x decreases and decreases as the value of x increases.

In both cases, k is the constant of variation.

Copyright © Mometrix Media. You have been licensed one copy of this document for personal use only. Any other reproduction or redistribution is strictly prohibited. All rights reserved.
This content is provided for test preparation purposes only and does not imply an endorsement by Mometrix of any particular political, scientific, or religious point of view.

PROPERTIES OF FUNCTIONS

There are many different ways to classify functions based on their structure or behavior. Important features of functions include:

- **End behavior**: the behavior of the function at extreme values ($f(x)$ as $x \to \pm\infty$)
- **y-intercept**: the value of the function at $f(0)$
- **Roots**: the values of x where the function equals zero ($f(x) = 0$)
- **Extrema**: minimum or maximum values of the function or where the function changes direction ($f(x) \geq k$ or $f(x) \leq k$)

CLASSIFICATION OF FUNCTIONS

An **invertible function** is defined as a function, $f(x)$, for which there is another function, $f^{-1}(x)$, such that $f^{-1}(f(x)) = x$. For example, if $f(x) = 3x - 2$ the inverse function, $f^{-1}(x)$, can be found:

$$x = 3(f^{-1}(x)) - 2$$
$$\frac{x+2}{3} = f^{-1}(x)$$

$$f^{-1}(f(x)) = \frac{3x - 2 + 2}{3}$$
$$= \frac{3x}{3}$$
$$= x$$

Note that $f^{-1}(x)$ is a valid function over all values of x.

In a **one-to-one function**, each value of x has exactly one value for y on the coordinate plane (this is the definition of a function) and each value of y has exactly one value for x. While the vertical line test will determine if a graph is that of a function, the horizontal line test will determine if a function is a one-to-one function. If a horizontal line drawn at any value of y intersects the graph in more than one place, the graph is not that of a one-to-one function. Do not make the mistake of using the horizontal line test exclusively in determining if a graph is that of a one-to-one function. A one-to-one function must pass both the vertical line test and the horizontal line test. As such, one-to-one functions are invertible functions.

A **many-to-one function** is a function whereby the relation is a function, but the inverse of the function is not a function. In other words, each element in the domain is mapped to one and only one element in the range. However, one or more elements in the range may be mapped to the same element in the domain. A graph of a many-to-one function would pass the vertical line test, but not the horizontal line test. This is why many-to-one functions are not invertible.

A **monotone function** is a function whose graph either constantly increases or constantly decreases. Examples include the functions $f(x) = x$, $f(x) = -x$, or $f(x) = x^3$.

An **even function** has a graph that is symmetric with respect to the y-axis and satisfies the equation $f(x) = f(-x)$. Examples include the functions $f(x) = x^2$ and $f(x) = ax^n$, where a is any real number and n is a positive even integer.

An **odd function** has a graph that is symmetric with respect to the origin and satisfies the equation $f(x) = -f(-x)$. Examples include the functions $f(x) = x^3$ and $f(x) = ax^n$, where a is any real number and n is a positive odd integer.

> **Review Video: Even and Odd Functions**
> Visit mometrix.com/academy and enter code: 278985

Constant functions are given by the equation $f(x) = b$, where b is a real number. There is no independent variable present in the equation, so the function has a constant value for all x. The graph of a constant function

Copyright © Mometrix Media. You have been licensed one copy of this document for personal use only. Any other reproduction or redistribution is strictly prohibited. All rights reserved. This content is provided for test preparation purposes only and does not imply an endorsement by Mometrix of any particular political, scientific, or religious point of view.

is a horizontal line of slope 0 that is positioned b units from the x-axis. If b is positive, the line is above the x-axis; if b is negative, the line is below the x-axis.

Identity functions are identified by the equation $f(x) = x$, where every value of the function is equal to its corresponding value of x. The only zero is the point $(0, 0)$. The graph is a line with slope of 1.

In **linear functions**, the value of the function changes in direct proportion to x. The rate of change, represented by the slope on its graph, is constant throughout. The standard form of a linear equation is $ax + cy = d$, where a, c, and d are real numbers. As a function, this equation is commonly in the form $y = mx + b$ or $f(x) = mx + b$ where $m = -\frac{a}{c}$ and $b = \frac{d}{c}$. This is known as the slope-intercept form, because the coefficients give the slope of the graphed function (m) and its y-intercept (b). Solve the equation $mx + b = 0$ for x to get $x = -\frac{b}{m}$, which is the only zero of the function. The domain and range are both the set of all real numbers.

> **Review Video: Linear Functions**
> Visit mometrix.com/academy and enter code: 200735

Algebraic functions are those that exclusively use polynomials and roots. These would include polynomial functions, rational functions, square root functions, and all combinations of these functions, such as polynomials as the radicand. These combinations may be joined by addition, subtraction, multiplication, or division, but may not include variables as exponents.

> **Review Video: Common Functions**
> Visit mometrix.com/academy and enter code: 629798

ABSOLUTE VALUE FUNCTIONS

An **absolute value function** is in the format $f(x) = |ax + b|$. Like other functions, the domain is the set of all real numbers. However, because absolute value indicates positive numbers, the range is limited to positive real numbers. To find the zero of an absolute value function, set the portion inside the absolute value sign equal to zero and solve for x. An absolute value function is also known as a piecewise function because it must be solved in pieces—one for if the value inside the absolute value sign is positive, and one for if the value is negative. The function can be expressed as

$$f(x) = \begin{cases} ax + b \text{ if } ax + b \geq 0 \\ -(ax + b) \text{ if } ax + b < 0 \end{cases}$$

This will allow for an accurate statement of the range. The graph of an example absolute value function, $f(x) = |2x - 1|$, is below:

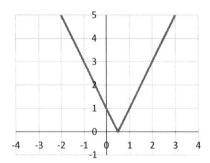

Copyright © Mometrix Media. You have been licensed one copy of this document for personal use only. Any other reproduction or redistribution is strictly prohibited. All rights reserved.
This content is provided for test preparation purposes only and does not imply an endorsement by Mometrix of any particular political, scientific, or religious point of view.

PIECEWISE FUNCTIONS

A **piecewise function** is a function that has different definitions on two or more different intervals. The following, for instance, is one example of a piecewise-defined function:

$$f(x) = \begin{cases} x^2, & x < 0 \\ x, & 0 \leq x \leq 2 \\ (x-2)^2, & x > 2 \end{cases}$$

To graph this function, we'd simply graph each part separately in the appropriate domain. The final graph would look like this:

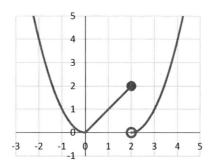

Note the filled and hollow dots at the discontinuity at $x = 2$. This is important to show which side of the graph that point corresponds to. Because $f(x) = x$ on the closed interval $0 \leq x \leq 2$, $f(2) = 2$. The point $(2, 2)$ is therefore marked with a filled circle, and the point $(2, 0)$, which is the endpoint of the rightmost $(x - 2)^2$ part of the graph but *not actually part of the function*, is marked with a hollow dot to indicate this.

> **Review Video: Piecewise Functions**
> Visit mometrix.com/academy and enter code: 707921

RATIONAL FUNCTIONS

A **rational function** is a function that can be constructed as a ratio of two polynomial expressions: $f(x) = \frac{p(x)}{q(x)}$, where $p(x)$ and $q(x)$ are both polynomial expressions and $q(x) \neq 0$. The domain is the set of all real numbers, except any values for which $q(x) = 0$. The range is the set of real numbers that satisfies the function when the domain is applied. When you graph a rational function, you will have vertical asymptotes wherever $q(x) = 0$. If the polynomial in the numerator is of lesser degree than the polynomial in the denominator, the x-axis will also be a horizontal asymptote. If the numerator and denominator have equal degrees, there will be a horizontal asymptote not on the x-axis. If the degree of the numerator is exactly one greater than the degree of the denominator, the graph will have an oblique, or diagonal, asymptote. The asymptote will be along the line $y = \frac{p_n}{q_{n-1}} x + \frac{p_{n-1}}{q_{n-1}}$, where p_n and q_{n-1} are the coefficients of the highest degree terms in their respective polynomials.

SQUARE ROOT FUNCTIONS

A **square root function** is a function that contains a radical and is in the format $f(x) = \sqrt{ax + b}$. The domain is the set of all real numbers that yields a positive radicand or a radicand equal to zero. Because square root values are assumed to be positive unless otherwise identified, the range is all real numbers from zero to infinity. To find the zero of a square root function, set the radicand equal to zero and solve for x. The graph of a square root function is always to the right of the zero and always above the x-axis.

Copyright © Mometrix Media. You have been licensed one copy of this document for personal use only. Any other reproduction or redistribution is strictly prohibited. All rights reserved.
This content is provided for test preparation purposes only and does not imply an endorsement by Mometrix of any particular political, scientific, or religious point of view.

Example graph of a square root function, $f(x) = \sqrt{2x + 1}$:

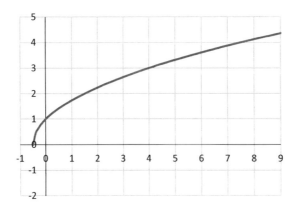

PRACTICE

P1. Martin needs a 20% medicine solution. The pharmacy has a 5% solution and a 30% solution. He needs 50 mL of the solution. If the pharmacist must mix the two solutions, how many milliliters of 5% solution and 30% solution should be used?

P2. Describe two different strategies for solving the following problem:

> Kevin can mow the yard in 4 hours. Mandy can mow the same yard in 5 hours. If they work together, how long will it take them to mow the yard?

P3. A car, traveling at 65 miles per hour, leaves Flagstaff and heads east on I-40. Another car, traveling at 75 miles per hour, leaves Flagstaff 2 hours later, from the same starting point and also heads east on I-40. Determine how many hours it will take the second car to catch the first car by:

(a) Using a table.

(b) Using algebra.

PRACTICE SOLUTIONS

P1. To solve this problem, a table may be created to represent the variables, percentages, and total amount of solution. Such a table is shown below:

	mL solution	% medicine	Total mL medicine
5% solution	x	0.05	$0.05x$
30% solution	y	0.30	$0.30y$
Mixture	$x + y = 50$	0.20	$(0.20)(50) = 10$

The variable x may be rewritten as $50 - y$, so the equation $0.05(50 - y) + 0.30y = 10$ may be written and solved for y. Doing so gives $y = 30$. So, 30 mL of 30% solution are needed. Evaluating the expression, $50 - y$ for an x-value of 20, shows that 20 mL of 5% solution are needed.

P2. Two possible strategies both involve the use of rational equations to solve. The first strategy involves representing the fractional part of the yard mowed by each person in one hour and setting this sum equal to the ratio of 1 to the total time needed. The appropriate equation is $1/4 + 1/5 = 1/t$, which simplifies as $9/20 = 1/t$, and finally as $t = 20/9$. So the time it will take them to mow the yard, when working together, is a little more than 2.2 hours.

Copyright © Mometrix Media. You have been licensed one copy of this document for personal use only. Any other reproduction or redistribution is strictly prohibited. All rights reserved.
This content is provided for test preparation purposes only and does not imply an endorsement by Mometrix of any particular political, scientific, or religious point of view.

A second strategy involves representing the time needed for each person as two fractions and setting the sum equal to 1 (representing 1 yard). The appropriate equation is $t/4 + t/5 = 1$, which simplifies as $9t/20 = 1$, and finally as $t = 20/9$. This strategy also shows the total time to be a little more than 2.2 hours.

P3. (a) One strategy might involve creating a table of values for the number of hours and distances for each car. The table may be examined to find the same distance traveled and the corresponding number of hours taken. Such a table is shown below:

Car A		Car B	
x (hours)	*y* (distance)	*x* (hours)	*y* (distance)
0	0	0	
1	65	1	
2	130	2	0
3	195	3	75
4	260	4	150
5	325	5	225
6	390	6	300
7	455	7	375
8	520	8	450
9	585	9	525
10	650	10	600
11	715	11	675
12	780	12	750
13	845	13	825
14	910	14	900
15	975	15	975

The table shows that after 15 hours, the distance traveled is the same. Thus, the second car catches up with the first car after a distance of 975 miles and 15 hours.

(b) A second strategy might involve setting up and solving an algebraic equation. This situation may be modeled as $65x = 75(x - 2)$. This equation sets the distances traveled by each car equal to one another. Solving for x gives $x = 15$. Thus, once again, the second car will catch up with the first car after 15 hours.

TRIGONOMETRY
PYTHAGOREAN THEOREM

The side of a triangle opposite the right angle is called the **hypotenuse**. The other two sides are called the legs. The Pythagorean theorem states a relationship among the legs and hypotenuse of a right triangle: $(a^2 + b^2 = c^2)$, where a and b are the lengths of the legs of a right triangle, and c is the length of the hypotenuse. Note that this formula will only work with right triangles.

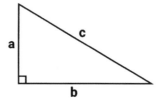

Review Video: **Pythagorean Theorem**
Visit mometrix.com/academy and enter code: 906576

Copyright © Mometrix Media. You have been licensed one copy of this document for personal use only. Any other reproduction or redistribution is strictly prohibited. All rights reserved.
This content is provided for test preparation purposes only and does not imply an endorsement by Mometrix of any particular political, scientific, or religious point of view.

TRIGONOMETRIC FORMULAS

In the diagram below, angle C is the right angle, and side c is the hypotenuse. Side a is the side opposite to angle A and side b is the side opposite to angle B. Using ratios of side lengths as a means to calculate the sine, cosine, and tangent of an acute angle only works for right triangles.

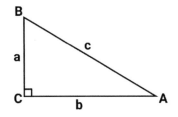

$$\sin A = \frac{\text{opposite side}}{\text{hypotenuse}} = \frac{a}{c} \qquad \csc A = \frac{1}{\sin A} = \frac{\text{hypotenuse}}{\text{opposite side}} = \frac{c}{a}$$

$$\cos A = \frac{\text{adjacent side}}{\text{hypotenuse}} = \frac{b}{c} \qquad \sec A = \frac{1}{\cos A} = \frac{\text{hypotenuse}}{\text{adjacent side}} = \frac{c}{b}$$

$$\tan A = \frac{\text{opposite side}}{\text{adjacent side}} = \frac{a}{b} \qquad \cot A = \frac{1}{\tan A} = \frac{\text{adjacent side}}{\text{opposite side}} = \frac{b}{a}$$

LAWS OF SINES AND COSINES

The **law of sines** states that $\frac{\sin A}{a} = \frac{\sin B}{b} = \frac{\sin C}{c}$, where A, B, and C are the angles of a triangle, and a, b, and c are the sides opposite their respective angles. This formula will work with all triangles, not just right triangles.

The **law of cosines** is given by the formula $c^2 = a^2 + b^2 - 2ab(\cos C)$, where a, b, and c are the sides of a triangle, and C is the angle opposite side c. This is a generalized form of the Pythagorean theorem that can be used on any triangle.

Review Video: <u>Upper Level Trig: Law of Sines</u>
Visit mometrix.com/academy and enter code: 206844

Review Video: <u>Law of Signs</u>
Visit mometrix.com/academy and enter code: 158911

PRACTICE

P1. Calculate the following values based on triangle MNO:

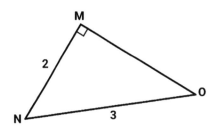

(a) length of $\overline{MO}$

(b) $\sin(\angle NOM)$

(c) area of the triangle, if the units of the measurements are in miles

PRACTICE SOLUTIONS

P1. (a) Since triangle MNO is a right triangle, we can use the simple form of Pythagoras theorem to find the missing side length:

$$\left(\overline{MO}\right)^2 + 2^2 = 3^2$$
$$\left(\overline{MO}\right)^2 = 9 - 4$$
$$\overline{MO} = \sqrt{5}$$

Copyright © Mometrix Media. You have been licensed one copy of this document for personal use only. Any other reproduction or redistribution is strictly prohibited. All rights reserved. This content is provided for test preparation purposes only and does not imply an endorsement by Mometrix of any particular political, scientific, or religious point of view.

(b) Recall that sine of an angle in a right triangle is the ratio of the opposite side to the hypotenuse. So, $\sin(\angle NOM) = 2/3$

(c) Since triangle MNO is a right triangle, we can use either of the legs as the height and the other as the base in the simple formula for the area of a triangle:

$$A = \frac{bh}{2}$$
$$= \frac{(2 \text{ mi})\left(\sqrt{5} \text{ mi}\right)}{2}$$
$$= \sqrt{5} \text{ mi}^2$$

DEGREES, RADIANS, AND THE UNIT CIRCLE

It is important to understand the deep connection between trigonometry and circles. Specifically, the two main units, **degrees** (°) and **radians** (rad), that are used to measure angles are related this way: 360° in one full circle and 2π radians in one full circle: $(360° = 2\pi \text{ rad})$. The conversion factor relating the two is often stated as $\frac{180°}{\pi}$. For example, to convert $\frac{3\pi}{2}$ radians to degrees, multiply by the conversion factor: $\frac{3\pi}{2} \times \frac{180°}{\pi} = 270°$. As another example, to convert 60° to radians, divide by the conversion factor or multiply by the reciprocal: $60° \times \frac{\pi}{180°} = \frac{\pi}{3}$ radians.

Recall that the standard equation for a circle is $(x - h)^2 + (y - k)^2 = r^2$. A **unit circle** is a circle with a radius of 1 $(r = 1)$ that has its center at the origin $(h = 0, k = 0)$. Thus, the equation for the unit circle simplifies from the standard equation down to $x^2 + y^2 = 1$.

Standard position is the position of an angle of measure θ whose vertex is at the origin, the initial side crosses the unit circle at the point $(1, 0)$, and the terminal side crosses the unit circle at some other point (a, b). In the standard position, $\sin \theta = b$, $\cos \theta = a$, and $\tan \theta = \frac{b}{a}$.

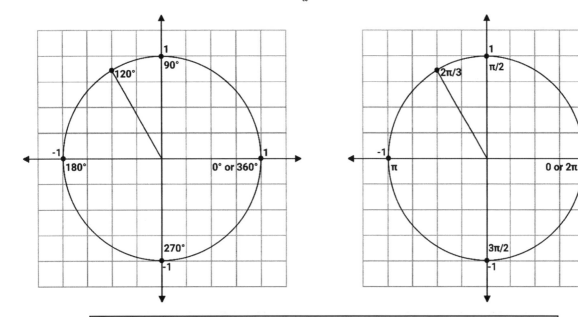

Review Video: Upper Level Trig: Unit Circle
Visit mometrix.com/academy and enter code: 333922

Copyright © Mometrix Media. You have been licensed one copy of this document for personal use only. Any other reproduction or redistribution is strictly prohibited. All rights reserved.
This content is provided for test preparation purposes only and does not imply an endorsement by Mometrix of any particular political, scientific, or religious point of view.

BASIC TRIGONOMETRIC FUNCTIONS
SINE

The **sine** (sin) function has a period of 360° or 2π radians. This means that its graph makes one complete cycle every 360° or 2π. Because $\sin 0 = 0$, the graph of $y = \sin x$ begins at the origin, with the x-axis representing the angle measure, and the y-axis representing the sine of the angle. The graph of the sine function is a smooth curve that begins at the origin, peaks at the point $\left(\frac{\pi}{2}, 1\right)$, crosses the x-axis at $(\pi, 0)$, has its lowest point at $\left(\frac{3\pi}{2}, -1\right)$, and returns to the x-axis to complete one cycle at $(2\pi, 0)$.

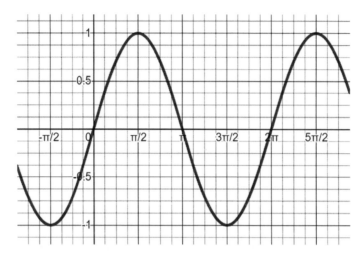

Review Video: Upper Level Trig: Sine
Visit mometrix.com/academy and enter code: 193339

COSINE

The **cosine** (cos) function also has a period of 360° or 2π radians, which means that its graph also makes one complete cycle every 360° or 2π. Because $\cos 0° = 1$, the graph of $y = \cos x$ begins at the point $(0, 1)$, with the x-axis representing the angle measure, and the y-axis representing the cosine of the angle. The graph of the cosine function is a smooth curve that begins at the point $(0,1)$, crosses the x-axis at the point $\left(\frac{\pi}{2}, 0\right)$, has its

Copyright © Mometrix Media. You have been licensed one copy of this document for personal use only. Any other reproduction or redistribution is strictly prohibited. All rights reserved.
This content is provided for test preparation purposes only and does not imply an endorsement by Mometrix of any particular political, scientific, or religious point of view.

lowest point at $(\pi, -1)$, crosses the x-axis again at the point $\left(\frac{3\pi}{2}, 0\right)$, and returns to a peak at the point $(2\pi, 1)$ to complete one cycle.

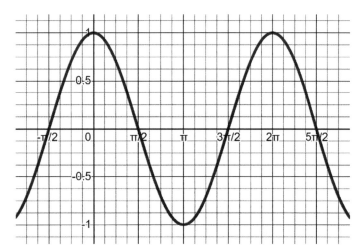

Review Video: Upper Level Trig: Cosine
Visit mometrix.com/academy and enter code: 361120

TANGENT

The **tangent** (tan) function has a period of 180° or π radians, which means that its graph makes one complete cycle every 180° or π radians. The x-axis represents the angle measure, and the y-axis represents the tangent of the angle. The graph of the tangent function is a series of smooth curves that cross the x-axis at every 180° or π radians and have an asymptote every $k \times 90°$ or $\frac{k\pi}{2}$ radians, where k is an odd integer. This can be explained by the fact that the tangent is calculated by dividing the sine by the cosine, since the cosine equals zero at those asymptote points.

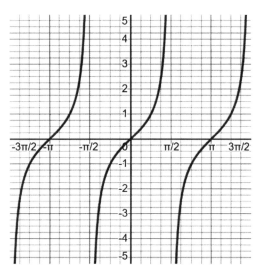

Review Video: Upper Level Trig: Tangent
Visit mometrix.com/academy and enter code: 947639

Copyright © Mometrix Media. You have been licensed one copy of this document for personal use only. Any other reproduction or redistribution is strictly prohibited. All rights reserved.
This content is provided for test preparation purposes only and does not imply an endorsement by Mometrix of any particular political, scientific, or religious point of view.

DEFINED AND RECIPROCAL FUNCTIONS

The tangent function is defined as the ratio of the sine to the cosine: $\tan x = \frac{\sin x}{\cos x}$

To take the reciprocal of a number means to place that number as the denominator of a fraction with a numerator of 1. The reciprocal functions are thus defined quite simply.

Cosecant	$\csc x$	$\frac{1}{\sin x}$
Secant	$\sec x$	$\frac{1}{\cos x}$
Cotangent	$\cot x$	$\frac{1}{\tan x}$

It is important to know these reciprocal functions, but they are not as commonly used as the three basic functions.

Review Video: Defined and Reciprocal Functions
Visit mometrix.com/academy and enter code: 996431

INVERSE FUNCTIONS

Each of the trigonometric functions accepts an angular measure, either degrees or radians, and gives a numerical value as the output. The inverse functions do the opposite; they accept a numerical value and give an angular measure as the output. The inverse of sine, or arcsine, commonly written as either $\sin^{-1} x$ or $\arcsin x$, gives the angle whose sine is x. Similarly:

The inverse of $\cos x$ is written as $\cos^{-1} x$ or $\arccos x$ and means the angle whose cosine is x.
The inverse of $\tan x$ is written as $\tan^{-1} x$ or $\arctan x$ and means the angle whose tangent is x.
The inverse of $\csc x$ is written as $\csc^{-1} x$ or $\text{arccsc } x$ and means the angle whose cosecant is x.
The inverse of $\sec x$ is written as $\sec^{-1} x$ or $\text{arcsec } x$ and means the angle whose secant is x.
The inverse of $\cot x$ is written as $\cot^{-1} x$ or $\text{arccot } x$ and means the angle whose cotangent is x.

Review Video: Inverse Functions
Visit mometrix.com/academy and enter code: 156054

IMPORTANT NOTE ABOUT SOLVING TRIGONOMETRIC EQUATIONS

When solving for an angle with a known trigonometric value, you must consider the sign and include all angles with that value. Your calculator will probably only give one value as an answer, typically in the following ranges:

- For $\sin^{-1} x$, $\left[-\frac{\pi}{2}, \frac{\pi}{2}\right]$ or $[-90°, 90°]$
- For $\cos^{-1} x$, $[0, \pi]$ or $[0°, 180°]$
- For $\tan^{-1} x$, $\left[-\frac{\pi}{2}, \frac{\pi}{2}\right]$ or $[-90°, 90°]$

It is important to determine if there is another angle in a different quadrant that also satisfies the problem. To do this, find the other quadrant(s) with the same sign for that trigonometric function and find the angle that has the same reference angle. Then check whether this angle is also a solution.

- In the first quadrant, all six trigonometric functions are positive.
- In the second quadrant, sin and csc are positive.
- In the third quadrant, tan and cot are positive.
- In the fourth quadrant, cos and sec are positive.

Copyright © Mometrix Media. You have been licensed one copy of this document for personal use only. Any other reproduction or redistribution is strictly prohibited. All rights reserved. This content is provided for test preparation purposes only and does not imply an endorsement by Mometrix of any particular political, scientific, or religious point of view.

If you remember the phrase, "ALL Students Take Classes," you will be able to remember the sign of each trigonometric function in each quadrant. ALL represents all the signs in the first quadrant. The "S" in "Students" represents the sine function and its reciprocal in the second quadrant. The "T" in "Take" represents the tangent function and its reciprocal in the third quadrant. The "C" in "Classes" represents the cosine function and its reciprocal.

DOMAIN, RANGE, AND ASYMPTOTES IN TRIGONOMETRY

The domain is the set of all possible real number values of x on the graph of a trigonometric function. Some graphs will impose limits on the values of x.

The range is the set of all possible real number values of y on the graph of a trigonometric function. Some graphs will impose limits on the values of y.

Asymptotes are lines that the graph of a trigonometric function approaches but never reaches. Asymptotes exist for values of x in the graphs of the tangent, cotangent, secant, and cosecant. The sine and cosine graphs do not have any asymptotes.

DOMAIN, RANGE, AND ASYMPTOTES OF THE SIX TRIGONOMETRIC FUNCTIONS

The domain, range, and asymptotes for each of the trigonometric functions are as follows:

- In the **sine** function, the domain is all real numbers, the range is $-1 \le y \le 1$, and there are no asymptotes.
- In the **cosine** function, the domain is all real numbers, the range is $-1 \le y \le 1$, and there are no asymptotes.
- In the **tangent** function, the domain is $x \in$ all real numbers; $x \ne \frac{\pi}{2} + k\pi$, the range is all real numbers, and the asymptotes are the lines $x = \frac{\pi}{2} + k\pi$.
- In the **cosecant** function, the domain is $x \in$ all real numbers; $x \ne k\pi$, the range is $(-\infty, -1]$ and $[1, \infty)$, and the asymptotes are the lines $x = k\pi$.
- In the **secant** function, the domain is $x \in$ all real numbers; $x \ne \frac{\pi}{2} + k\pi$, the range is $(-\infty, 1]$ and $[1, \infty)$, and the asymptotes are the lines $x = \frac{\pi}{2} + k\pi$.
- In the **cotangent** function, the domain is $x \in$ all real numbers; $x \ne k\pi$, the range is all real numbers, and the asymptotes are the lines $x = k\pi$.

In each of the above cases, k represents any integer.

TRIGONOMETRIC IDENTITIES
SUM AND DIFFERENCE

To find the sine, cosine, or tangent of the sum or difference of two angles, use one of the following formulas where α and β are two angles with known sine, cosine, or tangent values as needed:

$$\sin(\alpha \pm \beta) = \sin\alpha\cos\beta \pm \cos\alpha\sin\beta$$
$$\cos(\alpha \pm \beta) = \cos\alpha\cos\beta \mp \sin\alpha\sin\beta$$
$$\tan(\alpha \pm \beta) = \frac{\tan\alpha \pm \tan\beta}{1 \mp \tan\alpha\tan\beta}$$

HALF ANGLE

To find the sine or cosine of half of a known angle, use the following formulas where θ is an angle with a known exact cosine value:

$$\sin(\theta/2) = \pm\sqrt{(1 - \cos\theta)/2}$$
$$\cos(\theta/2) = \pm\sqrt{(1 + \cos\theta)/2}$$

Copyright © Mometrix Media. You have been licensed one copy of this document for personal use only. Any other reproduction or redistribution is strictly prohibited. All rights reserved.
This content is provided for test preparation purposes only and does not imply an endorsement by Mometrix of any particular political, scientific, or religious point of view.

To determine the sign of the answer, you must recognize which quadrant the given angle is in and apply the correct sign for the trigonometric function you are using. If you need to find an expression for the exact sine or cosine of an angle that you do not know, such as sine 22.5°, you can rewrite the given angle as a half angle, such as $\sin\left(\frac{45°}{2}\right)$, and use the formula above:

$$\sin\left(\frac{45°}{2}\right) = \pm\sqrt{(1 - \cos(45°))/2} = \pm\sqrt{\left(1 - \frac{\sqrt{2}}{2}\right)/2} = \pm\sqrt{(2 - \sqrt{2})/4} = \pm\frac{1}{2}\sqrt{(2 - \sqrt{2})}$$

To find the tangent or cotangent of half of a known angle, use the following formulas where θ is an angle with known exact sine and cosine values:

$$\tan\frac{\theta}{2} = \frac{\sin\theta}{1 + \cos\theta}$$
$$\cot\frac{\theta}{2} = \frac{\sin\theta}{1 - \cos\theta}$$

These formulas will work for finding the tangent or cotangent of half of any angle unless the cosine of θ happens to make the denominator of the identity equal to 0.

The Pythagorean theorem states that $a^2 + b^2 = c^2$ for all right triangles. The trigonometric identity that derives from this principle is stated in this way: $\sin^2\theta + \cos^2\theta = 1$

Dividing each term by either $\sin^2\theta$ or $\cos^2\theta$ yields two other identities, respectively:

$$1 + \cot^2\theta = \csc^2\theta$$
$$\tan^2\theta + 1 = \sec^2\theta$$

DOUBLE ANGLES

In each case, use one of the double angle formulas. To find the sine or cosine of twice a known angle, use one of the following formulas:

$$\sin(2\theta) = 2\sin\theta\cos\theta$$

$$\cos(2\theta) = \cos^2\theta - \sin^2\theta$$
$$= 2\cos^2\theta - 1$$
$$= 1 - 2\sin^2\theta$$

To find the tangent or cotangent of twice a known angle, use the formulas where θ is an angle with known exact sine, cosine, tangent, and cotangent values:

$$\tan(2\theta) = \frac{2\tan\theta}{1 - \tan^2\theta}$$
$$\cot(2\theta) = \frac{\cot\theta - \tan\theta}{2}$$

Copyright © Mometrix Media. You have been licensed one copy of this document for personal use only. Any other reproduction or redistribution is strictly prohibited. All rights reserved.
This content is provided for test preparation purposes only and does not imply an endorsement by Mometrix of any particular political, scientific, or religious point of view.

PRODUCTS

To find the product of the sines and cosines of two different angles, use one of the following formulas where α and β are two unique angles:

$$\sin \alpha \sin \beta = \frac{1}{2}[\cos(\alpha - \beta) - \cos(\alpha + \beta)]$$
$$\cos \alpha \cos \beta = \frac{1}{2}[\cos(\alpha + \beta) + \cos(\alpha - \beta)]$$
$$\sin \alpha \cos \beta = \frac{1}{2}[\sin(\alpha + \beta) + \sin(\alpha - \beta)]$$
$$\cos \alpha \sin \beta = \frac{1}{2}[\sin(\alpha + \beta) - \sin(\alpha - \beta)]$$

COMPLEMENTARY

The trigonometric cofunction identities use the trigonometric relationships of complementary angles (angles whose sum is 90°). These are:

$$\cos x = \sin(90° - x)$$
$$\csc x = \sec(90° - x)$$
$$\cot x = \tan(90° - x)$$

TABLE OF COMMONLY ENCOUNTERED ANGLES

$0° = 0$ radians, $30° = \frac{\pi}{6}$ radians, $45° = \frac{\pi}{4}$ radians, $60° = \frac{\pi}{3}$ radians, and $90° = \frac{\pi}{2}$ radians

$\sin 0° = 0$	$\cos 0° = 1$	$\tan 0° = 0$
$\sin 30° = \frac{1}{2}$	$\cos 30° = \frac{\sqrt{3}}{2}$	$\tan 30° = \frac{\sqrt{3}}{3}$
$\sin 45° = \frac{\sqrt{2}}{2}$	$\cos 45° = \frac{\sqrt{2}}{2}$	$\tan 45° = 1$
$\sin 60° = \frac{\sqrt{3}}{2}$	$\cos 60° = \frac{1}{2}$	$\tan 60° = \sqrt{3}$
$\sin 90° = 1$	$\cos 90° = 0$	$\tan 90° =$ undefined
$\csc 0° =$ undefined	$\sec 0° = 1$	$\cot 0° =$ undefined
$\csc 30° = 2$	$\sec 30° = \frac{2\sqrt{3}}{3}$	$\cot 30° = \sqrt{3}$
$\csc 45° = \sqrt{2}$	$\sec 45° = \sqrt{2}$	$\cot 45° = 1$
$\csc 60° = \frac{2\sqrt{3}}{3}$	$\sec 60° = 2$	$\cot 60° = \frac{\sqrt{3}}{3}$
$\csc 90° = 1$	$\sec 90° =$ undefined	$\cot 90° = 0$

The values in the upper half of this table are values you should have memorized or be able to find quickly and those in the lower half can easily be determined as the reciprocal of the corresponding function.

RECTANGULAR AND POLAR COORDINATES

Rectangular coordinates are those that lie on the square grids of the Cartesian plane. They should be quite familiar to you. The polar coordinate system is based on a circular graph, rather than the square grid of the Cartesian system. Points in the polar coordinate system are in the format (r, θ), where r is the distance from the origin (think radius of the circle) and θ is the smallest positive angle (moving counterclockwise around the circle) made with the positive horizontal axis.

Copyright © Mometrix Media. You have been licensed one copy of this document for personal use only. Any other reproduction or redistribution is strictly prohibited. All rights reserved.
This content is provided for test preparation purposes only and does not imply an endorsement by Mometrix of any particular political, scientific, or religious point of view.

To convert a point from rectangular (x, y) format to polar (r, θ) format, use the formula (x, y) to $(r, \theta) \Rightarrow r = \sqrt{x^2 + y^2}; \theta = \arctan\frac{y}{x}$ when $x \neq 0$

If x is positive, use the positive square root value for r. If x is negative, use the negative square root value for r. If $x = 0$, use the following rules:

- If $y = 0$, then $\theta = 0$
- If $y > 0$, then $\theta = \frac{\pi}{2}$
- If $y < 0$, then $\theta = \frac{3\pi}{2}$

To convert a point from polar (r, θ) format to rectangular (x, y) format, use the formula (r, θ) to $(x, y) \Rightarrow x = r \cos \theta \,; y = r \sin \theta$

DE MOIVRE'S THEOREM

De Moivre's theorem is used to find the powers of complex numbers (numbers that contain the imaginary number i) written in polar form. Given a trigonometric expression that contains i, such as $z = r \cos x + ir \sin x$, where r is a real number and x is an angle measurement in polar form, use the formula $z^n = r^n(\cos nx + i \sin nx)$, where r and n are real numbers, x is the angle measure in polar form, and i is the imaginary number $i = \sqrt{-1}$. The expression $\cos x + i \sin x$ can be written cis x, making the formula appear in the format $z^n = r^n$ cis nx.

Note that De Moivre's theorem is only for angles in polar form. If you are given an angle in degrees, you must convert to polar form before using the formula.

PRACTICE

P1. Convert the following angles from degrees to radians:

(a) 56°

(b) 12°

(c) 199°

P2. Convert the following angles from radians to degrees:

(a) 3

(b) 3π

(c) 33

P3. Simplify the following trigonometric expressions:

(a) $\dfrac{\sin x \tan x + \cos x}{\sec x}$

(b) $\dfrac{4 \cos 2x}{\sin^2 2x} + \sec^2 x$

Copyright © Mometrix Media. You have been licensed one copy of this document for personal use only. Any other reproduction or redistribution is strictly prohibited. All rights reserved.
This content is provided for test preparation purposes only and does not imply an endorsement by Mometrix of any particular political, scientific, or religious point of view.

PRACTICE SOLUTIONS

P1. Multiply each by the conversion factor $\frac{\pi}{180°}$:

(a) $56° \times \frac{\pi}{180°} \cong 0.977$

(b) $12° \times \frac{\pi}{180°} \cong 0.209$

(c) $199° \times \frac{\pi}{180°} \cong 3.473$

P2. Multiply each by the conversion factor $\frac{180°}{\pi}$:

(a) $3 \times \frac{180°}{\pi} \cong 171.9°$

(b) $3\pi \times \frac{180°}{\pi} = 540° = 180°$

(c) $33 \times \frac{180°}{\pi} \cong 1890.8° \cong 90.8°$

P3. (a) Utilize trigonometric identities and definitions to simplify. Specifically, $\tan x = \frac{\sin x}{\cos x}$, $\sec x = \frac{1}{\cos x}$, and $\sin^2 x + \cos^2 x = 1$:

$$\frac{\sin x \tan x + \cos x}{\sec x} = \left(\sin x \frac{\sin x}{\cos x} + \cos x\right)\cos x$$
$$= \frac{\sin^2 x}{\cos x}\cos x + \cos^2 x$$
$$= \sin^2 x + \cos^2 x$$
$$= 1$$

(b) Utilize trigonometric identities and definitions to simplify. Specifically, double angle formulas, $\sin^2 x = (\sin x)^2$, and $\sin^2 x + \cos^2 x = 1$:

$$\frac{4\cos 2x}{\sin^2 2x} + \sec^2 x = \frac{4(\cos^2 x - \sin^2 x)}{4\sin^2 x \cos^2 x} + \sec^2 x$$
$$= \frac{\cos^2 x - \sin^2 x}{\sin^2 x \cos^2 x} + \sec^2 x$$
$$= \frac{\cos^2 x}{\sin^2 x \cos^2 x} - \frac{\sin^2 x}{\sin^2 x \cos^2 x} + \sec^2 x$$
$$= \frac{1}{\sin^2 x} - \frac{1}{\cos^2 x} + \sec^2 x$$
$$= \csc^2 x - \sec^2 x + \sec^2 x$$
$$= \csc^2 x$$

FINANCIAL PRINCIPLES

TIME VALUE OF MONEY

When money is invested in a safe banking type institution, it can accumulate or accrue **interest**. The amount of interest earned is called the **accrued amount**. The interest amount is based on the amount of the investment, the length of time it is invested, and the interest percentage rate. If the money is invested over several time cycles then the interest is calculated differently. At the end of each time cycle, the interest is calculated on the increased investment amount which is known as **compounded interest**. The effective interest rate is the

Copyright © Mometrix Media. You have been licensed one copy of this document for personal use only. Any other reproduction or redistribution is strictly prohibited. All rights reserved.
This content is provided for test preparation purposes only and does not imply an endorsement by Mometrix of any particular political, scientific, or religious point of view.

interest rate between compounding cycles. If the effective interest rate is calculated over a year it is known as the effective annual interest rate.

CASH FLOW AND CASH FLOW DIAGRAMS

The analysis of money going in and out of an entity is **cash flow**. If the rent is due on Thursday and you are paid on Friday, you have a cash flow problem. All cash flow analysis is dependent upon the business entity of interest. A cash flow out from one business entity is a cash flow in for another entity. Paying the rent is a cash flow out for the renter but is an inflow of cash for the landlord. A **cash flow diagram** is a chart with the horizontal axis of time with money coming in as an up arrow and money going out as a down arrow. At any point in time, the sum of cash in and out can be represented by individual arrows or a single arrow with the sum. Money cash flow can be a single payment, a uniform series of equal values of money at regular time intervals, or gradient series of increasing or decreasing values of money at regular time intervals.

BENEFIT COST ANALYSIS

One of the five common economic comparisons is the **benefit cost analysis**. Of the five economic comparison techniques, the benefit cost analysis is easily the most complicated to perform and is also most subjective in nature. In simple terms, the benefit cost analysis looks at where benefits will occur for different users and total cost to everyone. Benefit cost analysis is not normally applied to commercial projects unless they are extremely large and is normally applied to government projects. The sum of the benefits divided by the sum of the costs should be greater than one for an acceptable project. When comparing multiple projects, the highest ratio will determine the best project. The exact sum of benefits and costs are sometimes difficult to accurately determine—a benefit to one group may be a cost to another group.

BREAK EVEN ANALYSIS

One of the five common economic comparisons is **break even analysis**. In the simplest terms, break even analysis looks at the shortest time or minimum number of units until the project pays for itself. This analysis is sometimes known as determining the payback period. To use break even analysis, the projects must have costs and generate revenue so this is usually limited to commercial ventures and not government infrastructure projects. If a project ends before the break even or pay back occurs, then the project will be a net loss for the company. At any time after the break even occurs, the company will expect a new profit.

RATE OF RETURN COST ANALYSIS

One of the five common economic comparisons is the **rate of return cost analysis** or simply known as **ROR**. The rate of return analysis looks for the highest interest rate of competing cash flow projection scenarios. A simpler definition is, "How much interest would I earn if I put that amount of money in a bank?" Coincidentally, that is also a helpful measure in determining whether the project should be done: "Would the money have been better off sitting in a bank instead of risked on this venture?" This minimum acceptable interest rate is known as the **minimum attractive rate of return** or **MARR** and is established by the company. Some companies use different MARR values for different projects or project lengths.

Suppose Rachel has invested $12,000 in restoring an antique car, and $7,000 in Ace Shipping Company. After four years, the antique car sells for $18,000. She sells her shares in Ace Shipping for $9,500 after a year. After calculating the return on investment for both investments and adjusting for time duration, they can be compared.

$$ROI_{car} = \frac{18,000 - 12,000}{12,000} = 0.5$$

$$ROI_{Ace} = \frac{9,500 - 7,000}{7,000} = 0.357$$

Copyright © Mometrix Media. You have been licensed one copy of this document for personal use only. Any other reproduction or redistribution is strictly prohibited. All rights reserved.
This content is provided for test preparation purposes only and does not imply an endorsement by Mometrix of any particular political, scientific, or religious point of view.

Note that to get a more accurate picture of the viability of the investments, the time duration has to be taken into account. To calculate annual ROI, divide ROI by the duration of the investment.

$$Annual\ ROI_{car} = \frac{0.5}{4} = 0.125$$

$$Annual\ ROI_{Ace} = \frac{0.357}{1} = 0.357$$

PRESENT WORTH AND ANNUAL COST ANALYSIS

Two of the five common economic comparisons are present worth and annual cost analysis. These two comparisons are very similar despite one being opposite signs or values. In simple terms, **present worth analysis** looks for the maximum present worth of competing scenarios. **Annual cost analysis** simply looks for the minimum Equivalent Uniform Analysis Cost (EUAC) and is sometimes referred to as annual return method or the capital recovery method. Both these comparisons use standard discount factors to calculate the present worth or the annual cost of the respective scenarios. Both of these analyses require the projects of interest to be mutually exclusive. Both of these types of analysis are simple to apply to commercial or government projects, although present worth is rarely used for government analysis.

NET PRESENT VALUE

Net present value (**NPV**) is based on the principle that money now is worth more than money later, known as the *time value of money*. This is because money can be used to make more money, whether that money is supporting a business, invested in the stock market, or put into a bank. NPV is the difference between the present values of cash inflows minus the present values of cash outflows. To calculate it, all cash flows must first be converted from future values to present values. This is accomplished by the following equation:

$$PV = \frac{FV}{\left(1 + \frac{i}{n}\right)^{(nt)}}$$

where

PV is the present value of the money

FV is the future value of the money

i is the decimal interest rate

n is the number of times interest is compounded per year

t is the number of years

Suppose Ethan's good friend asks to borrow $1,000 from him today, and repay him $1,150 in two years. To determine if it is a good investment, Ethan must first calculate the present value of the sum. Assuming money can be invested elsewhere at a rate of 6% annually,

$$PV = \frac{\$1,150}{\left(1 + \frac{0.06}{1}\right)^{(1 \times 2)}} = \$1,023.50$$

To calculate the net present value of the investment, take the difference between the cash outflow and cash inflow: -$1,000 + $1,023.50 = $23.50. Thus, it would be a sound investment for Ethan to lend to this friend.

Copyright © Mometrix Media. You have been licensed one copy of this document for personal use only. Any other reproduction or redistribution is strictly prohibited. All rights reserved.
This content is provided for test preparation purposes only and does not imply an endorsement by Mometrix of any particular political, scientific, or religious point of view.

LIFE CYCLE COST

While capital cost is usually very easy to compare between two different possible purchases, it is only a portion of the total costs that will occur during an asset's lifetime. **Life cycle cost analysis (LCCA)** takes into account the total cost of ownership of the asset, including acquisition costs, operating costs, maintenance costs, disposal costs, and residual value.

For example, consider the life cycle cost of a commercial kitchen mixer. Suppose the purchase price is $8,400, and it uses $30 of electricity every month. Every two years, a technician is paid $200 to service it. After 20 years, the mixer is replaced, and the residual value is $1,000. The life cycle cost of this mixer would then be

$$LCC_{mixer} = \$8,400 + \left(\$30 \times \frac{12 \text{ mo.}}{1 \text{ yr.}} \times 20 \text{ yr.}\right) + (\$200 \times 9) - \$1,000 = \$16,400$$

Note that the mixer is only serviced nine times because there would be no need to service it right before replacement.

FUNCTIONAL NOTATION

There are many discount tables that convert cash flows from one type to another equivalent type. The names for these tables are not standardized and take many characters to identify, so a short hand version has been devised known as **functional notation**. Functional notation uses three terms separated by commas between parentheses. The first term indicates the first letter of the *type* of cash flow you are starting with and the type of cash flow you wish to calculate separated by a vertical line. The four cash flows are identified by Present (P), Future (F), Annual (A), or Gradient (G). The second term of the functional notation is the *interest rate* and the third term is the number of *cycles*. If you want the discount factor for present value given a future value at five percent annual interest rate for four years, you would look for the (P|F,5%,4) discount factor.

DISCOUNT FACTORS AND EQUIVALENCE

A technique for comparing various cash flows is the use of **discount factors**. The comparison of cash flows can be done at the current time called the *present worth*, or it can be done at some time later known as the *future worth*. Cash flows can also be compared on an annual amount basis. There are tables of discount factors for one-time cash flows in or out known as single payment compound amount factor. There are also discount factor tables for cash flows that repeat and are known either as uniform series, if the amount is unchanging, or gradient series, if the amounts increase or decrease over time. When you calculate present or future worth of two or more cash flows and they are the same value, then the cash flows are **equivalent**. Typically, equivalence is not the goal of cash flow calculations; normally you are trying to minimize negative cash flows or maximizing positive cash flows.

CONTINUOUS COMPOUNDING

For almost all normal investment or loan situations, interest is calculated on a **discrete** time basis such as monthly, quarterly, or yearly. The discrete compound interest discount factors can be found in tables. There are some situations where the interest is compounded every day, such as credit cards where purchases are made while there is an outstanding balance. Compounding interest every day is more often known as **continuous compound interest**. The continuous interest discount factors are not normally listed in tables and can be calculated using exponential equations using the nominal interest rate, r, and the time period in years, n.

DISCONTINUOUS AND RANDOM COMPOUNDING

Normally, interest on an investment or a loan is compounded on some recurring basis; thus, it is called **compound interest**. This recurring basis may or may not be an annual time period. If it is not annual, then it is simply known as the **nominal interest rate** or for money invested in banks, it is sometimes referred to as the yield, identified by r. Between the periods of compounding, interest may be calculated on the investment or

Copyright © Mometrix Media. You have been licensed one copy of this document for personal use only. Any other reproduction or redistribution is strictly prohibited. All rights reserved. This content is provided for test preparation purposes only and does not imply an endorsement by Mometrix of any particular political, scientific, or religious point of view.

loan amount. The **effective interest rate**, identified as i, is the nominal interest rate divided by the number of time periods between the compound time periods.

BOOK VALUE

The book value, **BV**, is a calculated amount that starts with the purchase price and subtracts the accumulated depreciation, or the sum of all the depreciations, regardless of how the depreciation is calculated. The **book value** is normally calculated at the end of each year, although some companies apply depreciation on a monthly basis. The original book value is the same as the purchase price until depreciation is applied, whether that is a month or at the end of the year, whichever is used by the company. The book value, or the ratio of the book value to the initial purchase price, is used by many depreciation schemes.

STRAIGHT LINE AND ACCELERATED DEPRECIATION

For most people, depreciation is the decrease in value in a piece of equipment due to use or misuse over time. For the Internal Revenue Service, depreciation is the calculated annual expense that takes a single large purchase and distributes it over several years. The current tax laws, type of purchase, and amount determine how large a purchase has to be to be depreciated and how it should be calculated. First, the **depreciation basis** must be calculated which is the purchase price minus the salvage value. The simplest depreciation calculation is called the **straight-line depreciation** method which uses the depreciation basis divided by the number of years between the purchase and the salvage time. The Accelerated Cost Recovery System (ACRS) or the Modified Accelerated Cost Recovery System (MACRS) use a series of factors to determine the amount of depreciation each year. Depreciation is in engineering economics because comparing similar purchases may have different depreciation basis or depreciation schedules.

CAPITALIZED COST

Capitalized cost is the present worth of an infinitely long cash flow scenario that requires no other expenses to continue the scenario by way of compound interest. The idea is if someone had the entire **capitalized cost** sitting in the bank earning interest, the project would never run out of money. The discount factors for infinite time periods are not listed, but the present value of an infinite series is the equivalent uniform annual cost (EUAC) divided by the interest rate. Since capitalized cost is expenses, a negative number means that incoming future money exceeds the cost of the cash flow scenario which is typical in commercial ventures but rarely occurs with large infrastructure projects.

EUAC

Besides comparing the value or cost of various cash flows at present or future worth, there is another common technique known as the **Equivalent Uniform Annual Cost** or **EUAC**. The EUAC is useful for comparing large infrastructure projects that may have very different lifetimes. Where present or future worth provide positive values for incoming monies and negative values for outgoing monies, the EUAC is a cost, so positive values are for outgoing monies and negative values for incoming monies. Thus, the Equivalent Uniform Annual Cost, as it sounds, is the sum of all the negative cash flows minus the sum of all the positive cash flows divided by the number of years the cash flows occur.

ALTERNATIVE ECONOMIC COMPARISONS

Engineering projects rarely have no design tradeoffs. When the outcomes of these design tradeoffs produce similar results, then the preferred approach must be selected using some form of economic analysis. There are five normal **economic comparison tools** commonly used with pros and cons for each tool. The comparisons are *Present Worth Analysis* which simply looks for the maximum present worth of competing scenarios, *Annual Cost Analysis* which simply looks for the minimum EUAC, *Rate of Return Analysis* which looks for the highest interest rate, *Benefit-Cost Analysis* which looks at where benefits for different users and cost to all, and *Break-Even Analysis* which looks at the shortest time until the project pays for itself.

Copyright © Mometrix Media. You have been licensed one copy of this document for personal use only. Any other reproduction or redistribution is strictly prohibited. All rights reserved.
This content is provided for test preparation purposes only and does not imply an endorsement by Mometrix of any particular political, scientific, or religious point of view.

BOND, FACE VALUE, DATE OF MATURITY, BOND VALUE, AND YIELD

A bond is a financial agreement usually between an investor and a government entity that promises the government entity will repay the principal plus interest at a certain set time, usually long term in nature. **Face value** is a bond's stated principal amount. Usually, bonds are purchased for an amount lower than the face value. Some bonds continue to accrue interest beyond the face value. **Date of maturity** is the agreed upon date when a bond attains the face value. For some bonds, the interest may continue to earn interest after this date.

Bond value is, at any time, the redeemable value of the bond. **Yield** is the nominal interest rate for a bond including the original purchase price, any interest earned, as well as the final value when the bond is redeemed.

ENGINEERING CALCULATIONS

STATICS

Newton's second law says that force is equal to mass times acceleration. When dealing with **statics**, the subset of mechanics that deals with rigid bodies in static equilibrium, the acceleration in Newton's equation is zero. This means that the sum of all forces applied to non-moving objects is also equal to zero.

> **Review Video: Mechanical Calculations**
> Visit mometrix.com/academy and enter code: 606847

VECTORS

Vectors are quantities with both direction and magnitude. In two-dimensional space, **vectors** can have *horizontal* (x-direction) and *vertical* (y-direction) components. Vector x- and y-components are calculated by multiplying the magnitude of the factor by its angle from horizontal:

$$A_x = A\cos(\theta)$$

$$A_y = A\sin(\theta)$$

where

A_x is the horizontal component

A_y is the vertical component

θ is the angle between the positive direction on the horizontal axis and the vector, measured counter clockwise

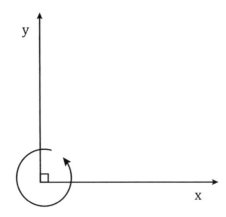

Copyright © Mometrix Media. You have been licensed one copy of this document for personal use only. Any other reproduction or redistribution is strictly prohibited. All rights reserved.
This content is provided for test preparation purposes only and does not imply an endorsement by Mometrix of any particular political, scientific, or religious point of view.

To add vectors together, first sum the x-components and y-components:

$$R_x = A_x + B_x$$

$$R_y = A_y + B_y$$

Find the magnitude of the resultant vector by taking the square root of the sum of the components squared:

$$R = \sqrt{R_x{}^2 + R_y{}^2}$$

Finally, determine the angle of the resultant vector by taking the inverse tangent of R_y divided by R_x:

$$\theta = \tan^{-1}\frac{R_y}{R_x}$$

MOMENTS

Although a moment, or **torque**, is the product of a particular force and distance, a **moment** can be either thought of as a rotational force, or more accurately, as a measure of how much a force will contribute to potential rotation. Moments may sound unnatural when described this way, but they are quite intuitive as a twisting force. The moment about a point is defined as the magnitude of the acting force multiplied by the distance between it and the line of action, given by the equation:

$$M = F \times d$$

where M is the moment, F is the force, and d is the distance perpendicular to the force to the point. In the diagram below, a wrench is used to tighten a lug nut.

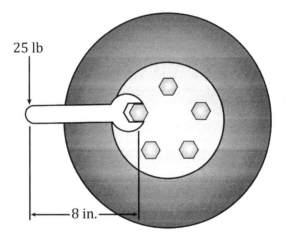

If 25 pounds of force are applied to the end of the 8-inch wrench, the moment applied to the nut can be calculated as

$$M_n = 25 \text{ lb} \times \left(8 \text{ in} \times \frac{1 \text{ ft}}{12 \text{ in}}\right) = 16.67 \text{ lb} \cdot \text{ft}$$

Note that, although moments can be set as positive in either the clockwise or counterclockwise directions, this product will use the moments acting counterclockwise in the x-y plane as positive.

Copyright © Mometrix Media. You have been licensed one copy of this document for personal use only. Any other reproduction or redistribution is strictly prohibited. All rights reserved.
This content is provided for test preparation purposes only and does not imply an endorsement by Mometrix of any particular political, scientific, or religious point of view.

VENTILATION

Ventilation is defined as the mechanical system or equipment used to circulate air or to replace stale air with fresh air. The key quantity in ventilation is the **volume flow rate**. It uses the units of cubic feet per minute, or cfm in the following equation

$$Q = VA$$

where

Q is the quantity of moving air

V is the velocity at which it is moving

A is the cross-sectional area the air is moving through

For example, if a fan pushes air through a 1-foot-diameter circular ventilation duct at a rate of 1000 feet per minute, it can be calculated that the fan is moving air at a rate of

$$\frac{1000 \text{ ft.}}{1 \text{ min.}} \times \left(\frac{\pi \times 1 \text{ ft.}^2}{4} \right) = 785.4 \text{ cfm}$$

There are three types of pressure in ventilation ducts: total, static, and velocity. **Total pressure** is the sum of static and velocity pressure in a duct:

$$P_T = P_S + P_V$$

where P_T is total pressure, P_S is static pressure, and P_V is velocity pressure. **Static pressure** is a resistance to flow, equal in all directions and independent of air velocity. **Velocity pressure** is a function of both air velocity and density. It cannot be measured directly, but can be calculated by measuring total pressure and subtracting static pressure. To perform the measurement, a pitot tube is inserted into the duct with the tip facing the direction of airflow. The total pressure port is connected to the positive side of a manometer, and the static pressure port is connected to the negative side. The manometer reading now displays velocity pressure, usually in inches of water. To calculate air velocity from velocity pressure, the following equation is used, assuming clean, dry air at atmospheric pressure:

$$V = 4005\sqrt{P_V}$$

FIRE SUPPRESSION

Volume flow rate can also describe the volume of **fluid** that passes through a certain area per unit time. When referring to liquids, it is usually given in cubic feet per minute or gallons per minute. It also uses the equation

$$Q = VA$$

where Q is volume flow rate, V is the velocity of the fluid, and A is the cross-sectional area of the pipe it is flowing through. For example, if a fire sprinkler requires 20 gallons per minute (gpm) of water to operate, water must flow through a 1-inch diameter pipe at a speed of:

$$V = \frac{\frac{20 \text{ } gallons}{1 \text{ } minute} \times \frac{1 \text{ } ft^3}{7.38 \text{ } gallons}}{\pi \times \left(0.5 \text{ } inches \times \frac{1 \text{ } foot}{12 \text{ } inches} \right)^2} = 490 \text{ feet per minute or } 8.17 \text{ ft/s}$$

Copyright © Mometrix Media. You have been licensed one copy of this document for personal use only. Any other reproduction or redistribution is strictly prohibited. All rights reserved.
This content is provided for test preparation purposes only and does not imply an endorsement by Mometrix of any particular political, scientific, or religious point of view.

Mass flow rate, similarly, is the mass of fluid that passes through a certain area per unit time. It is calculated by multiplying the density of the fluid by its volume flow rate:

$$m = \rho Q = \rho V A$$

where ρ (rho) is fluid density in pounds per cubic foot. Just as electric current is constant in series circuits, mass flow rate is constant in individual pipes. Because fluid density is constant, velocity is inversely proportional to area.

$$m = \rho V_1 A_1 = \rho V_2 A_2$$

Suppose a 1-foot-diameter pipe has water flowing through it at a rate of 8 feet per second. If the diameter of the pipe decreases by 20%, the water is flowing at a rate of:

$$V_2 = \frac{V_1 A_1}{A_2} = \frac{8 \times (\pi \times 1^2)}{(\pi \times 0.8^2)} = 12.5 \text{ ft/s}$$

NFPA 13 classifies occupancies as light, ordinary, and extra hazard depending on their levels and intensity of combustibles. In general, **light hazard occupancies** have low quantity and/or combustibility of contents, and fires with relatively low rates of heat release are expected. Examples include offices, restaurants, and theaters. **Ordinary hazard occupancies** have low to high amounts of combustibles, with moderate rates of heat release. Examples include machine shops, mills, and parking garages. **Extra hazard occupancies** have either very high combustibility of contents or a large quantity of flammable or combustible liquids. Examples include print shops, plastic processing plants, and metal works.

NOISE

Noise is measured in decibels (dB), but OSHA uses a slightly different scale (dBA) that more closely matches the human ear's perception of sound. The most important thing to know about the decibel scale is that it is *logarithmic*, not linear. This means that an addition of ten decibels indicates that sound intensity (SI) has been multiplied by a factor of ten. Sound intensity level (SIL) is calculated using the equation

$$IL(dB) = 10 \times \log\left(\frac{I}{I_0}\right)$$

where

IL is sound intensity level (dBA)

I is sound intensity (W)

I_0 is the reference sound intensity, 10^{-12} (W)

Suppose there is a grinding machine that produces a sound intensity level of 60 dBA. The sound intensity can be calculated by

$$I = I_0 \times 10^{\left(\frac{IL}{10}\right)} = 10^{-12} \times 10^{\left(\frac{60}{10}\right)} = 10^{-6} \text{ W}$$

If a second identical machine is turned on, the sound intensity will double, 2×10^{-6}. Plugging this new value into the sound intensity level equation yields

$$IL = 10 \times \log\left(\frac{2 \times 10^{-6}}{10^{-12}}\right) = 63.01 \text{ dBA}$$

Copyright © Mometrix Media. You have been licensed one copy of this document for personal use only. Any other reproduction or redistribution is strictly prohibited. All rights reserved.
This content is provided for test preparation purposes only and does not imply an endorsement by Mometrix of any particular political, scientific, or religious point of view.

CLIMATE CONDITIONS

According to NOAA, the **Wet Bulb Globe Temperature (WBGT)** is a measure of the heat stress in direct sunlight, which takes into account temperature, humidity, wind speed, sun angle, and cloud cover (solar radiation). It is measured with a special device that combines several climate measurements into a single temperature reading. This reading is used to calculate the ratio of work to rest that workers should use to avoid heat-induced illnesses. WBGT temperature is calculated according to the following equation:

$$WBGT = 0.7T_w + 0.2T_g + 0.1T_d$$

where

T_w is natural wet-bulb temperature

T_g is globe thermometer temperature

T_d is actual air temperature, or dry-bulb temperature.

CABLES

An ideal cable has no mass, and tension is constant throughout the length. To determine the tension in **cables**, apply the equilibrium equations. For example, in the diagram below, two cables support a weight of 2,000 pounds.

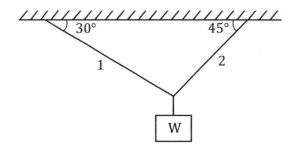

To calculate the **tension** in each cable, write equilibrium equations for the system. The weight is not accelerating in the x direction, so the sum of the x-components of the cable tensions must be zero.

$$\Sigma F_x = 0 = T_{1_x} + T_{2_x}$$

Once again, there is zero acceleration, so the sum of the weight and the y-components of the cable tensions must be zero.

$$\Sigma F_y - 0 = \text{-}2{,}000 + T_{1_y} + T_{2_y}$$

The x- and y-components of the tension in both cables can be solved with trigonometry:

$$T_{1_y} = T_1 \times \sin(30°) \qquad T_{1_x} = T_1 \times \cos(30°)$$

$$T_{2_y} = T_2 \times \sin(45°) \qquad T_{2_x} = T_2 \times \cos(45°)$$

Substituting these equations in for the original equilibrium equations results in

$$T_1 \times \cos(30°) + T_2 \times \cos(45°) = 0$$

$$\text{-}2{,}000 + T_1 \times \sin(30°) + T_2 \times \sin(45°) = 0$$

Copyright © Mometrix Media. You have been licensed one copy of this document for personal use only. Any other reproduction or redistribution is strictly prohibited. All rights reserved.
This content is provided for test preparation purposes only and does not imply an endorsement by Mometrix of any particular political, scientific, or religious point of view.

Now T_1 and T_2 can be calculated by solving for T_1 in the first equation and substituting it in the second equation:

$$T_1 = \frac{T_2 \times \cos(45°)}{\cos(30°)}$$

$$0 = -2{,}000 + \frac{T_2 \times \cos(45°)}{\cos(30°)} \times \sin(30°) + T_2 \times \sin(45°)$$

Therefore, T_2 equals 1,793 pounds and T_1 equals 1,464 pounds.

PULLEYS

A pulley is a wheel with a grooved rim around which a rope passes. It acts to change the direction of a force applied to the rope, and is chiefly used for lifting heavy weights. An ideal **pulley** has no mass or friction. In a simple configuration with two equal masses suspended from a single pulley, the force on both rope segments is equal to F, therefore the force on the cable holding the pulley up must be $2 \times F$.

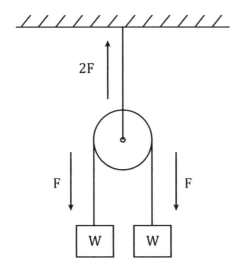

More complex pulley systems can also be analyzed by applying the equations of static equilibrium.

DISTRIBUTED LOADS

Unlike a point load, a distributed load acts upon a length or area of an object. To calculate the effect of a **distributed load**, it must first be reduced to a resultant load that acts on one point of the length or surface. The magnitude of the resultant force is equal to the area under the curve of the distributed load. The location of the force is at the centroid, or weighted center, of the distributed load.

Copyright © Mometrix Media. You have been licensed one copy of this document for personal use only. Any other reproduction or redistribution is strictly prohibited. All rights reserved.
This content is provided for test preparation purposes only and does not imply an endorsement by Mometrix of any particular political, scientific, or religious point of view.

For example, the beam in the diagram below has a triangle-shaped distributed load on it.

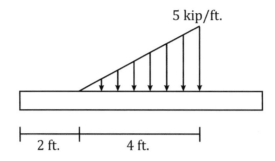

The magnitude of the resultant force can be calculated as such:

$$Area_{triangle} = \frac{1}{2}bh = \frac{1}{2} \times 4 \text{ ft} \times \frac{5 \text{ kips}}{1 \text{ ft}} = 10 \text{ kips}$$

The center of mass of this triangle can be found by plugging the equation of the load into the following equation:

$$\bar{x} = \frac{\int_0^L x \times w(x)\, dx}{\int_0^L w(x)\, dx} = \frac{\int_0^4 x \times \frac{5}{4}x\, dx}{\int_0^4 \frac{5}{4}x\, dx} = 2.66 \text{ ft}$$

Because the load starts two feet down the beam, the actual location of the resultant is at 2+2.66 ft = 4.66 ft.

FREE-BODY DIAGRAMS

Free-body diagrams are essential to understanding the statics of rigid bodies. A correctly drawn diagram allows one to identify and calculate all of the unknown *forces* and *moments* acting on such a body. To begin drawing a **free-body diagram**, separate the member of interest from the rest of the system at the joints or points of contact with other members. Draw a sketch of the member, and include all applied forces and moments, as well as support reactions or joint forces. In the figure below, a block rests on a ramp. To the right, a free-body diagram is drawn on the block, showing the three forces acting on it.

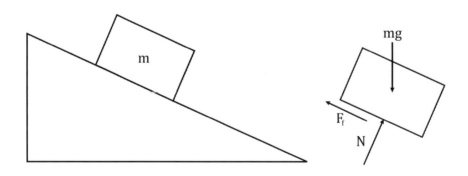

Copyright © Mometrix Media. You have been licensed one copy of this document for personal use only. Any other reproduction or redistribution is strictly prohibited. All rights reserved.
This content is provided for test preparation purposes only and does not imply an endorsement by Mometrix of any particular political, scientific, or religious point of view.

Consider the following crane structure.

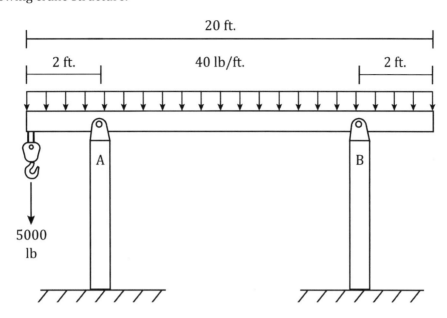

Suppose the crane can lift up to 5,000 pounds, and the top beam weighs 40 pounds per foot. The maximum load on any column can be calculated by drawing free-body diagrams, and applying equilibrium equations. The first step is converting the distributed load of the beam into a point load.

$$A_{rectangle} = l \times w = 20 \text{ ft} \times 40 \text{ lb/ft} = 800 \text{ lb}$$

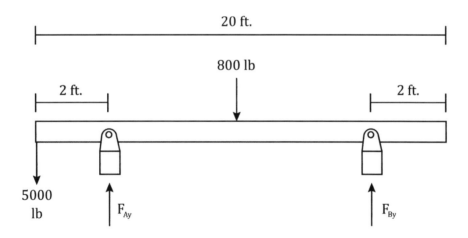

The **center of mass** of the new point load is at the center of beam, because it is equally distributed. Because the structure is in equilibrium, the sum of moments around point A is zero. This allows the calculation of the vertical force on column B:

$$\Sigma M_A = 0 = (2 \text{ ft} \times 5{,}000 \text{ lb}) - (8 \text{ ft} \times 800 \text{ lb}) + (16 \text{ ft} \times F_{B_y})$$

$$F_{B_y} = \text{-}225 \text{ lb}$$

Copyright © Mometrix Media. You have been licensed one copy of this document for personal use only. Any other reproduction or redistribution is strictly prohibited. All rights reserved.
This content is provided for test preparation purposes only and does not imply an endorsement by Mometrix of any particular political, scientific, or religious point of view.

Then F_{By} can be substituted into the sum of y-direction forces, allowing the calculation of F_{Ay}.

$$\Sigma F_y = 0 = \text{-}5{,}000 + F_{A_y} - 800 - 225$$

$$F_{A_y} = 6{,}025 \text{ lb}$$

Thus, column A will bear the greater load of the two columns, a maximum of 6,025 pounds.

RIGGING

The most common types of **slings** used in rigging are wire rope, chain, synthetic web, round, and metal mesh slings. The most common types of **hitches** are vertical, choker, basket, and 3- or 4-legged hitches. All slings come from the manufacturer stamped or labeled with a **working load limit (WLL)**. This is not the breaking threshold of the equipment, but the maximum load the manufacturer has designed it to carry on a regular basis. When slings or sling legs of any kind are used at an angle other than vertical, their WLL decreases accordingly. This reduction is called the **sling angle factor**. For basket and multi-legged slings, the sling angle factor is calculated by taking the sine of the angle between the load and the sling:

$$Sling\ angle\ factor\ =\ \sin(angle\ between\ load\ and\ sling\ leg)$$

To calculate the total WLL for sling configurations, multiply the sling angle factor by the number of legs in the sling and by the vertical WLL of one leg:

$$Adjusted\ WLL\ =\ Vertical\ WLL\ \times\ number\ of\ legs\ \times\ sling\ angle\ factor$$

For example, consider a 4-legged wire rope sling configured with 45-degree angles between the load and each leg.

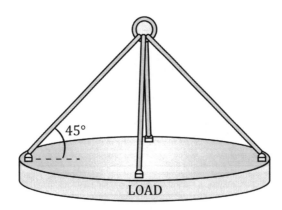

It is important to note that for chain slings, a 4-legged sling's adjusted WLL uses 3 legs in the equation. This is because of the difficulty in rigging a chain sling to distribute the load equally among four legs. Riggers often apply the same reduction to 4-legged slings of any material for increased safety factor.

If each leg of the sling has a vertical WLL of 5,000 lb, the reduced WLL of this sling would be calculated as

$$Adjusted\ WLL\ =\ 5{,}000\ \text{lb} \times 3\ \text{legs} \times \sin(45°) = 10{,}606\ \text{lb}$$

Statistics for Interpreting Data

MEASURES OF CENTRAL TENDENCY

A **measure of central tendency** is a statistical value that gives a reasonable estimate for the center of a group of data. There are several different ways of describing the measure of central tendency. Each one has a unique

Copyright © Mometrix Media. You have been licensed one copy of this document for personal use only. Any other reproduction or redistribution is strictly prohibited. All rights reserved.
This content is provided for test preparation purposes only and does not imply an endorsement by Mometrix of any particular political, scientific, or religious point of view.

way it is calculated, and each one gives a slightly different perspective on the data set. Whenever you give a measure of central tendency, always make sure the units are the same. If the data has different units, such as hours, minutes, and seconds, convert all the data to the same unit, and use the same unit in the measure of central tendency. If no units are given in the data, do not give units for the measure of central tendency.

MEAN

The **statistical mean** of a group of data is the same as the arithmetic average of that group. To find the mean of a set of data, first convert each value to the same units, if necessary. Then find the sum of all the values, and count the total number of data values, making sure you take into consideration each individual value. If a value appears more than once, count it more than once. Divide the sum of the values by the total number of values and apply the units, if any. Note that the mean does not have to be one of the data values in the set, and may not divide evenly.

$$\text{mean} = \frac{\text{sum of the data values}}{\text{quantity of data values}}$$

For instance, the mean of the data set $\{88, 72, 61, 90, 97, 68, 88, 79, 86, 93, 97, 71, 80, 84, 89\}$ would be the sum of the fifteen numbers divided by 15:

$$\frac{88 + 72 + 61 + 90 + 97 + 68 + 88 + 79 + 86 + 93 + 97 + 71 + 80 + 84 + 89}{15} = \frac{1242}{15}$$
$$= 82.8$$

While the mean is relatively easy to calculate and averages are understood by most people, the mean can be very misleading if it is used as the sole measure of central tendency. If the data set has outliers (data values that are unusually high or unusually low compared to the rest of the data values), the mean can be very distorted, especially if the data set has a small number of values. If unusually high values are countered with unusually low values, the mean is not affected as much. For example, if five of twenty students in a class get a 100 on a test, but the other 15 students have an average of 60 on the same test, the class average would appear as 70. Whenever the mean is skewed by outliers, it is always a good idea to include the median as an alternate measure of central tendency.

A **weighted mean**, or weighted average, is a mean that uses "weighted" values. The formula is weighted mean $= \frac{w_1 x_1 + w_2 x_2 + w_3 x_3 \dots + w_n x_n}{w_1 + w_2 + w_3 + \dots + w_n}$. Weighted values, such as $w_1, w_2, w_3, \dots w_n$ are assigned to each member of the set $x_1, x_2, x_3, \dots x_n$. When calculating the weighted mean, make sure a weight value for each member of the set is used.

MEDIAN

The **statistical median** is the value in the middle of the set of data. To find the median, list all data values in order from smallest to largest or from largest to smallest. Any value that is repeated in the set must be listed the number of times it appears. If there are an odd number of data values, the median is the value in the middle of the list. If there is an even number of data values, the median is the arithmetic mean of the two middle values.

For example, the median of the data set $\{88, 72, 61, 90, 97, 68, 88, 79, 86, 93, 97, 71, 80, 84, 88\}$ is 86 since the ordered set is $\{61, 68, 71, 72, 79, 80, 84, \mathbf{86}, 88, 88, 88, 90, 93, 97, 97\}$.

The big disadvantage of using the median as a measure of central tendency is that is relies solely on a value's relative size as compared to the other values in the set. When the individual values in a set of data are evenly dispersed, the median can be an accurate tool. However, if there is a group of rather large values or a group of rather small values that are not offset by a different group of values, the information that can be inferred from the median may not be accurate because the distribution of values is skewed.

Copyright © Mometrix Media. You have been licensed one copy of this document for personal use only. Any other reproduction or redistribution is strictly prohibited. All rights reserved.
This content is provided for test preparation purposes only and does not imply an endorsement by Mometrix of any particular political, scientific, or religious point of view.

MODE

The **statistical mode** is the data value that occurs the greatest number of times in the data set. It is possible to have exactly one mode, more than one mode, or no mode. To find the mode of a set of data, arrange the data like you do to find the median (all values in order, listing all multiples of data values). Count the number of times each value appears in the data set. If all values appear an equal number of times, there is no mode. If one value appears more than any other value, that value is the mode. If two or more values appear the same number of times, but there are other values that appear fewer times and no values that appear more times, all of those values are the modes.

For example, the mode of the data set {**88**, 72, 61, 90, 97, 68, **88**, 79, 86, 93, 97, 71, 80, 84, **88**} is 88.

The main disadvantage of the mode is that the values of the other data in the set have no bearing on the mode. The mode may be the largest value, the smallest value, or a value anywhere in between in the set. The mode only tells which value or values, if any, occurred the greatest number of times. It does not give any suggestions about the remaining values in the set.

> **Review Video: Mean, Median, and Mode**
> Visit mometrix.com/academy and enter code: 286207

MEASURES OF DISPERSION

A **measure of dispersion** is a single value that helps to "interpret" the measure of central tendency by providing more information about how the data values in the set are distributed about the measure of central tendency. The measure of dispersion helps to eliminate or reduce the disadvantages of using the mean, median, or mode as a single measure of central tendency, and give a more accurate picture of the dataset as a whole. To have a measure of dispersion, you must know or calculate the range, standard deviation, or variance of the data set.

RANGE

The **range** of a set of data is the difference between the greatest and lowest values of the data in the set. To calculate the range, you must first make sure the units for all data values are the same, and then identify the greatest and lowest values. If there are multiple data values that are equal for the highest or lowest, just use one of the values in the formula. Write the answer with the same units as the data values you used to do the calculations.

> **Review Video: Statistical Range**
> Visit mometrix.com/academy and enter code: 778541

STANDARD DEVIATION

Standard deviation is a measure of dispersion that compares all the data values in the set to the mean of the set to give a more accurate picture. To find the standard deviation of a sample, use the formula

$$s = \sqrt{\frac{\sum_{i=1}^{n}(x_i - \bar{x})^2}{n-1}}$$

Note that s is the standard deviation of a sample, x represents the individual values in the data set, $\bar{x}$ is the mean of the data values in the set, and n is the number of data values in the set. The higher the value of the standard deviation is, the greater the variance of the data values from the mean. The units associated with the standard deviation are the same as the units of the data values.

> **Review Video: Standard Deviation**
> Visit mometrix.com/academy and enter code: 419469

Copyright © Mometrix Media. You have been licensed one copy of this document for personal use only. Any other reproduction or redistribution is strictly prohibited. All rights reserved.
This content is provided for test preparation purposes only and does not imply an endorsement by Mometrix of any particular political, scientific, or religious point of view.

VARIANCE

The **variance of a sample** is the square of the sample standard deviation (denoted s^2). While the mean of a set of data gives the average of the set and gives information about where a specific data value lies in relation to the average, the variance of the sample gives information about the degree to which the data values are spread out and tell you how close an individual value is to the average compared to the other values. The units associated with variance are the same as the units of the data values squared.

OUTLIERS

An outlier is an extremely high or extremely low value in the data set. It may be the result of measurement error, in which case, the outlier is not a valid member of the data set. However, it may also be a valid member of the distribution. Unless a measurement error is identified, the experimenter cannot know for certain if an outlier is or is not a member of the distribution. There are arbitrary methods that can be employed to designate an extreme value as an outlier. One method designates an outlier (or possible outlier) to be any value less than $Q_1 - 1.5(IQR)$ or any value greater than $Q_3 + 1.5(IQR)$.

CONFIDENCE INTERVAL

A confidence interval consists of three components: a statistic, a margin of error, and a confidence level.

The format is $sample\ statistic \pm margin\ of\ error\ with\ confidence\ level\ of\ XX\%$. The margin of error is the square root of the estimate of the variance, and it is calculated from sample data.

When the distribution of the variable is known, the confidence level may be calculated by the area under the probability distribution function (pdf) and between the upper and lower limits of the confidence interval of the variable. This area is listed in the table for the distribution function, for example the standard normal table.

There is no single way of constructing the confidence interval of an unobservable population parameter, θ. It depends on the statistical variable whose interval is to be estimated and the distribution of that statistical variable (if any exist). The first rule of constructing an interval is that the upper and lower end-points, U and L, are both functions of the statistical variable X. In other words, the confidence interval will be $(L(X), U(X))$. The probability Pr that the confidence interval $(L(X), U(X))$ includes the unobservable population parameter θ at the $(1 - \alpha)(100\%)$ confidence level is:

$$Pr\big(L(X) < \ \theta < U(X)\big) = (1 - \alpha).$$

MEANING OF A CONFIDENCE LEVEL

A confidence level of 95% means that if the same sampling method were repeated a total of 100 times and the confidence interval was calculated each time, the true population parameter would fall inside 95 of the calculated confidence intervals.

Copyright © Mometrix Media. You have been licensed one copy of this document for personal use only. Any other reproduction or redistribution is strictly prohibited. All rights reserved.
This content is provided for test preparation purposes only and does not imply an endorsement by Mometrix of any particular political, scientific, or religious point of view.

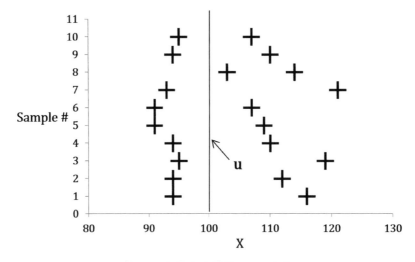

Example: A normally distributed variable X is sampled 10 times. The standard deviation and 95% confidence interval are calculated. This process is repeated 10 times. For a normal distribution, 95% of the values are between $\mu - 1.96\sigma$ and $\mu + 1.96\sigma$. The results for the 10 estimates of the 95% confidence interval are,

#	$\bar{x}_{10} - 1.96s_n$	$\bar{x}_{10} + 1.96s_n$
1	94	116
2	94	112
3	95	119
4	94	110
5	91	109
6	91	107
7	95	121
8	102	114
9	94	110
10	95	107

It turns out that $\mu = 100$, therefore, the true population mean does not fall in the confidence interval for sample #8, but it does fall within 9 of the 10 confidence intervals which is reasonably close to the 95% confidence level.

PROBABILITY

Probability is the likelihood of a certain outcome occurring for a given event. An **event** is any situation that produces a result. It could be something as simple as flipping a coin or as complex as launching a rocket. Determining the probability of an outcome for an event can be equally simple or complex. As such, there are specific terms used in the study of probability that need to be understood:

- **Compound event**—an event that involves two or more independent events (rolling a pair of dice and taking the sum)
- **Desired outcome** (or success)—an outcome that meets a particular set of criteria (a roll of 1 or 2 if we are looking for numbers less than 3)
- **Independent events**—two or more events whose outcomes do not affect one another (two coins tossed at the same time)
- **Dependent events**—two or more events whose outcomes affect one another (two cards drawn consecutively from the same deck)
- **Certain outcome**—probability of outcome is 100% or 1
- **Impossible outcome**—probability of outcome is 0% or 0

Copyright © Mometrix Media. You have been licensed one copy of this document for personal use only. Any other reproduction or redistribution is strictly prohibited. All rights reserved.
This content is provided for test preparation purposes only and does not imply an endorsement by Mometrix of any particular political, scientific, or religious point of view.

- **Mutually exclusive outcomes**—two or more outcomes whose criteria cannot all be satisfied in a single event (a coin coming up heads and tails on the same toss)
- **Random variable**—refers to all possible outcomes of a single event which may be discrete or continuous.

Review Video: Intro to Probability
Visit mometrix.com/academy and enter code: 212374

THEORETICAL PROBABILITY

Theoretical probability can usually be determined without actually performing the event. The likelihood of an outcome occurring, or the probability of an outcome occurring, is given by the formula:

$$P(A) = \frac{\text{Number of acceptable outcomes}}{\text{Number of possible outcomes}}$$

Note that $P(A)$ is the probability of an outcome A occurring, and each outcome is just as likely to occur as any other outcome. If each outcome has the same probability of occurring as every other possible outcome, the outcomes are said to be equally likely to occur. The total number of acceptable outcomes must be less than or equal to the total number of possible outcomes. If the two are equal, then the outcome is certain to occur and the probability is 1. If the number of acceptable outcomes is zero, then the outcome is impossible and the probability is 0. For example, if there are 20 marbles in a bag and 5 are red, then the theoretical probability of randomly selecting a red marble is 5 out of 20, ($\frac{5}{20} = \frac{1}{4}$, 0.25, or 25%).

COMPLEMENT OF AN EVENT

Sometimes it may be easier to calculate the possibility of something not happening, or the **complement of an event**. Represented by the symbol $\bar{A}$, the complement of A is the probability that event A does not happen. When you know the probability of event A occurring, you can use the formula $P(\bar{A}) = 1 - P(A)$, where $P(\bar{A})$ is the probability of event A not occurring, and $P(A)$ is the probability of event A occurring.

ADDITION RULE

The **addition rule** for probability is used for finding the probability of a compound event. Use the formula $P(A \text{ or } B) = P(A) + P(B) - P(A \text{ and } B)$, where $P(A \text{ and } B)$ is the probability of both events occurring to find the probability of a compound event. The probability of both events occurring at the same time must be subtracted to eliminate any overlap in the first two probabilities.

MULTIPLICATION RULE

The **multiplication rule** can be used to find the probability of two independent events occurring using the formula $P(A \text{ and } B) = P(A) \times P(B)$, where $P(A \text{ and } B)$ is the probability of two independent events occurring, $P(A)$ is the probability of the first event occurring, and $P(B)$ is the probability of the second event occurring.

The multiplication rule can also be used to find the probability of two dependent events occurring using the formula $P(A \text{ and } B) = P(A) \times P(B|A)$, where $P(A \text{ and } B)$ is the probability of two dependent events occurring and $P(B|A)$ is the probability of the second event occurring after the first event has already occurred. Before using the multiplication rule, you MUST first determine whether the two events are *dependent* or *independent*.

Use a **combination** of the multiplication rule and the rule of complements to find the probability that at least one outcome of the element will occur. This is given by the general formula $P(\text{at least one event occurring}) = 1 - P(\text{no outcomes occurring})$. For example, to find the probability that at least one even number will show when a pair of dice is rolled, find the probability that two odd numbers will be rolled (no even numbers) and subtract from one. You can always use a tree diagram or make a chart to list the possible outcomes when the

Copyright © Mometrix Media. You have been licensed one copy of this document for personal use only. Any other reproduction or redistribution is strictly prohibited. All rights reserved.
This content is provided for test preparation purposes only and does not imply an endorsement by Mometrix of any particular political, scientific, or religious point of view.

sample space is small, such as in the dice-rolling example, but in most cases, it will be much faster to use the multiplication and complement formulas.

> **Review Video: Multiplication Rule**
> Visit mometrix.com/academy and enter code: 782598

PARETO ANALYSIS

The Pareto analysis system is a decision-making model which assumes that approximately 80% of the benefits that an organization receives from a particular task are the result of 20% of the effort that the various individuals within the organization put into the task. It also assumes that 80% of the problems that the organization faces are produced by approximately 20% of the factors that may be causing them. The first step necessary in using the Pareto analysis system is to list all of the problems that need to be addressed and/or the choices that are available. Next, each of those problems or choices should be grouped so that the choices offering similar benefits and/or the factors leading to larger related problems are grouped together. Each group is then given a score based on how much that particular group affects the overall organization. The group(s) which reflect the greatest gain for the least effort should be targeted first. In so doing, the organization can focus its efforts on improving things that will have the greatest effect.

Research Methodology

DATA DEFINITION AND COLLECTION OF DATA

Data definitions must be based on a solid understanding of statistical analysis and epidemiological concepts. Specific issues that must be addressed include the following:

- **3 S's:**
  - *Sensitivity*: The data should include all positive cases, taking into account variables, decreasing the number of false negatives.
  - *Specificity*: The data should include only those cases specific to the needs of the measurement and exclude those that may be similar but are a different population, decreasing the number of false positives.
  - *Stratification*: Data should be classified according to subsets, taking variables into consideration.
- **2 R's:**
  - *Recordability*: The tool/indicator should collect and measure the necessary data.
  - *Reliability*: Results should be reproducible.
- **UV:**
  - *Usability*: The tool or indicator should be easy to utilize and understand.
  - *Validity*: Collection should measure the target adequately, so that the results have predictive value.

POPULATION/SAMPLING

Defining the **population** is critical to data collection and the criteria must be established early in the process. The population may be comprised of a particular group of individuals, objects, or events. In some cases, data is gathered on an entire population, such as all cases with a particular disease, all deaths, or all workers in a particular discipline, usually within a specified time frame. In other cases, **sampling,** using a subset of a population, may be done to measure only part of a given population and to generalize the findings to the larger target population while accurately representing the target population. There are a number of considerations with sampling:

- The sampling must have the characteristics of the target population.
- The design of the collection must specify the size of the sample, the location, and time period.

Copyright © Mometrix Media. You have been licensed one copy of this document for personal use only. Any other reproduction or redistribution is strictly prohibited. All rights reserved.
This content is provided for test preparation purposes only and does not imply an endorsement by Mometrix of any particular political, scientific, or religious point of view.

- The sampling technique must ensure that the sampling represents the target population accurately.
- The design of the collection must ensure that the sampling will not be biased.

TYPES OF SAMPLING

Depending upon the goal of data collection, different **types of sampling** or combinations of sampling may be utilized. Sampling should have a *confidence level* of 95% (.05 level), meaning that there is a 95% chance that the sample represents the population and results can be replicated. Types include non-probability and probability.

NON-PROBABILITY SAMPLING

This type of sampling is intentionally biased (not everyone has an equal chance of being included), and results cannot be generalized to an entire population. It utilizes qualitative judgment.

- *Convenience*: This is a type of opportunity sampling when those available are sampled, such as all those in a clinic during a certain time frame.
- *Quota*: A stratified population is divided into subgroups (such as male and female) and then a proportion is sampled, such as 5% of females over 16 with HIV. Sometimes specified numbers may be counted, such as 50 males and 50 females.
- *Purpose*: Sampling of members of a particular population, such as all women over 60 with breast implants.

PROBABILITY SAMPLING

Probability sampling occurs when there is an equal chance for any member of a group to be part of the sample, allowing generalization of results to the entire population. Probability sampling is usually more expensive than non-probability sampling. There are a number of sub-types:

- *Cluster*: The target population is divided into clusters or groups, and then a number of these groups are selected at random and all members of the population within the selected groups are sampled.
- *Multi-stage*: This method is similar to cluster sampling, except that instead of all members of the population in selected groups being sampled, a sample of the selected groups is used, utilizing any of the methods of choosing members of a population, such as simple random sampling.
- *Simple random:* The cases in a given population are chosen randomly using a standard Table of Random Digits. This is the easiest and most commonly used method of sampling.
- *Stratified:* This is two-tier sampling method in which a group is divided into strata (mutually exclusive groups) with 2 or more homogenous characteristics. Then, a specified number of participants from each stratum are sampled.
- *Systematic (interval) random:* This involves random selection of the first member of the population and then other members at regular intervals. For example, if the desired sampling were 100 out of 500, then the *sampling interval* would be 5 (1 out of every 5). A random number between 1 and 5 is chosen as the *random start* and then every 5th member is sampled to a total of 100.
- *Multi-phase:* This sampling is usually done in two phases, but more can be used. In this type of sampling, certain data are obtained from an entire specified population, and then based on that data, further data are obtained from a subgroup within the original population.

CHARACTERISTICS OF A WELL-CONDUCTED SURVEY

The characteristics of a well-designed and well-conducted survey are the selection of sample units or clusters with probabilistic methods that can provide estimates of sampling error, and the absence of bias.

A unit/participant is an element of the population (i.e., one person).

A probabilistic method consists of constructing a sample frame with a selection procedure and a data collection method. A sample frame may consist of the entire population or an identifiable subset of the

Copyright © Mometrix Media. You have been licensed one copy of this document for personal use only. Any other reproduction or redistribution is strictly prohibited. All rights reserved.
This content is provided for test preparation purposes only and does not imply an endorsement by Mometrix of any particular political, scientific, or religious point of view.

population (i.e., names in a telephone directory, names from the DMV, social security numbers, electoral register). The sampling error is expressed as a confidence interval or a margin of error. For example, a 95% confidence interval for a mean says there is a 2.5% chance the mean is above the interval and a 2.5% chance it is below the interval. The margin of error is half the width of the confidence interval.

Major sources of bias are under-coverage bias, non-response bias, selection bias, and measurement bias.

Note: A population in a survey is generally not homogeneous with respect to the observations being made; rather, it often consists of homogeneous subsets.

INTERNAL AND EXTERNAL VALIDITY, GENERALIZABILITY, AND REPLICATION

Internal validity is concerned with the accuracy of the results of an experiment or study. If an experiment or study has internal validity, it demonstrates a cause-and-effect relationship between the variables that truly exists.

External validity is concerned with whether or not the results of an experiment or study are representative of the larger population.

Generalizability is concerned with whether or not the results of an experiment or study apply to other populations than the one studied.

Replication is concerned with whether the same results will be obtained if an experiment or study is repeated. The results of an experiment are considered to be sound if an experiment or study can be repeated and the same results are obtained.

Microbiology

GERM THEORY OF DISEASE

The **germ theory of disease** states that most infectious diseases are caused by germs or disease-causing microbes or pathogens. The germ theory is the foundation of microbiology and modern medicine. Pasteur studied the fermentation of wine and the spoiling of milk. He discovered that yeast caused the fermentation of wine and bacteria caused the spoiling of milk. He developed the process of pasteurization of milk that killed the harmful microbes without ruining the taste of the milk. Then he studied diseases in silkworms and was able to determine that the causes of those diseases are protozoa and bacteria. Pasteur also thought that microbes in hospitals came from preexisting microbes instead of spontaneous generation. He disproved **spontaneous generation** with his work with bacteria and broth. He discovered that weakened microbes could be used in **vaccines** or **immunizations** to prevent or protect against the diseases caused by those microbes. Pasteur discovered viruses in his work, developing the rabies vaccine and treatments for those already infected with the rabies virus.

BLOODBORNE PATHOGENS

The Occupational Safety and Health Administration (OSHA) (29 CFR 1910.1030) defines a **bloodborne pathogen** as any pathogenic microorganism that can be found in human blood that causes disease in humans. Although the bloodborne pathogen standard focuses on hepatitis B and HIV, there are numerous bloodborne pathogens, including hepatitis C and hepatitis A.

Any bodily fluid that is visibly contaminated with blood, any unfixed organ from a human, or known contaminated cell cultures that could cause an exposure are referred to as **other potentially infectious material (OPIM).** Exposure by blood or OPIM can occur by way of contact with a mucous membrane or non-intact skin, ingestion of the fluid, or injection into the body (such as a contaminated syringe or other sharp object).

Copyright © Mometrix Media. You have been licensed one copy of this document for personal use only. Any other reproduction or redistribution is strictly prohibited. All rights reserved. This content is provided for test preparation purposes only and does not imply an endorsement by Mometrix of any particular political, scientific, or religious point of view.

CONTROLLING BLOODBORNE PATHOGEN HAZARDS

Procedures that can protect workers from **bloodborne pathogens** in the workplace include the following:

- Treating all bodily fluids as if they are contaminated.
- Using self-sheathing needles, leakproof specimen containers, and puncture-proof containers for sharp objects.
- Providing handwashing stations with antiseptic hand cleaners and requiring workers to wash their hands after removing gloves that could be contaminated.
- Prohibiting employees from eating or drinking in areas where bloodborne pathogens could be present.
- Providing gloves, goggles, respirators, aprons, and other personal protective equipment.
- Regularly decontaminating and cleaning equipment and potentially contaminated areas.
- Labeling potential biohazards.

A **bloodborne pathogens policy** should be developed before any employees test positive for a disease. Preparing in advance allows the company to spend time determining appropriate actions instead of having to react quickly. A bloodborne pathogens policy needs to include at least three elements: employee rights, testing, and education. It should define the rights of employees who have been diagnosed with a bloodborne pathogen, including reasonable accommodations that will be made. The policy will also include whether employees will be tested for bloodborne diseases. Finally, the policy should include procedures for educating workers on how bloodborne pathogens can be transmitted and prevented.

NANOTECHNOLOGY

Nanotechnology involves science, engineering, and technology at a scale of approximately 1 to 100 nanometers. One nanometer is one billionth of a meter, which is smaller than the wavelength of visible light but still significantly larger than the average atom. Two applications of nanotechnology include nanowires and carbon nanotubes. Nanowires are wires with extremely small diameters that are excellent conductors of electricity. Carbon nanotubes are essentially rolled graphene sheets that are 10 times stronger than steel but 6 times lighter. Products with nanotechnology include sunscreen, self-cleaning glass, liquid-crystal displays (LCDs), wrinkle-resistant clothing, scratch-resistant coatings, antibacterial bandages, cosmetics, and batteries.

Chapter Quiz

Ready to see how well you retained what you just read? Scan the QR code to go directly to the chapter quiz interface for this study guide. If you're using a computer, simply visit the bonus page at **mometrix.com/bonus948/csp** and click the Chapter Quizzes link.

Copyright © Mometrix Media. You have been licensed one copy of this document for personal use only. Any other reproduction or redistribution is strictly prohibited. All rights reserved. This content is provided for test preparation purposes only and does not imply an endorsement by Mometrix of any particular political, scientific, or religious point of view.

Management Systems

Transform passive reading into active learning! After immersing yourself in this chapter, put your comprehension to the test by taking a quiz. The insights you gained will stay with you longer this way. Scan the QR code to go directly to the chapter quiz interface for this study guide. If you're using a computer, simply visit the bonus page at **mometrix.com/bonus948/csp** and click the Chapter Quizzes link.

Benchmarks and Performance Standards

SAFETY MANAGEMENT SYSTEMS

A **safety management system** is a system of procedures, practices, and policies designed to reduce the risk of occupational injury and illness within an organization. The system outlines organization-wide roles and responsibilities in a **top-down** manner to implement and maintain effective safety measures. The system is designed to be integrated into the business, similar to other management systems (e.g., quality, human resources, finance, etc.), and reinforces the business benefits of a safe work environment. Relying on the concept of **continual improvement**, the process seeks to identify risks and reduce them to the lowest acceptable level.

The National Safety Council identifies **five P's** of an effective safety management system:

- **People** - Responsible parties for all aspects of the system, emphasizing an engaged and committed work force.
- **Planning** - Assessments and audits to proactively identify hazards.
- **Programs** - Written programs that are references for employees and that standardize both procedures and expectations.
- **Progress** - Implement the concept of continual improvement to compare the system to regulatory and legal requirements and review these assessments with upper management on a routine basis.
- **Performance** - Compare injury and illness data to internal and external criteria to evaluate how well the system is performing, making changes as necessary.

BENCHMARKING

In general terms, **benchmarking** is a process wherein an organization compares its performance to other organizations to identify gaps or opportunities for improvement. Benchmarking is most valuable when metrics are compared to leaders within the industry an organization operates. This process can also be performed across industries to provide a more comprehensive assessment and to seek novel solutions.

Benchmarking is a deliberate process that involves **planning, data collection, assessment,** and **interpretation**. To start, an organization must determine what aspect of its operation it wants to improve. The next step is to establish a team to conduct the evaluation. The evaluation consists of collecting and comparing internal and external data. As differences are identified, the causes of the differences must be deduced and followed by establishing plans to address the identified gaps or deficiencies.

This process can be applied to safety management systems in an effort to reduce the risk of occupational injuries.

Safety benchmarking can be done internally, between departments, or between organizations. The process is most effective when organizations that are identified as safety leaders are selected for comparison.

Copyright © Mometrix Media. You have been licensed one copy of this document for personal use only. Any other reproduction or redistribution is strictly prohibited. All rights reserved.
This content is provided for test preparation purposes only and does not imply an endorsement by Mometrix of any particular political, scientific, or religious point of view.

Health and safety data is also published by the Bureau of Labor Statistics (BLS) for several industries and can be used for benchmarking. BLS data includes injury rates, lost days, and days of modified work. Data obtained from other organizations can include financial losses, near misses, employees trained, and number of inspections conducted.

PERFORMANCE STANDARDS

A **standard** is a document that specifies minimum requirements for practices or operations. **Performance standards** outline which practices or operations an entity must have in place, but does not explicitly describe how such practices or operations are to be done. Performance standards are **goal-oriented** in that they seek to achieve an end-product or result, but do not place restrictions on how the goal is to be achieved.

The standards promulgated by the Occupational Health and Safety Administration (OSHA) include both specification and performance standards. The performance standards describe the hazard to be addressed and allows for flexibility and interpretation by the varied workplaces that the standards apply to, such as the requirement to issue "appropriate protective equipment."

SPECIFICATION STANDARDS

A **specification standard** outlines the practices or operations a person or organization must institute and delineates specific requirements for materials, components, or systems to meet those guidelines. This type of standard not only states what must be done, but also how it must be done. A specification applies to an object, product, or process and may be dependent on the exact situation or circumstances. Specifications are set forth by agencies or organizations based on **best practices** and may be rigid or have ranges.

The Occupational Safety and Health Administration (OSHA) publishes both performance and specification standards. Specification standards describe the hazard to be addressed and designate the proper control, such as specific guardrail height requirements for elevated work platforms.

Organizational Culture

Organizational culture is the set of values and activities held as important in a business. Improving culture to create a more positive work environment in which people are working toward a common goal can be achieved through several initiatives. There should be clearly stated roles and responsibilities so that the people in each job function are aware of how they are participating in a larger whole. There should be transparency given by upper management into decisions that are made, the direction of the company, and the goals that are set. There should be two-way communication that emphasizes shared values and goals rather than hierarchical policies. According to each job function and role, tailored training should be given so that employees have the tools they need to achieve their objectives. Promotions and accolades should be awarded based on objective merit rather than friendship. Managers and supervisors should remember that actions speak louder than words; in the case of safety objectives, if the only consideration employees hear spoken of are financial and production objectives, this will be taken as indication that these goals are more important than employee safety.

MAINTAINING ORGANIZATIONAL CULTURE

Culture encompasses every facet of an organization and comprises four **key elements** including norms, artifacts, values, and core assumptions. Shared **norms** are not always defined or obvious but often inferred by specific situations. For example, punctuality and professionalism are reflected by group practice. Likewise, the collective beliefs, ideals, and feelings of the members of an organization construct its cultural **values**. Alternatively, cultural **artifacts** are tangible traits that portray core beliefs such as behaviors, language, and symbols. An organization's shared **assumptions** reveal the basis of how people think. This can be reflected by the measure of controls management imposes upon line staff. Organizational culture can be maintained through employee selection and disciplinary procedures, rewards systems, recognition ceremonies, stories, symbols, and leadership reactions to achievements and problems.

Copyright © Mometrix Media. You have been licensed one copy of this document for personal use only. Any other reproduction or redistribution is strictly prohibited. All rights reserved. This content is provided for test preparation purposes only and does not imply an endorsement by Mometrix of any particular political, scientific, or religious point of view.

MODIFYING ORGANIZATIONAL CULTURE

The following are the six core steps for modifying organizational culture:

1. Conduct a **culture audit** by performing interviews to identify current values and beliefs.
2. Assess the **need for change** by evaluating whether the current culture is appropriate for the company's size and mission. Determine whether it solves or creates problems for the firm.
3. **Unfreeze** the current culture. This often happens during times of extreme events, such as the loss of a partner, a merger, or the announcement of drastic operational or technological changes. Modifications to the culture are often most successful when the need is well communicated, and organizational members believe the changes are important.
4. Encourage support from the **leadership team**; they establish the code of conduct and are the cultural elite of an organization.
5. Implement an **intervention strategy** that might include frequent communications, revised training policies, revised rewards programs, restructuring or defining new roles, team-building and involvement activities, or even announcing a new slogan or mission statement.
6. Monitor and evaluate the **transitional change process** over an extended period of time.

Incident Investigation

EVENT AND CAUSAL FACTOR ANALYSIS

The goal of any incident investigation is to identify all factors that contributed to the negative result. A **causal factor** can be described as an unplanned or unintended contributor to an incident that, if eliminated, would have resulted in a different outcome. Causal factors include the **environment**, **people**, and **equipment**.

Event and Causal Factor Analysis (ECFA) identifies the **root causes** and **causal factors** associated with an accident. The events that led to the incident are charted out chronologically. Events are represented as rectangular boxes and conditions are represented as ovals. As the chart is developed, it may have branches for secondary events or parallel paths that are ultimately determined to be contributory. Events are derived logically and directly from the preceding event to create a clear path both to and from the event. The process results in identifying the cause and effect of a chain of events and how they contributed to the incident. Once the causes are identified, measures can be taken to prevent future incidents.

ROOT CAUSE ANALYSIS

Both the Occupational Safety and Health Administration (OSHA) and the Environmental Protection Agency (EPA) recommend that employers conduct a **root cause analysis** for incident investigation. A **root cause** is an underlying, fundamental system-related reason for the accident. The root cause is the system failure that allowed the dangerous condition to exist. When done thoroughly and objectively, this process will identify the factors that contributed to the event, both **directly** and **indirectly**. If an investigation only identifies **immediate causes**, then the underlying conditions and system failures that resulted in the incident are not addressed, thereby setting up the organization for similar incidents in the future. Where an immediate cause may be termed "fault-finding," root cause determination can be referred to as "fact-finding."

IMMEDIATE CAUSE

An **immediate cause** is the obvious reason for an occupational incident. It is the object, item, or action that caused the injury. For example, an employee walking through a warehouse slips on a fluid spill and twists their ankle. The immediate cause is the fluid on the floor presenting a slip hazard.

If an incident investigation only identifies the immediate cause, the **system failure** that allowed that condition to exist remains and the incident will likely recur. Therefore, incident investigations must identify the immediate cause and then seek to deduce why that condition was allowed to exist, thereby identifying the **root cause** of the incident.

Copyright © Mometrix Media. You have been licensed one copy of this document for personal use only. Any other reproduction or redistribution is strictly prohibited. All rights reserved.
This content is provided for test preparation purposes only and does not imply an endorsement by Mometrix of any particular political, scientific, or religious point of view.

For example, the cause of the fluid spill is traced to the leaking brake system of a cart. The brake system leak was not detected because the cart had not been serviced in several years. Thus, the root cause of the injury was the lack of a company-wide routine maintenance program for carts. Failure to implement a cart maintenance program could lead to more slip-related injuries from fluid leaks.

Management of Change

A Management of Change (MOC) system is a documented process to alter work flows or standard operating procedures. Proper use of an MOC system provides every department an opportunity to review and comment on proposed changes and provides a verifiable and auditable trail of documentation of process changes and approvals. The most important elements of the documented MOC process are the origination, the changes to any written documents, the complete scope of affected departments, and approvals of the change. An example is a process change that requires input from the production manager, the quality manager, and the environmental manager. The MOC process is started, and each department manager in turn can review the change and recommend alterations. Ancillary documents or training programs that are affected by the change can then be considered and documented, with these documents attached to verify that they were completed.

System Safety Analysis

FAULT TREE ANALYSIS

Fault tree analysis is an approach to evaluating advanced systems within a safety program. This approach employs Boolean logic to analyze an incident. Fault tree analysis actually resembles the structure of a tree. The incident being considered is at the top. Factors that influenced the incident are identified and broken down further into causes of the incident. This resembles the branches of a tree. This approach also uses probability to evaluate the incident and other possible incidents. The pattern of analysis is to start with general and use inference and reasoning to progress to more specific considerations, paying close attention to the relationship between an incident and each component considered. After the tree has been built, specific measurements and evaluations of quality of relationships can be conducted. Computers are often used in fault tree analysis for efficiency and effectiveness.

The following fault tree analysis events are defined as follows:

- A **basic event** is an incident or element that does not need to be broken down further or evaluated; shown on the fault tree as a circle at the end of a branch
- An **undeveloped event** is an incident or element that the evaluator might choose not to consider further and its cause may be clearly understood; on the fault tree it is shown as a diamond or double diamond
- A **normal event** is an expected and desired occurrence evaluated based on whether it happened or not; shown on the fault tree analysis as a house shape; statistical probability of this event is usually assigned as 1.0 or 0.0
- A **fault event** is an undesired or unexpected incident of primary concern usually placed at the top of the tree for later evaluation; shown on the fault analysis tree as a rectangle

Fault tree analysis begins with an undesired event as the root of the tree. Expanding outward, are each of the possible causes for that event and those causes. Fault tree analysis is often facilitated by specifically designed computer software. This approach is commonly applied to the design stage of a product or process in order to carefully evaluate potential causes of undesired events. When constructing a fault tree, events are shown as blocks and are connected using gates. Gates are designated as *AND* or *OR*. Fault trees can be simple or elaborate and pay close attention to the relationship among all events shown. A possible situation that would indicate the use of a fault tree analysis is the installation of new safety devices that read pressure on a compressor running a tank of hazardous gas. In order to evaluate the risk of rupture under extreme conditions, a fault tree could be constructed.

125

Copyright © Mometrix Media. You have been licensed one copy of this document for personal use only. Any other reproduction or redistribution is strictly prohibited. All rights reserved.
This content is provided for test preparation purposes only and does not imply an endorsement by Mometrix of any particular political, scientific, or religious point of view.

An event is a component of a fault tree that shows an occurrence. These occurrences could be routine episodes in an operation or might be component or system failures or problems. An occurrence of failure stops normal production or functioning. In an operation, a track that stops moving is an example of a failure. A fault is an aspect or characteristic of an element or entire system that can lead to an undesired event. In a fault tree, causal events can be divided into four groups. Primary events are those related to an integral part of the system. Secondary events are related to objects or actions separate from the actual system. Primary fault refers to occurrences that are outside routine functions in a system. Secondary fault indicates an occurrence induced by something outside of the system itself.

Fault-tree analysis is an important tool for safety professionals to understand causes of accidents and overall operations of a system. Using fault-tree analysis to look at safety can proactively expose possible unintended events. Each component of the fault-tree can be considered to determine what would cause these unintended events. Hazard controls can be implemented to reduce this risk. Considering a chain of events will be most successful if a tree branch is examined either from the top or the bottom event. Statistically, events that are connected on the tree by an OR gate have a greater probability of occurring, while those connected by AND gates happen less frequently. Using indicators of probability can allow an analyst to give priority consideration to events that are most likely to happen. This allows quicker response to the most pressing dangers that are present in the system.

FAILURE MODES EFFECTS ANALYSIS (FMEA)

Failure modes effects analysis is a step-by-step, bottom-up evaluation of all possible failures in a system and what effect each would have on the process. A system or process is divided into functions and each function is evaluated for how all possible failures could happen ("mode"). A failure can be an error or a defect in the final product. FMEA uses a **cross-functional team** to identify and prioritize a failure based on the impact of its consequence, the frequency, and how easily it can be detected. Consequences are evaluated for their impact on the system, subsystems, products, services, and customer experience. The goal of FMEA is to reduce or eliminate failures, starting with the most impactful. This process can be used during the design phase to prevent failures and can also be used once the process is implemented to control failures. FMEA can also be implemented as a continual improvement tool during the life cycle of the process.

Business Continuity and Contingency Plans

BUSINESS CONTINUITY PLANS

A business continuity plan is a documented plan backed by a multifunctional planning process that defines how a business will continue its key operations in the event of a natural or man-made disaster that interrupts business as usual. The planning process should include representatives from the key functional areas of the business: operations, human resources, safety and risk management, finance, information technology, and logistics. Planning considerations should be made for a variety of small and large disasters, for example, planning for localized natural disasters such as flooding or planning for business continuity in the event of a fire or tornado. In addition, plans should be made for wider disasters such as pandemic flu or earthquake. The plan should document lines of communication to employees and customers and should consider backup sources of major supplies, transportation, telecommunication, and computer systems. Finally, the plan should be communicated to key employees so that it is accessible and useful in the event of an emergency.

EMERGENCY CONTINGENCY PLANS

Emergency and contingency plans for large scale worksite accidents and occurrences should begin with recognition of the potential dangers.

- Step One: Identify and evaluate the types of accidents and injuries which might occur. Will responders have to deal with chemical release, fire, poisons, etc.? A projection of the type of injuries which might occur, the number of persons who might be affected, and whether nearby communities will be affected should all be part of the initial evaluation.

Copyright © Mometrix Media. You have been licensed one copy of this document for personal use only. Any other reproduction or redistribution is strictly prohibited. All rights reserved.
This content is provided for test preparation purposes only and does not imply an endorsement by Mometrix of any particular political, scientific, or religious point of view.

- Step Two: The emergency contingency plan should describe arrangements and contacts within hospitals, emergency response teams, and disaster teams. Note that the local fire department is usually in the role of incident commanders responsible for coordination of activities.
- Step Three: Enlist the participation of the manufacturers of hazardous materials in a coordinated emergency plan which involves Local Emergency Planning Committees (LEPC) and the State Emergency Response Committee (SERC). LEPCs and SERCs must have obtained all available scientific data pertaining to the handling of hazardous chemicals.

Leading and Lagging Safety, Health, Environmental, and Security Performance Indicators

LEADING INDICATORS

A leading indicator is an objective measure that is used to assess actions taken proactively to improve organizational performance. This is a useful measure in evaluating the impact of an occupational health and safety management system because it measures what the organization is doing to prevent injuries and improve effectiveness in a proactive manner instead of reacting to incidents. Examples of **leading indicators** are: the number of training courses given, the number of safety meetings held, the number of behavioral safety observations completed, the number of area safety inspections completed, and the number of near miss root cause analyses completed. These leading indicators can be used to assess overall proactive performance, and thorough implementation of the leading indicator activities can strengthen the occupational health and safety program.

NEAR MISS REPORTING

A near miss is an incident that comes very close to being an occupational injury but does not result in injury. Examples include having something fall off a highly stacked pallet of material and nearly hit a worker standing nearby, or two forklifts backing up toward each other and nearly crashing into each other, or an employee using a box cutter that slips and cuts his glove but misses cutting his hand. Diligent monitoring of **near misses** and responding to them as if they were injury incidents by completing *root cause analyses* and developing *action plans* to prevent recurrences can put into place the systems, procedures, and practices that create a safe work environment that responds to incidents before they occur.

INSPECTION FREQUENCY AND RESPONSE

Routinely scheduled inspections are an integral part of an effective occupational health and safety system. The **frequency of inspections** must be aligned with the degree of risk posed by the operation, in conjunction with regulatory requirements. Inspections that are conducted too infrequently are a sign of a lax occupational health and safety management system that potentially allows noncompliance or nonconformance to exist without correction between inspections. Moreover, the timeliness and attention paid to correcting issues identified in inspections is an indicator of the effectiveness of the health and safety system. Companies that recognize the importance of timely corrective action will realize the benefits of maintaining a safe work environment that promptly **responds** to issues identified.

LAGGING INDICATORS

Lagging indicators in occupational health and safety are those metrics that have happened after the fact, or after a workplace injury has occurred. They are a useful indicator of the effects of incidents and can be managed, but they do not provide a proactive opportunity for improvement. Examples of **lagging indicators** are the number of lost workdays, the number of days an employee is on restricted duty, the cost incurred for medical visits, and the number of recordable injuries. While it is essential to track lagging indicators and target improved performance over time, they do not provide a snapshot of future performance. Lagging indicators are often used to assess actual regulatory compliance and are essential for reporting purposes.

Copyright © Mometrix Media. You have been licensed one copy of this document for personal use only. Any other reproduction or redistribution is strictly prohibited. All rights reserved. This content is provided for test preparation purposes only and does not imply an endorsement by Mometrix of any particular political, scientific, or religious point of view.

CALCULATING INCIDENCE RATES

The **total case incident rate (TCIR)** is a health and safety metric that calculates the total number of OSHA recordable injury cases in a year and is weighted by the number of total hours worked by employees at the organization during the year to allow comparison between companies in similar industries. The formula to calculate the TCIR is as follows:

$$\text{TCIR} = \frac{\text{Number of recordable injuries in calendar year} \times 200{,}000}{\text{Total hours worked}}$$

The **days away, restricted duty, or transfer (DART)** is a measure of the number of injury cases that involved days off work, on restricted duty, or transferred to another job. Note that the calculation uses the number of cases, not the total number of days. The calculation is as follows:

$$\text{DART} = \frac{\text{Number of cases with days away, job restriction, or transfer} \times 200{,}000}{\text{Total hours worked}}$$

Ideally, the DART is lower than the TCIR. The 200,000 hours figure refers to the number of hours worked in a year by a company with 100 full-time employees.

DIRECT COSTS OF INCIDENTS

The direct costs of an incident are actual monetary costs attributable to the incident. In the case of an injury, the **direct costs** are the medical bills for the treatment of the injured worker, the money paid to a worker as worker's compensation payments during lost work time, the cost of medications, and the cost of transportation to and from the clinic to attend doctors' appointments. These costs can be readily identified by collecting the invoices from these various services and totaling them. However, in the case of an injury, the direct costs are usually borne by the insurance company and are not readily apparent to the organization.

Safety, Health, and Environmental Management and Audit Systems

ISO 14001

The **ISO 14001 series of environmental management standards** is a voluntary environmental management system standard that sets a broad framework that any type of organization can use to improve environmental performance. It is a management system that requires commitment from top management to be truly effective. It is up to the organization to assess its environmental aspects and use a ranking process to determine its significant environmental impacts. Those significant environmental impacts are used to guide the establishment of environmental performance objectives. An example objective would be to reduce energy consumption of a processing facility by 10 percent over the next two years. The objective would have a written set of planned activities to achieve the objective, and the organization would periodically assess its progress toward meeting the objective. Over time, environmental performance (measured environmental impact) is improved with systematic implementation of an ISO 14001 environmental management system.

The ISO 14001 environmental management system is built upon the **Plan, Do, Check, Act model**. It requires management commitment for its implementation. The clauses of the standard require that the organization establish an environmental policy, that they commit to compliance with all applicable environmental regulations, that they communicate their environmental programs to employees and make their policy available to the public, that they properly train their employees to do their tasks and to understand their role in the organization's achievement of its environmental objectives, that specific and measurable environmental objectives are established, that the organization maintain document and record control, that the organization conduct periodic internal audits to determine conformance with the standard, and that a system of corrective and preventive actions be implemented. The capstone of the system is the **management review process**, in which top management periodically review the organization's environmental performance and set objectives and allocate resources for the upcoming year.

Copyright © Mometrix Media. You have been licensed one copy of this document for personal use only. Any other reproduction or redistribution is strictly prohibited. All rights reserved.
This content is provided for test preparation purposes only and does not imply an endorsement by Mometrix of any particular political, scientific, or religious point of view.

ISO 45001

The International Standards Organization's (ISO) Standard 45001 provides the framework for an effective **occupational safety and health management system.** The goal of the standard is to assist organizations in creating and maintaining a safe work environment for employees.

This voluntary standard is the first international effort to standardize health and safety system requirements. Building off other management system standards, such as ISO 9001 and 14001, the Standard integrates health and safety into the overall management plan for the organization. ISO 45001 emphasizes **management's role and responsibility** in creating an environment that reduces the risk of injury and illness. The system is designed to be flexible, expandable, and emphasizes continual improvement.

The standard is divided into 10 clauses:

- **Scope**: Establishes the intent of the standard and its application
- **Normative references**: No entry for ISO 450001
- **Terms and definitions**: Terms used in the standard to maintain context
- **Context of the organization**: Requires the organization to identify internal and external factors, as well as the integration of health and safety into core business practices
- **Leadership and worker participation**: Establishes accountability for the success of the system, roles and responsibilities for top management, and two-way communication for health and safety topics within the organization
- **Planning**: Requires risk assessment processes be used to identify, assess, and re-evaluate workplace hazards on a recurring basis
- **Support**: Requires organizations to devote resources in support of health and safety
- **Operation**: Incorporates the use of the hierarchy of hazard controls and includes a change management provision
- **Performance evaluation**: Mandates evaluating the system periodically using the plan-do-check-act cycle, with management reviewing the findings to plan future goals
- **Improvement**: Requires incidents be evaluated for their root cause and stresses continual improvement to prevent injuries

ISO 19011

The document "Guidelines for Quality and/or Environmental Management Systems Auditing, ISO 19011" is part of the ISO series of standards, but is not a stand-alone standard to which a company can be certified to. Instead, it sets out best management practices for auditors to use when planning an audit, selecting the audit team, executing the audit, and following up on audit findings. It sets expectations for conducting a quality audit by first defining what the scope of the audit will be and what the audit criteria are. The document then discusses the qualifications of auditors, specifies that the auditors should be independent from the work they are auditing, that audit findings must be grounded in objective evidence, and that auditors must conduct themselves in an ethical and professional manner. The document also discusses the differences between first-, second-, and third-party audits, the responsibilities of the auditor, and the elements that should be included in a well-prepared audit report.

ANSI/AIHA Z10

The purpose of the ANSI/AIHA Z10 standard is to lay out a framework for an effective occupational health and safety management system. The main elements of the standard require management commitment to the implementation of the standard demonstrated by allocation of resources and attention to its implementation, participation of the organization's employees in the occupational health and safety system, risk assessment, planning of the occupational health and safety system to address the risks identified, followed by evaluation of the system and appropriate corrective action. The system is completed by management review to assess achievement of objectives and adjustment of targets due to newly identified occupational health and safety issues or business objectives.

Copyright © Mometrix Media. You have been licensed one copy of this document for personal use only. Any other reproduction or redistribution is strictly prohibited. All rights reserved.
This content is provided for test preparation purposes only and does not imply an endorsement by Mometrix of any particular political, scientific, or religious point of view.

The main objective of the ANSI/AIHA Z10 American National Standard for Occupational Health and Safety Management Systems is to set a framework for a management system. This systemic approach, while it encompasses compliance as a foundation, seeks to evaluate the organization's risks holistically, and to respond to them in a proactive rather than a reactive manner. The objective is to identify risks before they result in injury or harm, and systematically engage various elements of the organization in planning for risk management. The organization then evaluates its progress and performs root cause analysis to provide corrective action. This management system serves the overall objective to create a safe workplace that goes beyond compliance.

Applicable Requirements for Plans, Systems, and Policies

OSHA STANDARD COMPLIANCE PLANS

There are several OSHA standards that require written compliance and training plans:

Hazard Communication (29 CFR 1910.1200) is a written plan that must cover employee exposures to hazardous chemicals in the workplace, what measures are in place to minimize exposure, and how employees are trained to protect themselves from exposure.

Lead Protection Plans (29 CFR 1910.1025) are required to describe the tasks that result in lead exposure, how much the exposure is, how employees are protected from lead exposure, and the medical monitoring program implemented to monitor exposure.

Respiratory Protection Plans (29 CFR 1910.134) are required to document what type of exposure to hazardous chemicals requires respiratory protection, what type of respirators are available to employees, and how employees will be medically evaluated for fitness to wear a respirator.

Hearing Protection Plans (29 CFR 1910.95) are required to document noise-monitoring results, where hearing protection is required, the audiometric testing that will be conducted, and the steps the organization will take if an employee is found to have a threshold shift in annual audiometric testing.

CONTINGENCY PLANS

A **contingency plan** is a document required by the Environmental Protection Agency (EPA) for any facility that stores or generates **hazardous waste** or hazardous waste components. The plan is designed to protect people and the environment in the event of a fire, explosion, or unplanned release of hazardous waste onto soil or into the water or air.

The contingency plan must describe the actions an employer will take in the event of an unintentional release. The plan must:

- Describe the arrangements made with local **emergency response agencies** to provide support, including hospitals.
- List contact information of the organization's **emergency response coordinator**, who must be reachable at any time.
- List all the **response equipment** located at the facility, including fire extinguishing systems, spill control equipment, communications systems, alarm systems, and decontamination equipment. The list must include a description, physical location, and an explanation of each item's capabilities.
- Include **evacuation plan** for employees, including primary and secondary evacuation routes, as well as evacuation alarm signals.

EMERGENCY RESPONSE PLANS

An **emergency response plan (ERP)** is the employer's process for responding to the unintended release of a hazardous material. The ERP can be part of an organization's **contingency plan**, but differs in that it is specific

Copyright © Mometrix Media. You have been licensed one copy of this document for personal use only. Any other reproduction or redistribution is strictly prohibited. All rights reserved.
This content is provided for test preparation purposes only and does not imply an endorsement by Mometrix of any particular political, scientific, or religious point of view.

for those employers who will have employees respond to the release in some fashion. The extent of the program and training required for staff under the Hazardous Waste Operations and Emergency Response standard (HAZWOPER) will depend on whether employees will simply prevent entry to the release area or if they will actively try to stop the release, leak, or spill.

At a minimum, ERPs should include:

- Pre-emergency **planning and coordination** with local emergency response agencies
- **Identifying** staff with the necessary **training** who will respond to the spill
- How staff will **recognize** a release and the **actions** they are to take
- Establishing **safe distances** and **places of refuge**
- How **site security** will be established and maintained during emergency activities
- **Decontamination procedures** for contaminated staff and emergency responders
- Emergency **medical treatment and first aid**, including coordination with local hospitals
- The procedures used to **alert** staff and initiate a response
- A method for **post-response critique** for continual improvement

EMERGENCY ACTION PLANS

The Occupational Safety and Health Administration (OSHA) requires an **emergency action plan (EAP)** whenever such a plan is required by another standard. An EAP is designed to safely **evacuate** staff in the event of an emergency. The EAP addresses several different types of emergencies, including natural disasters, man-made emergencies, fires, and industrial accidents. OSHA establishes the following minimum components for any EAP:

- Procedures for **alerting** both employees and first responders that an emergency condition exists, such as fire, earthquake, or active shooter
- **Evacuation procedures** for employees, including when to evacuate and designated evacuation routes (Procedures typically include floor plans denoting primary and secondary evacuation routes for each area of the facility.)
- Procedures for employees who must remain in the building to safely shut down **critical operations**, such as chemical reactions, furnaces, or other sensitive operations
- A means to **account** for all employees after an evacuation
- Procedures for staff who may perform **rescue or medical duties**. If such duties will not be conducted by staff, the EAP should state who is responsible for those duties.
- Who employees can contact for questions about the EAP
- A provision for **training** on the EAP so that employees can be familiar with the process and ask questions before an emergency condition occurs

Document Retention

DIGITAL AND PHYSICAL DOCUMENT RETENTION

Regarding document retention, a policy should first be established to determine what records to keep, how they will be stored, and for how long. First consider regulatory requirements; for example, files on employee audiometry and respiratory protection are supposed to be kept for thirty years after the employee leaves the organization. Whether kept electronically or physically, files can be organized several ways. One way that works well is to organize them by regulatory agency or program with separate subfolders for plans, agency inspections, permits, and violations. Physical or digital files must be protected from theft or unauthorized access by use of passwords, in the case of electronic files, and with a locked file cabinet in the case of physical files. Records should be kept of when files are discarded and who authorized the removal of the files.

Copyright © Mometrix Media. You have been licensed one copy of this document for personal use only. Any other reproduction or redistribution is strictly prohibited. All rights reserved.
This content is provided for test preparation purposes only and does not imply an endorsement by Mometrix of any particular political, scientific, or religious point of view.

RECORD CYCLE

The life of a record begins the moment it is created and continues until it is finally deleted or destroyed. A decision is made at creation regarding **record retention**, or how long a record must be kept. Decisions are also made during different times of the record cycle as to its use, filing, and whether it is kept or deleted. The key steps of the record cycle are the creation of the record, utilization of the record, retention of the record, transfer of the record to storage, and disposal of the record.

A **record's retention schedule** is developed by the department creating it, the people who use the record, and the manager in charge of the organization's records. This schedule estimates the time the record will be kept in active storage for daily use, in inactive storage for reference, and when it may be destroyed. During this process, records are evaluated for their value. A record's value depends on its use and is evaluated according to its primary and secondary value. Records that are active and needed currently have primary value. They may have administrative, legal, fiscal, or research value. Records kept in semi-active or inactive storage have secondary value. These may have historical or archival importance.

A record may be transferred from active to inactive storage and vice versa. This depends on the record's use. It may also be physically removed and transferred to a records facility or within a computer system. Two methods of transferring records are perpetual transfer and periodic transfer. Using **perpetual transfer**, a record can be transferred anytime it is no longer needed. Future use of the record will be limited. An example would be in a law firm: once a court case has been closed, the records are transferred immediately to inactive storage. During **periodic transfer**, records are transferred at a specific date each year. An example is a business that transfers all records from active to inactive storage on December 31 of each year. Records are often analyzed at this time to see if they are needed for further use or if they can be destroyed.

When a record is no longer needed for the business, it can be destroyed or deleted from the system. The department that created or used the record is first notified to see if the file should be destroyed. The retention schedule for the record is often checked because it gives the length of time the record should be kept. Purging is the process of deleting the contents of an electronic record. As this takes place, each record is analyzed to see if it has further use. However, deleting the electronic copy of the record does not mean all the information is gone. The information is deleted from the location but could still be somewhere else in the system. The method of the destruction of paper, microform, or magnetic records is important since such documents may contain confidential information. Common ways to destroy these records include shredding, pulverizing, and incinerating.

CENTERS FOR MAINTAINING RECORDS

Record centers are the locations where a business stores its records, whether they are active, semi-active, or inactive. Sometimes businesses will prepare duplicate records digitally or on paper. Duplicating records in hard copy form and storing them at a separate place is known as **dispersal**.

Records are stored at either onsite or offsite locations. **Onsite storage units** are located at the business. These include vaults, for more sensitive documents, and special file rooms. **Offsite storage units** are located somewhere other than the business. These can be either owned by the business or rented. Advantages of offsite storage include lower costs, and since the business doesn't publicize the location, greater security.

Management Leadership

MANAGEMENT THEORIES

EARLY THEORIES

Early management theories, unlike more modern ones, focused more on the efficiency of the factory or business. (Theories that are more modern have a larger emphasis on the actual people performing the work.) Some of the early theorists were Frederick W. Taylor, Lillian and Frank Gilbreth, Henry L. Gantt (his "Gantt chart" was an early graphic aid for planning and controlling operations), William H. Leffingwell, Max Weber,

Copyright © Mometrix Media. You have been licensed one copy of this document for personal use only. Any other reproduction or redistribution is strictly prohibited. All rights reserved.
This content is provided for test preparation purposes only and does not imply an endorsement by Mometrix of any particular political, scientific, or religious point of view.

and Henri Fayol. These early theorists generally divided their ideas into two camps: scientific and administrative management. The scientific principle of management was described in 1911 in Taylor's *Principles of Scientific Management*, which is credited with being the first presentation of management theories.

SCIENTIFIC MANAGEMENT

Scientific management focuses less on the personnel aspect and more on the production side of operations. The originator of the theory is Frederick W. Taylor, who used the scientific method as a means to determine the most efficient method for a particular task. He divided a team into two parts: management and workers. Each had specific tasks and the job duties did not overlap. Lillian and Frank Gilbreth also believed in Taylor's ideas, and they added to them by creating a system of hand movements, each known as a "therblig," used when studying the physical motions used in task completion.

The first person to begin to shift the focus from purely one of efficiency to one involving the workers was Henry L. Gantt. William H. Leffingwell's *Scientific Office Management* added more elements to the management spectrum, including ways to plan, schedule, and evaluate the work being performed, and the incentive of employee reward.

ADMINISTRATIVE MANAGEMENT

Administrative management signaled a shift in the trend of scientific management (focused on production) by describing the duties of a good manager. Early administrative management was described by Henri Fayol in *General and Industrial Management*, in which he defined some of the principles that are still used today. First, he said a manager is supposed to have four tasks: plan, organize, activate, and control. The manager-worker relationship is based on: labor division, positions of authority, appropriate discipline, proper initiative, equality, tenured positions and stability, a common goal, common movements (towards the goal), appropriate and fair wages, positive and cohesive attitudes, keeping order, suspending one's own goals in favor of the general goals of the company, the scalar chain (levels of the chain of command), and centralizing operations.

THEORY X AND THEORY Y

Douglas McGregor, an early researcher into management theory, believed that employees are treated differently by their managers depending on how their managers perceive them to be as workers and human beings. McGregor believed that managers who felt that workers were naturally lazy or unmotivated, tended to try to avoid work, or were only working for the money believed in what he called "Theory X" (and thus, the managers offered money and controlled their employees in order to make them produce). In contrast, Theory Y described managers who viewed their employees as good workers who cared about their jobs, had pride in their work, and who were eager to please. Theory Y managers tended to treat their workers more as team members.

HUMAN RELATIONS MANAGEMENT THEORY

The **human relations management theory** is the most modern of the management approaches. The theory is based on the concept that the people performing the jobs have needs that should be considered equal to or above the needs of the organization. Some big names in human relations management are Fritz Roethlisberger and Elton Mayo, who conducted the "Hawthorne studies" that analyzed the correlation between employees' satisfaction, safety, and comfort with successful and productive work. The studies focused on employees, who seemed to work better while being studied; however, when the study was over, they went back to their old working habits. The conclusion was that employees worked better when they were being paid attention to. This showed management personnel that by considering their employees' needs, overall productivity would improve. Two related theories include Maslow's hierarchy of needs and Herzberg's motivation-hygiene theory.

Copyright © Mometrix Media. You have been licensed one copy of this document for personal use only. Any other reproduction or redistribution is strictly prohibited. All rights reserved. This content is provided for test preparation purposes only and does not imply an endorsement by Mometrix of any particular political, scientific, or religious point of view.

LEADERSHIP THEORIES

TRAIT THEORY OF LEADERSHIP

According to the trait theory of leadership, all successful leaders have certain personal characteristics in common: initiative, ambition; energy, desire for improvement, self-assurance, competence, and a firm grasp of the strengths and weaknesses of others.

Stogdill's Handbook of Leadership identifies the following traits common to good leaders:

- *Capacity*: knowledge, intelligence, focus, creativity, and judgment
- *Achievement*: accomplishments and education
- *Responsibility*: persistence, reliability, and determination
- *Participation*: cooperation, friendliness, helpfulness, and selflessness
- *Status*: popularity, reputation, and deference from colleagues

One criticism of this leadership theory is that it places all the emphasis on the leader, ignoring the employee, and it fails to differentiate between traits.

BEHAVIORAL THEORY OF LEADERSHIP

The behavioral theory of leadership, which began with the early work of Rensis Likert and his colleagues at the University of Michigan who identified job-centered and employee-centered leader behaviors. There are two leadership behaviors at the center of the behavioral theory of leadership: task accomplishment and sensitivity for the feelings of subordinates. A leader who demonstrates both of these behaviors will always be effective. In the work of Likert and his associates, there was special attention to three leadership behaviors:

- *Task performance behavior*: related to specific processes and performance of work tasks
- *Group maintenance behavior*: teambuilding and supportive leadership
- *Decision-making*: may be either autocratic or democratic

An autocratic decision-making style may result in higher performance, but the democratic style seems to result in happier employees. Leaders who make no decisions (that is, leaders who have adopted a laissez-faire style) create low performance and low employee satisfaction. Leaders who pay great attention to maintenance behavior tend to retain their employees far longer.

SITUATIONAL OR CONTINGENT LEADERSHIP THEORY

According to contingent (also known as situational) leadership theorists, the most effective strategy for leading a group depends on the circumstances. In other words, there is no one set of leadership skills that works in every case. Situational leadership centers around three approaches:

- The first approach emphasizes harmony between manager and situation
- The second approach emphasizes the probability that a manager will have to modify his or her approach in a given situation
- The third approach centers on the way some situations can mitigate or neutralize the skills and style of the leader

At this point, most leadership theorists believe that the second approach is the most consistent with reality.

TRANSFORMATIONAL LEADERSHIP THEORY

Transformational leadership theory (Burns, Bass) stresses the impact that leaders can have to facilitate change. Instead of a transactional style of leadership in which change is brought about through a system of rewards and punishments (or withholding of rewards), a transformational leader leads change through showing respect and consideration for individuals, challenging them intellectually, and inspiring and influencing them. Transformational leaders are often personally charismatic and tend to lead through example

Copyright © Mometrix Media. You have been licensed one copy of this document for personal use only. Any other reproduction or redistribution is strictly prohibited. All rights reserved.
This content is provided for test preparation purposes only and does not imply an endorsement by Mometrix of any particular political, scientific, or religious point of view.

rather than control. The transformational leader identifies those things that need change along with old methods that are inefficient. They then work with other members of the team to motivate them, help them to find solutions, and develop new and more efficient methods of doing things. The transformational leader provides a sense of direction and empowers others to do their best, all while focusing on collective purpose, pride in work, and achievement.

MOTIVATION

Today's motivation theories fall into three categories: process, content, and reinforcement. The goal of each is to explain why people behave as they do.

Process theories focus on the decisions a person makes while pursuing a goal. The most well-known process theory is the equity theory penned by John Stacey Adams, which considers how people feel they are being treated when comparing themselves to others. For example, if a person is doing more work but being paid less than a coworker, motivation will be lost. If the same person feels that he or she is being paid fairly and on par with peers, the motivation is present to be productive at work. Victor Vroom proposed that people who expect to do well and also believe they will receive a positive reward are able to complete a task (expectancy theory).

Content theory looks at the needs (achievement, power, social affiliation) of individuals that are met when they are motivated. For example, if they desires to feel a sense of achievement, they would be motivated to do a challenging job well.

Reinforcement theory is another way to look at motivation. Since reinforcement is received after behaving in a specific way (whether the reinforcement is positive or negative), the person will remember the reward or punishment from a past action and will apply those thoughts to a current project. For example, if in the past an employee completed a report on time and was praised by his or her superiors, the positive reinforcement (praise) would be motivation to do well on the next report assignment. If the same employee were chided for being late to work, he or she would strive to avoid the negative repercussions by arriving on time. A series of positive reinforcements (rewards), the theory states, will result in a productive and motivated worker.

HERZBERG'S MOTIVATION-HYGIENE THEORY

Frederick Herzberg's **motivation-hygiene theory** is based on the idea that people are influenced by both internal, positive rewards (motivation) and negative repercussions (which he called **hygiene factors**). He felt that motivation comes from within each employee, and that negative hygiene factors come from those things outside the employees' control (such as things controlled or influenced by supervisors or others in a company). Dissatisfaction results from poor working conditions, work relationships, salary issues, company policies or procedures with which the employee disagrees, poor supervision, bad relations with coworkers, etc. Satisfaction and motivation occur when the employee feels responsible, has a chance to advance, enjoys the work, feels accomplished, and is rewarded for a job well done through some sort of recognition. Interestingly, Herzberg believed that hygiene factors and motivators were mutually exclusive. In other words, if one is dissatisfied with the work he or she is producing, a change in a hygiene factor will not be able to restore satisfaction. Or if a person is not allowed the level of responsibility desired, a salary increase still cannot produce satisfaction and the person will most likely—eventually—leave the position.

DISCIPLINE

A manager must maintain discipline, a function essential to successful employee relations and company productivity. Broadly speaking, **discipline** regards the process by which managers direct actions towards those who do not follow the appropriate procedures, rules, or policies. A systematic approach to discipline is the fairest method, and the one that allows the least problems with employee morale. The discipline applied to employees must be consistent, uniform, and fair. The manager must use judgment to determine the amount and type of discipline called for as each situation arises. There are a number of theories regarding the administration of discipline, and two current ones are known as "progressive discipline" and "discipline without punishment."

Copyright © Mometrix Media. You have been licensed one copy of this document for personal use only. Any other reproduction or redistribution is strictly prohibited. All rights reserved. This content is provided for test preparation purposes only and does not imply an endorsement by Mometrix of any particular political, scientific, or religious point of view.

Progressive discipline includes five specific steps, each progressively more serious than the last. For the first infraction, the manager simply discusses the problem with the employee. The second infraction receives an informal warning and a copy is put in the employee's file. The third one earns a formal warning, which involves a discussion between employee and manager (and possibly a supervisor of the manager as well), a written warning, and a rundown of what will happen if the infraction occurs again. The fourth violation earns the employee a suspension from duties, a warning of dismissal on the next infraction, an oral reprimand, a notice placed in the employee's file, and possibly a demotion. The fifth violation is cause for dismissal of the employee. The company, by following the series of steps, has protected itself against threats of lawsuits filed for unfair dismissal, and further documentation at the time of dismissal is added to the file in case the employee decides to sue or protest at a future time.

Discipline without punishment is a series of four steps that are followed if an employee violates a policy, procedure, or rule. Each step increases the severity of the discipline, but none entails formal punishment. The first step is the oral warning, with a note placed in the employee's file. The second step is a formal notification from manager to employee, stating (in writing) the problem, a suggested correction, and a warning about what will happen if the issue occurs again. The third step is a 'day of decision' in which the employee is given a paid day off to think about his or her desire to have a future with the company. The fourth step is a dismissal (this could occur as the third step for major violations such as sexual harassment or drug use) and is only used after the first three steps have failed. In many cases, being sent home for a day embarrasses the employee and leads to improved behavior (as coworkers know the reason for the absence) so dismissal is a last resort.

COMMUNICATION STYLES

PERSUASIVE

The purpose of the **persuasive communication** is to convince people to do or believe something, a crucial skill in any environment. The essential steps to persuasive communication include:

- **Understanding the audience**: The message should be directed at the needs of the listeners and should be presented in language appropriate to their levels of education and experience, avoiding excess data and statistics.
- **Getting attention**: The speaker should begin with an anecdote or interesting information to get people's attention rather than immediately launching into the direct purpose of the communication.
- **Establishing credibility**: The speaker should outline authority or expertise.
- **Outlining benefits**: The listener's biggest concern is often how something will affect them personally, so explaining how they will benefit is crucial.
- **Using appropriate body language**: This may vary according to audience, but should generally include making frequent eye contact, smiling, avoiding closed body positions (arms folded), and using a persuasive tone of voice.

ASSERTIVE

Assertive communication occurs when the individual expresses opinions directly and actions correlate with words. Assertive communicators are respectful of others and do not bully, but they are firm and honest about opinions. They frequently use "I" statements to make their point: "I would like..." Communication usually includes **cooperative statements**, such as "What do you think?" and distinguishes between fact and opinion. Assertive communicators often engender trust in others because they are consistent, honest, and open in communicating with others. The assertive communicator feels free to express disagreement and anger but does so in a manner that is nonthreatening and respectful of others' feelings. Assertive communication requires a strong sense of self-worth and the belief that personal opinions have value. Assertive communicators tend to have good listening skills because they value the opinions of others and feel comfortable collaborating.

Copyright © Mometrix Media. You have been licensed one copy of this document for personal use only. Any other reproduction or redistribution is strictly prohibited. All rights reserved.
This content is provided for test preparation purposes only and does not imply an endorsement by Mometrix of any particular political, scientific, or religious point of view.

PASSIVE

Passive communication occurs when the individual does not express an opinion directly or verbally but may communicate in a **non-direct or non-verbal manner**. The passive communicator may be non-committal and submissive, often contributing little to a conversation and unwilling to take sides in a conflict. The person may believe that personal opinions are not important and may avoid direct eye contact and appear nervous and fidgety if confronted. The individual may show signs of anxiety, such as wringing hands and crossing the arms. The passive communicator may respond inappropriately when angry, such as by laughing, and may believe that disagreeing with another person will be upsetting to that person or result in conflict, which the communicator wants to avoid. The passive communicator benefits by rarely being blamed for failures (since the person took little part in decision making) and by avoiding conflict (at least in the short term).

AGGRESSIVE

Aggressive communication has some of the same characteristics as assertive communication but lacks the respect for others. The aggressive communicator expresses opinions directly and forcefully but does not want to hear the opinions of others and may denigrate those who speak up or disagree. The aggressive communicator often **bullies** others into agreement but is usually disliked, and this can increase social anxiety and resentment, which may lead to further aggression. The aggressive communicator may use sarcasm or insults, frequently interrupt or talk over other speakers, and intrude on others' personal space. They often believe they are superior to others or more intelligent and may take an aggressive stance (standing upright, feet apart, hands on hips). Hand gestures may include making fists and pointing fingers at others. The benefits of aggressive communication are being in control, getting one's own way, and feeling powerful.

PASSIVE-AGGRESSIVE

A key aspect of **passive-aggressive communication** is negativity, which influences people's thoughts and communication strategies. These communicators often appear quite passive but are angry and resentful. They may appear to be in agreement or cooperating while obstructing or undermining communication efforts. They often complain to others about what someone has said or done but fail to confront the person directly; consequently, they tend to be loners with few friends, and this results in increased feelings of powerlessness. Passive aggressive communicators attempt to get their way **indirectly** by convincing others to support their positions. Facial expressions may be at odds with words, and they may make sarcastic comments meant to belittle the other person. If others don't agree with their positions, passive-aggressive communicators may resort to sabotage but often deny there is a problem and cannot acknowledge their underlying anger.

Project Management

PLANNING FOR PROJECT COSTS

Effective planning for project costs is an important step in creating the budget for the project, and for ultimately delivering the project on or under budget. To accurately **plan for costs**, it is important to have all steps and aspects of the project delineated and planned. Unless the project planner has very recent cost information about a certain aspect of the project, it is important to get actual quotes and cost information for the project from potential vendors. It is then important to take into account how far in the future each aspect of the project will occur—if it is more than six months or so, one should factor increases for inflation or vendor price increases, or at least a contingency factor to account for future uncertainties. As the project progresses and actual invoices are received, these must be tracked and referenced back to the project plan to determine whether the project has stayed within its budget.

TIMELINE, DELIVERABLES, AND OBJECTIVES

A project timeline is a description of the various elements of a project according to the order in time in which they will be achieved. The **timeline** allows the project manager to obtain an overall picture of the time it will take to complete the project. In addition, considering how much time it takes to accomplish the various steps in a project ensures that elements that take longer can be started sooner, so that all are accomplished within

Copyright © Mometrix Media. You have been licensed one copy of this document for personal use only. Any other reproduction or redistribution is strictly prohibited. All rights reserved.
This content is provided for test preparation purposes only and does not imply an endorsement by Mometrix of any particular political, scientific, or religious point of view.

the project's overall goal. A **project deliverable** is a tangible work product. Within a complex project, there will be many deliverables by various participants in the project. For example, in a construction project there will be deliverables along the way, such as completion of the project drawings, completion of the project work plan, submittal of the permit applications, and completion of the construction itself in phases. At each point, the deliverable should be a well-defined outcome that can be assessed as part of the project completion.

SCHEDULING PROJECTS AND MEETING DEADLINES

The first step in scheduling a project is to ensure that a full project plan has been assembled that accounts for how long each step of the project will take, and documents which parts of the project must be completed before others can be. The most obvious example is in building a house—one must lay the foundation before the walls can be built, and the electrical wiring must be installed before the walls are finished. In a complex project with many deadlines, a large wall calendar or computerized equivalent can be used to graph the project elements according to time and to provide a visual representation of progress. If the various tasks require different contractors or work teams, advance notification of the estimated schedule for their work must be completed. As it gets closer to the time for each contributor to do their part of the project, continued communication on timing is important to ensure that **deadlines** are met.

PROJECT PERFORMANCE

The criteria used to assess project performance should be determined in advance for each phase and aspect of the project. Common metrics used to **assess performance** include the following:

- **Budget**: Is the project at, under, or over budget?
- **Time**: Has the project or phase been completed on time? If not, how many days overdue is it?
- **Quality**: Has the work met or exceeded quality standards? For example, has the project passed inspections?
- **Conflict**: Has the project phase created conflict among the team members?
- **Safety**: Has the project phase been completed without safety incidents?

SCOPE, GANTT CHART, AND TASK ANALYSIS

The project scope refers to the objectives and parameters of a particular project. Defining the **scope** in writing is the first step in project management and allows the project manager to assess the tasks and resources necessary to achieve the objectives. Defining the scope also ensures consideration can be made for necessary permits and personnel that need to be involved in the planning and execution of the project. A **GANTT Chart** is a project planning tool that graphically represents the project plan in a bar chart format. The tasks necessary to complete a project are listed on the left side of the chart in a column, starting with the first task and proceeding sequentially. The x-axis of the chart represents time. Bars in the chart represent the duration of each task and illustrate the overlapping nature of each task. The GANTT Chart also provides a visual way to show that certain tasks must be accomplished before others. **Task analysis** refers to a detailed method of defining the varied elements that make up an undertaking and provide a way to document resources that will be necessary in its achievement. It takes into account personnel requirements, tool requirements, documentation requirements, skills necessary (both internal to the organization and external), and how the resources will be provided.

RACI CHARTS

A RACI chart is a method of documented roles and responsibilities for a given project, process, or management system. The RACI is an acronym as follows:

- **R**esponsible—This is the main responsible party for the project or implementation.
- **A**ccountable (or Approver)—This person is accountable for the deliverable or approves the document.
- **C**onsulted—This person is consulted as the technical expert or one affected by the change.
- **I**nformed—This person or group is informed of the change once it has occurred.

Copyright © Mometrix Media. You have been licensed one copy of this document for personal use only. Any other reproduction or redistribution is strictly prohibited. All rights reserved. This content is provided for test preparation purposes only and does not imply an endorsement by Mometrix of any particular political, scientific, or religious point of view.

A RACI chart is used to document how cross-functional teams relate to and are impacted by a proposed change or process. This charting is useful in many large, multifunctional organizations where one's work and projects involve many departments or subject areas that do not directly report to the same line of authority. The RACI chart can provide clarity and ensure that all aspects are considered and documented.

Chapter Quiz

Ready to see how well you retained what you just read? Scan the QR code to go directly to the chapter quiz interface for this study guide. If you're using a computer, simply visit the bonus page at **mometrix.com/bonus948/csp** and click the Chapter Quizzes link.

Copyright © Mometrix Media. You have been licensed one copy of this document for personal use only. Any other reproduction or redistribution is strictly prohibited. All rights reserved.
This content is provided for test preparation purposes only and does not imply an endorsement by Mometrix of any particular political, scientific, or religious point of view.

Risk Management

Transform passive reading into active learning! After immersing yourself in this chapter, put your comprehension to the test by taking a quiz. The insights you gained will stay with you longer this way. Scan the QR code to go directly to the chapter quiz interface for this study guide. If you're using a computer, simply visit the bonus page at **mometrix.com/bonus948/csp** and click the Chapter Quizzes link.

Risk can have different meanings in different industries. In the financial sector, it refers to the probability of losing money in an investment. In the hospital setting, risk evaluates the potential of an error that can negatively impact a patient's safety. In an occupational setting, risk refers to the probability of an employee getting injured while performing a task as well as how severe the injury would be. Risk can also evaluate the fiscal loss due to accidents, both to property and to employees.

Hazard Identification and Analysis Methods

JOB SAFETY ANALYSIS

Job safety analysis (JSA) is an approach to safety that determines specific behaviors within a defined operation that are appropriate. JSA evaluates an operation by looking at each activity performed by employees and then identifying all risks that correspond to those activities. JSA provides specific instructions and procedures for completing each of the identified actions appropriately to minimize risks and maximize safety. This analysis also considers a variety of different job components including motion, efficiency based on time, specific movements, and pace. It looks at both normal job conditions as well as examining job activities related to possible emergencies or non-routine conditions, which is when accidents most commonly occur. JSA is often incorporated into safety training programs and operations guides.

HAZOP (HAZARD AND OPERABILITY STUDY)

A Hazard and Operability Study (HAZOP) systematically examines and breaks down a complex process or system. The primary goal is to identify problems in the design or engineering issues that have not yet been found. Once issues are identified, the team is tasked with finding competent solutions to mitigate the hazard. A team with various specialties takes the complex process or system and breaks it down into smaller units called nodes. A minimum team of 4 or 5 experts is recommended. And teams should not exceed 7 or 8 people as larger groups tend to slow the process considerably. A standard set of guide words is applied to the various parts of each node. For example, the guide words *no* and *not* indicate a complete negation of the design intent. Other guide words include *reverse*, *more*, and *less*, which can be applied to parameters such as flow rate, temperature, level, and pressure. The result of a careful and well executed HAZOP is greater safety and process efficiency.

QRA (QUANTITATIVE RISK ANALYSIS)

A Quantitative Risk Analysis is a technique of project management. The outcomes of such an analysis can impact: costs, schedules, resources, and budgets. In a QRA, the probability of a given risk is ascertained along with the impact of such an event happening. These risks are quantified using probability, which measures how likely a risk is to happen and the level of significant impact should the event occur. There are many methods available to do this, including conducting interviews, reviewing historical data, analyzing threats, strengths and weaknesses, etc. Often QRA is used to analyze human health risk from exposure to toxic substances. Models take into account ingestion, inhalation, and absorption pathways. Once the risk probability and impact are determined, ways to mitigate such risks can be strategized.

Copyright © Mometrix Media. You have been licensed one copy of this document for personal use only. Any other reproduction or redistribution is strictly prohibited. All rights reserved. This content is provided for test preparation purposes only and does not imply an endorsement by Mometrix of any particular political, scientific, or religious point of view.

HAZARD IDENTIFICATION STUDY

A Hazard Identification Study (HAZID) is conducted early in the design process. It is a technique used to identify hazards related to the process, causes of those hazards, potential consequences should the hazard be realized, and appropriate safeguards for personnel, environment, and equipment. It makes use of Process Flow Diagrams (PFDs), and a team of professionals from different disciplines including, engineering, safety, drafting, etc. HAZID is used to design a process and facility that minimizes risks and mitigates known hazards of the process to environment, equipment, and personnel. This process enables a ranking of risk that can then be used to focus resources on eliminating the most likely and severe risks.

PRELIMINARY HAZARD ANALYSIS (PHA)

Preliminary hazard analysis (PHA) is a method to identify, describe, and rank major hazards of a process. It is typically applied in the early stages of process development, but has also been adapted for broader applications. A portion of the process ("task") is evaluated for hazards by identifying the number of employees exposed, the probability of occurrence, and severity of the injury or loss. The output is typically a code or numerical value that allows for hazards to be ranked by impact. PHA has an advantage in that it can be done in a relatively short period of time if the team is experienced in the process.

SUB-SYSTEM HAZARD ANALYSIS (SSHA)

The **sub-system hazard analysis (SSHA)** method examines subsystems within a process to identify how normal performance, degradation, failure, unintended function, or inadvertent function (proper function but at the wrong time or place) can create hazardous conditions.

Typically done in the design phase of a process, this method is used to address these potential outcomes prior to implementation. Remediation can include redesign to eliminate or minimize the hazard, incorporation of safety devices, or identification of procedures to address the hazard.

In this method, a process or task is broken down into components or sub-systems and related hazards are identified. Each hazard is classified by its **severity** and **likelihood**. Hazards are ranked by their **overall risk,** which is the severity multiplied by likelihood. The design of the sub-system is then evaluated to determine if the hazard can be eliminated, controls or warnings installed, or whether a procedure can be developed to eliminate or minimize the hazard. These controls are then incorporated into the final design of the system.

FISHBONE DIAGRAMS

A **fishbone diagram** (also known as **cause/effect diagrams** or **Ishikawa diagrams)** is a visual technique designed to identify all contributing factors to a failure or negative event. Originally developed as a quality control tool, it can also be applied to determining the **root cause** of a system failure. A failure or negative consequence is identified and placed on one end of a horizontal line. Next, general contributing factors are identified (e.g., people, equipment, systems, materials, etc.) and written at the end of diagonal lines attached to the central line, thus resembling the bones of a fish. Potential causes of a failure for each factor are brainstormed and recoded as branches of the factor line. Likely causes can then be identified from the potential causes and can be addressed to prevent similar failures.

WHAT-IF/CHECKLIST ANALYSIS

A **what-if/checklist analysis** combines a "what-if" analysis with a checklist process to produce a failure evaluation tool that is more robust than either of the two would be on their own.

What-if is a brainstorming technique that is used to identify events and their potential outcomes that could impact a process. A **team leader** guides the group through the process to keep the team within the confines of the process being evaluated. The phrase "what if…" is used to identify potential negative events. Once events have been identified, the team assesses each one for the likely source of errors and whether the result has an acceptable level of risk. For those events deemed unacceptable, **corrective actions** are identified and

Copyright © Mometrix Media. You have been licensed one copy of this document for personal use only. Any other reproduction or redistribution is strictly prohibited. All rights reserved. This content is provided for test preparation purposes only and does not imply an endorsement by Mometrix of any particular political, scientific, or religious point of view.

implemented before the event can occur. This process is limited in that only events that are considered can be evaluated and has a high level of subjectivity.

A **checklist analysis** relies on published standards, codes, or industry practices to determine whether a process meets all the criteria. Responses can be "yes," "no," or "not applicable." This method relies on a walk-through method to verify the existence of necessary controls or processes.

The **what-if/checklist** combination uses the brainstorming process to identify controls necessary to address the failures anticipated by the group.

CHANGE ANALYSIS

Change within an organization, be it a process or policy, can result in altering the existing risk level in an organization. Thus, any proposed change should be analyzed for its impact on the process or organization and whether the resultant risk level is still acceptable to management.

Aspects to be evaluated should include the difference in the organization both before and after the change is implemented, the financial impact of the change, any safety impacts of the change, and who, both inside and outside of the organization, will be impacted by the change and how. The assessment should also identify the needed training, personnel, equipment, or program modifications, as well as the associated costs necessary to reach the new operational state.

ENERGY TRACE AND BARRIER ANALYSIS (ETBA)

Energy trace and barrier analysis (ETBA) is a qualitative method that identifies potential hazards by tracing **energy flow** through a system or process, evaluating any point where energy enters a system, how the energy interacts with the system, and where the energy exits the system. In this model, a "mishap" is identified by an undesired transfer of energy to a "target." A **target** can be a person, process, or property that receives the energy. If the energy transferred has an unwanted result, a **barrier** or control must be identified. A barrier must either contain or direct the hazardous energy to avoid the target or reduce the impact. Barriers can include physical (engineering controls) and procedural (administrative controls) means. ETBA is often a component of a management oversight risk tree (MORT) risk assessment.

SYSTEMATIC CAUSE ANALYSIS TECHNIQUE (SCAT)

Systematic cause analysis technique (SCAT) is a post-incident technique that is used to quickly identify the root cause of accidents and near misses. The intent is to determine the **system failures** that need to be corrected to prevent similar losses, damage, or injuries in the future. The foundational theory of SCAT is that all accidents have the same basic causes and that all causes are mainly due to **management system** inadequacy.

Utilizing a chart, the incident is analyzed sequentially by way of a "domino-effect" back to the root cause. Starting with the incident, the team first classifies the type of event and then identifies the **immediate cause** (sub-standard acts or conditions that allowed the event to occur). Continuing along the chart, the team next identifies **basic causes** (personal or system factors) which ultimately lead to the control areas that resulted in the incident, such as inadequate programs, standards, or compliance that management can address. The chart utilizes **standardized event and cause descriptions** so that the tool is broadly applicable to most incidents or near misses.

Risk Analysis

Risk assessment is one of the elements of risk management. Risk assessment includes determination, appraisal, and analysis of risk. The personal attitudes and biases of individuals involved in this process often impact the outcome. Risk assessment can be separated into two different main areas: risk determination and risk evaluation. Risk determination is the process of using investigative techniques and statistical probability to pinpoint possible risks, the likelihood of a resulting accident, and the potential undesired outcomes. Risk

Copyright © Mometrix Media. You have been licensed one copy of this document for personal use only. Any other reproduction or redistribution is strictly prohibited. All rights reserved. This content is provided for test preparation purposes only and does not imply an endorsement by Mometrix of any particular political, scientific, or religious point of view.

evaluation takes a closer look at the identified risks and can be further divided into two areas: risk aversion and risk acceptance. Risk aversion seeks to evaluate how effective certain safety programs, equipment, or training might be at eliminating the risk or at least reducing it. Risk acceptance analyzes risks by weighing factors such as financial and non-monetary costs to determine which risks are acceptable to the organization and do not warrant action.

The following risk analysis approach combines efforts to maximize designated financial resources in accomplishing the highest or most effective level of risk reduction. It can be divided into six steps:

1. A risk index should be calculated based on analysis of the known risks and controls that are currently in place. This involves generating hazard and control scores for further analysis.
2. An initial ranking should be constructed of different departments or identified elements in the operation by determining the relative risk associated with each. The element with the highest risk index often has extensive resources already designated and may not need further attention.
3. A percent risk index should also be determined for each element
4. Total financial exposure, known as composite exposure dollars, for each department or element should be calculated
5. Total composite risk for each department or element should be calculated utilizing composite exposure dollars and the percent risk index
6. The final step is determining the final ranking of each department or element for guiding decisions on resource allocation

CHEMICAL RISK ASSESSMENT

The National Academy of Sciences has identified the following four elements of chemical risk assessment:

- Hazard identification – this process considers numerous elements of operations and calculates risks using probability and also incorporates an engineer failure assessment
- Dose-response assessment – details the connection between the number of incidents involving injury or illness and the level and duration of exposure to hazards; this evaluation constructs formulas that describe the relationship of exposure, or dose, to injury and illness
- Exposure assessment – determines the number of people exposed to hazards, as well as the characteristics of that population, and the overall level of exposure
- Risk characterization – this evaluation considers all elements of an exposure and the related information in a single analysis

Risk Evaluation

Quantitative calculations for risk typically require numeric values for **probability**, **frequency**, and **severity**, to arrive at a final statement of risk. Expressed as a formula, $R = p \times f \times s$. Values for probability, frequency, and severity must be determined in an objective fashion so that the result of the calculation provides meaningful guidance for management. For example, values must be established such that the resultant value for a cut requiring stitches and a fatality have widely varying values. The last element is to determine ranks (e.g., High/Medium/Low, Danger/Caution/Warning) so that, when evaluated side-by-side, an action plan that is both economically feasible and effective at protecting employee health and safety can be created.

RISK ASSESSMENT MODELS

Two commonly cited models of risk management are the history, vulnerability, maximum threat, and probability (HVMP) model used by the US Federal Emergency Management Agency (FEMA) and the

Copyright © Mometrix Media. You have been licensed one copy of this document for personal use only. Any other reproduction or redistribution is strictly prohibited. All rights reserved. This content is provided for test preparation purposes only and does not imply an endorsement by Mometrix of any particular political, scientific, or religious point of view.

seriousness, manageability, urgency, and growth (SMUG) model developed by the Australian Natural Disasters Organization. Both methods tend to produce similar results.

- HVMP—For each risk, the four factors of history, vulnerability, maximum threat, and probability are assigned a score and a weighting factor, the product and summary of which are the quantified threat level; the higher the score, the higher the risk.
- SMUG—Each risk is assessed using four factors: seriousness, manageability, urgency, and growth. Similar to the FEMA model, each factor is assigned a qualitative score of high, medium, and low and then assigned a numerical score. The sum of the individual scores represents the quantified threat level; again, the higher the score, the higher the risk.

RISK FINANCING

Risk financing includes analysis and decision making regarding the allocation of risks, whether retained by the facility or transferred via insurance purchase. This involves:

- Tracking and trending data regarding losses and potential exposures for the organization
- Completing insurance applications and renewals
- Collaborating with brokers, underwriters, and actuaries to determine risk financing needs for the organization
- Evaluating lines of coverage, limits, and deductibles to ensure that potential exposures are adequately covered
- Exploring risk financing options, including insurance purchase, retention, captives, and risk retention groups and determining the best options to meet the needs of the organization
- Monitoring and evaluating the effectiveness of the organization's risk financing program

The Risk Management Process

The risk management process typically involves five steps to complete when addressing issues:

1. Identify and analyze loss exposures — The process of **risk identification** helps determine those risks that create loss exposure to the organization. The process of **risk analysis** attempts to determine the potential severity of loss to the organization should the identified risk occur.
2. Consider alternative risk techniques — Risk techniques involve two strategies:
   a. **Risk control** — preventing or mitigating the impact of losses
   b. **Risk financing** — paying for unavoidable losses
3. Select those risk management techniques that are best suited to manage the specific risk.
4. Implement the selected risk management technique.
5. Evaluate and monitor the effectiveness of the chosen technique in managing the identified risk.

RISK MANAGEMENT PLANS

The **risk management plan** is a written document that outlines the purpose, structure, and key responsibilities of the organization's risk management program. The plan should identify the **authority** and any delegation of authority for operation of the risk management program. A common example of this would be a statement such as "The governing body has the ultimate responsibility for worker safety, and it delegates authority for implementation of a risk management program to the organization's administration." The **scope** of the program is summarized in the plan, including such activities as identification, assessment, and control of losses. **Program elements and objectives** of the program are outlined, including specific elements such as insurance administration, claims management, and complaint resolution. The plan should also outline the **key job roles** required to operationalize the program, along with a summary of how risk management integrates with other operations in the organization. Finally, the plan should include the **approval** of the program, along with the attestation of required approvers.

Copyright © Mometrix Media. You have been licensed one copy of this document for personal use only. Any other reproduction or redistribution is strictly prohibited. All rights reserved. This content is provided for test preparation purposes only and does not imply an endorsement by Mometrix of any particular political, scientific, or religious point of view.

DEVELOPING RISK MANAGEMENT PLANS

Proper risk management planning procedures must consider all potential risks, the likelihood of each risk, and a plan for mitigating the risks. It will include being prepared for events that disrupt production processes, damage the company's reputation, injure employees, or result in a release of hazardous chemicals. Risks to be considered include the following:

Natural Disasters – What natural disasters are likely in the area? For example: flooding, earthquakes, tornadoes, hurricanes, etc. What physical and structural measures are in place to mitigate the effects?

Product Malfunction or Contamination – Depending on the business type, an extreme product malfunction or product contamination (in the case of food) is a potential risk. Risk management planning for these types of risks should include a communication plan and a recall plan.

Pandemic flu or other widespread disease outbreak – Planning for disease outbreaks should include how workers will be protected, how workers will be notified if the facility must close, and protocols regarding medicine or vaccine distribution to workers.

Labor strike – Although the business itself may not be unionized; it can be affected by labor strikes in related businesses. For example, a strike in the transportation sector can disrupt a business. Proper risk management planning includes being prepared for disruptions in external services such as transportation and shipping.

Training Lapse – Consider the possibility and likelihood that an employee has not received the proper training or has not remembered the proper procedure. Management systems should be in place to evaluate whether employees have received the proper training and that they understand how to apply the training in a given situation.

Equipment Failure – Consider what types of equipment failure would be catastrophic. Risk management includes developing a relevant preventive maintenance program and stocking relevant spare parts to prevent equipment failures and respond to them if they occur.

Document Loss – Important documents may be lost through failure to implement robust data backup and file storage (both onsite and offsite) and through failure to enforce policies that require employees to store important documents on central servers rather than individual computers. Risk management should consider which documents are essential to the running of the business and to regulatory compliance and take steps to ensure that they are protected from loss.

The Costs and Benefits of Risk Assessment Process

Performing a risk analysis with costs and benefits assigned to alternative outcomes can help to provide a business case for implementing control measures. For example, if the problem to be analyzed is high levels of lead found in workers blood screens, begin by finding the current costs related to medical treatment, time lost from sickness, etc. Then, determine the costs and benefits related to implementing various control measures. Assign costs to the periodic industrial hygiene and medical monitoring testing required for high lead exposure. Consider the implementation of various control measures; for example, ventilation can be improved, process changes may be able to be made, or hygienic practices could be improved. Assign costs to each of these control measures, and then determine the benefit of a certain percentage of blood lead levels being decreased below the OSHA action level. Ensure that the costs and benefits are compared on an equal time frame.

Copyright © Mometrix Media. You have been licensed one copy of this document for personal use only. Any other reproduction or redistribution is strictly prohibited. All rights reserved.
This content is provided for test preparation purposes only and does not imply an endorsement by Mometrix of any particular political, scientific, or religious point of view.

Insurance and Risk Transfer Principles

METHODS OF MANAGING RISK

Risk transfer is when the degree of potential loss is known or unknown and is no longer managed by the primary entity. Risk can be transferred by hiring subcontractors to conduct the work, purchasing insurance, or by including contractual language such as indemnification.

Risk control is when the degree of potential loss is known and measures are put in place to keep the risk at an established threshold. Control methods can include contractual language, such as establishing parameters for a project or by environmental, physical, or chemical hazard control methods, such as engineering, administrative, and personal protective equipment methods.

Risk acceptance is when the degree of potential loss is known and is below the predetermined acceptable threshold established by management. Risk can never be completely eliminated—the goal is to reduce it to the lowest level possible while still considering economic, personnel, and industry standards.

INSURANCE

Insurance of all types operates on the principle of spreading out risk over a large pool of people or businesses by charging a fee (called a premium) based upon the likelihood of a loss or claim against the insurance. The insurance company will then cover the cost of the loss, whether it's the cost of replacing a car if lost in an accident or the cost of treating an employee's injury. In worker's compensation insurance, the premium is calculated based on the job classification of the employees covered and the employer's history of work-related injuries compared to other companies in similar businesses. To calculate this last portion, the past three years' history (in terms of number of recordable injuries and total costs) are combined into an experience modifier, or x-mod. Having a better injury record than others in the same SIC code results in an x-mod of less than 1.0 and becomes an economic advantage because the company will pay less for worker's compensation insurance.

Important insurance terms to note:

- **Insurance:** the transfer of risk from an organization to an insurance company, which reimburses the organization for losses.
- **Insurance policy:** a legal agreement between the insured (who transfers risk) and the insurer (who accepts risk) whereby the insurer agrees to pay for certain losses incurred by the insured.
- **Declarations page:** a document that names the insured and lists the type of coverage and other identifiers such as the policy number, term dates, policy limits, and deductibles.
- **Exclusions:** items listed in the policy that the insurer will not pay. A common exclusion in a professional liability policy is an intentional or criminal act or a punitive damages award.

REDUCING RISK IN CONTRACTS

Insurance and indemnification provisions are two critical methods of reducing risk in contracts. Indemnification provisions require the parties to a contract to hold each other harmless (i.e., release from liability) for its own negligent acts. An effective indemnification provision within a contract specifies that each party is responsible for its own actions and will reimburse the second party for any damages arising from its own actions. A second critical method is to require the parties to obtain and maintain insurance in amounts sufficient to satisfy the indemnification obligations of the contract. Specific insurance requirements will vary with the type of contract. For example, a contract for professional services will require the service provider to

Copyright © Mometrix Media. You have been licensed one copy of this document for personal use only. Any other reproduction or redistribution is strictly prohibited. All rights reserved. This content is provided for test preparation purposes only and does not imply an endorsement by Mometrix of any particular political, scientific, or religious point of view.

maintain professional liability insurance, whereas a maintenance contract might require property, automobile, and workers' compensation coverage.

Chapter Quiz

Ready to see how well you retained what you just read? Scan the QR code to go directly to the chapter quiz interface for this study guide. If you're using a computer, simply visit the bonus page at **mometrix.com/bonus948/csp** and click the Chapter Quizzes link.

Copyright © Mometrix Media. You have been licensed one copy of this document for personal use only. Any other reproduction or redistribution is strictly prohibited. All rights reserved.
This content is provided for test preparation purposes only and does not imply an endorsement by Mometrix of any particular political, scientific, or religious point of view.

Advanced Application of Key Safety Concepts

Transform passive reading into active learning! After immersing yourself in this chapter, put your comprehension to the test by taking a quiz. The insights you gained will stay with you longer this way. Scan the QR code to go directly to the chapter quiz interface for this study guide. If you're using a computer, simply visit the bonus page at **mometrix.com/bonus948/csp** and click the Chapter Quizzes link.

Safety Through Design

The best time to consider how a project or process can be designed to positively impact safety is in the design phase. Proper process design yields a work flow and layout that does not provide the opportunity for human error that will result in injuries. For example, material handling is performed to eliminate lifting of loads more than 26 pounds. Machines are designed with appropriate guarding to eliminate pinch point hazards and with safety interlocks that prevent operation out of sequence. Designing processes to eliminate hazards is always the best course of action because humans are difficult to prevent from making mistakes 100% of the time; people often make unsafe choices out of hurriedness or ignorance. In addition, unsafe acts may not always result in injury, but injuries do often result from unsafe acts.

BASIC SAFETY THROUGH DESIGN

The hierarchy of controls refers to the preferred methods of controlling health and safety hazards. In order of most preferred first, these include the following:

1. Elimination is completely eliminating the hazard through process changes.
2. Substitution is substituting a lesser hazard, for example, changing from an organic solvent parts washer to an aqueous parts washer.
3. Engineering controls are physical modifications to a work station that serve to reduce or eliminate hazards. An example of engineering controls is to install duct work and exhaust ventilation to remove fumes from the breathing zone of the worker.
4. Administrative control refers to worker management as a means of controlling the hazards. An example of administrative controls is job rotation to limit an employee's exposure to repetitive motion.

Copyright © Mometrix Media. You have been licensed one copy of this document for personal use only. Any other reproduction or redistribution is strictly prohibited. All rights reserved. This content is provided for test preparation purposes only and does not imply an endorsement by Mometrix of any particular political, scientific, or religious point of view.

5. PPE is garments or auxiliary equipment used to protect workers. Examples of PPE include respirators, gloves, Tyvek suits, welding hoods, and steel-toed boots. This is the last item in the hierarchy because PPE is often uncomfortable to wear, and its effectiveness relies on employee compliance, whereas the other methods of hazard elimination do not.

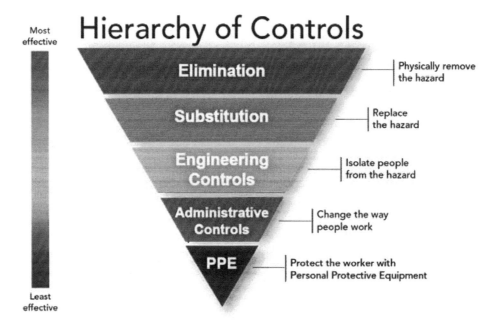

ELIMINATION OF HAZARDS AND SUBSTITUTION TO MITIGATE HAZARDS

Elimination of hazards refers to making process changes that completely eliminate the hazard rather than developing a work-around or protective device. An example would be changing a process to eliminate solvent use. Another example of elimination of hazards would be to change the way parts are delivered to an assembly line that eliminates the need to lifting heavy boxes. Substitution is another mechanism to mitigate hazards. Examples of substitution include substituting chemicals in a process that are of lower toxicity than the original chemical or substituting a tool that requires awkward, forceful grasping with one that uses a more ergonomically favorable grip.

Engineering Controls

Engineering controls to mitigate occupational hazards are changes in the way the process is designed or the physical controls on the process that make it unlikely or impossible to be injured by the hazard. An example of engineering controls is installing ventilation systems to remove hazardous vapors from the worker's breathing zone, eliminating chemical or hazardous dust exposure. Another example is to install permanent access platforms with proper guardrails to provide elevated machinery access that will eliminate the hazard of using an aerial lift or ladder to access at heights. Another example of an engineering control is to install a switch on an electrical testing device or press brake that requires two hands to activate it; this eliminates the possibility of inserting one's hands into the point of operation while it is operational.

VENTILATION

Ventilation refers to the movement of air and exchange of fresh air for trapped air. Ventilation is important in all indoor environments but is especially important if toxic or harmful vapors are in the work area. For example, in a laboratory setting, ventilation hoods are installed, and workers are instructed to use all volatile solvents inside the ventilation hood. The ventilation hood is equipped with a fan to pull air out of the hood and exhaust it outside. This keeps the vapors out of the work area and away from the breathing zone of the worker. In industrial environments, ventilation hoods operate similarly and evacuate vapors to the exterior of the

Copyright © Mometrix Media. You have been licensed one copy of this document for personal use only. Any other reproduction or redistribution is strictly prohibited. All rights reserved.
This content is provided for test preparation purposes only and does not imply an endorsement by Mometrix of any particular political, scientific, or religious point of view.

building, either with capture technology or without depending on the contaminant. The American Conference of Governmental Industrial Hygienists (ACGIH) publishes "Industrial Ventilation: A Manual of Recommended Practice for Design," which outlines ventilation recommendations for types of chemical atmospheres and work environments and is the standard reference text.

MACHINE GUARDING

Machine guarding is a means of providing physical protection between moving machinery parts and a worker's hands, arms, or other body parts. Machine guarding can include shields of physical barriers between the machine and the employee. For example, a shield that encloses the drill bit on a drill press is one type of machine guard; an enclosure around exposed gears and pulley systems is another. Machine guarding also includes safety interlock systems such as light curtains or two-hand switches that protect employees by preventing their hands from coming into the working zone of a machine. An example of a light curtain is a beam of laser light that goes across the working plane of a press brake; if an object (such as the operator's hands) breaks the plane of the light beam, the press mechanism does not come down and cannot injure the hands. Machine guards are an essential aspect of machine safety and prevention of injuries as they do not rely on employee compliance to provide protection.

ISOLATION

Isolating hazards can be an effective way to prevent injuries at lower cost. For example, if one operation produces a very noisy environment, it may be possible to isolate and enclose the operation that prevents noise exposure to a wider area. This will potentially eliminate the need for a hearing protection program among the wider employee population. Another example of isolating hazards applies to painting operations; isolating the painting in a booth allows for localized ventilation control and prevents exposure to harmful organic vapors to employees not directly engaged in painting. A third example of isolating hazards is isolating a laboratory that does microbial pathogen analysis from the larger laboratory. A separate enclosure with separate ventilation can ensure that pathogenic bacteria do not leave the designated work area.

Administrative Controls

Engineering controls for hazards require a redesign of a work process or physical environment that makes it very unlikely that employees will continue to be exposed to the hazard. Examples of engineering controls include installation of ventilation systems to remove hazardous dust from the workplace, installing assistive lifting devices in a manufacturing assembly line to eliminate lifting, and reconfiguring an electrical testing station so that two hands are needed to activate the on switch, therefore, keeping the worker's hands out of electrical shock hazards.

JOB ROTATION

Job rotation is an important consideration to reduce ergonomic risk factors. Once engineering solutions have been considered and implemented to the extent possible, job rotation can be used to ensure that workers do not repetitively use the same muscle groups for their entire work shift. To implement job rotation correctly, one should first do ergonomic evaluations of all job functions of each role to determine what muscle groups are used, how much lifting and reaching a position requires, and how repetitive the tasks are. One can then design a job rotation schedule that rotates jobs to use different muscle groups. Ideally, the rotations are done every two hours, but rotations every four hours are acceptable. One should aim for a mix of upper and lower body work and to mix standing with sitting positions along with some walking movement.

CHEMICAL SUBSTITUTION

Substitution of safer chemicals for more toxic or dangerous chemicals should always be explored as part of harm reduction. A safer chemical is one that is less toxic to workers or poses fewer physical hazards such as flammability. A safer chemical can also result in a product that is safer for use by the end user or public. Using safer chemicals can save a company money on personal protective equipment (not required if employees are

Copyright © Mometrix Media. You have been licensed one copy of this document for personal use only. Any other reproduction or redistribution is strictly prohibited. All rights reserved. This content is provided for test preparation purposes only and does not imply an endorsement by Mometrix of any particular political, scientific, or religious point of view.

not exposed). It can also greatly decrease associated hazardous waste disposal costs if toxic waste does not have to be disposed of.

Personal Protective Equipment

Personal protective equipment is any specialized clothing or equipment worn or used to protect a person from hazards. Personal protective equipment can include HAZMAT suits, goggles, gloves, respiration equipment, hard hats, and more. Personal protective equipment can form an essential part of a safety plan, but it should never be a primary means for controlling hazards. Personal protective equipment forms a barrier between the user and a hazard, but it does not remove the hazard. It is far better to remove the hazard, if possible. Personal protective equipment has limited success because the user must have the right equipment and know how to use it properly, often in an emergency situation. In addition, the personal protective equipment must fit properly and must be well-maintained.

In order to be effective, a program for personal protective equipment must include detailed, written procedures that address how to select, manage, use, and maintain personal protective equipment. These procedures must be enforced and supported by management and should include standards and rules for the following:

- Wearing and using personal protective equipment
- Inspecting and testing personal protective equipment to ensure it is in good condition and working properly
- Maintaining, repairing, cleaning, and replacing personal protective equipment

Another important element of a personal protective program is to ensure that users understand and accept the importance of personal protective equipment. Allowing users to participate in selecting the personal protective equipment they will wear can help them "buy into" the program and be more likely to use their personal protective equipment when it is needed.

EYES AND EARS

Eyes need to be protected from flying particles and objects, splashing liquids, excessive light, and radiation. Types of eye protection include spectacles, with or without side shields, and goggles. Spectacles and goggles protect the eyes from frontal impact injuries, particles, splashes, etc. Side shields are needed for spectacles if there is any danger of particles hitting the eyes from the side. Spectacle lenses can be tinted to prevent light damage and include radiation filters. Different types of spectacles and goggles are available for different tasks. For example, employees working with lasers need laser safety goggles that can filter the specific wavelength and intensity of the laser beam. Hearing needs to be protected from excessive noise, or hearing loss can result. Two main types of hearing protection are muffs and earplugs. Muffs are best for very noisy environments. For the noisiest environments, muffs and plugs can be used together.

HEAD AND FACE

Personal protective equipment for the head can protect wearers from being hit by falling or flying objects, from bumping their heads, and from having their hair caught in a machine or set on fire. Helmets, bump caps, and hard hats are examples of this type of head protection. Hoods and soft caps are another type of head protection that also protect the face and neck. Hoods may include hardhat sections as well as air supply lines, visors, and other protective features. They provide protection from heat, sparks, flames, chemicals, molten metals, dust, and chemicals. Head protection can also aid sanitation by keeping hair and skin particles from contaminating the work. This is especially important in processes involving food and clean room work. Hairnets and caps offer this type of protection. Face shields and welding helmets protect the face from sparks, molten metal, and liquid splashes. They should always be used in conjunction with eye protection such as goggles or spectacles.

Copyright © Mometrix Media. You have been licensed one copy of this document for personal use only. Any other reproduction or redistribution is strictly prohibited. All rights reserved.
This content is provided for test preparation purposes only and does not imply an endorsement by Mometrix of any particular political, scientific, or religious point of view.

HANDS, FINGERS, ARMS, FEET, AND LEGS

Hands, feet, arms, fingers, and legs need protection from heat and cold, sharp objects, falling objects, chemicals, radiation, and electricity. Gloves and mittens protect the hands and fingers and can even extend up the wrist and arm. They can be made of different materials according to the protection needed: for example, lead is used for radiation protection and leather for protection from sparks. Gloves can be fingerless to protect just the hands; finger guards are used to protect just the fingers. Creams and lotions also protect hands and fingers from water, solvents, and irritants. Feet can be protected by the appropriate type of shoes: safety shoes with steel toes and insoles; metatarsal or instep guards; insulated shoes; and slip-resistant, conductive, or non-conductive soles. Rubber or plastic boots provide protection against water, mud, and chemicals while non-sparking and non-conductive shoes are useful for people working around electricity or where there is a danger of explosion. Shin guards and leggings protect legs from falling and moving objects and from cuts from saws and other equipment.

RESPIRATORY PROTECTION

Respiratory protection can mean ensuring that air for breathing is of good quality or it can mean cleaning air before it is inhaled. Two types of equipment ensure that air is of good quality: self-contained respirators and supplied-air respirators. Air-purifying respirators clean air before it is inhaled. Self-contained breathing apparatuses (SCBA) are an example of a self-contained respirator. SCBAs are usually enclosed in a backpack and provide users with clean, breathable air. Hose masks, air-line respirators, and air-supplied suits and hoods are all examples of supplied-air respirators. These units provide breathable air to the wearer through a hose from an outside source. Air-purifying respirators use filters, cartridges, or canisters to remove particulates and gases from air. Different types of filters, cartridges and canisters are available for different types of contaminants.

BODY PROTECTION

Personal protective equipment for the body provides protection from hazardous materials, biohazards, heat, fire, sparks, molten metal, and dangerous liquids. This clothing is often combined with other types of personal protective equipment, such as respiratory equipment and eye protection. Types of personal protective equipment for the body include the following:

- Coats and smocks to protect clothing from spills
- Coveralls, which may include hoods and boots
- Aprons, which protect the front of a person from spills and splatters
- Full body suits for working with substances that present a danger to life or health (may include cooling units to help lower the wearer's body temperature)
- Fire entry suits
- Rainwear
- High-visibility clothing for people working on road construction or in traffic
- Personal flotation devices for people working around or on water
- Puncture-resistant or cut-resistant clothing for protection from ballistic objects, power saws and other cutting equipment

Some personal protective equipment is designed to be disposable, especially clothing contaminated with hazardous materials.

Chemical Process Safety Management

Chemical process safety management is an OSHA regulation designed to provide safe operation of highly hazardous chemical processes, such as in refineries and large chemical manufacturing plants. The regulation may be found in 29 CFR 1910.119. The overall required elements must document the process, the chemicals used, and the reactor vessel construction and must conduct a hazard analysis that takes into account potential failure paths and how catastrophic releases and explosions can be prevented. In the case of pressure relief

Copyright © Mometrix Media. You have been licensed one copy of this document for personal use only. Any other reproduction or redistribution is strictly prohibited. All rights reserved.
This content is provided for test preparation purposes only and does not imply an endorsement by Mometrix of any particular political, scientific, or religious point of view.

systems, consideration must be made to install and document the type of pressure relief system, and it must be ensured that the valve materials are compatible with the chemicals in the process. Pressure relief systems may be spring-loaded, which provide simple overpressure protection for a tank or piping system. A second type of pressure relief system is a balanced bellows or balanced piston system, which is appropriate to use when superimposed backpressure is variable. Chemical compatibility of tanks, piping, valves, and tools with the reactant and product chemicals must be investigated and documented.

In chemical process safety, detailed process flow diagrams of the entire process must be produced. The process chemistry must be thoroughly documented, and maximum inventories of chemical reactants, intermediates, and products must be accounted for. Safe upper and lower limits of temperature, pressure, and flows must be calculated and documented. Once this is completed, a robust management of change to the process must be implemented that includes a full assessment of potential impacts of process changes. For each change, a documented technical basis for the change must be completed along with an analysis of its impact on employee safety, a list of operational procedures that will need to be altered due to the change, a timeline for the change, and a consideration of authorization needed to implement the change. The hazard assessment portion of chemical process safety can be any accepted method that considers potential failures of the process and how to prevent a resulting catastrophe. Examples of acceptable hazard assessment methods include failure mode analysis, fault tree analysis, and a hazard and operability study.

Redundancy Systems

ENERGY ISOLATION

Hazardous energy is any energy (electrical, mechanical, hydraulic, pneumatic, chemical, thermal, or gravity) whose release, if not properly controlled, can result in injury or death. Hazardous energy is controlled by way of **a lockout/tagout (LOTO) system**.

An **energy isolation device** is a mechanical device that prevents the release or transmission of hazardous energy. Such devices include manual circuit breakers, disconnect switches, line valves, and blocks. **Tagout devices** are warnings attached to energy-isolating devices, prohibiting use of the device or re-energizing during maintenance or service.

In the **tagout-plus** process, the employer opts to use tags on an energy isolation device that has the ability to be locked into the safe position. However, the employer is required to implement additional safeguards that will provide the same level of protection as a lockout device. These safeguards may include removing the switch assembly, physically blocking the switch, opening an additional isolation device, or removing valve handles.

VENTILATION

LABORATORIES

Laboratory **ventilation systems** are used to remove hazardous contaminants from the breathing zone of employees. International Mechanical Code requires mechanical exhaust whenever the environment exceeds 25% of the lower explosive limit or the airborne concentration exceeds 1% of the listed median lethal dose (LD_{50}) of any substance used in the area.

In past design specifications, each **zone** (e.g., fume hood or storage location) was required to have an independent duct and fan system. Changes to the International Mechanical Code have allowed system designs to include ventilation **manifolds** for separate zones. While this has the advantage of reducing the energy cost and space required for multiple discrete ventilation systems, the disadvantage is that multiple zones are tied to a single fan. Thus, the Code has instituted the requirement of a **redundant fan system** which can continue to remove contaminants in the event of a failure or planned maintenance of the primary fan. The redundant or backup fan must be able to maintain equivalent volume discharge as the primary unit.

Copyright © Mometrix Media. You have been licensed one copy of this document for personal use only. Any other reproduction or redistribution is strictly prohibited. All rights reserved. This content is provided for test preparation purposes only and does not imply an endorsement by Mometrix of any particular political, scientific, or religious point of view.

FACILITIES THAT WORK WITH RADIOACTIVE MATERIALS

The Department of Energy specifies the system requirements for ventilation systems in facilities that handle or process radioactive materials. The ventilation system maintains a **negative pressure** in each zone so that any material that escapes does not contaminate occupied areas. Systems are designed so that air flows from a **secondary confinement zone** (areas containing airborne radioactive particles or designed as safety buffers) into the **primary confinement zone** (areas of high airborne radiation concentration where personnel are excluded from entering).

This ventilation system must have a redundant system of fans, fan motors, or backup power supplies in the event of a power outage, emergency, or planned maintenance. The systems must maintain a negative pressure throughout all zones to prevent radiation from entering occupied areas.

Common Workplace Hazards

ELECTRICAL HAZARDS AND CONTROLS

Electricity is dangerous due to the potential for shock and electrical burns. Basic electrical safety for non-electricians includes the following: never use tools or equipment with worn or frayed wiring or that do not have the wire insulation intact, never use cords with damaged prongs or if the ground (round) prong is missing, do not use electricity around water (water is a good conductor of electricity and amplifies the risk), do not enter electrical panels, especially if they are high voltage, always be aware of the voltage you are working with, be familiar with basic first aid for victims of electrical shock, and never attempt repairs if you are not trained and qualified for electrical work.

The Occupational Safety and Health Administration (OSHA) Electrical Safety Standard (29 CFR 1910.303) considers that guarding and personal protective equipment (electrical safety gloves or other measures) must be taken when employees are exposed to live electrical wires greater than 50 volts. Many companies have adopted more stringent requirements that require protection if exposure levels are greater than 30 volts. Electrical safety gloves must be worn, and untrained and unauthorized employees must stay at least 10 feet from the energized parts. There must be a means of triggering an emergency stop available to the employee, and there must be personnel on site who are trained in first aid measures for electric shock if employees will be exposed to electricity above these threshold levels.

ARC FLASH

Arc flash is an event in which electrical current jumps (or flows) through an air gap between two conductors; for example, broken or torn wire insulation can cause conditions that promote arc flash, as can dust buildup in an electrical panel. Arc flash is an extremely dangerous condition due to the tremendous energy released during the event. The arc flash explosion can cause severe burns, and the explosive concussion can throw an employee some distance from the event. It can also cause hearing damage. Unfortunately, the susceptibility of a given electrical panel to arc flash is not apparent to the naked eye, making an arc flash assessment and electrical panel labeling program important.

All electrical workers must be trained in the basic elements of arc flash safety. All electrical panels must be evaluated by qualified personnel to determine the arc flash potential. This evaluation considers the potential release of energy that would occur (based on voltage and load) were there to be an arc flash in that panel. From this, the panel is rated on a scale of 0 to 4. Personnel that will be working in the panel must wear personal protection suits rated for the appropriate arc flash hazard level. In addition, workers must be trained to set up appropriate exclusion zones around areas where work will occur on electrical panels. Workers must be trained in emergency procedures and first aid procedures for victims of electrical shock and burns.

GFCI

A Ground Fault Circuit Interrupter (GFCI) protects against the most common type of electrical shock, a ground fault. A ground fault occurs when an electrical current finds an alternate 'path of least resistance' to the ground

Copyright © Mometrix Media. You have been licensed one copy of this document for personal use only. Any other reproduction or redistribution is strictly prohibited. All rights reserved.
This content is provided for test preparation purposes only and does not imply an endorsement by Mometrix of any particular political, scientific, or religious point of view.

(or earth) than the ground wire. A person receives a shock when this path of least resistance is through their body. GFCIs are commonly used and required in wet areas such as bathrooms or kitchens, since the presence of water increases the chance that electrical current will experience a ground fault. Water is very conductive and provides an easy path for electrical current. The GFCI works by comparing the current that exits the unit to the current returning to it; if a significant difference is detected, it immediately cuts off the electricity flow through the circuit and protects from the risk of electrical shock.

HAZARDS AND CONTROLS ASSOCIATED WITH WORKING AT HEIGHTS

Elevated work platforms or working at heights pose a fall hazard that can be fatal if an employee falls on his or her head. When using a platform, there should be guardrails that conform to Occupational Safety and Health Administration (OSHA) guardrail guidelines. Employees should be trained in and use fall protection harnesses; the harness must be tied to a place that will safely arrest the fall and not tip over any equipment. If the height is accessible using a ladder, make sure the ladder is on a stable surface and that a coworker is available to hold the ladder and position it so that reaching from the ladder is not necessary. Never stand on the top step of the ladder.

SIX-FOOT REGULATION PERTAINING TO FALL PROTECTION SYSTEMS

Personal fall arrest systems (harnesses, for example), guardrails, and safety net systems must be used whenever workers are employed in construction or walking in work areas six feet or more from the lower level.

OSHA regulations require that the "six-foot" rule be applied to the following situations:

- Workers must be protected from falling through holes or floor openings like skylights or stairwells. Skylights may be covered with solid structural materials. Another method may be to erect a guardrail system around floor openings or skylights.
- Workers employed in framework or reinforcing steel frame construction must be protected by personal arrest systems and/or safety nets.
- Workers who must walk through or work near trenching areas or excavations must be protected by fences, barricades, or guardrail systems if the excavation is six feet or more.

TYPES OF FALL PROTECTION SYSTEMS

When determining what type of fall protection to employ, it is important to consider the task the worker will be performing while using the system. For tasks that do not require much side-to-side moving, a vertical lifeline may be best. If the job includes multiple workers, a horizontal lifeline system may be best. To calculate the clearance required to use a vertical lifeline system, add the lanyard length and maximum elongation distance to the height of the worker's back D-ring. Then add a margin of safety: three feet is common. Suppose a 5'6" worker is attached to a 10' lanyard that has an elongation distance of 3'6". His back D-ring is mounted between his shoulder blades at a height of 4'6". The fall clearance to safely use this lanyard system would be 10' + 3'6" + 4'6" + 3' = 21 feet.

SAFE PRACTICES FOR USING FALL PROTECTION SYSTEMS

For effective fall protection, OSHA recommends that companies adhere to the following practices:

- The company should have a written fall protection plan as part of its overall health and safety plan. The plan should include company rules for how and when to use fall protection equipment.
- The company should follow standard fall protection requirements when fall protection equipment must be used, usually when an employee in a general industry is four feet above the floor, when an employee of a construction company is six feet above the ground, or when an employee is on scaffolding 10 feet above the ground.
- The company should provide correct fall protection equipment and ensure that it is not only used, but is used properly.

Copyright © Mometrix Media. You have been licensed one copy of this document for personal use only. Any other reproduction or redistribution is strictly prohibited. All rights reserved. This content is provided for test preparation purposes only and does not imply an endorsement by Mometrix of any particular political, scientific, or religious point of view.

- The company should inspect, maintain, repair, and replace fall protection equipment regularly.
- The company should provide supervisors and workers with training on how to recognize fall-related hazards and how and when to use fall protection equipment.

A fall protection system can limit or prevent falls. A fall protection system can include safety belts, safety harnesses, lanyards, hardware, grabbing devices, lifelines, fall arrestors, climbing safety systems, and safety nets. Most of these elements stop a fall that has already started and must meet specific standards. Safety belts are worn around the waist while harnesses fit around the chest and shoulders and occasionally the upper legs. Safety harnesses lessen the number and severity of injuries when they arrest a fall because the force is distributed over a larger part of the body. Lanyards and lifelines connect safety harnesses to an anchoring point while grabbing devices connect lanyards to a lifeline. Lanyards absorb energy, so they reduce the impact load on a person when the fall is arrested.

PERSONAL FALL ARREST SYSTEMS

A personal fall arrest system is a method of stopping a worker from falling from the heights at which he or she is working. Some personal fall arrest systems involve harnesses, hooks, belts, and loops of rope or other suspension mechanisms designed to catch a falling worker. Fall arrest systems must:

- Not subject an employee to a force greater than 900 pounds if a body belt is used
- Not subject an employee to a force greater than 1800 pounds if a body harness is used
- Not allow an employee to fall more than six feet nor come in contact with the floors or objects below

Personal fall arrest systems must also be able to sustain two times the impact caused by an employee falling six feet. The deceleration distance of travel can be no longer than 3.5 feet.

AERIAL LIFTS AND SCISSOR LIFTS

An aerial lift is a basket on an extended arm for lifting workers to heights. A scissor lift accomplishes the same thing but is conveyed upward vertically. Both have guard rails around the platform. Per 29 CFR 1910.67(c)(2)(v), OSHA mandates that workers working from an aerial lift must wear an acceptable personal fall arrest or travel restraint system.

HAZARDS AND CONTROLS ASSOCIATED WITH EXCAVATIONS
TRAINING REQUIREMENTS

As part of a comprehensive injury prevention plan and hazard communication plan, workers who work in an excavation site must be trained on the hazards of an excavation and how they are protected from injury. They should be trained in site-specific emergency procedures. If wearing a harness, the employee must be trained in how to use the harness and how to inspect it to ensure it is working optimally.

SAFETY CONSIDERATIONS WHEN PLANNING PROJECTS

A trenching or excavation project poses many safety hazards that must be carefully considered through a site-specific pre-job planning process; potential cave-ins are the greatest risk. Considerations must be given to the type of soil to be excavated, and cave-in prevention measures will be taken according to the type of soil, location of underground and overhead utility lines, the weather forecast, and the potential for a hazardous atmosphere in the trench or excavation. Consideration must be made for the types of personal protective equipment (PPE) the employees will need. Everyone should wear a high-visibility vest, and if entering excavations of a deep and confined space, employees must wear a harness and lifeline. Provisions should be made for daily inspections for excavation integrity; inspections should also be done when conditions have changed in the excavation (e.g., due to weather).

SOIL TYPES

The type of soil being excavated is important in determining the proper safety measures that must be taken. A qualified soil classification specialist must perform the determination and make the recommendations. The

Copyright © Mometrix Media. You have been licensed one copy of this document for personal use only. Any other reproduction or redistribution is strictly prohibited. All rights reserved. This content is provided for test preparation purposes only and does not imply an endorsement by Mometrix of any particular political, scientific, or religious point of view.

unconfined compressive strength must be evaluated, either in the field or in the laboratory. The unconfined compressive strength is the load at which the soil will fail. The basic soil types are as follows:

- Stable rock—this is natural solid material that can be excavated and remain intact while work is performed in the excavation.
- Type A soil—this is soil that has an unconfined compressive strength of 1.5 tons per square foot or greater. These soils are described as clay, silty clay, sandy clay, or clay loam.
- Type B soil—this is soil that has an unconfined compressive strength of 0.5 to 1.5 tons per square foot. It may be described as crushed rock, angular gravel, silt loam, or sandy loam.
- Type C soil—this is soil that has an unconfined compressive strength of less than 0.5 tons per square foot. This type of soil may have water seeping from it or may be a layered system that reaches into the trench or excavation.

SAFETY REQUIREMENTS

The risk of a cave-in is the greatest risk at an excavation site. Any excavation of greater than five feet deep must have a protective system in place to prevent cave-ins (barricades, sloping side, benching, etc.). If the excavation is greater than twenty feet deep, this protective system must be designed by a registered professional engineer. There are several types of cave-in protection available, such as shoring the sides, sloping the sides to reduce the vertical edge, benching the sides, and shielding workers from the sides. A qualified individual should be consulted when choosing cave-in protection, as site conditions such as soil type, moisture level, and the amount of activity around the excavation must be taken into consideration. Access and egress to the excavation area and the excavation itself must be controlled with barricades and work practice controls. A ladder or ramp must be provided as a means of egress if the depth of the excavation is four feet or greater. The route to the means of egress cannot be more than 25 feet for any employee who may be working in the excavation. The spoil pile (the soil removed from the pit) must be set back from the edge of the excavation at least two feet. This prevents material falling on workers and makes an even walking surface at the edge of the excavation.

CONDUCTING THE REQUIRED DAILY INSPECTION OF AN ONGOING EXCAVATION SITE

Daily inspections of excavation sites are required as a minimum, but inspections can be made at any time a change in work, weather, or environmental conditions makes more frequent inspections desirable. The safety inspector must be alert to all hazardous conditions affecting worker safety, but there are certain commonalities of concern:

- Examine for failure of protective systems, hazardous atmospheres, water accumulation and the ground signs which may indicate a potential collapse of excavation walls
- Means of exit or egress should be inspected. Stairways, ladders, ramps or other safe means of evacuation from trenches are required in ditches or trenches that are 4 feet or more in depth. A worker should not have to travel more than 25 feet to reach a means of safe exit.
- Stability of adjoining walls, buildings, or other nearby structures should be inspected for settling, leaning, or other signs of tipping

HAZARDS AND CONTROLS ASSOCIATED WITH WORKING IN CONFINED SPACES

A confined space is an area with limited entry and exit access that is not designed for regular employee occupancy but is routinely entered for maintenance or other activities. The definition includes spaces that even arms are placed into, not just spaces that can accommodate the entire body. Confined spaces are dangerous because they cannot be exited easily in an emergency, they may have oxygen-deficient atmospheres, and there may be dust or vapors present that can pose a hazard to employees entering them. For this reason, Occupational Safety and Health Administration (OSHA) requires assessments and inventories of potential confined spaces to determine appropriate entry procedures.

Copyright © Mometrix Media. You have been licensed one copy of this document for personal use only. Any other reproduction or redistribution is strictly prohibited. All rights reserved.
This content is provided for test preparation purposes only and does not imply an endorsement by Mometrix of any particular political, scientific, or religious point of view.

PERMIT-REQUIRED AND NON-PERMIT-REQUIRED CONFINED SPACES

There is a significant difference between a permit-required and non-permit required confined space. Confined spaces are areas not designed for continuous employee occupancy, and which have limited means of egress. They may also have the potential for a hazardous atmosphere, either oxygen deficiency, presence of chemical vapors, or extreme temperatures. For this reason, Occupational Safety and Health Administration (OSHA) requires assessments and inventories of potential confined spaces to determine appropriate entry procedures. Entry into a confined space using a permit system is required when there is a potential for oxygen deficiency, explosive atmosphere, and/or chemical vapor exposures. The permit provides a mechanism to track entries and to document that the proper pre-entry procedures have been followed, such as measuring oxygen levels and measuring chemical vapors. Employees must also have an attendant, also known as a hole watch, immediately outside the confined space at all times and emergency equipment on hand in case of emergency.

Permits issued for this purpose must:

- Identify the space to be entered
- Identify the type and nature of the work to be performed and provide substantial justification for issuing a permit
- Be date stamped with the date of authorization and the number of hours or days in which confined-space work has been authorized
- Identify the person or persons who are authorized to enter the confined space. This section of the permit should specify the type of tracking and monitoring system used to control entrance and egress.

WORKING IN PERMIT-REQUIRED CONFINED SPACES

A confined space has the following characteristics:

- A confined space has an area sufficient in size as to accommodate a worker of normal size to enter and perform assigned work with necessary tools and uniform (including PPE).
- A confined space has limited entry and/or egress points which are so constructed as to limit the free passage of employees or rescuers into the area. Holding tanks, grain silos, manure pits, and entry passages to sewage tunnels are confined spaces requiring special methods of access and preparatory measures taken to ensure health and safety under poor atmospheric conditions.
- A confined space is one in which continuous employee occupancy for work purposes cannot be expected to last for an entire 8-hour period of time as would be the case under normal working conditions. OSHA limits the amount of time a worker may be exposed to confined spaces with limited or extremely hazardous atmospheres.

CONFINED SPACE PROGRAMS

A confined space program must contain an inventory of all confined spaces at a site, a formal documented assessment of the potential hazards posed by the space (e.g., Is there a danger of oxygen deficiency? Are there potentially hazardous vapors or fumes present? Is there a risk of high or low temperature environment?). A confined space entry permit must be developed and required to be used for all permit-required confined spaces. All confined spaces must be labeled as such, and the label should identify whether the space is permit required or not. The employees that will enter the confined space must receive appropriate training in the entry procedures and what appropriate emergency procedures are.

To fully implement a confined space safety program, one must be able to evaluate whether a hazardous atmosphere exists inside the confined space. The first assessment that must be made is to determine whether there is an oxygen-deficient atmosphere. For this, an oxygen level meter is needed to confirm that the oxygen content of the air inside the confined space is at least 19.5 percent. Second, if there is any possibility that flammable dust or vapors exist, the air must be analyzed for either dust or organic vapors. Organic vapors can be analyzed using a handheld organic vapor analyzer, and the results can be used to establish whether

Copyright © Mometrix Media. You have been licensed one copy of this document for personal use only. Any other reproduction or redistribution is strictly prohibited. All rights reserved.
This content is provided for test preparation purposes only and does not imply an endorsement by Mometrix of any particular political, scientific, or religious point of view.

respiratory protection is necessary. The confined space entry plan and testing plan should ideally be overseen by an industrial hygienist to ensure that no potential hazards are overlooked.

CONTROLS FOR WORKING IN CONFINED SPACES

Confined spaces include such work areas as tank cars, boilers, silos, underground tunnels, and railroad boxcars. All these spaces have limited entrances and exits and require specific controls to ensure worker safety. Hazards that workers in confined spaces face include toxicity, potential oxygen deficiency, and fire or explosion from flammable or combustible gases or dust. To protect workers, the following actions should be taken:

- Always evaluate a confined space for hazards before workers enter.
- Ensure that the confined space has adequate ventilation.
- Include equipment for suppressing fires and removing smoke and fumes.
- Train workers on safety procedures they need to follow when working in a confined space.
- Institute a buddy system for confined spaces so two workers are always present.

LOCKOUT/TAGOUT

Lockout/tagout refers to the process of isolating hazardous energy during maintenance activities to prevent employee injury. Lockout refers to physically placing a lock on the power source (to isolate electrical energy) or other means of starting the source of hazardous energy. Tagout refers to placing a tag on the switch to indicate that the energy source is isolated and should not be turned back on without following proper procedures. Tagout systems should not be used unless accompanied by the more robust and undefeatable lockout system, although tagout is a best practice for notifying who has placed the equipment in lockout.

TRAINING REQUIREMENTS

The Occupational Safety and Health Administration (OSHA) lockout/tagout regulation lists specific training requirements for employees both initially and on an annual basis. The training must cover the types of hazardous energy that can/should be controlled (not just electrical energy), what are authorized and affected employees, the specific lockout procedures for equipment they will be locking out, the difference between lockout and tagout, why tagout alone is not an approved control of hazardous energy, and the process to commence safe start-up of equipment after lockout.

AUTHORIZED AND AFFECTED EMPLOYEES

An authorized employee under the lockout/tagout regulations is an employee who has been thoroughly trained in the reasons for lockout and the methods to lock out equipment, and has been issued a lock to use. The lock should be personalized by color coding, and/or by the use of personalized tags to notify others who is responsible for a particular lockout. An affected employee is one that has a general awareness of what lockout/tagout is and works near machinery that will be locked out from time to time. However, these employees are not responsible themselves for performing the lockout or for following the steps to safe start-up of equipment after lockout.

HAZARDS ASSOCIATED WITH WORKING AROUND WATER

Although water is essential for human life, in certain work environments it can pose a hazard. Water on walking and working surfaces almost always increases the slipperiness of the surface and contributes to slip, trip, and fall hazards. Water in the work environment can increase the humidity depending on temperature and ventilation; increasing humidity in a warm environment can make employees more susceptible to heat stress. Water that continually moistens an area may contribute to mold and mildew growth, which acts as an irritant to some people. Finally, water is an excellent conductor of electricity. Water amplifies any electrical exposure due to exposed wiring or other electrical hazards and greatly increases the likelihood of electric shock.

Copyright © Mometrix Media. You have been licensed one copy of this document for personal use only. Any other reproduction or redistribution is strictly prohibited. All rights reserved.
This content is provided for test preparation purposes only and does not imply an endorsement by Mometrix of any particular political, scientific, or religious point of view.

'CAUGHT IN' AND 'STRUCK BY' HAZARDS

OSHA defines 'caught-in or between' injuries as harm caused by a person being squeezed, caught, crushed, pinched, or compressed between machinery or parts of equipment. This type of hazard and injury can cause broken bones, amputations, strangulation, or internal injuries. The best control measure for this type of risk is to construct physical machine guards that prevent any body parts from insertion in or near the equipment. Also, workers can help mitigate potential harm by not wearing jewelry (necklaces, and other things that dangle) or loose clothing (un-tucked shirts, etc.). OSHA defines 'Struck by' as an injury caused by the contact or impact of a piece of equipment or object and the injured person. The impact of the object with the person is the cause of the injury. Types of 'Struck by' hazards include: flying objects, falling objects, swinging objects, and rolling objects. These can cause severe injury. Control measures to prevent struck by injuries include enforcing height limits on pallet stacking, toe boards and other barriers, proper training for those operating various equipment and vehicles, etc. Finally, proper PPE is critical, especially hard hats. The hard hat is the best piece of PPE to prevent 'Struck by' injuries due to falling objects.

HAZARDS AND CONTROLS ASSOCIATED WITH HOT WORK

Hot work refers to work capable of generating a source of ignition, such as brazing, welding, soldering, cutting with a torch, and drilling or grinding that potentially create a fire hazard. Employees engaged in hot work must be trained in the hazards posed by the work and how to mitigate them. A hot work program must include assessment of industrial hygiene hazards (exposure to metal dusts and fumes), assessment of noise hazards, assessment of proper personal protective equipment (PPE; eye protection, proper gloves, and respiratory protection if required) and must include an assessment of fire hazards posed by the hot work.

HOT WORK PERMIT SYSTEMS

A hot work permit ensures that safety precautions have been taken for welding or torch cutting activities. The permit is designed as a job aid to check that the work area has been prepared for flying sparks by removing **flammable debris** in a radius around the work area. The work permit should prompt a check that the **fire sprinkler protection system** is in place and functional, and that fire extinguishers of the correct type are staged and ready. The permit should include a provision to test the work environment to ensure there is no **explosive atmosphere**. The permit should document that the employees have received the required training and have the proper PPE available. The permit should include a provision to have a **fire watch** in place for at least thirty minutes after the hot work has been completed, and for the area to be periodically monitored for at least six hours after the work is completed.

SUPERVISOR'S DUTIES FOR HOT WORK

Supervisors are responsible for planning the work and ensuring that the hot work permit system is implemented. The use of the hot work permit checklist is a means of ensuring the proper safety precautions are taken and planning is completed prior to the hot work beginning. The supervisor is responsible for ensuring employees have the proper PPE on hand. Supervisors are responsible for providing the proper manpower and personnel to have a designated fire watch employee if necessary. The supervisor is also responsible for ensuring that employees have received the required safety and operational training to conduct the hot work.

FIRE WATCH

Proper planning for hot work or welding includes having a person to act as fire watch. This is necessary for any activities that have a fire risk. The fire watch person should be trained in the duties and should understand the requirements of the **hot work permit**. The person should be stationed in the area and remain alert for sparks or embers emitted during the work. The person must be prepared to use a fire extinguisher and to alert other workers and authorities in the event of an emergency. Fire watch duties must extend for a minimum of thirty minutes after the hot work is finished, until there is absolutely no chance that any embers remain that could cause a fire. If the fire watch must leave the work area at any time during work, work must be stopped until he or she returns.

Copyright © Mometrix Media. You have been licensed one copy of this document for personal use only. Any other reproduction or redistribution is strictly prohibited. All rights reserved.
This content is provided for test preparation purposes only and does not imply an endorsement by Mometrix of any particular political, scientific, or religious point of view.

WELDING PROJECT HAZARDS

There are several hazards to consider when planning a welding project. The safe use of the compressed gases used must be considered. The types of metals to be welded should be considered to determine whether hazardous metal fumes or dusts will be generated that will require respiratory protection (and specialized equipment that will fit under a welding helmet). The eye hazard posed by exposure to the wavelengths of light emitted by the welding process must be considered and the appropriate welding glasses or face shield obtained. The risk of fire and sparks must be considered, and appropriate protective clothing should be worn.

HEALTH HAZARDS ASSOCIATED WITH HOT WEATHER WORK

Heat exhaustion and heat prostration are different names for the same illness. They are caused by a victim failing to drink enough water to replace fluids lost to sweat when working in a hot environment. Symptoms include the following: cold, clammy skin; fatigue; nausea; headache; giddiness; and low, concentrated urine output. Treatment requires moving the victim to a cool area for rest and replacing fluids. Heat cramps are muscle cramps during or after work in a hot environment. They occur because of excess body salts lost during sweating. Treatment involves replacing body salts by drinking fluids such as sports drinks. Heat fatigue occurs in people who aren't used to working in a hot environment. Symptoms include reduced performance at tasks requiring vigilance or mental acuity. Victims need time to acclimate to the hot environment and training on ways to work safely in a hot environment.

A heat illness is any illness primarily caused by prolonged exposure to heat. Heat stroke occurs when a person's thermal regulatory system fails. Symptoms include lack of sweating, hot and dry skin, fever, and mental confusion. Victims need to be cooled immediately or loss of consciousness, convulsion, coma, or even death can result. Sunstroke is a type of heat stroke caused by too much sun exposure. Heat hyperpyrexia is a mild form of heat stroke with lesser symptoms. Heat syncope affects individuals who aren't used to a hot environment and who have been standing for a long time. The victim faints because blood flows more to the arms and legs and less to the brain and they will need to lie down in a cool area. Heat rash is also called prickly heat. It occurs when sweat glands become plugged, leading to inflammation and prickly blisters on the skin. Treatment can include cold compresses, cool showers, cooling lotion, steroid creams, and ointments containing hydrocortisone. During treatment, victims must keep their skin dry and avoid heat.

CONTROLS FOR REDUCING AND ELIMINATING HEAT STRESS AND THERMAL INJURIES

The keys to reducing heat stress and thermal injuries are stated below:

- Control the source by keeping heat sources away from occupied areas.
- Modify the environment through ventilation, shielding, barriers, and air conditioning.
- Adjust activities by making the work easier, limiting time spent in hot environments, and requiring periodic rest breaks.
- Provide protective equipment such as water-cooled and air-cooled clothing, reflective clothing, protective eyewear, gloves, and insulated materials.
- Incorporate physiological and medical examinations and monitoring to identify high-risk people.
- Develop a training program to help workers acclimatize to hot environments and learn safe work habits.

HEALTH HAZARDS ASSOCIATED WITH COLD WEATHER WORK

Trench foot occurs when a person spends an extended time inactive with moist skin, at temperatures that are cold but not freezing. Bloods vessels in the feet and legs constrict, causing numbness, a pale appearance, swelling, and, eventually, pain. Treatment involves soaking the feet in warm water. However, the numbness can last for several weeks even after the feet are warmed. Chilblains are an itching and reddening of the skin caused by exposure to the cold. Fingers, toes, and ears are the most susceptible. Gentle warming and treatment with calamine lotion or witch hazel can lessen chilblains. Itchy red hives can occur in some people when their

Copyright © Mometrix Media. You have been licensed one copy of this document for personal use only. Any other reproduction or redistribution is strictly prohibited. All rights reserved.
This content is provided for test preparation purposes only and does not imply an endorsement by Mometrix of any particular political, scientific, or religious point of view.

bodies develop an allergic reaction to the cold. The hives may be accompanied by vomiting, rapid heart rate, and swollen nasal passages. Cold compresses, cool showers, and antihistamines can help relieve the symptoms.

Frostbite and hypothermia are the most dangerous cold hazards. Frostbite occurs when the temperature of body tissue goes below the freezing point leading to tissue damage. The amount of damage depends on how deeply the tissue is frozen. Severe frostbite can lead to the victim losing a damaged finger or toe. Frostbitten skin is usually white or gray and the victim may or may not feel pain. To treat frostbite, the damaged body part must be submerged in room-temperature water so it can warm up slowly. Hypothermia occurs when a victim's body temperature drops below normal. Symptoms include shivering, numbness, disorientation, amnesia, and poor judgment. Eventually, unconsciousness, muscular rigidity, heart failure, and even death can result. Warm liquids and moderate movement can help warm a victim who is still conscious. An unconscious victim needs to be wrapped warmly and taken for medical treatment.

CONTROLS FOR REDUCING AND ELIMINATING COLD STRESS AND THERMAL INJURIES

A cold environment can be measured according to the air temperature, humidity, mean radiant temperature of surrounding surfaces, air speed, and core body temperature of people in extremely cold temperatures. The keys to preventing injury from cold environments are as follows:

- Modifying the environment by providing heat sources and using screens or enclosures to reduce wind speed
- Adjusting activities to minimize time in cold areas and requiring regular breaks in a warm area
- Providing protective clothing with insulated layers that both wick away moisture and provide a windscreen
- Providing gloves, hats, wicking socks, and insulated boots to protect vulnerable extremities
- Allowing employees time to become acclimated to the cold environment
- Training employees on practices and procedures for staying safe in a cold environment

HAZARDS AND CONTROLS FOR INFRARED RADIATION AND LASERS

Sources of infrared radiation include fire, stoves, and heating elements. This **radiation** can cause eye disorders such as scotoma, swelling, hemorrhages, lesions, and cataracts. Controlling these dangers requires limiting exposure to the infrared radiation and wearing protective eye gear. Sources of **high-intensity visible light** include welding, carbon arc lamps, and some lasers. This type of light can damage the eyes. To prevent or control the damage, the following actions should be taken:

- Enclose the source of light.
- Limit the intensity of the source.
- Use shields, guards, or filters to protect eyes from the light source.
- Require workers to wear protective eye gear.

Lasers are used in multiple fields, including construction, mining, health, and weapons. Lasers can damage the eyes and skin depending on the laser's intensity, wavelength, and duration. To control the hazards related to lasers, the following actions should be taken:

- Enclose the laser source.
- Eliminate reflective surfaces.
- Require protective clothing and eye gear.
- Train users on safe procedures for using lasers.

Copyright © Mometrix Media. You have been licensed one copy of this document for personal use only. Any other reproduction or redistribution is strictly prohibited. All rights reserved.
This content is provided for test preparation purposes only and does not imply an endorsement by Mometrix of any particular political, scientific, or religious point of view.

Facility Life Safety Features

PUBLIC SPACE SAFETY

Public spaces are governed from a life safety standpoint by the Uniform Fire Code and Uniform Building Code. There are regulations that govern the use of public spaces regarding ensuring fire extinguishers are available, that occupancy limits are observed, and that there are no open flames used. Routes of emergency egress must be clearly marked and available. There must be an unobstructed path from each area of a public space to the exit of no more than fifty feet. Exits must not be blocked, there must be emergency lighting, and the exits must be marked. The emergency exit doors must open with a push bar (i.e., people are not required to turn doorknobs in an emergency to get out of the room). Fire sprinklers are always required in new construction and are often required as retrofits. Fire alarm systems must be in place and tested on a routine basis.

MAXIMUM FLOOR AND OCCUPANCY LOADS

For life safety reasons, uniform fire and building codes specify the maximum occupancy loads. The purpose of a maximum occupancy load is to ensure that a room or space is not so crowded that people will not be able to make an orderly escape in the event of an emergency. Occupancy loads are dependent upon the classification of the space (e.g., retail, commercial, industrial, and assembly) and upon the area of the space. Other factors that are considered are the number of exits available and the size of the exits (e.g., double doors can accommodate more people exiting than single doors). Maximum floor loads are important when considering how many people can be on an elevated or supported structure. An example is on a mezzanine, balcony, or elevated deck structure. OSHA regulations on walking and working surfaces (29 CFR 1910.22) also require employers to ensure floors can support workers at elevated heights, including the weight of any equipment on the elevated surface. One should engage the services of a structural engineer to make the calculations.

Fleet Safety

Fleet safety is comprised of the policies and procedures implemented by management to protect employees and vehicles in a commercial fleet. A fleet safety program should address the following elements:

1. **Identify** all drivers: Evaluate all jobs and determine everyone who will be driving company vehicles as part of their work duties.
2. **Express** management's commitment to fleet safety.
3. Insert a robust **hiring process** for drivers, including background checks.
4. **Train** all drivers on safe driving habits and on any specialized equipment, such as forklifts.
5. Institute a method of continual or periodic **monitoring** driving habits.
6. **Manage accidents** immediately by having procedures in place for responding to and investigating all incidents and near misses.
7. Have written policies and procedures.
8. Institute a vehicle **inspection and maintenance** program.

Safe driving behavior starts before an employee gets behind the wheel. **Training** on defensive driving behavior, both initially and on a recurring basis, provide the employee with management's expectations before they drive a company vehicle. **Testing** employees after they have been trained and periodically during their employment is one method to **evaluate** their knowledge of safe driving behavior.

Continuous monitoring of driver behavior is an essential element of any fleet safety program. Ride-along evaluations, public hotline numbers, accident investigations, and onboard computer monitoring systems (**telematic systems**) can provide feedback on driver behavior and adherence to policies. Management can review the data generated from these methods to evaluate the continued application of safe driving behavior. Deficiencies can be identified and addressed, preferably before an employee-involved accident.

Copyright © Mometrix Media. You have been licensed one copy of this document for personal use only. Any other reproduction or redistribution is strictly prohibited. All rights reserved. This content is provided for test preparation purposes only and does not imply an endorsement by Mometrix of any particular political, scientific, or religious point of view.

DEFENSIVE DRIVING

Defensive driving is when a driver uses strategies to minimize risk in order to avoid accidents. The goal of defensive driving is to predictively identify potential hazards and determine a way to avoid them. Once the hazard is identified and the avoidance strategy is determined, the driver then acts decisively and immediately to avoid the hazard.

Defensive driving strategies include avoiding distracted driving, yielding the right of way, using appropriate following distances, avoiding emotional driving, and driving within the speed limit. Other methods include pre-driving checks, avoiding substances and medications that interfere with driving, using indicator lights, obeying all traffic laws, and regular vehicle maintenance.

DISTRACTED DRIVING

Driving is a process wherein a person must process multiple streams of information simultaneously. The National Highway Traffic Safety Administration (NHTSA) defines **distracted driving** as any activity that diverts the driver's attention away from the primary task of driving. Whenever a person attempts to perform another task in addition to driving, such as eating or communicating on a mobile device, they are being distracted. Some studies have shown that drivers distracted by texting perform equivalent to an individual with a blood alcohol level of 0.08.

Distracted driving is any time when a driver does not apply all of their attention to the driving task. Distractions can be **mental** (daydreaming), **physical** (adjusting the AC), or **visual** (looking at a text message). Distractions can lead to accidents resulting in employee injuries and financial losses. In today's connected world, drivers often receive directions, updates, or changes in real time when they are behind the wheel.

Organizations can reduce losses from distracted driving through **training** and **policies**. Initial and recurring training on defensive driving strategies can reduce the chance of accidents. Policies that prohibit employees from answering calls or texts while driving, setting GPS before starting the vehicle, and scheduling stops to communicate with dispatch can reduce the distractions for the driver.

DAILY DRIVER VEHICLE INSPECTIONS

A daily driver vehicle inspection is a requirement for commercial drivers but should also be a part of any company-owned vehicle program. Drivers should check **daily** that the following safety features are operational: brakes, rearview mirrors (inside and side mirrors), brake lights, headlights, reversing lights, emergency brakes, and regular brakes. The steering should be checked to ensure it's not too loose, gears should be checked for smooth operation, and it should be confirmed that a fire extinguisher is present. Any paperwork that should be in the vehicle should be checked, such as registration and insurance information, accident reporting forms, and any permits or licenses held.

RECORD-KEEPING REQUIREMENTS FOR VEHICLE INSPECTIONS

Commercial drivers are required to do daily vehicle inspections and sign the inspection form to indicate who performed the inspection. These **records** must be kept for a minimum of thirty days. Any deficiencies that are discovered during inspections must be repaired before the vehicle is used, and the driver must re-inspect to show that all agree the repair has been completed. Documentation of repairs must be kept on file as well. Commercial vehicles that are used for hazardous materials hauling must also be inspected for engine and proper operation every ninety days; again, any deficiencies must be corrected, and documentation must be maintained.

ENGINEERED SAFETY FEATURES OF VEHICLES

There are several engineered safety features in motor vehicles that help prevent injuries. For example, seat belts restrain occupants in the event of a crash and minimize the chance of the occupant hitting his or her head or breaking bones. Antilock brakes prevent the brakes from locking up when pressed quickly and forcefully and failing to engage. This minimizes the chance that the car won't be able to stop in an emergency. Brighter

Copyright © Mometrix Media. You have been licensed one copy of this document for personal use only. Any other reproduction or redistribution is strictly prohibited. All rights reserved.
This content is provided for test preparation purposes only and does not imply an endorsement by Mometrix of any particular political, scientific, or religious point of view.

brake lights alert the vehicles behind a car that it is stopping, thereby preventing collisions. Air bags that inflate when there is a collision cushion the occupants from hitting the dashboard or steering wheel and decrease likelihood of injury or death. Designers of industrial processes can learn about incorporating safety into design from studying **automobile safety engineering**.

MAINTENANCE SCHEDULES

Proper fleet maintenance schedules can have a positive impact on safety. Standard operating procedure is for each driver to do a daily driver's inspection before operating a vehicle and to document this inspection. The inspection sheet should be submitted to the maintenance manager for review. Any items noted on the inspection sheet that can adversely impact safety (e.g., broken or missing mirrors, tail lights, etc.) must be fixed immediately before the vehicle is operated. Every ninety days, at minimum, a skilled and trained mechanic should inspect the vehicle for mechanical issues such as fluid levels, tire wear, and the presence of safety features. This inspection should also be documented and any deficiencies immediately corrected. Preventive maintenance schedules such as these are important to catch problems before they become a catastrophic failure point that causes an accident that injures the driver or others.

MONITORING EQUIPMENT

GPS trackers can monitor the location and speed of a vehicle at any time and record this information for later review or for accessing remotely. They can increase fleet safety by allowing for monitoring of a driver's speed habits. It will be obvious from review of the data if a driver is exceeding speed limits; excessive speed is a known safety risk. In addition, analysis of data from GPS fleet trackers can be used to create more efficient routes; reducing unnecessary trips and miles driven will improve safety because fewer miles driven means fewer opportunities for accidents. GPS trackers can also alert the driver to unsafe road conditions on the route, so they can be avoided or circumvented.

Transportation Safety

Hazardous materials are moved by air, sea, and land. Shipping a hazardous material, also referred to as a **dangerous good**, requires information **identifying** the material or the hazards presented, **training** for the transport operators, and **shipping papers**. Each mode of transportation (truck, rail, plane, or ship) has specific requirements to reduce the risk during shipment and limit the impact of any incident that may occur during shipping.

The individual container and the outside of the vehicle must have information identifying the materials carried within the vehicle. This can take the form of product name, **UN numbers**, or placards. There are requirements for product containers, bulk containers, and external shipping containers depending on the potential impact of a spill or accident involving the material.

TRANSPORTING HAZARDOUS MATERIALS

Operators of vehicles transporting hazardous materials must be trained on the **hazards** of the materials they transport, **safety measures**, **security** measures, **packaging** requirements, **shipping paper** requirements, **emergency response** measures, and other requirements specific for the mode of transportation. An operator must be able to understand what they are shipping; how to do it safely; and what to do if a release is noted, including in the event of an accident involving the shipment.

Shipping papers are required as a tracking mechanism for hazardous materials. The papers must include a **description** of the items, **quantity** being shipped, and the **number** of packages. Each mode (land, sea, air) has additional requirements as determined by the agency responsible for overseeing the transport. The shipping papers are to ensure that all materials placed in the container arrive at the destination and to inform first responders of the potential hazards if there is an incident during shipment.

Copyright © Mometrix Media. You have been licensed one copy of this document for personal use only. Any other reproduction or redistribution is strictly prohibited. All rights reserved.
This content is provided for test preparation purposes only and does not imply an endorsement by Mometrix of any particular political, scientific, or religious point of view.

DANGEROUS GOODS REGULATION

The International Air Transport Association (IATA) is a trade association that establishes global standards for the airline industry. IATA has developed the **Dangerous Goods Regulation (DGR)** for the transport of hazardous materials by air. DGR is a United Nations-based standard that has been adopted by the **Federal Aviation Association (FAA).** Therefore, in the United States, DGR applies to both domestic and international shipments. DGR regulations outline proper packaging, labeling, weight/volume limits, and excluded materials. Failure to abide by the regulation can result in a rejected shipment or an enforcement action.

UN SPECIFICATION PACKAGING

UN specification packaging refers to international codes for shipping containers that verify that a package configuration (box, barrel, or other type of container) is certified to carry a designated chemical or dangerous good. In the United States, it is a method for the Department of Transportation to ensure that the materials listed are packaged in a manner to prevent release during shipment. The UN packaging codes for a specific material are listed in Section 14 of a Safety Data Sheet (SDS).

The alphanumeric code describes the following information for a package configuration:

1. Type (such as barrel, drum, or box)
2. Material (plastic, aluminum, fiberboard, etc.)
3. Category (open or closed top)
4. Packing group
5. Maximum gross mass or specific gravity
6. Solids or inner packaging
7. Year of manufacture
8. Location of manufacture

FEDERAL RAILROAD ADMINISTRATION

The movement of hazardous materials by rail is governed by the Department of Transportation's **Federal Railroad Administration (FRA).** Hazardous materials, as defined in Title 49 of the Code of Federal Regulations, must be properly classed, labeled, marked, packaged, and the cars or tanks must be placarded.

Additional regulations for rail include identifying **time-sensitive** shipments (such as acetylene, hydrogen, and hydrogen chloride) that require shipment within certain time frames of receiving from the shipper. Shipping papers must not only include the identity and amount of the material(s), but also their **position** within the train. Documentation must include the amount of material being shipped, proper shipping name, hazard class, UN identifier, packing group, and emergency response phone number.

All cars containing hazardous materials must be inspected prior to leaving the site for compliance with train makeup, adequate **buffer cars** between hazardous cars, load stability, and temperature control equipment (if necessary). The visual inspection must also check for leaks, proper labeling and placarding, properly secured closures, and any suspicious devices or signs of tampering.

Materials Handling

Materials handling involves lifting, moving, and placing items, whether manually or with equipment. Equipment frequently used for materials handling includes jacks, hoists, backhoes, escalators, derricks, and cranes. As many as 20-25 percent of disabling work-related injuries involve materials handling. Hazards stemming from materials handling differ depending on the material being handled and on the equipment being used. Materials may be heavy, toxic, radioactive, hazardous, or flammable: each involves a different set of hazards. Equipment used may be mobile, such as a forklift, and could hit someone. Other times, items can fall off a hoist or a crane can collapse. Electrically powered equipment poses electricity hazards such as shock.

Copyright © Mometrix Media. You have been licensed one copy of this document for personal use only. Any other reproduction or redistribution is strictly prohibited. All rights reserved.
This content is provided for test preparation purposes only and does not imply an endorsement by Mometrix of any particular political, scientific, or religious point of view.

Moving items manually also poses hazards. For example, lifting too heavy a load or using improper lifting techniques can cause sprains or strains.

Developing and enforcing procedures for materials handling can help **reduce accidents**. Procedures should include how to do the following:

- Select the correct equipment for the job.
- Communicate during the materials transfer, whether using hand signals, two-way radios, or other forms of communication.
- Deal with problems that could occur during the materials handling activity.

The procedures should also include step-by-step instructions for actually completing the materials handling activity. Other actions that can help **prevent materials handling accidents** include the following:

- Create a safe materials handling environment with good lighting, wide aisles, and proper ventilation.
- Institute traffic controls to keep lift areas clear of people.
- Regularly maintain, inspect, and repair equipment used for materials handling.
- Train workers to properly use materials handling equipment, hand signals, and rigging.
- Train workers on safe techniques for manually moving materials, such as techniques for lifting heavy loads.
- Eliminate materials handling whenever possible.

SAFE LIFTING TECHNIQUES FOR MANUAL MATERIALS HANDLING

Training workers on safe lifting techniques is important because improper lifting can cause sprain and strain injuries. As many as 25% of workers' compensation claims are for lower back injuries. To decrease the chances of injury when lifting, you need to do the following:

- Check the weight of the item to be lifted. If it is higher than the RWL (recommended weight limit), take steps to lighten the load, whether by using equipment to pick up the item or by splitting the load into two or more loads.
- Ensure the floor is not slippery.
- Spread your feet for a more stable stance.
- Keep your back straight.
- Hold the load close to your body.
- If an item is on the floor, bend down, grasp it firmly, and then stand up slowly and steadily.

RWL stands for **recommended weight limit**. The RWL is the weight that healthy workers could lift for up to eight hours without causing musculoskeletal injuries. To calculate the RWL, you need to multiply LC (load constant) × HM (horizontal multiplier) × VM (vertical multiplier) × DM (distance multiplier) × AM (asymmetric multiplier) × FM (frequency multiplier) × CM (coupling multiplier).

LI stands for **lifting index**. It measures the physical stress associated with lifting. As the LI goes up, the chance of injury also goes up. To calculate LI, you divide the load weight by the RWL.\

It is important to know the RWL and the LI because they can help in the following ways:

- Identify tasks where injuries are more likely to occur.
- Help you develop procedures for safe lifting tasks.
- Identify which lifting tasks need to be redesigned first (generally those with higher LIs).

Copyright © Mometrix Media. You have been licensed one copy of this document for personal use only. Any other reproduction or redistribution is strictly prohibited. All rights reserved.
This content is provided for test preparation purposes only and does not imply an endorsement by Mometrix of any particular political, scientific, or religious point of view.

Ultimately, knowing the RWL and LI can lead to safer lifting procedures and fewer injuries. In order to determine the RWL, you must know the weight of the object. You must also know the following task variables:

- H (**horizontal distance**) – distance of the hands away from the midpoint between the ankles.
- V (**vertical location**) – distance of the hands above the floor.
- D (**vertical travel distance**) – number of inches or centimeters the object is lifted.
- A (**asymmetry angle**) – distance from 0 to 135 degrees that a worker turns during the lift.
- F (**lifting frequency**) – the average number of lifts per minute, measured over a 15-minute time span.
- C (**coupling classification**) – defined as good, fair, or poor depending on the type of grip (such as handles) and the type of container (box or bag; rigid or non-rigid, standard or irregular shape, etc.).

SAFE OPERATION OF FORKLIFTS
DAILY INSPECTION CHECKLIST ELEMENTS FOR FORKLIFTS

Daily forklift inspections must be conducted by each driver before driving the forklift. Inspection elements include the following: check that horns and alerts are operational; check the parking brake works; check the mast operation for smooth operation and no broken chain links; check the forks for signs of cracks or wear that would weaken the forks; check the tires; check the fluid levels in the forklift, and check for leaks; ensure the seat belt is present and operational; and if there is a propane tank, check for leaks and rust.

FORKLIFT TRAFFIC

A well-designed traffic pattern plan for forklift traffic can greatly increase the safety of the workplace. "Rules of the road" should be established that are enforceable for all forklift drivers and pedestrians. Similar to public roadways, there should be designated lanes of travel for forklifts. Pedestrian walkways should be designated and separate from forklift lanes. Intersections should be posted with a "Stop" sign for forklifts to stop at each intersection. Speed limits should be established and enforced (maximum of eight miles per hour). High traffic areas such as receiving docks should restrict pedestrian access.

PEDESTRIAN SAFETY AROUND POWERED INDUSTRIAL TRUCKS

Although pedestrians always have the right of way, it is important for pedestrians to observe best management practices when walking in areas with forklift traffic. At all intersections, forklifts are instructed to stop and sound their horn; pedestrians should stop at all intersections and look for forklifts. Pedestrians should be aware that forklifts may be backing out of inventory rows. Pedestrians should stop and wait for an acknowledgment to pass through the path of a traveling forklift to ensure that the driver sees them and will stop for them. Never walk under raised forklift forks.

FORKLIFT-ATTACHABLE DEVICES

Devices can be purchased that are cages meant for lifting workers to heights using a standard forklift. These must meet specifications with regard to securely fastening to the forks of the forklift, they must be equipped with guard rails of an approved height, the access gate must swing inward instead of outward, and they must undergo regular inspections. Under no circumstances should homemade work platforms be used because they must be engineered for strength and load limits. In addition, OSHA regulations do specify that if one is using such a cage as a man lift, one should obtain a letter from the forklift manufacturer specifying what the load limits are using the cage and that the capacity decal should be changed accordingly [29 CFR 1910.178(a)(4)].

TRAINING REQUIREMENTS FOR OPERATING FORKLIFTS

Occupational Safety and Health Administration (OSHA) regulations governing forklift training requirements are found in 29 CFR 1910.178(l). All employees who will drive a forklift must be trained both in the classroom and on the job and must not be allowed to operate a forklift without direct supervision until they have passed exams to demonstrate proficiency. The classroom training portion should cover the principles of safe forklift operation (the stability triangle), how to determine the load limits of a forklift, how to conduct an inspection of a forklift, how to drive the forklift on ramps, how to carry loads that obstruct the view, and forklift traffic rules.

Copyright © Mometrix Media. You have been licensed one copy of this document for personal use only. Any other reproduction or redistribution is strictly prohibited. All rights reserved.
This content is provided for test preparation purposes only and does not imply an endorsement by Mometrix of any particular political, scientific, or religious point of view.

The classroom knowledge should be tested by a written test, and a minimum score for passing the test should be established. Finally, the employee must pass a behind-the-wheel proficiency test to demonstrate skilled and safe operation of the forklift.

LOAD LIMIT OF FORKLIFTS

The forklift generally has two front wheels and one back wheel that pivots around when turning the unit. This three-point triangle formed by the three wheels is the "stability triangle." One must be mindful of the center of gravity in relation to this stability triangle in determining the load limit of the forklift. Manufacturers establish the load limit for various loads relative to the load's center. For example, a 48-inch pallet has a load center of 24 inches. Lifting loads in the air also affects the center of gravity. The load limit therefore depends on three factors: the load center of the object being lifted or transported, the height the load will be lifted, and the counterbalanced weight of the forklift itself.

All forklifts are equipped with a capacity plate affixed by the manufacturer. This plate lists the load limit of the forklift for several common load centers (such as 24 inches and 36 inches). This will be the amount of weight the forklift can safely carry and move, given a certain load center. This load limit assumes that the forklift will be operated at a reasonable speed, especially around corners. Turning corners quickly can quickly shift the load center outside of the stability triangle, causing the forklift to turn over and potentially crushing an employee. Any changes to the forklift that affect the stability triangle or maximum mast height will affect the load limit and the manufacturer must be consulted to determine the new load limit.

BATTERY CHARGING STATIONS

Forklift batteries contain a strong acid. Therefore, it is important to observe proper training and precautions when recharging batteries. Battery charging stations should be located outdoors if at all possible. OSHA requires that an eyewash station be available in the battery charging area. Proper PPE must be available to the employee that will be handling the batteries. Gloves must be worn to plug in and unplug the batteries; extra precautions must be taken if a person will be checking the water level in the battery and adding water. Additional PPE to wear when servicing batteries includes acid-resistant gloves, safety glasses and a face shield. Water should only be added to the batteries after charging and once the battery has a full charge. Only deionized water can be used to fill the batteries. The level should be checked at least once per week and water added to the fill line if it is low. If there is any acid spilled on the outside of the battery, it should be cleaned up using appropriate precautions while wearing proper PPE.

SAFE OPERATION OF CRANES AND LIFTING DEVICES

Cranes account for a high percentage of workplace injury and accidents on worksites. The safety professional can implement several strategies to minimize injury from unsafe conditions:

PRE-OPERATION INSPECTION

- Before operating, the crane's hydraulic lift controls should be inspected and determined to be in proper working order. The out rigging hydraulic extenders should be solidly placed and fully extended to guarantee utmost stability.
- The weight of intended loads must be within the crane's specified load capacity.
- Human walking traffic should be barricaded from the crane's area of operation. At no time should loads be moved over the heads of workers.
- Cranes must be situated and operated at safe distances from electric power lines or onsite distributive power lines needed for small equipment.
- Rigging and brakes must be examined and trial tested before use. Inspect cable, chains, and hook.

DAILY CRANE INSPECTION

A daily crane inspection program is an essential part of safe crane operation. The presence of appropriate personal protective equipment (PPE) should be confirmed, and it should be checked that access to the area that the crane will be used is controlled. Check the disconnect switch for correct operation, that the hoist is not

Copyright © Mometrix Media. You have been licensed one copy of this document for personal use only. Any other reproduction or redistribution is strictly prohibited. All rights reserved.
This content is provided for test preparation purposes only and does not imply an endorsement by Mometrix of any particular political, scientific, or religious point of view.

loose or broken, that the wire rope is seated properly and not twisted or bent, that the push button controls have no damage, that the controls have the required American National Standards Institute (ANSI) tag, that the controls operate as they should (e.g., the crane goes up when that button is triggered), that hooks have no cracks or gouges, that the wire ropes are not frayed, and that the capacity plate is present and visible.

MONTHLY CRANE INSPECTION

There are additional inspection elements for a monthly crane inspection above the daily requirements. All inspections must be conducted by qualified personnel. Items to be inspected include looking for deformed, cracked, or corroded members; loose bolts and rivets; cracked or worn sheaves and drums; worn bearings, pins, shafts, or gears; and excessive wear on brake system and parts. Check that the load indicators function correctly over the full operating range, and check for excessive wear on chain drive sprockets.

CRANE LOAD RATINGS

Manufacturers of cranes design them for a certain load capacity. The load capacity is the maximum that the crane can safely lift; however, it is not good practice to lift approaching the capacity limit unless the crane is designed for that type of use. Cranes are classified as follows:

- Class A: Standby service—crane on standby or used infrequently
- Class B Light service—used at slow speeds and infrequently
- Class C Moderate service—Average 50 percent of rated capacity, five to ten lifts per hour
- Class D Heavy service—Used at 50 percent of rated capacity constantly through the work day
- Class E Severe service—Used approaching capacity 20 times per hour
- Class F Continuous severe service—Used approaching capacity continuously throughout its life

SAFETY PROCEDURES ASSOCIATED WITH RIGGING AND HOISTING
PRE-JOB INSPECTION OF RIGGING EQUIPMENT

A pre-job safety inspection must be conducted before any rigging job. Ensure all lines to be used are not frayed or broken. Ensure all employees are aware of how the job is planned to be conducted and are aware of their respective roles. Ensure the controls on the equipment operate as planned and that the equipment is parked in a stable surface and will not rock once the load is engaged and lifted. Inspect hydraulic lines for leaks, and ensure there are proper levels of hydraulic fluid. Evaluate the need for tag lines, and employ them if necessary.

TAG LINES

Tag lines are used with cranes and hoisting equipment to attach to and stabilize the object being lifted. Lifting and moving an object with a crane will cause the load to swing on the end of the cable like a pendulum, which is potentially dangerous to employees. The tag lines are affixed to the load and to the ground to stabilize the load and prevent it from swinging. The tag lines must be made of soft material such as nylon or sisal, not of wire rope. Tag lines are required when the risk to employees of being hit by a swinging load exists or when there are overhead electrical lines that may be hit by a swinging load or crane.

WIRE ROPE USED IN RIGGING

The use of wire rope for rigging must meet OSHA specifications:

- There cannot be more than three full tucks in a wire rope. Other permitted types of connection may be used if they meet safety specifications.
- Wire ropes used for hoisting or lowering must be constructed of a continuous length of rope without knot or splice except for the eye splices at the end of the rope.
- The eyes in wire rope slings or bridles must not be comprised of wire rope clips or knots.
- Wire rope should not be used if the total number of visible broken wires is in excess of ten percent of the total number of wires, or if the rope shows other signs of excessive corrosion or wear.

Copyright © Mometrix Media. You have been licensed one copy of this document for personal use only. Any other reproduction or redistribution is strictly prohibited. All rights reserved. This content is provided for test preparation purposes only and does not imply an endorsement by Mometrix of any particular political, scientific, or religious point of view.

- Store rigging properly, out of sunlight and away from moisture and chemicals that can cause it to deteriorate.
- Inspect rigging regularly to ensure it is not deteriorating or wearing out.
- Follow load capacity charts for rigging to guard against overloading.

HAND SIGNALS FOR COMMUNICATING IN A RIGGING AND HOISTING JOB

Hand signals should be used whenever the crane operator cannot see the load or landing area or cannot see the path of travel or when the load is close to power lines. Signals should be communicated bare-handed. The common signals are as follows:

- HOIST: Raise the arm at the elbow with the index finger pointing up, then move hand in a horizontal circle.
- LOWER: Lower the arm straight down with the index finger down, then move the hand in a horizontal circle, pointing down.
- BOOM UP: Extend right arm to the side with fingers closed and thumb pointing up.
- BOOM DOWN: Extend right arm to the side with fingers closed and thumb pointing down.
- TROLLEY TRAVEL: With palm up, move the thumb in the direction of travel.
- TRAVEL FORWARD (BOTH TRACKS): With closed fists, rotate hands in a circle towards the body to indicate going forward (rotate away from the body for backwards).
- STOP: Extend the arm straight out with palm down; move arm back and forth horizontally.
- EMERGENCY STOP: With the arm extended straight out, palm down, move rapidly right and left.

PERSONNEL HOISTING

When conventional means of moving workers to higher levels are not feasible, a crane can be used to hoist personnel, so long as the following cautionary procedures are observed:

- The crane must be on level ground. The angle between crane base and the ground cannot exceed **one percent**.
- Total weight of personnel hoisted plus the weight of the platform itself cannot exceed **fifty percent of the rated capacity** of the crane or derrick.
- If workers must be hoisted aloft by crane, the **platform** should be moved in a slow, cautious and controlled manner.
- **Carrying load lines** must be capable of supporting seven times the weight of the load. If anti-rotation rope is used, it should be of a type capable of supporting ten times the intended carry weight.
- All **brakes and locking devices** on the crane must be engaged when the personnel platform is stopped.

PERSONNEL PLATFORMS

When conventional means of hoisting personnel to higher building levels are unavailable or infeasible, a **personnel platform** may be used. OSHA regulations require that such platforms be designed by a qualified engineer or other qualified competent person.

- The platform must be designed to **minimize tipping** when workers move or shift their weight on the platform.
- The platform itself (without guardrails or fall arrest systems attached) must be able to support **five times the maximum intended load**.
- **Guardrails and grab rails** should be installed around the entire perimeter of the platform.
- **Gates** for access must not be outward swinging. A fail-safe device must be installed to prevent accidental opening of the gate or entrance.

Copyright © Mometrix Media. You have been licensed one copy of this document for personal use only. Any other reproduction or redistribution is strictly prohibited. All rights reserved.
This content is provided for test preparation purposes only and does not imply an endorsement by Mometrix of any particular political, scientific, or religious point of view.

- Platform or cage must be of a height permitting employees to stand **upright**.
- The platform or cage must be provided with **overhead protection** to prevent injury from falling objects.

Foreign Material Exclusion (FME) and Foreign Object Damage (FOD)

Foreign material exclusion (FME) is the process of preventing **foreign object damage (FOD)** by making sure that vulnerable systems and components are free from damaging foreign material. FOD can result in damage to equipment, loss of product quality, environmental damage, injury, or economic loss.

Foreign material exclusion is simply keeping objects out of places they should not be. Objects can be debris, vermin, tools, or even people. Areas vulnerable to FOD must be identified, potential impacts of FOD (e.g., injury or chemical release) must be assessed, and prevention methods must be implemented. Prevention methods can include an emphasis on cleanliness, a workplace culture of accountability, inspections, visibility or monitoring of the area, and a tracking system for tools and materials into and out of the vulnerable area.

Foreign object damage (FOD) is a safety and quality control concept wherein an object not native to the environment can result in damage, injury, production delays, or create a hazard. Any particle, substance, or item present in an undesignated location that causes the damage is called foreign object debris. The object can be small pieces of debris, loose objects such as tools or spare parts, vermin, or even a person.

The damage caused by the foreign object can impact the **quality** of the product, result in **damage** to equipment, or result in an **injury**. An example would be a screwdriver used to remove a faceplate that falls into a working fan housing, causing the fan blades to break, which then ejects pieces of blade into the nearby environment.

Foreign object damage can be mitigated by the principal of **foreign material exclusion (FME)** and includes proper housekeeping, routine cleaning, routine inspections, and systems for organizing and accounting for parts and tools.

Hazardous Materials Management

THE GLOBALLY HARMONIZED SYSTEM OF CLASSIFICATION AND LABELING OF CHEMICALS (GHS)

Hazard communication refers to the Occupational Safety and Health Administration (OSHA) Hazard Communication Standard found in 29 CFR 1910.1200. The Hazard Communication Standard governs the requirements to notify workers of chemical hazards faced at work and to provide information on protection from hazards. GHS refers to an international standard developed by the United Nations to guide hazardous chemical labeling, warning systems, and safety data sheets. The GHS was developed to standardize hazard warning terminology, pictograms, and safety data sheets worldwide so that international commerce could be improved and language barriers overcome. The OSHA Hazard Communication Standard has recently been updated to include the requirements of the GHS. As of 2015, all workplaces in the United States are required to have safety data sheets available on site that conform to the GHS system and to use these in their notification and training programs.

SDS (SAFETY DATA SHEETS)

Safety Data Sheets (formerly Material Safety Data Sheets) provide information on the physical and chemical properties of a substance as well as potential health and environmental concerns. OSHA requires that all chemicals be labeled appropriately and that SDS be readily available in the workplace. The hazard

Copyright © Mometrix Media. You have been licensed one copy of this document for personal use only. Any other reproduction or redistribution is strictly prohibited. All rights reserved.
This content is provided for test preparation purposes only and does not imply an endorsement by Mometrix of any particular political, scientific, or religious point of view.

communication standard also requires employees to be trained, and for the employer to maintain records of the training given. The format for SDS includes sixteen sections. The required sections are as follows:

I -- Identification
II -- Hazard Identification
III -- Composition/Information on Ingredients
IV -- First Aid Measures
V -- Firefighting Measures
VI -- Accidental Release Measures
VII -- Handling/Storage Requirements
VIII -- Exposure Controls/Personal Protection
IX -- Physical/Chemical Properties
X -- Stability/Reactivity
XI -- Toxicological Information
XII -- Ecological Information
XIII -- Disposal Considerations
XIV -- Transportation Information
XV -- Regulatory Information
XVI -- Other Information

SDS provide a number of indicators for possible health threats of a particular chemical. They are required to provide all known information regarding carcinogenicity of a substance (known or potential cancer-causing risks). Carcinogenic risks are published in the National Toxicology Program report (NTP), the International Agency for Research on Cancer (IACR), and Occupation Safety and Health Administration (OSHA). Toxicity levels are indicated by numbers called the LD_{50} and the LC_{50}. LD_{50} refers to the dose at which 50% of the test subjects were killed. LC_{50} is the lethal concentration at which 50% of test subjects were killed. Dosages are typically normalized to include the mass of the possible toxin divided by the mass of the test subject. LD_{50} values may also include descriptors that indicate the mode of administration of the dose (intravenously or orally) and the timeframe for death after administration. Limits for exposure to a particular chemical are also provided. These can be measured as the OSHA permissible exposure limit (PEL) and/or the Threshold Limit Values (TLV), which are published by the American Conference of Governmental Industrial Hygienists (ACGIH).

SDS often recommend the usage of chemical protective clothing (CPC). Protective eye goggles with splash guards and air vents should be used when handling chemicals. Face shields should be used when working with large quantities of a substance and are most effective when used in conjunction with safety goggles. If the mode of possible hazard is through contact and/or absorption on skin, appropriate gloves should be worn. Gloves are chosen based upon their permeability to and reactivity with the chemical in use. Personal respiratory equipment may be indicated if fume hoods do not provide adequate ventilation of fumes or airborne particulates. Body protection depends on the level of protection needed and ranges from rubberized aprons to full suits that are evaluated for their permeability and leak protection. Closed-toed protective shoes should always be used when working with chemicals.

REQUIREMENTS FOR LABELS

The term "label" under the GHS of Classification and Labeling of Chemicals refers to the label on the container. Under GHS, it's required to contain certain elements; these requirements apply whether the label is affixed by the manufacturer or whether the chemical is placed into a smaller, secondary container in the workplace. The label must include the identification of the chemical, the manufacturer's name and contact information, the applicable GHS pictograms, the applicable signal words (either "danger" or "warning," as applicable), and precautionary statements (measures to reduce risk from exposure to the chemical).

Copyright © Mometrix Media. You have been licensed one copy of this document for personal use only. Any other reproduction or redistribution is strictly prohibited. All rights reserved.
This content is provided for test preparation purposes only and does not imply an endorsement by Mometrix of any particular political, scientific, or religious point of view.

PICTOGRAMS

The pictograms used in the GHS system are simple pictures used to convey hazards posed by the chemical. They are meant to be universally understandable by people with diverse language and reading fluencies. They are as follows:

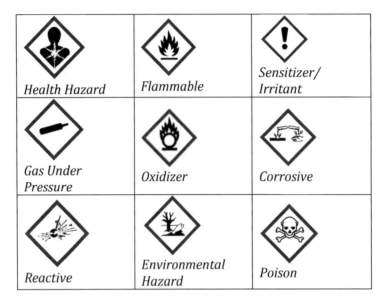

SIGNAL WORDS

Under the GHS hazard communication and safety data sheet system, the term "signal word" is used to describe one word that summarizes the degree of danger posed by the substances. There are only two signal words: "danger" and "warning." The word "danger" is used for more hazardous substances that present immediate hazards such as flammability, reactivity, poison, and so on. The word "warning" is used for lesser hazards such as irritants, environmental hazards, and less toxic substances. The signal word is used on the label to provide a quick and easily understandable indication of the degree of hazard posed by the substance.

NFPA 704 DIAMOND

The NFPA 704 diamond is a graphic representation of the various hazards confronted by personnel or responding fire officials to a dangerous site. It consists of a diamond shaped placard with numbers, colors, and codes to identify different hazards to which people may be exposed.

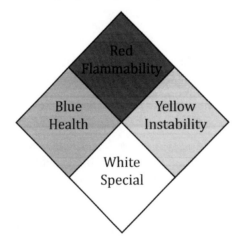

Categories of the placard identify health, flammability, instability and other factors impacting emergency responders. As the graphic shows, the blue color represents health hazards. Red indicates flammables, yellow

Copyright © Mometrix Media. You have been licensed one copy of this document for personal use only. Any other reproduction or redistribution is strictly prohibited. All rights reserved.
This content is provided for test preparation purposes only and does not imply an endorsement by Mometrix of any particular political, scientific, or religious point of view.

means reactivity or instability, and white is a special category which can indicate a variety of conditions like corrosive characteristics, radiation, or oxidizers. The NFPA 704 standards were developed by the US National Fire Protection Association. While it involves more than fire conditions, the graphic is often called the "fire diamond."

The NFPA 704 diamond is a graphic representation of the various hazards confronted by personnel or responding fire officials to a dangerous site. Categories of the placard identify health, flammability, instability and other factors impacting emergency responders.

- Blue Color: indicates a health condition with intensity ranging from zero (no health hazard) to four. A Blue health indicator of four means that a very short exposure could cause death or serious injury.
- Red Color: indicates flammability with a numerical rating from zero (water) to four. An example of the highest numerical rate of flammability (four) would be propane gas.
- Yellow Color: indicates instability or reactivity. Oxidizers are a prime example. Levels of volatility range from zero to four as in other categories.
- White Color: indicates a special category substance like corrosives, biohazards, or substances which react with water.

The NFPA 704 placarding standards use four colors and a numerical rating to identify hazardous substance types and levels of danger. The white category is a special category which may identify substances which may not have direct relationships to others in the same category:

- A "W" with a line crossing indicates a substance which, when wet, will react dangerously. Cesium and sodium are examples.
- OXY refers to an oxidizer. An oxidizer is a substance which supports the combustion of fuel. Hydrogen peroxide in high concentrations is an oxidizer, as is potassium perchlorate.

The preceding two standards are the only official standards of the NFPA but others are being considered and are often used:

- COR indicates the presence of a corrosive like sulfuric acid.
- BIO indicates a biohazard like smallpox virus.
- CRYO means cryogenic and is used to indicate the presence of extreme low temperatures.

DOT WARNING LABEL SYSTEM

The DOT mandates that hazardous materials being transported on roads be marked with the approved warning labels or sign. This label or sign is a 4 × 4 diamond shape that is color coded and marked with a class number at the bottom of the sign for further identification. Class numbers are broken into sub-classes that can dictate the use of certain signs. Additionally, some signs contain written descriptions or warnings. The signs must be placed on all sides of a vehicle. This system aids emergency workers respond safely. Emergency Response Guidelines, published by the DOT in joint effort with the transportation authorities of Canada and Mexico, can be referenced for detailed explanation of signs.

Color Coding	Class Number Identification
Red = flammable gas or liquid	1 = Explosives
Orange = explosive material	2 = Gasses
White = poisonous	3 = Flammable liquids
Black & White = corrosive	4 = Flammable solid
Yellow = oxidizer	5 = Oxidizers
Green = non-flammable gas	6 = Poisonous or diseased
Yellow & White = radioactive	7 = Radioactive
	8 = Corrosive
	9 = Other dangerous materials

Copyright © Mometrix Media. You have been licensed one copy of this document for personal use only. Any other reproduction or redistribution is strictly prohibited. All rights reserved.
This content is provided for test preparation purposes only and does not imply an endorsement by Mometrix of any particular political, scientific, or religious point of view.

STORAGE AND HANDLING OF HAZARDOUS CHEMICALS

OSHA standard 1910.119 outlines the regulations for the usage, handling, and storage of highly hazardous chemicals. The focus is on preventing the release of chemicals whose chemical properties such as toxicity, flammability, and reactivity have a high potential for disastrous consequences. The regulation requires employers to partner with employees and those with process expertise in developing a system for safe management of the chemicals, including a documented and well-communicated emergency response plan. Appendix A of 1910.119 provides a list of chemicals for which this regulation is mandatory. Common examples include aqueous ammonia solutions that are greater than 44% by weight ammonia, including anhydrous (without water) ammonia. Arsine and boron trifluoride have very low threshold quantity (TQ) limits and are sometimes used in the semiconductor industry. Hydrogen fluoride, hydrogen cyanide, and concentrated hydrogen peroxide are included. Halogen gases (F_2, Cl_2, Br_2, I_2) are all highly reactive and are included in the list of regulated chemicals.

Hazardous waste materials must be handled by an employer designated HAZMAT team. OSHA recognizes all chemicals listed in CERCLA 101(14) as hazardous chemicals requiring special handling and disposal. CERCLA is the Comprehensive Environmental Response, Compensation, and Liability Act that authorizes ATSDR (Agency for Toxic Substances & Disease Registry) and the EPA to develop biannually updated lists of such substances. Examples include arsenic, lead, chloroform, and phenol. OSHA has also embraced all chemicals listed in the DOT 49 CFR 172.101, including those listed in the appendix. OSHA includes biological and/or disease-causing agents as hazardous. Such substances have a high risk of causing death, reproduction interference, or birth defects if released into the environment, regardless of the mode of toxicity.

Chemicals should be stored separately according to key physical and/or chemical properties. They may be stored alphabetically, but only within a designated group. For example, oxidizing agents should NEVER be stored near organic solvents. Additionally, some chemicals are limited in the amounts that can be stored on site at any one time. Chemicals must be stored in appropriate containers. For example, some organic solvents will dissolve some types of plastic. Alkaline solutions often etch glass containers. The containers must be appropriately sealed to minimize escape of vapors. Such chemicals are often stored in a cabinet that is vented into the exhaust system. Bottles of chemicals must be scrupulously labeled with the name as provided on the SDS sheet, potential hazards, and the contact information of the manufacturer. Caution signs should be posted at entrances to chemical storage rooms that warn of the particular hazard(s) present. Finally, chemicals must be in a secure location at the proper temperature and pressure needed to ensure stability.

HANDLING OF DRUMS AND CONTAINERS OF HAZARDOUS MATERIALS

The OSHA regulations in 1910.120 describe the special handling treatment of drums and containers of hazardous substances and contaminated liquids. Prior to the Environmental Protection Act and other legislation designed to protect workers and communities, it was fairly commonplace to store 55-gallon drums by burying. Regulations require that this situation be ameliorated by interventions.

- Whenever possible, drums and containers should be inspected and tested for contamination before being moved. If this is impractical, then the containers should be moved to an area which is more hospitable to inspection of contents.
- Currently, there are stringent regulations regarding labeling and storage of containers. If an unlabeled or unidentified container is found at a worksite, it should be handled according to existing regulations for the handling of hazardous materials and wastes until the substance is identified.
- Well-planned worksites should be controlled so that movement of containerized chemicals and substances is minimal or non-existent.
- Employees occupied in the on-site movement of containers and drums must be trained in the potential hazards and informed of the potential for health effects.

Copyright © Mometrix Media. You have been licensed one copy of this document for personal use only. Any other reproduction or redistribution is strictly prohibited. All rights reserved. This content is provided for test preparation purposes only and does not imply an endorsement by Mometrix of any particular political, scientific, or religious point of view.

MOVING AND STORING COMPRESSED GAS CYLINDERS

Compressed gas cylinders are dangerous when dropped, exposed to ignition sources or corroded. Precautions are to be taken when moving and storing cylinders of compressed gas:

- Valve protection caps should be placed over all valves. Valve protection caps are not "handles" and should not be used for lifting and moving cylinders.
- Before hoisting cylinders aloft, compressed gas cylinders must be stabilized on a cradle, slingboard, or pallet. Magnets or choker slings may not be used for moving gas cylinders.
- When moving cylinders, they should not be dropped or permitted to crash into each other violently. The recommended method is to tilt them and roll them on their bottom edges.

Precautions are to be taken when moving cylinders of compressed gas by motor vehicle.

- It is important to recognize that cylinders of oxygen must be separated from gas cylinders or other combustible materials when moving them by truck.
- If moved and then stored, the oxygen cylinders must be set apart a distance of 20 feet or more. If this cannot be done, then a noncombustible barrier must be erected to a height of at least 5 feet. The barrier must have a fire-resistance rating of at least ½ hour.
- Cylinders moved by motor vehicle must be loaded in a vertical position. Unless a special carrier is used, gas regulators must be removed and replaced with valve protection caps before the cylinders are moved.
- Unless transported by a dedicated cylinder truck with racks, a chain or stabilizing device should be used to maintain cylinders in an upright position.

STORAGE AND HANDLING OF FLAMMABLE MATERIALS

Flammable liquids must be stored in approved flammable containers; for example, flammable liquids will generally be supplied in glass bottles or metal drums, not in plastic containers. If a secondary container is to be used (e.g., to transport a small quantity of gasoline), the container must be approved to hold flammable liquids. Flammable liquids must be stored in approved flammable liquid storage cabinets or in segregated rooms that have separate ventilation and whose walls meet fire resistance ratings. Aisles must be maintained at 3 feet in width, and egress routes must be kept clear in areas where flammable liquids are stored.

STORAGE AND HANDLING OF CORROSIVE MATERIALS

Corrosive materials are those that can dissolve metal and severely damage human tissue upon contact. They are usually of either a very high pH (greater than 12) or low pH (less than 2) but can also be other types of chemicals. Because they can dissolve metal, they should be stored in plastic containers. Corrosive materials must be stored away from flammable materials and incompatible metals. Acids and bases should be stored separately from one another due to the risk of exothermic (heat-producing) reactions if they are accidentally mixed. If possible, they should be stored in an enclosed cabinet or room with ventilation that does not go into the work area.

CHEMICAL INCOMPATIBILITY

Incompatibility refers to one or more chemicals that when mixed together, create a hazardous reaction. A hazardous reaction can refer to generation of heat (to the point of starting a fire), creation of a hazardous gas (e.g., hydrogen gas, which is flammable), or creation of a toxic gas. Common incompatibilities are strong acids and strong bases (heat and hydrogen gas), ammonia and bleach (toxic fumes), and strong acids with oxidizers. Incompatible chemicals must be stored in well-ventilated areas well apart from one another to ensure they do not mix accidentally.

Copyright © Mometrix Media. You have been licensed one copy of this document for personal use only. Any other reproduction or redistribution is strictly prohibited. All rights reserved.
This content is provided for test preparation purposes only and does not imply an endorsement by Mometrix of any particular political, scientific, or religious point of view.

Hazardous Materials Containment

Hazardous materials containment refers to properly containing hazardous materials in the event of an unexpected spill. Considerations should be made when designing containment as follows:

- Containment capacity: What should the containment capacity be? The design criteria are to contain 110 percent of the largest container or 10 percent of the aggregate volume stored. In addition, if the area is subject to storm water, containment capacity must be provided to contain the storm water also.
- Compatibility: Ensure that the materials of construction of the containment device are compatible with the hazardous materials being contained.
- Inspection frequency: Plans should be made to inspect the containment for spilled material on a regular basis. A corrective action process should be put in place to address any deficiencies discovered.
- Emergency planning: What will be the procedure if material is spilled in the containment? Who will be notified, and how will the material be cleaned up?

If the spill is small and the hazards are known, the spill can generally be cleaned up by personnel using appropriate personal protection gear and methods specific to the chemical involved. Exceptions include mercury and radioactive substances. Spills can typically be handled using specifically designed adsorption spill kits or via neutralization. Powdered neutralizers should be applied to the spill from the outside to the inside of the spill in a circular manner. Depending on the chemical, the neutralized material should be placed in a carefully labeled container for appropriate disposal. All sources of ignition must be controlled if the substance is flammable. At least two people should be present in case the person cleaning the spill needs emergency assistance. If large amounts of chemicals have spilled or there is a possibility the spill can result in an uncontrolled release of a hazardous substance, the designated HAZMAT team must be summoned.

Multi-Employer Worksite Issues

Ways in Which the General Contractor Can Communicate Hazardous Standards Information to Subcontractors

On multi-employer sites, it is of utmost importance that the general contractor (sometimes referred to as the Controlling Employer) educates and informs subcontractors as to the location, handling, and use of hazardous materials stored at the workplace. The general contractor must communicate the location and availability of the overall safety program and provide opportunities for meeting to review and alter the process as work progresses.

- The program must indicate the manner in which SDS information will be provided to the sub-contractor, indicating where in the workplace it can be read and reviewed.
- The program must indicate precautionary measures such as the use of Personal Protective Equipment and other protections.
- The program must indicate methods and schedules for training sub-contractors regarding the labeling system for the hazardous materials.

Contractual Control

Having "contractual control" over a worksite means that a Controlling Employer has been designated in written contracts as an entity responsible for preventing and correcting violations.

- A key ingredient of "contractual control" is that it requires an employer to exercise high standards of "reasonable care" in complying with worker safety regulations.
- "Contractual Control" extends from the general contractor to all subcontractors with the general contractor being responsible for administration of safety compliance measures to be taken for worker safety.

Copyright © Mometrix Media. You have been licensed one copy of this document for personal use only. Any other reproduction or redistribution is strictly prohibited. All rights reserved. This content is provided for test preparation purposes only and does not imply an endorsement by Mometrix of any particular political, scientific, or religious point of view.

- The "reasonable care" standard of contractual control means that the general contractor may be issued a citation for a safety violation as the Exposing Contractor or Employer. The standard of "reasonable care" for a Controlling Employer, however, is not as high as it is for Exposing Employers, Correcting Employers, or Creating Employers.

CREATING EMPLOYER, EXPOSING EMPLOYER, CORRECTING EMPLOYER, AND CONTROLLING EMPLOYER

The terms are often used in the inspection of multi-employer worksites. It is common practice on construction sites to have more than one contractor on a specific job since framers, electricians, masons, plumbers may not all fall under the authority of a single parent company. In most cases, there is a joint responsibility and liability.

- The Creating Employer is the one who creates the hazard. If this employer is a sub-contractor, this sub-contractor has the responsibility for observing safety policies and practices.
- The Controlling Employer has the authority to ensure that hazardous conditions are corrected.
- The Correcting Employer is responsible for correcting the hazard.
- The Exposing Employer is the contractor whose employees are exposed to the hazard.

Any or all of these employers may be cited for violation if found responsible.

REASONABLE CARE

Controlling Employers can be cited for OSHA violations if it is found that they did not exercise "reasonable care" in preventing or correcting violations. A Controlling Employer is presumed to have knowledge of and authority for correcting hazardous conditions in the workplace. However, the standards for making the determination are not as high as they are for Exposing Employers, Correcting Employers, or Creating Employers.

The Controlling Employer or construction manager is not routinely required to conduct safety inspections as often as the employers who are sub-contracted for specific tasks and functions. Nor is the Controlling Employer expected to have the same degree of technical expertise in the various construction fields. The general contractor who sub-contracts to other entities cannot be expected to have simultaneous expertise in electrical worker safety, masonry work safety, plumbing work safety, heavy equipment operation safety, and so forth.

The Controlling Employer isn't expected to have as much specific trade expertise as a subcontractor in a specialized field. The factors which come into play in making a determination of "reasonable care" may include:

- The physical size or scale of the project.
- The amount of knowledge the Controlling Employer has about the type of work being performed and the safety compliance integrity of the subcontractor(s) being hired.
- Evidence of an effective safety and health program which combines training of workers with established protocols for the use of PPE.
- A system with designated persons for the identification and correction of hazardous conditions which crop up on the job.
- Are safety meetings and training regularly conducted and reviewed?
- Is there a history of previous violations and citations? And if there is, has the employer taken appropriate steps to remedy past problems?

Copyright © Mometrix Media. You have been licensed one copy of this document for personal use only. Any other reproduction or redistribution is strictly prohibited. All rights reserved.
This content is provided for test preparation purposes only and does not imply an endorsement by Mometrix of any particular political, scientific, or religious point of view.

Sources of Information on Hazard and Risk Management Options

Planning for external threats such as natural disasters is an essential part of any business continuity plan. There are many resources available online to assess hazards and develop risk control measures. For natural disaster risk and response planning, consult federal government web sites such as www.ready.gov and resources posted on the Federal Emergency Management Agency web site. To assess occupational hazards posed by the physical environment, consult the OSHA web site. The OSHA website provides regulations, best practices for managing risks, and interpretations of the standards. For technical and research information, consult the National Institute of Occupational Safety and Health web site (NIOSH). For information on the toxicity of chemicals and related data, consult the Integrated Risk Information System (IRIS) database, which is maintained by the US EPA. Trade associations and professional associations can also be valuable sources of information, especially the American Conference of Government and Industrial Hygienists (ACGIH) web site. They publish technical information on ventilation design and guidelines for exposure to toxic chemicals (the Threshold Limit Values, or TLVs).

SDS

The abbreviation SDS (previously MSDS) refers to the safety data sheet. This form is mandatory for all products containing hazardous chemicals in a concentration higher than one percent. Other facts about the SDS:

- If a substance is carcinogenic or potentially cancer causing, the SDS is required at concentration levels of only 0.1%.
- An SDS has sixteen basic categories of information provided about the chemical product, though not all categories are relevant to certain products.
- Required information provided on an SDS includes identifying information for:
  o company of origin
  o type of chemical
  o type of hazardous effect the chemical may have on workers
  o first aid and firefighting measures
  o handling and storage
  o personal protective measures to be used
  o stability, reactivity, disposal concerns, and other categories which may or may not pertain
- SDS labeling must be done in English. This rule applies even though a workforce may consist of a population more than fifty percent foreign-language speaking. SDS labeling in other languages may accompany the English language labels, but this is at the discretion of shippers and receivers.
- SDS must be kept for thirty years because, like worker exposure records, they are part of the employee's medical records.
- Additional training must be conducted every time a new SDS (and material) is introduced into the workplace.

Safety Design Criteria for Workplace Facilities, Machines, and Practices

PREVENTION THROUGH DESIGN

The National Institute of Occupational Safety and Health (NIOSH) has supported the **Prevention Through Design (PtD)** initiative as a way to reduce occupational injuries. The PtD concept is that hazards and risk can be reduced in the early phases of development of processes, equipment, tools, and work organization. By focusing on the worker and how they will interact with the final system, hazards can be anticipated and designed out, thereby reducing future costs associated with retrofitting or replacement later in the life cycle.

The PtD concept relies on recognizing potential hazards and addressing them in the design or redesign process. For example, if a particular machine requires an employee to observe material movement from an

Copyright © Mometrix Media. You have been licensed one copy of this document for personal use only. Any other reproduction or redistribution is strictly prohibited. All rights reserved. This content is provided for test preparation purposes only and does not imply an endorsement by Mometrix of any particular political, scientific, or religious point of view.

elevated location, the platform or catwalk can be designed with guardrails or tie-off points for fall restraint equipment.

SAFETY DESIGN CRITERIA

Safety design criteria establishes the design, construction, fabrication, testing, and performance requirements for safety equipment, processes, and systems. While the Occupational Safety and Health Administration (OSHA) establishes health and safety standards, it does not establish the criteria for equipment or systems that can be used to meet the standards. To that end, private or quasi-governmental agencies have taken the lead on safety design and their work products (specifications, testing standards, or performance standards) may be referenced in OSHA standards. For example, the OSHA respiratory protection standard requires the use of respirators certified by the National Institute of Occupational Safety and Health (NIOSH), but does not state what the certification entails. Some of the more recognized bodies that establish and certify those standards are:

- **Underwriters' Laboratory (UL)**: An independent testing laboratory that conducts quality and safety testing for a wide variety of products to determine if they meet relevant standards.
- **The National Fire Prevention Association (NFPA)**: Creates standards related to fire and electrical safety, including establishing requirements for fire suppression systems, fire extinguishers, and emergency exits.
- **National Institute of Occupational Safety and Health (NIOSH)**: Conducts research and makes recommendations to reduce occupational injuries and fatalities, such as studies in relation to exposure limits for toxic chemicals and respirator requirements.
- **Factory Mutual Global (FMG)**: One of the world's largest insurance and risk management companies and specializes in property loss prevention services. A product that is marked "FM Approved" has been evaluated to conform to the highest standards of safety and property loss prevention.

Tools, Machines, Practices, and Equipment Safety

HAZARDS AND CONTROLS ASSOCIATED WITH HAND AND POWER TOOLS

HAZARDS AND INJURIES ASSOCIATED WITH TOOLS AND MACHINES

Hazards associated with tools and machines include the following:

- Being struck by a tool, machine, or machine part.
- Being struck by flying debris from materials the tool or machine is acting on, such as concrete chips.
- Getting caught in a machine or tool.

Less direct hazards also exist. For example, if a machine requires repetitive motion, cumulative stress disorders can result. For powered tools, electrical hazards are also present. Tools and machines are a major source of injury, including the following:

- Cuts
- Abrasions
- Puncture wounds
- Tissue tears
- Crushing injuries
- Fractures
- Carpal tunnel syndrome
- Bursitis
- Tendonitis

As many as 8% of injuries involving lost time are related to **hand tools**.

Copyright © Mometrix Media. You have been licensed one copy of this document for personal use only. Any other reproduction or redistribution is strictly prohibited. All rights reserved.
This content is provided for test preparation purposes only and does not imply an endorsement by Mometrix of any particular political, scientific, or religious point of view.

SAFE PRACTICES AND SAFEGUARDS FOR USING HAND TOOLS

Use the following safe practices when using hand tools:

- Choose the appropriate tool for the job.
- Know the hazards of using the tool.
- Use tools correctly.
- Inspect, maintain, and repair or replace tools.
- Store tools properly.

Hand tool safeguards further protect users of hand tools. Safeguards include tool guards and handle designs. The length, shape, and material of a handle can all affect its safety:

- Long handles on axes and hatchets keep the tool away from the user so long swings can safely be used.
- Short handles on tools such as hammers allow for closer body work.
- Bent handles can help prevent repetitive motion and tissue compression disorders.
- High-friction plastic handles can help users grip a tool more tightly and can be molded to individual users.

HAND TOOL INSPECTIONS

The term "hand tools" refers to handheld tools that are not powered. This includes screwdrivers, hammers, axes, scissors, box cutters, and pliers. All tools should be inspected before every use to ensure they are in good operational order. One should examine hand tools to ensure the metal is not cracked or thinning to the point that it may break during use. One should also check the handles to ensure they are firmly seated and that any grip coverings are in place and not loose. Tools that are comprised of several parts should be checked to make sure that the parts are securely attached.

POWER TOOL INSPECTIONS

Power tools refer to handheld tools powered by electricity, batteries, compressed air, or internal combustion engines. These tools include power saws, drills, nail guns, grinders, cutting tools, sanders, and riveters. Some inspection elements are common to other handheld tools, such as checking that the metal parts are not cracked or worn and that all parts are firmly seated and not loose. The electrical cord should be inspected to make sure it is not worn or the insulation frayed. The electrical prongs should be inspected to make sure they are not bent or missing (especially the round grounding prong). If there are cutting blades in the tool, they should be inspected to make sure they are not too worn or needing sharpening; dull blades are unsafe due to the extra force required to use them that may cause one's grip to slip.

HAZARDS AND CONTROLS FOR LADDERS AND SCAFFOLDS

Common hazards associated with ladders include the following:

- Falling off the ladder
- Slipping off the ladder rungs
- The ladder tipping over, the ladder sliding
- Metal ladders conducting electricity

To improve safety when using ladders, the following actions should be taken:

- Ensure that ladder rungs are slip-resistant.
- Place ladders far enough from the wall so the arch of the foot can fit on the rung, not just the toe.
- Inspect ladders frequently for damage such as cracks, bends, and other wear.
- Anchor or tie ladders to a support structure.
- Do not use metal ladders around electrical conductors.

Copyright © Mometrix Media. You have been licensed one copy of this document for personal use only. Any other reproduction or redistribution is strictly prohibited. All rights reserved.
This content is provided for test preparation purposes only and does not imply an endorsement by Mometrix of any particular political, scientific, or religious point of view.

Hazards associated with scaffolds include the following:

- Unsecured or loose planks
- Overloading and structural failure
- Tipping over, falls.

To improve safety when using scaffolds, the following actions should be taken: Select a scaffold that is rated for the load it will have to support; Inspect scaffolds before use, checking planks, bolts, ropes, outrigger beams, bracing, and clamps; Place the legs of the scaffold on a solid base. Tie the scaffold to a solid structure.

HAZARDS AND CONTROLS ASSOCIATED WITH WORKING AROUND PRESSURIZED SYSTEMS
PRESSURIZED STEAM

The most common source of pressurized steam in an industrial environment is created by a boiler system. Boilers are used to generate steam for heating (both process heating and comfort heating), sterilization, food processing, cleaning, humidification, and steam turbines to produce electricity. The use for steam extends beyond the industrial environment to high-rise office and apartment buildings.

There are several safety risks that must be considered when pressurized steam is used in industrial processes. The pipes that carry steam present a burn hazard, so they should either be insulated or there should be barriers erected, so employees do not inadvertently touch the pipes. Signs should be posted warning of the pressure and heat risk. Lockout points should be labeled, and employees should be instructed to bleed lines properly after locking out and before working on them. Fittings and valves should be regularly inspected to ensure that they do not leak or provide a failure point that will allow hot steam to escape into the work area.

COMPRESSED AIR

There are many systems that use compressed air; being aware of them will enable the safety officer to mitigate the risks posed. They are used to inflate tires and other items, power pneumatic tools, provide the air pressure to pneumatically convey materials, and power paint spray guns, sanding equipment, and sandblasting equipment. Air compressor systems must be inspected regularly for leaks, and care must be taken to ensure hoses are free of cracks and damage that may pose a dangerous leak.

Compressed air is a powerful and widely utilized industrial tool, but it poses many hazards that must be controlled. Compressed air produces noise, so noise exposure measurements must be conducted and a hearing conservation program implemented if necessary. Compressed air streams are an eye and skin hazard—if blown directly on the skin or into the eyes, the air can cause serious damage. Eye protection must be worn. Nozzles for compressed air must be Occupational Safety and Health Administration (OSHA)-approved to reduce the nozzle air pressure to below 30 psi. Any gauges used when inflating with compressed air must be tested to ensure they are accurate to minimize the risk of overinflating and causing a blowout.

HIGH-PRESSURE FLUIDS

High-pressure fluids are used in such tools as paint sprayers, fire hoses, and fuel injection devices. Hazards associated with these fluids include air and gas injuries, injection injuries, and whipping of lines. Air and gas injuries occur when pressurized air or gases rupture or injure bodily tissues. Injection injuries occur when a stream of air, gas, or liquid penetrates the skin and enters the body. The fluid can be toxic, or injected gas can cause embolisms. Whipping occurs when fluid moving through a nozzle makes the muzzle and hose whip around. The hose and nozzle can hit people and property, causing injuries and damage. To reduce the hazards of high-pressure fluids, you can lower the pressure level, keep hydraulic lines away from people, use solid lines instead of hoses, and use shields or guarding to separate sprays from people and property. It is also important to train workers using high-pressure fluids in safety procedures they need to follow.

Copyright © Mometrix Media. You have been licensed one copy of this document for personal use only. Any other reproduction or redistribution is strictly prohibited. All rights reserved.
This content is provided for test preparation purposes only and does not imply an endorsement by Mometrix of any particular political, scientific, or religious point of view.

HAZARDS AND CONTROLS WHEN WORKING WITH ROBOTS

When workers enter a robot's work envelope (total area in which a robot's moving parts move), they can be struck by the robot, trapped between the robot and another surface, or hit by a tool or other object that the robot drops or ejects. To reduce these hazards, workers should only enter a functioning robot's work envelope when they need to teach the robot a new motion. To keep workers safe when they do need to enter the work envelope, it needs to be well-lit with a clean floor that is clear of any obstructions. The work envelope needs to be kept clear of non-essential objects and any electrical and pneumatic components on the robot need to be covered by fixed covers and guards. Before entering the area, all lockout and test procedures need to be in place. Workers also need to ensure that they remove all tools and equipment from the work envelope when they leave.

Workplace Hazards

NANOPARTICLES

OSHA defines a **nanoparticle** as having dimensions between one and one hundred nanometers (0.000000001 meters). **Nanotechnology** involves manipulation of nanoparticles, including carbon nanotubes, titanium dioxide, and cadmium selenide for uses in healthcare, electronics, and consumer products.

Research has shown that nanoparticles may be inhaled and cause damage to the lungs and **respiratory system**. Some nanomaterials may pass through cell membranes and damage **cellular structures**, while others may be **carcinogens**. Additionally, such fine particles may be **combustible** and, due to their smaller size, may have lower explosive temperatures than the bulk material. There are also indications that materials that are generally non-toxic in larger particle size may pose health hazards when reduced to the nanoscale.

COMBUSTIBLE DUST

The Occupational Safety and Health Administration (OSHA) describes **combustible dust** as any finely divided airborne particle that presents a fire or deflagration hazard under certain conditions. Such fine particles can become airborne during cutting, blasting, grinding, polishing, sifting, conveying, or mixing dry materials. Only the dusts of specific materials are combustible, such as aluminum and magnesium metals, coal dust, wood dust, flour or sugar dust, soap, and some textile fiber dusts.

Where all dusts can be inhaled and may affect the respiratory system, combustible dusts have the added explosion hazard. Unconfined combustible dusts that are initiated can deflagrate and ignite other combustible materials, including flammable chemicals. If the dust is confined, then any ignition can cause an **explosion**. Explosions can cause concussion injuries, destroy structures or equipment, or may start fires.

INDUSTRIAL HEAT SYSTEMS

An **industrial heat system** is any thermal device used to prepare or process materials. In an industrial operation, industrial heat can be used to melt metal, produce glass, or liquefy plastics. The energy for the system can be derived from **fuel-based** sources (coal, natural gas, fuel oil, or biomass burners), **steam**, or **electricity**. Fuel-based sources create heat by burning, while electrical systems can heat by direct application or by heating filaments. Steam can be applied directly or indirectly to a system to increase the temperature.

The heat elements and heated materials can cause **burns** or **heat illness** in workers. In some operations, the heat source or molten material may produce **radiation** that is harmful to the eyes. Systems such as burners or steam nozzles may create an occupational **noise** hazard. Fuel-based systems will present **fire** and explosion hazards. Electrical systems will have **high-voltage** hazards and the potential to act as an ignition source for flammable materials.

Copyright © Mometrix Media. You have been licensed one copy of this document for personal use only. Any other reproduction or redistribution is strictly prohibited. All rights reserved. This content is provided for test preparation purposes only and does not imply an endorsement by Mometrix of any particular political, scientific, or religious point of view.

HIGH-PRESSURE SYSTEMS

High-pressure fluids can be used for cleaning, such as power washers or waterjet cutting. Compressed air is used in pneumatic devices and tools, while high-pressure gas cylinders are used in welding operations.

High-pressure systems are any fluid system that exceeds 100 pounds per square inch (psi) or any air system where the pressure exceeds 150 psi. Compressed gas cylinders can be filled as high as 2,900 psi, while hydraulic systems can operate as high as 10,000 psi or beyond.

High pressure systems present **injection hazards** in which the fluid or gas breaks through the skin and the material is injected into the body. Injected gases can enter the bloodstream and cause embolisms. If the high-pressure delivery system uses a flexible hose, loss of control of the device can result in a whipping hazard. Employees must also protect their eyes and mouth from any material that is dislodged by the high-pressure system.

RADIATION

Certain elements can undergo radioactive decay and release ionizing radiation. **Ionizing radiation**, in the form of **gamma rays**, **alpha particles**, and **beta particles**, has sufficient energy to damage tissue, cells, or even DNA. Ionizing radiation sources include x-ray machines and radioactive chemicals, such as uranium and polonium.

Acute exposure to very high levels of radiation can result in skin burns or **radiation sickness**. Symptoms of radiation sickness include nausea, vomiting, and even death in a matter of days or weeks. Chronic exposure to low levels of radiation can increase the risk of various **cancers**, with the risk being directly related to the total lifetime dose.

SILICA DUST

Silica is the most common material on the planet and exists in two primary forms: crystalline and non-crystalline. Materials containing **crystalline silica** are common in the construction industry, being found in brick, grout, concrete, stucco, and numerous other materials. When these materials are cut, blasted, ground, or otherwise formed into small particles, the dust that is created can be breathed in.

Crystalline silica exposure has been related to lung cancer, tuberculosis, chronic obstructive pulmonary disease (COPD), and silicosis. **Silicosis** is the scarring of the lung tissue created by the buildup of crystalline silica dust particles. Short-term silicosis symptoms include coughing, excessive phlegm production, and shortness of breath. Over time, the scar tissue obstructs the airways and stiffens the lungs, resulting in difficulty breathing, which can lead to fatigue, weight loss, and reduced blood oxygen levels.

SPRAY APPLICATIONS

Industrial coatings (like paint) can be applied in a variety of ways. **Spray application** is a common method of applying a coating to a variety of materials using a high-pressure system. Some metal products use **powder application**, where charged particles are sprayed onto a grounded metal surface that is then heated to form the coating.

Inhalation of the coating particles can cause asthma and other breathing problems. Spray applications may involve the use of solvents that pose a variety of health hazards if inhaled, such as narcosis or dizziness, and the solvent may be a **systemic toxin**. Eye and skin irritation are both possibilities if protective equipment is not used. Any high-pressure system exceeding 100 psi has the potential to cause **injection injuries** to unprotected skin. Powder coating processes expose the worker to **electrical** and **high temperature** hazards.

Copyright © Mometrix Media. You have been licensed one copy of this document for personal use only. Any other reproduction or redistribution is strictly prohibited. All rights reserved.
This content is provided for test preparation purposes only and does not imply an endorsement by Mometrix of any particular political, scientific, or religious point of view.

BLASTING

Abrasive blasting is any process that uses high-pressure streams of air or water mixed with an abrasive material to clean or polish surfaces. Materials used as abrasives include crushed garnet, coal slag, beaded or crushed glass, sand, or metal shot.

The use of high-pressure streams of air and water can create airborne debris that can enter the eyes or respiratory system. The abrasive agent may also have specific health hazards, including silicosis from sand blasting, lung damage from coal blasting, and the potential of traces of toxic metals in metal grit. **High-pressure** systems (greater than 100 psi) have the potential to cause injection injuries. The mechanical process of blasting generates high levels of occupational **noise**, which can be compounded in confined locations. Finally, the hose used to deliver the material can present a struck-by hazard if the workers lose control during operation.

MOLTEN METAL

Molten metal refers to any metal that has been heated past its melting point to be formed, molded, or applied to surfaces. The range of melting points of metals is large, ranging from lead (327 °C/621 °F) to iron (1538 °C/2600 °F). The extreme temperatures needed to liquefy metals creates a variety of hazards.

Improper heating of the metal or contamination of the molten material can cause hot liquid splashes that result in **burns**. Working in the foundry environment exposes employees to **heat stress** due to both the temperature required to liquefy metals and the protective equipment necessary to handle molten materials safely. Materials with high melting points may produce harmful **electromagnetic radiation**. Employees working in this environment must wear shielded lenses to protect their eyes from damaging infrared and ultraviolet radiation.

Human Performance

The Department of Energy defines **human performance** as a series of behaviors, what people say and do, in order to achieve the overall objectives of the organization. Recognizing that people make mistakes, human performance-based safety looks to identify the **organizational** and **internal factors** that cause a person to make unsafe decisions. Recognizing that accidents are rarely caused by intentionally unsafe acts, a human performance approach seeks to identify the disconnect between the intention and the result.

Human performance is based on five principles:

1. Humans make **mistakes**.
2. Errors are **predictable** and are therefore **preventable**.
3. Individual behavior is influenced by organizational **culture**.
4. High performance is achieved through encouragement and **positive reinforcement**.
5. Negative events can be avoided by learning from past mistakes.

ERROR

Error can be defined as unintended outcomes that occur while conducting a planned activity. An error is a product of the tools, tasks, and organizational environment in which employees work. It is understood that errors have underlying causes and result in injuries only if there is a hazard present. Errors can be caused by either intentional or unintentional acts, either of which can result in an accident under certain conditions.

Human error is not considered the cause of health and safety incidents, but rather the result of safety management system failures. When management clearly states goals, has clear procedures, provides employees with the necessary tools, and trains employees, performance increases and errors decrease. If any

Copyright © Mometrix Media. You have been licensed one copy of this document for personal use only. Any other reproduction or redistribution is strictly prohibited. All rights reserved. This content is provided for test preparation purposes only and does not imply an endorsement by Mometrix of any particular political, scientific, or religious point of view.

of those safety system elements are missing, then human performance theory recognizes that errors and the associated resultant injuries will occur.

Chapter Quiz

Ready to see how well you retained what you just read? Scan the QR code to go directly to the chapter quiz interface for this study guide. If you're using a computer, simply visit the bonus page at **mometrix.com/bonus948/csp** and click the Chapter Quizzes link.

Copyright © Mometrix Media. You have been licensed one copy of this document for personal use only. Any other reproduction or redistribution is strictly prohibited. All rights reserved. This content is provided for test preparation purposes only and does not imply an endorsement by Mometrix of any particular political, scientific, or religious point of view.

Emergency Preparedness, Fire Prevention, and Security

Transform passive reading into active learning! After immersing yourself in this chapter, put your comprehension to the test by taking a quiz. The insights you gained will stay with you longer this way. Scan the QR code to go directly to the chapter quiz interface for this study guide. If you're using a computer, simply visit the bonus page at **mometrix.com/bonus948/csp** and click the Chapter Quizzes link.

Emergency Response Planning and Business Continuity

FIRE EVACUATION DRILLS

The National Fire Prevention Association (NFPA) Standard 1 establishes the provisions for **evacuation drills**. Drills must:

- Be held with a **sufficient frequency** to familiarize occupants with the process (typically at least annually).
- Be managed in an **orderly and organized** fashion to convey individual responsibilities during a true emergency and not purely focused on speed of egress.
- Not always be held at the same time and manner to better **resemble an actual event.**
- Identify a **relocation area** to allow for all occupants to be accounted for.
- Be **documented** by way of a record noting the date, time, and type of drill.

COMPONENTS OF EMERGENCY RESPONSE PLAN PREPARATION

An **emergency** is any sudden and unexpected event that has the potential to harm life or the environment. Emergencies may be a result of natural or man-made causes. Companies that store or use hazardous materials must prepare an **emergency response plan** to reduce any potential harm that may be caused by a release. The ability to quickly respond and stabilize an emergency requires planning, practicing, evaluating, and adjusting.

- **Planning**: creating an emergency response plan in advance of an emergency is critical in managing the event. Planning allows for establishing **roles and responsibilities,** as well as allowing the company to procure necessary materials before they are needed. The overall goal of planning is to reduce the time between event and mitigation to reduce losses.
- **Practicing**: response team members must learn to use equipment, ask questions about their role, and troubleshoot the response plan elements before an actual emergency occurs. **Practicing and training** is the most effective method for team members to learn to work together without the stress of a real emergency.
- **Evaluating**: the effectiveness of a plan must continually be evaluated. Practicing an emergency response allows the team to identify **areas for improvement** before an emergency occurs. Robust plans are also evaluated after an emergency response. Evaluation should include identifying aspects that worked well, areas that can be improved, and things that failed to work as designed.
- **Adjusting**: the plan should be adjusted whenever improvements are identified. Response activities that worked well can be expanded to other aspects of the response. Areas that need correction can be adjusted and then practiced again to determine if the performance goals were achieved.

Copyright © Mometrix Media. You have been licensed one copy of this document for personal use only. Any other reproduction or redistribution is strictly prohibited. All rights reserved. This content is provided for test preparation purposes only and does not imply an endorsement by Mometrix of any particular political, scientific, or religious point of view.

EMERGENCY PLANNING AND COMMUNITY RIGHT TO KNOW ACT

The Environmental Protection Agency (EPA) is assigned responsibility for enforcing the **Emergency Planning and Community Right to Know Act (EPCRA)**. This Act was created to help communities plan for chemical emergencies that could originate from companies in or around their area that store or handle toxic chemicals. The intent of the EPCRA is to increase community knowledge and access to information regarding chemicals at facilities, their uses, and provisions to manage releases. EPCRA addresses four main elements: planning, notification, information, and reporting.

- **Planning**: facilities that store large amounts of toxic or hazardous chemicals are required to cooperate with local agencies in preparing **emergency release response plans**.
- **Notification**: facilities must immediately report any release of hazardous substances that exceed a designated reportable quantity (RQ).
- **Information**: in order to inform the community, facilities must provide local response agencies with the safety data sheets (SDS) of those materials on-site and also an inventory form delineating those chemicals.
- **Toxic release inventory**: facilities must annually submit a report of the release of specified chemicals that exceed certain thresholds.

EMERGENCY ACTION PLANS VS. EMERGENCY RESPONSE PLANS

Emergency planning is a critical element for any organization to reduce losses to people, property, and the environment. A robust plan prepares for emergencies and outlines proper response activities to allow the business to respond quickly and effectively. There are two basic types of plans: an emergency action plan (EAP) and an emergency response plan (ERP).

The Occupational Safety and Health Administration (OSHA) in 29 CFR 1910.38 requires that businesses develop an **emergency action plan (EAP).** An EAP is for companies who will only respond to emergencies in a **defensive** fashion—meaning only evacuation and communication with first responders will take place. An EAP is a general guidance document that can be used for a variety of emergencies, from fires to mass violence incidents. The goal of the EAP is to ensure employee safety, not to address the emergency. The EAP must be in writing for employers having more than ten (10) employees and must include the following elements:

- Procedures for emergency reporting
- Procedures for evacuation
- The process for maintaining critical operations
- Procedures to account for employees after an evacuation
- Procedures for employees providing rescue or medical aid
- Procedures for those responsible for the plan

For facilities who will act as their own **first responders** for chemical emergencies, OSHA requires an **emergency response plan (ERP)** by way of 29 CFR 1910.120. The ERP establishes emergency response procedures, assigns roles and responsibilities, identifies necessary equipment, defines training requirements, and requires measures to prevent the spread of the chemical release to the surrounding environment. Within the ERP framework, employers can determine the level of response they will have their employees engage in before transitioning to external assistance.

EMERGENCY ACTION PLANS

The Occupational Safety and Health Administration (OSHA) requires that employees have plans in place to provide for the safe evacuation of employees during emergencies. This **emergency action plan (EAP)** is required in 29 CFR 1901.38, which outlines the necessary parts of the Plan. An EAP can be thought of as a collection of situation-specific plans written for each foreseeable emergency (e.g., fire, flood, tornado, earthquake, etc.). Each of these specific plans should have three main components: procedures, coordination, and assignments.

Copyright © Mometrix Media. You have been licensed one copy of this document for personal use only. Any other reproduction or redistribution is strictly prohibited. All rights reserved. This content is provided for test preparation purposes only and does not imply an endorsement by Mometrix of any particular political, scientific, or religious point of view.

Procedures: each individual plan within the EAP should have specific, step-by-step procedures describing the **actions** employees should take, beginning when the emergency occurs and ending when they are released to return home. Procedures should include notification systems, response actions, assembly areas for counting employees, and criteria for releasing employees.

Coordination: each action plan should include how the company will coordinate with responding agencies. This may differ for the various emergency events, or it may be a single local agency for all situations. Coordination should include identifying points of contact for each agency and a means to communicate with the agency in the event normal communication (i.e., cell phones) are not functioning.

Assignments and responsibilities: the EAP should clearly assign individuals who will be responsible for managing the actions outlined in the plan. From individuals responsible for ensuring the building is evacuated to identifying who will give the "all clear" to return, each role needs to be clearly assigned to an individual or position.

EMERGENCY EVACUATION PLANS

An effective **emergency evacuation plan** requires both pre-planning and training all staff on the plan. If employees do not know how to evacuate in an emergency, the risk of injury and loss of life increases dramatically. Information that staff should be informed of includes:

- Location of primary and secondary **evacuation routes,** including signage.
- Location of fire alarm pull stations.
- Primary and secondary **assembly areas** to report to after the building has been evacuated to account for all staff.
- Designating who is responsible for evacuating visitors.

In addition to staff responsibilities, the emergency coordinator must also account for:

- Employees and visitors with mobility, hearing, or sight impairments.
- Identifying medical aid for staff, including meeting with area hospitals to ensure they can address specific hazards at the facility, including chemical exposures and burns.

POST-EMERGENCY TRAUMA RESPONSE TEAMS

In addition to the loss of property and physical injuries after an emergency, companies should also be prepared to manage psychological injuries to their employees. Emergency situations may place people in highly stressful situations or expose them to sounds, images, or other experiences that may be disturbing. If left untreated, psychological trauma can result in post-traumatic stress disorder, which can have long-lasting effects on employees. Employers can assist employees through the post-emergency period using trauma response teams.

A **trauma response team (TRT)** is one or more persons who are psychologists or have specialized training in helping people who have been exposed to extremely stressful situations. Providing employees access to this support service as soon as possible after an emergency can help employees navigate the emotions related to the emergency. The TRT can work with employees individually or in group settings and, if necessary, can refer employees to additional mental health support services.

DISASTER RECOVERY PLAN TEAM MEMBERS

Although employers may put a lot of effort into emergency planning, equal effort must be put into recovery planning. **Recovery planning** is all the activities necessary to return the business to its pre-emergency functionality as quickly as possible. Recovering too slowly can have long-lasting impacts on the survival of a company. The plan should outline when and how the company will begin its efforts to move from response to recovery. A disaster recovery plan should have assignments for the following team members: recovery

Copyright © Mometrix Media. You have been licensed one copy of this document for personal use only. Any other reproduction or redistribution is strictly prohibited. All rights reserved.
This content is provided for test preparation purposes only and does not imply an endorsement by Mometrix of any particular political, scientific, or religious point of view.

coordinator, recovery teams, damage assessment team, salvage team, logistics coordinator, and technology coordinator.

The **recovery coordinator** is the individual with the ultimate responsibility and authority over recovery operations. They must have the authority to make decisions, delegate responsibilities, and approve resource allocation.

Recovery teams are task-specific groups assigned by the recovery coordinator. Depending on the facility, teams can include facility management, security, human resources, environmental protection, and technical work groups.

The **damage assessment team** is responsible for an inventory of all plant systems, equipment, goods, and stores that require repair or replacement. The damage assessment team must include representatives from the facilities or maintenance department who are familiar with all the facility's systems and may include external contractors, such as engineers or utility company representatives. The team should document all damage with photographs for insurance purposes.

Salvage teams are responsible for securing systems, equipment, goods, and stores that can be used during recovery and after normal operations have resumed. The salvage team should be able to report on the usability of items after they have been assessed by knowledgeable persons.

Logistics and supply line coordinators are responsible for reestablishing all vendor contacts and contracts after the emergency has subsided. Receiving necessary raw materials or goods and securing shipping of finished goods are critical in getting the business back up and running. If prior contacts and contracts are no longer feasible, then new suppliers and shippers must be procured.

Communication and technology coordinators are responsible for addressing the phone, data, and online services after the emergency. If systems cannot be brought online at once, they are responsible for prioritizing systems and coordinating with service providers to reestablish external communications.

INCIDENT COMMAND SYSTEM

The Federal Emergency Management Agency (FEMA) has implemented the **Incident Command System (ICS)** as a means of coordinating multi-agency responses to an emergency event. The intent is to use standardized assignments, language, and responsibilities to efficiently and effectively leverage the unique capabilities of multiple agencies that respond simultaneously to a large-scale emergency event. The ICS model eliminates redundancy, reduces overlap, and consolidates control to effectively manage emergency response actions. The ICS is designed to be scalable in that it can be used for small incidents with minimal staffing or for large multi-agency incidents.

COMMAND STAFF POSITIONS

All command staff report to the **incident commander,** who is not part of the command staff but directs its efforts. The command staff consists of the public information officer, safety officer, and liaison officer.

- The **public information officer** (PIO) communicates with the media and holds press briefings. The PIO should be the only individual providing updates to the public through the media or online platforms to maintain consistent messaging.
- The **safety officer** is responsible for the overall safety of the responders. They review the response plan to identify any hazardous situations. They also receive and review updates on changing hazards as well as conduct safety briefings for staff.
- The **liaison officer** acts as the point contact for all responding agencies. They maintain a list of all primary agency contacts and a knowledge of each agency's capabilities to provide input for response activities.

Copyright © Mometrix Media. You have been licensed one copy of this document for personal use only. Any other reproduction or redistribution is strictly prohibited. All rights reserved.
This content is provided for test preparation purposes only and does not imply an endorsement by Mometrix of any particular political, scientific, or religious point of view.

Promulgated by the Federal Emergency Management Agency, the **Incident Command System (ICS)** is a command-and-control system for emergency responses. The incident commander establishes the objectives of an emergency response and relies on specific functional groups to execute and support the **incident action plan (IAP)**. The ICS is divided into five functional areas, or sections: operations, planning, logistics, finance/administration, and intelligence. The intent of the division is to assign specific responsibilities to avoid redundancy. All functional area section chiefs report directly to the incident commander.

Operations: responsible for conducting the tactical operations for an incident and directing resources to execute the incident action plan.

Planning: responsible for developing and updating the incident action plan to achieve the objectives established by the incident commander. This section is also responsible for assessing resource utilization and coordinating additional resources with the logistics section.

Logistics: plans, acquires, and provides the resources needed by operations and other sections. In addition to tools and equipment, logistics also addresses personnel needs, such as hygiene, food, and rest areas.

Finance/administration: monitors costs and makes funds available for logistics. This functional area is also responsible for tracking and recording all activities to apply for applicable reimbursements after the emergency has abated.

Intelligence: an optional functional area that can be formed in specific responses, such as mass attacks. This functional area conducts investigations, manages evidence related to unlawful events, conducts missing persons investigations, and works to prevent additional attacks.

ROLE OF THE INCIDENT COMMANDER

The **incident commander** has overall responsibility for the incident and ultimately oversees the **Incident Command System**. All of the support sections relay information to and receive directions from the incident commander.

The incident commander is responsible for establishing the overall objectives for the response. They determine and approve the **incident action plan** and coordinate command staff and section chief activities. They establish the incident command post, which is the singular location for all information to funnel into for decision-making and prioritization. Lastly, it is the incident commander who determines when the Incident Command System can be deactivated.

ICS GENERAL STAFF

The Incident Command System (ICS) is overseen by the **incident commander,** who is directly supported by the general staff. The **general staff** is made up of the chiefs for each of the functional areas: operations, logistics, planning, and finance/administration. These positions report directly to the incident commander and can be filled by qualified persons from any agency or jurisdiction. If external personnel are not assigned as chiefs, interagency coordination can be facilitated by appointing agency representatives as deputy chiefs.

General staff can pass information horizontally or vertically within the system. However, all directions can only take place through their respective chains of command. For small scale events, positional responsibilities can be combined within a single individual as long as they are capable of executing all responsibilities effectively.

ICS COMMAND STAFF

The Incident Command System (ICS) is overseen by the **incident commander,** who is directly supported by the general staff. The **general staff** is made up of the chiefs for each of the functional areas: operations, logistics, planning, and finance/administration. The command staff provide additional support to the incident commander, but do not fall into any other functional area. The command staff consists of the public

Copyright © Mometrix Media. You have been licensed one copy of this document for personal use only. Any other reproduction or redistribution is strictly prohibited. All rights reserved.
This content is provided for test preparation purposes only and does not imply an endorsement by Mometrix of any particular political, scientific, or religious point of view.

information officer, safety officer, and liaison officer. Some responses may require additional expertise added to the command staff, such as legal counsel and a medical advisor.

Legal counsel may be added to advise the incident commander of issues pertaining to evacuations, emergency proclamations, and the media's right to access. In responses with large numbers of injuries or fatalities, a **medical advisor** may be necessary. This individual would direct the work of trained medical staff, coordinate transportation of the injured to hospitals, and coordinate with the coroner or medical examiner to manage the deceased and their families.

COMPARISON OF ICS TO OTHER SYSTEMS

The **Incident Command System** is the **field-level** emergency response structure. Based on a standardized structure, roles, and responsibilities, its primary purpose is to address an emergency incident.

The **Standardized Emergency Management System (SEMS)** is designed to be leveraged when an emergency exceeds the capabilities or resources of a local agency. SEMS is organized into five levels: **field, local, operational area, regional,** and **state.** As the resources of the local agency are exhausted or as the incident grows to impact multiple jurisdictions, SEMS coordinates resources between local and regional governments all the way up to the state level. Under SEMS, each level of government operates a coordinated emergency operations center, using the ICS terminology, to coordinate activities and resource allocation.

The **National Incident Management System (NIMS)** is the emergency response structure promulgated by the Federal Emergency Management Agency (FEMA). It requires agencies that will work together in emergency responses to adhere to similar basic principles, terminology, and structure. Where ICS is used at the field level, NIMS uses the same structure at the state operations center for statewide or regional responses.

TRAINING FOR COMMAND STAFF IN NIMS

The Federal Emergency Management Agency (FEMA) establishes and offers training on the elements of the **Incident Command System**, which is the basic response structure for emergencies. After Hurricane Katrina, FEMA established the NIMS Training Program. Federal, state, local, and private entities have the responsibility to identify personnel to be trained on the NIMS curriculum.

Command staff should complete, at a minimum, **IS-700 NIMS**: an introduction (which addresses the goals and objectives of the NIMS) and **IS-100 NIMS** Incident Command System (an introduction to the roles and terminology used in ICS). Additional, specialized training, including role-specific training, is available through FEMA.

BUSINESS CONTINUITY PLANS

A **business continuity plan** is a document that outlines the process for a business to recover from an unplanned event, such as a natural disaster. The plan should include elements addressing when it is to be implemented, assigning authority for initiating and terminating the plan, identifying critical systems, outlining the emergency response itself, identifying resources necessary for recovery, and delineating a method to test the plan prior to an emergency. The plan also identifies who in the organization is responsible for recovering systems and supply chains, lists external vendors or contractors to provide support, and prioritizes systems to return the business to productivity as soon as possible.

The goal of the plan is to reduce unanticipated downtime by reacting quickly and efficiently to emergencies in order to get back to servicing customers as soon as possible.

UTILITY OUTAGES

Utility outages can occur due to natural events or can be the result of human action, such as errors, accidents, or terrorism. Businesses should have plans in place to address any potential utility outage. **Vulnerable utilities** to natural events include power, natural gas, and water.

Copyright © Mometrix Media. You have been licensed one copy of this document for personal use only. Any other reproduction or redistribution is strictly prohibited. All rights reserved.
This content is provided for test preparation purposes only and does not imply an endorsement by Mometrix of any particular political, scientific, or religious point of view.

Businesses should assess the dependency of their operations on utilities and devise strategies in their **business continuity plan** to manage disruptions to one or any combination of said operations. The plan should identify critical processes necessary for operation and then devise ways to manage an interruption, both for short- and long-term timeframes. The exposure to disruption of any one utility will be dependent on the specific business and the operations at each location. Backup generators, alternate water supplies, and liquefied gas hookups can be used to reduce the down time associated with utility outages.

PLANNING FOR SPECIFIC TYPES OF EMERGENCIES

NUCLEAR INCIDENTS

A nuclear incident may occur if one is near a nuclear reactor or radiation sources are mishandled in a hospital or laboratory setting. In addition to normal disaster preparedness, local authorities should coordinate an external nuclear incident disaster response. Evacuate the premises if advised to do so. If not, shelter in place by closing all doors and windows, and close air-conditioning ventilation to ensure contaminated air does not enter the building. If one has already been exposed to radioactive dust particles, remove contaminated clothing if possible and seal them in a plastic bag. Take a shower to wash off contamination. If food has been contaminated with dust, it must be washed before consumption or thrown away. Shelter in place until advised by local authorities that this is no longer necessary.

NATURAL DISASTERS

Depending on the area of the country, the most likely natural disasters are tornadoes, earthquakes, and floods. To respond to a tornado, try to get into a basement or storm cellar. If this is not possible, get into an interior room. If outside, lie flat on the ground in a ditch. If in a vehicle, do not park under a bridge or overpass. During an earthquake, the safest place to take cover is under a sturdy piece of furniture or against an inside wall. If outdoors, stay outdoors. After an earthquake shaking stops, turn off gas and electricity lines until they can be inspected for damage. In the event of a flood, preparedness is the most important. Know the risk of flood, and pay attention to the news for announcements of flood risk. If in a flood zone, elevate water heaters and electrical panels, and install check valves on the sewer lines to prevent floodwater backup. Turn off electricity before a flood, and install sandbags at doorways if possible. Do not walk or drive through moving water; it is easy to be swept away in moving floodwater.

TERRORIST ATTACKS

Preparedness for a terrorist attack can be planning for a lone gunman or for a bomb situation. In the case of a lone gunman, authorities advise to plan to run, hide, and fight in that order. Run away from an active shooter if possible; if not hide in a locked office or closet or under a desk. If these are not options, group together to fight the shooter. In the case of a bomb attack, preparedness measures to take are to supply staff with flashlights and dust masks in the event of a bomb detonation. Stay away from windows during a detonation event. Evacuate the area if it is safe to do so, but do not use the elevator.

CHEMICAL SPILLS

An internal chemical spill should be prepared for by staging chemical spill kits at strategic locations in the facility and training personnel to use them. The source of the spill should at first be eliminated (e.g., close the valve or turn the drum upright so material does not continue to leak out of it). Large spills should be cleaned up by professional hazardous material cleanup contractors. If there is a major chemical release near one's workplace, look to local authorities to provide direction on whether evacuation or shelter in place is the safest response. If there is a possibility of shelter in place, one's disaster preparedness kit should be equipped with plastic sheeting and duct tape to seal off doorways and windows. Air-conditioning vents should be closed to keep contaminated air out. Stay indoors until local authorities advise it is safe to exit the building.

ACTIVE VIOLENT ATTACKS

The Department of Homeland Security (DHS) defines an **active shooter** event as when there is a person on the premises with the intent to injure or kill, typically using a firearm. The shooter may have one or more targets

Copyright © Mometrix Media. You have been licensed one copy of this document for personal use only. Any other reproduction or redistribution is strictly prohibited. All rights reserved.
This content is provided for test preparation purposes only and does not imply an endorsement by Mometrix of any particular political, scientific, or religious point of view.

in mind or may be targeting the facility indiscriminately. As active shooter events are typically brief, the arrival of law enforcement may occur after the event has subsided. Thus, businesses should prepare their employees for proper response.

The active shooter response plan should include **notification methods** for law enforcement, **evacuation routes**, and a **notification system** in the event a shooter is on site. Employees should be **trained** on the elements of the plan, how to interact with law enforcement, and what to do when the situation has stabilized. Like other emergency response incidents, training **exercises** should be conducted to familiarize employees with the process.

Fire Prevention, Protection, and Suppression Systems

CHEMICAL FIRES

Flash point is the minimum temperature where enough vapor exists above a material to ignite when exposed to an ignition source.

Lower flammable/explosive limit is the minimum concentration (expressed as a percentage) of flammable vapor in air that is capable of propagating a flame when exposed to an ignition source. Below this concentration, there is not enough fuel for the fuel/air mixture to ignite—the mixture is "too lean."

Upper flammable/explosive limit is the maximum concentration (expressed as a percentage) of a flammable vapor in air that is capable of propagating a flame when exposed to an ignition source. Above this concentration, there is too much fuel and not enough air for the mixture to burn—the mixture is "too rich." The area between the lower and upper flammable/explosive limit is called the **flammable range**. The difference between a flammable range and explosive range is determined by whether or not the fuel is contained within an enclosed space or container.

Auto-ignition temperature is that minimum temperature where a chemical will ignite without the presence of an ignition source. The energy in the environment is at a level high enough for combustion.

CONTROL MEASURES FOR CHEMICAL FIRES

Control measures for any hazard should follow the hierarchy of controls—**elimination, substitution, engineering controls, administrative controls,** and **personal protective equipment (PPE)**. In the case of preventing chemical fires, PPE will not be applicable.

Elimination: determine if the chemical is necessary or can be removed from the process. Eliminating a redundant cleaning step or unnecessary heating can remove the hazard.

Substitution: replacing the flammable chemical with a combustible or non-flammable substitute can address the fire hazard. If feasible, water-based solutions would be preferred to flammable mixtures.

Engineering controls: exhaust ventilation can be used to remove flammable vapors and combustible dusts from the environment. Containing or removing ignition sources, such as enclosing pilot lights or grounding equipment susceptible to static charge buildup, can reduce the chance of a chemical fire. Proper storage of flammable and combustible liquids, including the use of safety cans and fire-resistant storage cabinets and refrigerators for chemicals with low flash points, can prevent fuels from catching fire. Proper **separation** and **segregation** of incompatible materials can prevent chemical reactions from initiating a fire. Finally, intrinsically safe lighting in chemical storage areas and grounding of equipment that builds static charges can further eliminate sources of ignition.

Administrative controls: policies limiting the amount of flammable chemicals in an area or process can reduce the chance of fire. Adherence to standard operating procedures can assist in reducing the chance of fire due to operator error. Proper signage prohibiting open flames can remind employees to avoid ignition sources

Copyright © Mometrix Media. You have been licensed one copy of this document for personal use only. Any other reproduction or redistribution is strictly prohibited. All rights reserved.
This content is provided for test preparation purposes only and does not imply an endorsement by Mometrix of any particular political, scientific, or religious point of view.

in hazardous atmospheres. Finally, proper training of staff on chemical hazards, proper chemical handling, and how to respond to releases can further assist in preventing chemical fires.

VAPOR PRESSURE AND FLAMMABILITY

Vapor pressure is the force exerted by the vapor of a material. It is caused by the evaporation or sublimation of the material under normal conditions. The amount of material evaporating is dependent on temperature, with higher temperatures causing higher amounts of vapor above the material.

It is only the vapor of a material that burns, not the liquid or solid itself. Therefore, materials that have higher vapor pressures evaporate at lower temperatures. This means that at any temperature, the material will have a significant concentration of vapor above the material available to burn. The vapor will mix with available air to create **flammable mixtures**. Thus, materials with high vapor pressures have decreased lower flammable/explosive limits, higher upper flammable/explosive limits, and lower ignition temperatures.

PYROPHORIC AND WATER-REACTIVE CHEMICALS

Pyrophoric chemicals are those chemicals that spontaneously combust when exposed to air. To prevent combustion, these chemicals can be stored underwater. Examples of pyrophoric chemicals include metal hydrides, finely divided metal powders, and specialized chemical reagents.

Water reactive chemicals react, sometimes violently, with water. The degree of reaction can vary from forming a gas to a sustained flame to an explosion. These chemicals must be stored away from any source of water and may be stored under a heavy oil, such as kerosene. In certain climates, these chemicals can react with the humidity in the ambient air. Examples of water reactive chemicals include sodium metal, potassium metal, aluminum chloride, lithium metal, and phosphorus pentachloride.

ELECTRICAL FIRES

GROUNDING AND BONDING

Chemical fires can be initiated by **static discharge**. **Static electricity** is an electric charge that is at rest. A **static charge** can be formed whenever two dissimilar materials make contact and are then separated and neither of the materials can dissipate the charge. In chemical processes, this condition can arise by the friction of fluids or solids moving through pipes or agitation in their containers. This motion results in a charge being unequally distributed, resulting in a difference in potential. When the potential difference between two materials or containers becomes large enough and they are brought into contact with each other, the current moves between the materials or containers in the form of a discharge. In the presence of flammable liquids or dusts, a fire or explosion can result.

Bonding is a method of equilibrating the potential of the two containers so that no differential exists. Electrons move freely through a conductor so that the charge on both containers is equal. This is typically accomplished by way of a metal strap or wire that is attached to both containers. Bonding does not remove the charge from the containers but makes the charge equal, thereby preventing a discharge.

Grounding is the process of providing a path to earth that removes the charge from the container. The path for the charge must include a wire or rod that is in contact with bare earth to allow the charge to flow from the container. Grounding can be used in conjunction with bonding.

ARC FLASH HAZARDS

The arc flash hazard level is determined by calculating the expected energy of an arc flash at various distances from the source. It is an engineering calculation that takes into account the fault current of the panel or connection involved and determines the energy felt at various distances away from the work. The energy is calculated in units of calories per square centimeter. The distance used is generally three feet (an arm's length) for the workers who will be doing the work. The equation can also be used to determine the exclusion boundary around the work; this is the distance at which the incident energy is less than 4 cal/cm^2, and a

Copyright © Mometrix Media. You have been licensed one copy of this document for personal use only. Any other reproduction or redistribution is strictly prohibited. All rights reserved.
This content is provided for test preparation purposes only and does not imply an endorsement by Mometrix of any particular political, scientific, or religious point of view.

bystander can observe the work clad in regular work clothes. These are engineering calculations that must be performed by a qualified engineer.

The **Arc flash level of PPE** is presented in National Fire Protection Association (NFPA) 70E, Standard of Electrical Safety in the Workplace. The level of protection required to protect a worker from an arc flash hazard is determined by engineering calculations that estimate the amount of incident energy potentially released from an arc flash, measured in calories per square centimeter. There are four levels, numbered from one to four (category zero can be considered normal industrial protection—safety glasses, hard hat, gloves, and steel-toed boots). The categories are as follows:

- **Category 1**: up to 4 cal/cm^2—flame-resistant long-sleeved shirt, pants, and coveralls, plus face shield
- **Category 2**: up to 8 cal/cm^2—cotton underwear, plus flame-resistant long-sleeved shirt and pants, and face shield
- **Category 3**: up to 25 cal/cm^2—all of Category 2 plus Level 3 arc flash suit
- **Category 4**: up to 40 cal/cm^2—all of Category 2 plus Level 4 arc flash suit

FIRE SCIENCE
FIRE TETRAHEDRON

Fire is a rapid and self-sustaining chemical reaction involving oxygen, heat, and fuel. This can be visualized with the **fire triangle** or, if the chemical chain reaction is included, the **fire tetrahedron.** If any one of the four elements of the tetrahedron is removed, the fire cannot continue. Thus, fires can be extinguished by removing the oxygen, removing the fuel, cooling the fire down, or blocking the chemical reaction with an inert agent.

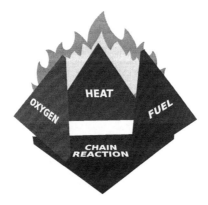

In the US, there are five **classifications** of fire, defined by the combustible they burn:

Class A: ordinary combustibles such as wood, paper, cloth, trash, and plastics

Class B: flammable liquids (or gases) such as gasoline, petroleum oil, and paint

Class C: energized electrical equipment

Class D: combustible metals such as potassium, sodium, aluminum, and magnesium

Class K: cooking oils and fats

Water and foam extinguishers are good for class A fires only. Carbon dioxide, clean agent, or halogenated extinguishers can be used on class B and C fires. Dry powder extinguishers are designed for class D fires. Wet chemical extinguishers are used on class K fires.

Copyright © Mometrix Media. You have been licensed one copy of this document for personal use only. Any other reproduction or redistribution is strictly prohibited. All rights reserved.
This content is provided for test preparation purposes only and does not imply an endorsement by Mometrix of any particular political, scientific, or religious point of view.

UPPER AND LOWER EXPLOSIVE LIMITS

The main difference between flammable liquids and gases is that **flammable gases** are ready to burn, but **flammable liquids** must be vaporized to burn. Vapor can only burn if the concentration in air is between the **lower flammability limit (LFL)** and **upper flammability limit (UFL)**. If the concentration is lower than the LFL, the mixture of gas and atmosphere is "too lean." If the concentration is higher than the UFL, it is "too rich." For example, gasoline has a flammable range of 1% to 8%, meaning it can only burn when the concentration of gasoline vapor in the air is between 1 and 8 percent.

The flammable range of a mixture of gases in air can be calculated by using **Le Chatelier's mixing rule** for combustible volume fractions:

$$LFL_{mix} = \frac{1}{\sum \frac{f_n}{LFL_n}}$$

where

LFL_{mix} = lower flammability limit of the mixture

f_n = fractional concentration of component n

LFL_n = lower flammability limit of component n

Note that the formula is the same for UFL, simply substituting UFL_{mix} for LFL_{mix} and UFL_n for LFL_n. For example, consider a gas mixture of 40% carbon monoxide, 10% octane, and 50% ammonia. Assuming the flammable ranges for these gases are 12-75%, 1-7%, and 15-28%, respectively, the upper flammability limit of the mixture can be calculated as such:

$$UFL_{mix} = \frac{1}{\sum \frac{f_n}{UFL_n}} = \frac{1}{\frac{0.4}{0.75} + \frac{0.1}{0.07} + \frac{0.50}{0.28}} = 0.267, \text{ or } 26.7\%$$

COMBUSTIBLE DUST

Dust explosions occur when fine particles of a material disperse in the air and then ignite. The dust can become airborne during a normal working procedure or when dust that has settled in a room is disturbed. Such explosions can occur in a series with an initial explosion disturbing settled dust, causing it to become airborne and ignite. In addition, oxidizing agents in the air can make a dust explosion even more severe. Most organic dusts are combustible in the air, as are some inorganic and metallic dusts. The *severity* of the explosion depends on numerous factors:

- Type of dust
- Size of the dust particles (Smaller particles ignite more easily)
- Concentration of particles in the air (Higher concentrations of particles are more flammable)
- Presence of oxygen (More oxygen pressure increases the likelihood of an explosion)
- Presence of impurities (Inert materials mixed in with the dust reduces its combustibility)
- Moisture content (Moisture increases the ignition temperature, making combustion less likely)
- Air turbulence (Combustion occurs more readily and explosions are more severe when air turbulence mixes the dust and air together)

The **combustible dust explosion pentagon** is similar to the fire triangle in that both require fuel, an oxidizer, and an ignition source to occur. In addition to these, a dust explosion must have dispersion and confinement of dust particles. These elements are created when dust particles are suspended in air in an enclosed space. If any of the five elements are not present, a dust explosion cannot occur.

Copyright © Mometrix Media. You have been licensed one copy of this document for personal use only. Any other reproduction or redistribution is strictly prohibited. All rights reserved. This content is provided for test preparation purposes only and does not imply an endorsement by Mometrix of any particular political, scientific, or religious point of view.

DETECTION SYSTEMS

Smoke detectors detect particulate matter in the air associated with smoke. There are two types: **ionization detectors** and **photoelectric detectors.** An ionization detector uses a small radioactive source and detector in a chamber. The source creates a charge that crosses a small chamber to complete the circuit. Smoke particles interrupt the current, thereby triggering an alarm. A photoelectric detector uses a light sensor system. A light source is directed away from the detector in the unit. When smoke particles enter the unit, the light is scattered and strike the sensor, initiating the alarm.

Heat detector: in environments where particulate matter may be present and a smoke detector would initiate false alarms, a heat detector may be a better choice. In these types of detectors, two thermistors are used, with one sealed from the environment and another exposed to the air temperature. A change in current between the exposed thermistor and the reference thermistor will cause a current to flow, thereby initiating the alarm.

Flame detector: these units will respond when they detect specific frequencies of light (ultraviolet, visible, or infrared) associated with combustion.

SUPPRESSION SYSTEMS, FIRE EXTINGUISHERS, SPRINKLER TYPES
CLASSES OF FIRE EXTINGUISHERS

The National Fire Protection Association's Standard 10 identifies five (5) different classes of portable fire extinguishers: **A, B, C, D,** and **K**. Selection of the appropriate extinguisher is based on the fuel type(s) present that would contribute to a fire and the amount of combustible material present (fuel load). Combination extinguishers, such as A/B, B/C, or A/B/C, can be used in environments where multiple fuel types exist.

Class A: primary fuel is ordinary combustibles, such as wood or paper, or paper-based materials, such as cardboard; may be water or a dry chemical-extinguishing material.

Class B: the main fuel source for this class would be petrochemical products, such as flammable liquids, combustible liquids, solvents, alcohols, and flammable gases; extinguishing material can be dry chemical, foam, or carbon dioxide.

Class C: fires that involve energized electrical equipment; extinguishing material is typically dry chemical or carbon dioxide.

Class D: this class is used for fires involving flammable metals that burn at very high temperatures, such as magnesium titanium, sodium, and lithium; extinguishing material is dry chemical, typically sodium chloride or graphite.

Class K: this class is used for kitchen fires involving grease and fat; extinguishing material is typically an alkaline mist, such as those containing potassium citrate, potassium acetate, or potassium carbonate.

EXTINGUISHERS FOR ELECTRICAL FIRES

A dedicated **Class C** extinguisher is recommended for use on fires that involve energized electrical equipment. This also refers to fires involving portable equipment that is still plugged in. The extinguishing medium must be non-conductive to prevent an electrocution hazard to the individual using the extinguisher.

However, these types of fires can cause surrounding materials to ignite. Thus, a dedicated Class C extinguisher may not be appropriate for the surrounding materials. If a dedicated Class C extinguisher is necessary for delicate electronic equipment, then a supplemental Class A or Combination A/B should also be available in the area. Another option is to select a Class A/B/C extinguisher for the area to address all available fuel types.

FIRE EXTINGUISHER INSPECTIONS

In Standard 10, the National Fire Protection Association (NFPA) establishes the requirements for portable extinguisher inspections. A **portable extinguisher** is any device that is hand-carried or on wheels that

Copyright © Mometrix Media. You have been licensed one copy of this document for personal use only. Any other reproduction or redistribution is strictly prohibited. All rights reserved.
This content is provided for test preparation purposes only and does not imply an endorsement by Mometrix of any particular political, scientific, or religious point of view.

contains an extinguishing agent under pressure. The goal of an inspection is to ensure the extinguisher is in the proper location and has not been actuated, damaged, or tampered with and is ready in an emergency. NFPA has established two types of inspections which must be recorded on a tag affixed to the extinguisher: **monthly** and **annual**.

The monthly extinguisher inspection serves to check that the unit is ready if needed and also that units are in their proper locations. The monthly visual inspection is recorded on the tag by way of initials and date of the individual conducting the inspection. The inspector must check the following:

- Area around extinguisher is clear, with a clearance of no less than 24 inches
- Pressure gauge is in the operable range
- Extinguisher contains agent, which is verified by lifting the unit
- Tamper seal and pin are in place and intact
- Unit is not visibly damaged

A record of the inspection is made by replacing and marking the tag on the unit. The annual inspection shall address all the elements of a monthly inspection and also the following (note: inspection frequency may vary based on the construction and type of extinguisher):

- Operating instructions are present and visible
- Hydrostatic test has not expired (6-year interval for most extinguishers)
- Pin removes from handle when pulled
- All boots, foot rings, and attachments are in good condition and are removed.
- Internal inspection

CARBON DIOXIDE SUPPRESSION SYSTEMS

Carbon dioxide-based extinguishing systems can be used when water may create additional hazards, such as the presence of water-reactive chemicals causing burning liquids to flow, or when water may damage sensitive equipment. Such systems can be found on ships, in certain metal processing industries, and in computer rooms. Carbon dioxide is an **inert gas** that removes the oxygen from the system to inhibit combustion. The gas is non-flammable, provides its own pressurization in the system, is non-reactive with other materials, works in three dimensions, and does not leave a residue after discharge.

However, there are issues to consider with carbon dioxide systems. Carbon dioxide systems are designed to achieve an airborne concentration of approximately 34%, which is lethal. Additionally, the agent is designed to reduce the **oxygen level** in the room, creating an IDLH environment. The National Fire Protection Association (NFPA) Standard 12 outlines the requirements for carbon dioxide systems. Wherever carbon dioxide systems are installed, **warning signs** must be visible informing employees to leave the area when the **alarm** sounds and not to re-enter until properly ventilated. Additional warnings must be posted in the gas storage area in the event the storage tanks leak. The system must also be outfitted with **audible and visual alarms** that actuate prior to system discharge to provide occupants time to evacuate. These alarms must be distinct from other alarm systems in the building and must be at least 90 dB. Audible alarms can be silenced after all entrances have been secured, while visual alarms must continue to function until the atmosphere is safe for re-entry.

WATER-BASED SPRINKLER SYSTEMS
INSPECTIONS FOR WATER-BASED SPRINKLER SYSTEMS

The National Fire Protection Association (NFPA) Standard 25 denotes the required inspection regimen for a **water-based automatic fire suppression system**. The major components of the system must be inspected on a recurring basis. The frequency of some inspections is dependent on the system components and, in some

Copyright © Mometrix Media. You have been licensed one copy of this document for personal use only. Any other reproduction or redistribution is strictly prohibited. All rights reserved.
This content is provided for test preparation purposes only and does not imply an endorsement by Mometrix of any particular political, scientific, or religious point of view.

locations, can vary in winter months to avoid freeze damage. These inspections must be recorded to demonstrate compliance at the frequency listed below:

- **Sprinklers** are to be inspected from the floor level annually. Sprinklers should be inspected for leakage, corrosion, damage, loss of fluid in heat detection element, and paint.
- **Standpipe and hose systems** shall be visually inspected annually, ensuring that the hydraulic design information sign is present and legible.
- Wet standpipe gauges shall be visually inspected quarterly, while dry standpipe gauges shall be inspected weekly.
- **Private fire hydrants** have components that must be inspected quarterly, semi-annually, and annually.
- **Pump systems**, if present, shall be visually inspected weekly for damage, leaks, and proper pressure.
- **Water storage tanks**, if present, have components that must be inspected daily, weekly, monthly, quarterly, annually, and at 3-5-year intervals, depending on the system.
- **Valve systems** must be inspected weekly, monthly, quarterly, or annually, depending on the system components.
- **Specialized systems**, such as water spray, mist, and foam-water systems have additional inspection requirements.

SPRINKLER REQUIREMENTS FOR STORAGE RACKS

Warehouses are designed to compactly store large amounts of materials. The storage capacity in any floor space is vastly increased with the use of **storage racks**. However, storage racks may contain a high **fuel load** of flammable or combustible materials stacked several feet high. This increases the fuel load for each square foot of storage space in the warehouse. For materials that are classified as **high-pile** (12 feet high or more), the National Fire Protection Administration (NFPA) Standard 13 describes the sprinkler system requirements. Fire and loss risk increase because high-piled materials can act like flues, increasing the rate of smoke generation and flame spread

Factors that are considered in system design include the type and amount of materials to be stored, density of the stored materials, the rack design, the height of the racks, aisle width, the slope of the roof, and the height of the roof. At a minimum, NFPA 13 requires sprinklers to be installed 18-54 inches above the storage rack, depending on the rack design and construction. The use of in-rack sprinklers with heads in between two levels of storage can also increase coverage and decrease losses in the event of a fire. Because of this, any sprinkler system for high-piled storage must be designed by an engineer.

FIRE SPRINKLER REPAIR REQUIREMENTS

The National Fire Protection Association (NFPA) Standard 25 outlines the inspection, maintenance, and testing requirements for water-based fire protection systems, including automatic sprinkler systems. The standard requires an annual inspection of spare sprinklers. Spare sprinklers must be immediately available in the event of damage or actuation of the system in order to return the system to a state of readiness as soon as possible. Spare sprinklers of each type used in the system must be kept on hand along with a wrench for each type. (A pipe wrench or crescent wrench cannot be used to substitute for manufacturer-recommended tools.) Replacement sprinklers must be the same style, orifice size, temperature rating, spacing requirements, deflector type, and system design ratings.

No less than six (6) new replacement sprinklers must be kept on the premises at all times. At least two (2) sprinklers of each type must be maintained. All sprinklers must be stored in a cabinet where the temperature will not exceed 100° F.

Copyright © Mometrix Media. You have been licensed one copy of this document for personal use only. Any other reproduction or redistribution is strictly prohibited. All rights reserved.
This content is provided for test preparation purposes only and does not imply an endorsement by Mometrix of any particular political, scientific, or religious point of view.

SEGREGATION AND SEPARATION

SEGREGATION OF HAZARDOUS MATERIALS FOR STORAGE

Hazardous materials must be properly segregated for storage. The materials should be classified according to hazard class. The US Department of Transportation hazard classification system provides a suitable guide for hazard classification. Strong acids must be segregated from storage near strong bases, because when the two mix a violent exothermic reaction can occur. Similarly, oxidizing materials must be stored away from flammable materials because oxidizers promote fire. Flammable or combustible materials must be stored away from any sources of heat or ignition (including a hot environment). Alkali metals must be stored under oil to prevent air contact and must be stored away from any flammable materials. Attention must be paid to possible chemical reactions; a good source of information for chemical incompatibility is the Safety Data Sheet.

STORING COMPRESSED GAS CYLINDERS

Commonly used hazardous materials that are supplied and stored in gas cylinders include oxygen, argon, acetylene, and helium. Care must be taken when storing and handling them to prevent release of the compressed gas or fires and explosions. The cylinders should be stored upright in a well-ventilated area and must be chained in place to prevent them toppling over. The caps that cover the valves should be tightly secured to prevent the valves being opened inadvertently. If cylinders are stored outside, they must be protected from ice, rain, and high temperatures and be stored on a fireproof surface. If stored inside, they must also be on a fireproof surface. Oxygen must always be stored segregated from fuel gases (such as acetylene) and separated by a distance of at least twenty feet or by a fire-resistant wall of at least five feet in height.

STORAGE AND HANDLING OF FLAMMABLE MATERIALS

Flammable liquids must be stored in approved flammable containers; for example, flammable liquids will generally be supplied in glass bottles or metal drums, not in plastic containers. If a secondary container is to be used (e.g., to transport a small quantity of gasoline), the container must be approved to hold flammable liquids. Flammable liquids must be stored in approved flammable liquid storage cabinets or in segregated rooms that have separate ventilation and whose walls meet fire resistance ratings. Aisles must be maintained at 3 feet in width, and egress routes must be kept clear in areas where flammable liquids are stored.

When storing flammable or combustible materials indoors, the following actions should be taken: Store only small amounts in occupied areas or buildings; larger amounts need to be stored in separate facilities. Follow National Fire Protection Association (NFPA) standards when designing storerooms for flammable and combustible materials, including standards for ventilation, static electricity grounding systems, explosion-proof light switches and fixtures, self-closing doors with raised sills, signage, and floor contours. Follow NFPA standards for storage cabinets designed to hold small quantities of flammable and combustible items. When transferring flammables from one container to another, ensure that the containers are touching each other or are connected to a grounding rod or line. Store flammable liquids in closed containers. When dispensing flammable liquids from drums, use gravity or suction pumps rather than pressurizing the drum. Use safety cans to move flammable liquids from their storage area to their point of use. Use plunger cans if you need to wet cleaning cloths with a flammable liquid. Store cloths that have been contaminated by flammable liquids in a small self-closing container that you empty regularly.

HOUSEKEEPING

Housecleaning refers to the process of cleaning an area: sweeping, wiping surfaces, throwing away trash, etc. **Housekeeping** means putting things away where they belong. Every tool, piece of equipment, and material should have a designated storage area. Hazardous materials should have special storage areas designed specifically for them.

Effective housekeeping is important from both environmental and safety standpoints. Poor housekeeping can increase the volume of waste generated by causing spills and by accumulating out-of-date materials that must be discarded. From a safety standpoint, poor housekeeping can create slip, trip, and fall hazards; can block emergency exits; and can block emergency equipment such as fire extinguishers. Setting **housekeeping**

Copyright © Mometrix Media. You have been licensed one copy of this document for personal use only. Any other reproduction or redistribution is strictly prohibited. All rights reserved.
This content is provided for test preparation purposes only and does not imply an endorsement by Mometrix of any particular political, scientific, or religious point of view.

policies and enforcing them, along with employee training and an inspection program, are the key elements of an effective housekeeping program. Effective housekeeping begins with only necessary materials in the work area, with everything having a designated location, and with clear communication of these guidelines (all elements of a 5S program). Employees should be trained to clean up as they go along throughout their shift and should set aside time at the end of shift to clean up completely. All tools should be replaced into storage lockers and containers returned to storage locations. Surfaces should be kept clean. Effective housekeeping promotes a safe workplace and increases job satisfaction because it is more pleasant to work in an orderly environment.

CONTROLLING HAZARDOUS CHEMICALS

Part of housekeeping is removing dust and cleaning up spills. **Hazardous dust** needs to be regularly vacuumed from surfaces so that it will not become airborne. A vacuum that traps the contaminants must be used. Materials can become airborne when they are loaded, unloaded, and transferred to other containers. Transferring within a closed transfer or exhaust system can protect workers from being exposed to airborne dust and vapors. For **liquids**, it is also helpful to use drip pans or containers to collect overfill spills and leaks. Leak detection programs can include both automatic sensors and regular visual inspections of valves and pipes. The sensors can trigger alarms or even shut down a process. Repairing leaks quickly minimizes any potential exposures. Workers and supervisors who use hazardous chemicals need to receive training on what hazards they face and how to protect themselves. This training will help them stay safe and is also required by OSHA standards and by law in some states.

Housekeeping is important in controlling fire hazards, especially storage and handling of rags and wipes soaked in flammable materials. If one accumulates rags and wipes soaked with solvents or similar materials, they should be stored in metal canisters rated for flammable rag storage and emptied daily into suitable containers. If rags and wipes soaked with flammable solvents are stored in piles outside of the metal canister, they can build up heat and create conditions favorable to spontaneous combustion. It is also important to store flammable liquids in an orderly manner in cabinets or rooms rated for flammable chemicals.

Transportation and Security of Hazardous Materials

TRANSPORTATION AND SECURITY OF HAZARDOUS MATERIALS

There are nine classes of hazardous materials which require the use of placards to warn safety personnel, workers, and responders of chemical or substance hazards associated with a shipping load. The proper use and placement of placards is described in 49 CFR 172.504:

- The type of hazard should be noted from the shipper's manifest and from the markings upon the shipping pallets of the substance. Placards must be placed upon the transport vehicle as soon as the hazardous substance is loaded.
- Placards must be placed in visible locations on the front and back ends of the vehicle and on both sides. This is the minimum requirement for placarding.
- Placards should be positioned where they can be easily seen and at least three inches from other graphics or writing. Words and numbers must be level and read from left to right.

TRANSPORTATION HAZARDS

Railroads present a number of hazards including derailment resulting in fire, explosion, environmental contamination, inappropriate transportation of hazardous materials, and accidents resulting from collisions with vehicles at crossings. Safety aboard railcars has been improved through the use of grab bars and ladders to facilitate climbing. Safety engineers are constantly improving warning devices at crossings. Tankers have been designed with insulation that keeps temperatures from rising to unsafe levels. Companies that ship hazardous materials must ensure that containers used are safe and appropriate for the material, packing methods are appropriate, transportation methods used are safe, and any storage in route is within safety guidelines for the material.

Copyright © Mometrix Media. You have been licensed one copy of this document for personal use only. Any other reproduction or redistribution is strictly prohibited. All rights reserved. This content is provided for test preparation purposes only and does not imply an endorsement by Mometrix of any particular political, scientific, or religious point of view.

The federal government passed the Transportation Safety Act in 1974 to address dangers associated with moving hazardous materials. This law regulates packaging, labeling, and moving hazardous materials and assigns penalties to companies or individuals who violate its mandates. This act organizes hazardous materials into different categories including radioactive, flammable, corrosive, combustible, and biological hazards. Risks are reduced by specifically designing safety guidelines for each category. Controls include identifying specific materials and associated hazards, establishing guidelines for labeling, placing limits on quantity or size of materials transported, monitoring movement of materials, mandating training, banning movement of some materials, and specifying packaging and container materials. The movement of hazardous materials is overseen by the Department of Transportation which publishes data on hazardous materials with daily updates on the Federal Register. Companies and individuals who move hazardous materials bear responsibility for knowing and complying with these guidelines and mandates.

Media regarding transportation of hazardous materials is published by a number of government agencies and private organizations including the National Highway Traffic Safety Administration, the Federal Motor Vehicle Safety Standards (FMVSS), the Society of Automotive Engineers (SAE), the Department of Transportation (DOT), and the Urban Mass Transportation Administration. All entities produce materials that establish safety standards and guidelines designed to reduce or control hazards associated with moving certain materials. These include identifying hazards through labeling, manifests, specific coded design of packaging using colors and symbols, established routes, and education for individuals involved. Additionally, federal agencies such as DOT set up specific rules related to packaging and containers for particular materials. These rules include both mandates on what can be shipped and how and also the identification procedures to be used.

Accidents and injuries commonly result from mistakes in the movement and handling of dangerous materials. Labeling all materials properly and generating accurate and detailed shipping manifests allows individuals involved in these activities to take proper precautions. Labeling should include identification of the materials as well as proper transportation and handling instructions. Federal regulatory agencies such as DOT mandate appropriate warning signage on all transportation vehicles such as trucks and trains. Hazardous materials shipments must also be tracked with a specific assigned number that can pull up all related data such as material type, quantity, and known hazards. Labeling on a container as well as shipment tracking allows faster response in case of emergencies.

Effective communication is one strategy for lessening the risks of moving hazardous materials. Common tools to facilitate this communication include incident reports and proper training for individuals involved in transporting hazardous substances. Informing appropriate supervisors and regulatory authorities of all non-routine incidents and accidents is important in limiting the negative impact of people and property. For example, the Department of Transportation should be informed of any unintended dispersal of dangerous substances during transport as well as any accidents, illness, or injuries related to moving these substances. All individuals involved in moving hazardous substances should be properly trained in risks, procedures, and emergency response. This even includes individuals with only incidental contact and those with no contact, but supervision over transportation decisions.

US DEPARTMENT OF TRANSPORTATION REQUIREMENTS

The US Department of Transportation requires hazardous materials and hazardous waste carriers to develop security plans (49 CFR Part 179.802) for materials that are flammable, explosive, or poisonous. The security plan must be in writing and include: plans to mitigate known hazards in the transportation and storage of the material; personnel security (background checks); unauthorized access (prevention of theft); identification of responsible person(s) involved in overseeing the entire project, as well as those directly responsible for transportation and storage; security duties of all those involved in the transportation and/or storage of the material; and hazmat training for all involved. Specific response procedures must be listed for all identified safety and security hazards.

Copyright © Mometrix Media. You have been licensed one copy of this document for personal use only. Any other reproduction or redistribution is strictly prohibited. All rights reserved.
This content is provided for test preparation purposes only and does not imply an endorsement by Mometrix of any particular political, scientific, or religious point of view.

Workplace Violence and Prevention

REDUCING WORKPLACE VIOLENCE

Managers can incorporate several strategies into the workplace to prevent or reduce **workplace violence**. Employers can provide a secure workplace.

- The workplace should be well-lit with no areas that are secluded or isolated.
- Work flows and traffic patterns should be easily observed so employees are never left in a vulnerable position. Employees should have freedom and control within their own area of the workplace but limited access to other areas.
- Surveillance cameras can allow for further monitoring of the workplace.
- Employers can also control access to the workplace. Fencing and locks can restrict trespassers from entering the work area. Security procedures that require visitors to check in reduce the risk of violence from outsiders.

ESTABLISHING A WORKPLACE VIOLENCE PROTECTION PROGRAM

A workplace violence protection program should establish a zero-tolerance policy toward threats and intimidation in the workplace. The policy must be communicated to all employees, managers, and supervisors.

- Personnel must be encouraged to promptly report observed or experienced incidents of violence or threats of violence in the workplace.
- Anonymous reporting procedures can be established and implemented in the form of a "complaint box."
- Written incident reports should be maintained detailing time, date, and nature of the threat incident. Part of the written report should be geared toward risk assessment and the likelihood of future occurrences.
- Liaison with law enforcement and social service agencies should be made so that appropriate referrals can be made when necessary.
- Training teams should be established to address, advise, and counsel employee groups with a view toward maintaining a civil and non-threatening work atmosphere.

PHYSICAL SECURITY PROGRAMS

Physical security is important in an industrial environment; it is unfortunately rather common for there to be instances of workplace violence that may have been prevented by a more robust physical security program. **Physical security programs** should include controlled and locked access points, the use of photo identification badges that are required to be worn in a visible location, and requiring badge entry at all entrances. Employees should be educated about the importance of physical security and not providing access to those who are not able to show a current badge for entry. Upon separation of an employee, badges should be confiscated immediately and deactivated.

Chapter Quiz

Ready to see how well you retained what you just read? Scan the QR code to go directly to the chapter quiz interface for this study guide. If you're using a computer, simply visit the bonus page at **mometrix.com/bonus948/csp** and click the Chapter Quizzes link.

Copyright © Mometrix Media. You have been licensed one copy of this document for personal use only. Any other reproduction or redistribution is strictly prohibited. All rights reserved. This content is provided for test preparation purposes only and does not imply an endorsement by Mometrix of any particular political, scientific, or religious point of view.

Occupational Health and Ergonomics

Transform passive reading into active learning! After immersing yourself in this chapter, put your comprehension to the test by taking a quiz. The insights you gained will stay with you longer this way. Scan the QR code to go directly to the chapter quiz interface for this study guide. If you're using a computer, simply visit the bonus page at **mometrix.com/bonus948/csp** and click the Chapter Quizzes link.

Toxicology

SIGNS AND SYMPTOMS OF CHEMICAL EXPOSURE

A **chemical exposure** symptom is the body's reaction to a chemical. Symptoms may become evident immediately after an exposure, while others may take years to develop. Common symptoms of exposure to a chemical can be found on the safety data sheet for the substance. The signs and symptoms of chemical exposure depend on the chemical itself and also the route of exposure, whether it be a dermal exposure, inhalation, or ingestion.

Symptoms of a **dermal contact** can include dryness, itching, cracking, burns, blisters, or redness near the point of contact.

Inhalation of chemicals are usually identified by a smell or taste followed by coughing, sneezing, itching or burning in throat, detectable chemical odor, shortness of breath, dizziness, lack of concentration, or cognitive difficulties.

Ingesting chemicals can lead to abdominal pains, nausea, vomiting, or acid reflux-like symptoms.

ACUTE AND CHRONIC EXPOSURE

Exposure to toxins is discussed in terms of dose (concentration), duration (length of time over which exposure occurred), and the nature of the toxin itself. As the terms imply, acute refers to an immediate impact and chronic to a long term, sometimes more subtle, impact. With chronic exposure, a person may experience negative consequences from low doses of the toxin if exposed over long periods of time. Remember, the concept of "low" is not the same for all toxins (see TLV or PEL for particular substances). The adverse effects of acute toxins are typically well known. A direct link between symptoms and toxin exposure is more difficult to make with chronic exposure than with acute exposure.

LC_{50} AND LD_{50}

The terms LC_{50} and LD_{50} refer to the results of scientific tests involving animals, usually laboratory mice or rats. LC_{50} and LD_{50} studies are standard scientific experimentation used to forecast the toxicity of hazardous substances. The only difference between the two terms is in the method of administration. LC_{50} refers to the **concentration** of an airborne substance in the presense of which one half of the subject animals will die. Similarly LD_{50} refers to the **dosage** of an ingested substance (or a substance absorbed through the skin) for which one half of the subject animals will die.

MUTAGENS

A mutagen is a chemical substance or radioactive particle that causes mutations in a cell's DNA. This is important in planning for toxic material hazards because mutagenesis is thought to be one mechanism by which toxic substances can cause cancer. A mutagen acts to disrupt the normal pattern of the building blocks of DNA (the genes) that code for proteins necessary for cell life. Normal cells have many redundant repair mechanisms that allow for repair; however, repeated assaults by a mutagen can overwhelm the normal repair

Copyright © Mometrix Media. You have been licensed one copy of this document for personal use only. Any other reproduction or redistribution is strictly prohibited. All rights reserved. This content is provided for test preparation purposes only and does not imply an endorsement by Mometrix of any particular political, scientific, or religious point of view.

mechanisms and allow mistakes in the DNA to persist. Tumors are cells that have malfunctioned and proliferate unimpeded, and eventually take over the organism. Examples of commonly encountered mutagens are polycyclic aromatic hydrocarbons (found in tar and charred meat), benzene (found in gasoline), and ionizing radiation (found in the sun's rays). It must be noted that mutagens are not necessarily carcinogens but are likely to promote carcinogenesis.

TERATOGENS

A teratogen is a chemical substance that causes birth defects when either the mother or father has been exposed to the substance before or during the conception and gestation of the baby. Many teratogens act in the first trimester of pregnancy, when a large amount of cell division and specialization occurs. Teratogens can be chemicals or medicines that are prescribed for common medical conditions. A common teratogen is ethyl alcohol; overexposure to alcohol during pregnancy can cause a cluster of problems in the child termed "Fetal Alcohol Syndrome." A teratogen of the 1960's was thalidomide; women who ingested the drug (prescribed for morning sickness) gave birth to babies with stunted limbs and other physical abnormalities. Because of these possible long-lasting effects, it is important to limit a pregnant woman's exposure to chemicals. There are substances that exert teratogenic effects in males, such as polychlorinated biphenyls and DBCP (a pesticide).

OTOTOXINS

An **ototoxin** is a chemical that can cause **hearing loss** or that **compounds** hearing loss when an employee is exposed to industrial noise. The results of exposure can be **tinnitus** (ringing in the ear), **hearing loss**, or **loss of balance**. Ototoxins can affect aural structures, such as the cochlea, or may impact the auditory nerve. Effects are dose-dependent and may be temporary or permanent, depending on the dose of the chemical. Ototoxicity is not a risk factor that is currently listed on Safety Data Sheets. Ototoxins can be **medications** or **industrial chemicals**.

Medications: chemotherapy drugs, certain antibiotics, and large doses of aspirin and ibuprofen

Chemicals: solvents such as toluene, carbon disulfide, and n-hexane; nitriles, including acrylonitrile; and certain metals, like mercury compounds, lead compounds, and tin.

Carcinogens

A **carcinogen** is any substance that is known or suspected of causing cancer or increasing the incidence of cancer. **Cancer** is a condition where normal cells are damaged so that they no longer undergo programmed cell death. The result is uncontrolled cell growth, which is manifested in the form of **tumors**. The tumors can interrupt normal physiological processes and, if left uncontrolled, can cause death. This condition can be caused by damage to the cell's DNA or disruption in the cellular metabolism. Disruption in cellular metabolism can cause a cell to become less specialized, which can mask it from the immune system's cell termination process.

Carcinogenic substances include radionuclides, certain wavelengths of radiation, and certain chemicals such as benzene, polynuclear aromatic hydrocarbons, and aflatoxins.

CARCINOGEN GROUPS

The **International Agency for Research on Cancer (IARC)** is an intergovernmental agency that is part of the World Health Organization (WHO). The goal of the Agency is to promote international collaboration in the fight against cancer. The Agency has four major objectives: monitor the global occurrence of cancer, identify causes of cancer, investigate the biological processes behind cancer-related diseases, and develop strategies to control

Copyright © Mometrix Media. You have been licensed one copy of this document for personal use only. Any other reproduction or redistribution is strictly prohibited. All rights reserved.
This content is provided for test preparation purposes only and does not imply an endorsement by Mometrix of any particular political, scientific, or religious point of view.

cancer. As part of their mission, the IARC groups substances based on their potential to cause cancer in humans using a numbered scale from 1-4, with Group 1 being the most hazardous.

- **Group 4**: substances designated at Group 4 are probably not carcinogenic in humans. Scientific evidence shows either a lack of cancer-causing results in humans and animals or an inadequate evidence of cancer-causing effects.
- **Group 3**: substances in this Group are considered not classifiable as causing cancer in humans. The substances either have inadequate information in humans and animals, or have caused cancer in animals but present no evidence that it may do so in humans. Substances in this Group are considered to need more research.
- **Group 2B**: substances in Group 2B are designated as possible human carcinogens. The substance has limited data on its effects on humans but has sufficient animal data. Additionally, substances in this group may have suggestions of being human carcinogens based on other data.
- **Group 2A**: substances in this Group are probably human carcinogens. A substance may be classified as Group 2A if it has similar data results as Group 2B but belongs to a class of substances designated as Group 2A or Group 1.
- **Group 1**: known human carcinogen. Substances in this Group have sufficient human or animal data and strong indications of cancer-causing mechanisms.

Ergonomics and Human Factors

Ergonomics is defined as the relationship between people and their environment, including tools, equipment, work area, vehicles, facilities, and printed material. Good ergonomics improves output and performance and reduces error and accidents by making the environment comfortable and user-friendly. The four general principles of ergonomics that apply to safety engineering are as follows:

- People versus machines: This principle states that people are better at some jobs, such as reasoning inductively and handling unexpected occurrences, while machines are better at other jobs, such as repetitive operations and deductive reasoning.
- Change the job, not the person: People have limits, and not recognizing those limits can cause errors, hazards, and accidents. It is better to change a job, equipment, or environment to fit the person rather than trying to change the person to fit the job.
- Work smart: Productivity can be improved and errors reduced by finding new and better ways to do a job.
- People are different: People differ in their age, height, weight, reaction time, strength, coordination, attitudes, etc. Designers and managers need to adjust jobs accordingly.

THE FOUR MAJOR ERGONOMIC STRESSORS

When considering the likelihood of an ergonomic injury, tasks must be evaluated with regard to four major stressors.

- Repetition—how often does a certain movement have to be repeated during the work day? Higher numbers of repetitions create more stress on bones, muscles, and tendons, thus increasing likelihood of injury.
- Force—how much force must be applied when performing the task? Force also includes how much weight must be lifted. Any lifting greater than 25 pounds is considered heavy. The heavier the lifting (or force), the greater the likelihood of injury.
- Posture—this refers to the orientation of the body or body part. Neutral postures are the least stressful. The farther from neutral the body is required to be, the greater the likelihood of injury.
- Vibration—this refers to the amount of vibratory movement required. Vibration is generally caused by holding power tools (e.g., a drill or jackhammer). Exposure to vibration for long periods of time can damage nerves.

Copyright © Mometrix Media. You have been licensed one copy of this document for personal use only. Any other reproduction or redistribution is strictly prohibited. All rights reserved. This content is provided for test preparation purposes only and does not imply an endorsement by Mometrix of any particular political, scientific, or religious point of view.

VISUAL ACUITY AND VISION

Proper work station ergonomics must include proper adjustments for lighting and distances to enhance visual acuity. The most comfortable position of the head is a neutral posture in which the head is not bent down or up. Therefore, the objects that must be used and seen the most must be situated within the 'normal line of sight', which is about ten degrees downward from the horizontal. The type of task determines how much visual acuity is required. Visual acuity is the ability to distinguish fine features and details. Tasks that require more visual acuity will require stronger and more consistent lighting.

ANTHROPOMETRICS

Anthropometrics is the science of measuring human body dimensions and physical characteristics. It is applied in the occupational setting through designing machines, vehicles, safety equipment, and PPE to correspond to the anthropometric measurements gathered and analyzed. Anthropometrics are critical in designing workplaces, machines, and PPE that are ergonomically sound and, therefore, less likely to cause strains or other adverse incidents. Current work in this area is done using three-dimensional computer-aided models that help design proper environments and equipment. Uses in occupational health and safety include using the data to design personal protective equipment for better fit and, therefore, better protection. Anthropometric measurements can be applied on an individual basis when setting up computer work stations or manual assembly stations. One of the ways this is done is providing adjustable height chairs and desks/tables. Anthropometric data is also used for designing items that cannot be adjusted, such as doorways and control panels. In this case, the principle is to design for the ninety-fifth percentile male when considering size or the fifth percentile female when considering reach. If a ninety-fifth percentile male can fit through a doorway or in a chair, so will smaller people. If a fifth-percentile female can reach a control, taller people will be able to reach it as well. It should be noted that there are a wide variety of body sizes and proportions and therefore the sample sizes must also be quite large in order to provide proper measurements for the various designs and to fit the worker in order to minimize risk.

NIOSH LIFTING EQUATION

The NIOSH lifting equation uses several factors to calculate a recommended weight limit (RWL) for a certain task. This RWL is the maximum weight that almost any worker can lift over an eight-hour shift without increased risk of musculoskeletal injury. The equation is as follows:

$$\text{RWL} = (51 \text{ lb}) \times (\text{Horizontal Multiplier}) \times (\text{Vertical Multiplier}) \times (\text{Distance Moved}) \times (\text{Asymmetry Angle}) \times (\text{Frequency Multiplier}) \times (\text{Coupling Multiplier})$$

The horizontal and vertical multipliers are how far the load must be moved in the horizontal and vertical directions. The asymmetry angle is the number of degrees from vertical the body must be moved. The frequency multiplier ranges from 0.2 to 15 times per hour. The coupling multiplier is a measure of how well the person's grip is on the load to be moved, ranging from 1 (good) to 3 (poor).

RAPID UPPER LIMB ASSESSMENT

A Rapid Upper Limb Assessment (RULA) is an ergonomic evaluation method that can be used to screen and quantify the degree of ergonomic risk from a given task or work flow. The tool requires observation and evaluation of a work task with regard to body posture, required application of force, and degree of repetition in the tasks. Body postures receive higher scores the more they deviate from neutral. Force or lifting is evaluated from 1 kilogram to 10 kilograms; any forces or lifting greater than 10 kilograms is assigned the highest score. Repetition is scored from intermittent to frequent. Each body part evaluated is assigned a number from 1 to 7. Scores of 1 to 2 are considered acceptable ergonomically, 3 to 4 may require change, 5 to 6 require change in the near time frame, and scores of 7 require immediate evaluation and change. The RULA is most appropriate for seated or sedentary tasks that do not involve the entire body.

Copyright © Mometrix Media. You have been licensed one copy of this document for personal use only. Any other reproduction or redistribution is strictly prohibited. All rights reserved. This content is provided for test preparation purposes only and does not imply an endorsement by Mometrix of any particular political, scientific, or religious point of view.

RAPID WHOLE-BODY ASSESSMENT

A Rapid Whole-Body Assessment (RWBA, also referred to as Rapid Entire Body Assessment or REBA) is an ergonomic evaluation tool used to assess degree of ergonomic strain or risk to the entire body from a given work task sequence. It is used as a screening tool to provide a relative risk ranking that can be used as a guide to determine which work tasks to redesign first. Assessment is similar to that of the RULA, and is expanded to the entire body—neck, arms, legs, trunk, and wrists. Scores obtained in the RWBA range from 1 to 15 and are evaluated as follows:

- 1–3: low risk
- 4–7: medium risk, action may be necessary in the future
- 8–10: high risk, action is necessary in the short term
- 11–15: very high risk, action is necessary immediately to redesign the work task

The RWBA is best applied to tasks that involve the entire body rather than just the upper body.

INDUSTRIAL FATIGUE

Industrial fatigue is the mental and physical exhaustion that occurs from performing work-related activities. The energy required for both the mental and physical demands of a job can result in a diminished capacity for job performance.

Industrial fatigue can be attributed to **personal factors**, such as poor or inadequate sleep, medications, or medical conditions; and **environmental factors**, including poor working conditions, tasks that require a large amount of mental activity, work-related anxiety, or job demands that exceed an individual's capacity.

The primary results of fatigue are the **loss of focus** and concentration that may result in mistakes which can impact quality or safety. Fatigue may also increase risk-taking behaviors and decrease reaction time, both of which can lead to accidents.

Employers can manage industrial fatigue in a variety of ways. Employers can monitor overtime and shift work to ensure an employee is allotted adequate time to rest and recover. Mandatory rest breaks can provide an employee time away from the job to recover mentally. Proper lighting, air temperature, and monitoring noise can improve employee alertness and prevent fatigue. Education on topics such as proper sleep, identifying symptoms of fatigue, the importance of proper nutrition, and stress management techniques can improve employee well-being, which can allow for better rest and sleep to reduce fatigue. Also, task rotation can improve an employee's focus as the environment and mental demands are varied.

Recognizing, Evaluating, and Controlling Occupational Exposures

RECOGNIZING OCCUPATIONAL EXPOSURES

Exposures to radiation, biological agents, and infectious disease agents are best recognized through job safety analysis and analysis of the operational process. Consideration of each step in a process or job function should take into account any chemicals used, equipment used, and unique aspects thereof. Some common sources of radiation exposure include use of instruments that have a radioactive source; for example, instruments that check the fill level in a bottle or jar can have a radioactive source. Symptoms of radiation exposure include burns, but exposure will not always produce an observable sign. Biological agents can be bacteria, fungi, or viruses that cause illness. Processes that may be sources of exposure to biological agents include working outdoors and stirring up dust where animals have been or being exposed to animal feces or dander. Biological agents may cause flu-like symptoms or respiratory illness. Infectious diseases commonly encountered include colds and flus that are transmitted through contact with coworkers and customers or through contact with bodily fluids. Medical professionals can best evaluate these symptoms.

Copyright © Mometrix Media. You have been licensed one copy of this document for personal use only. Any other reproduction or redistribution is strictly prohibited. All rights reserved. This content is provided for test preparation purposes only and does not imply an endorsement by Mometrix of any particular political, scientific, or religious point of view.

Nanoparticles are extremely small particles that are nanometers in diameter (a nanometer is one-billionth of a meter). Unfortunately, they can only be detected and analyzed by using an electron microscope; there are no real-time instruments available that can measure them. In addition, the health effects of these particles are poorly understood. The greatest exposure route is through inhalation, and the most common source of nanoparticles is diesel fuel combustion. Process analyses are the best sources to determine if nanoparticle exposure is a potential; nanoparticles are used in cosmetic manufacturing and are generated in powder-handling processes such as paint and pigment manufacturing, cement manufacturing, as well as welding operations. Adverse indoor air quality can be detected by analyzing the ventilation system of a building and evaluating whether there have been recent events that may contribute to poor indoor air quality, such as painting and carpet installation. Indoor air quality problems are most often detected by complaints from building occupants.

EVALUATING AND QUANTIFYING OCCUPATIONAL EXPOSURES

Handheld instruments are available to detect radiation and to differentiate among alpha, beta, and gamma radiation. These can be rented from environmental and industrial hygiene equipment vendors. Determining which radioactive elements are present to account for radiation requires sampling and submittal to a laboratory. Biological agents such as bacteria and fungi can be sampled from the air or surfaces using standard industrial hygiene techniques. The samples must then be submitted to an accredited laboratory that can culture the samples and identify the agents in the samples. Infectious disease agent identification also requires submittal of biological samples to a laboratory for identification. Laboratories often use DNA or RNA sequencing techniques to identify bacteria, fungi, and viruses. These methods are relatively low cost and are extremely accurate.

CONTROLLING OCCUPATIONAL EXPOSURES

Radiation exposure control is different for each type of radiation. Clothing stops alpha particles; wearing a respirator rated for alpha particles is important to eliminate the risk of breathing in the particles. Beta particles are also stopped by clothing and gloves, which can be discarded. Gamma radiation requires heavier shielding, such as lead-lined clothing, to stop it. Exposure to biological agents can be controlled through proper use of protective clothing that is carefully removed and discarded after each use, along with a respirator or self-contained breathing apparatus, depending on level of concern. Infectious disease exposures are similarly controlled. In a hospital setting, isolation rooms with positive forced-air ventilation may be necessary to ensure that exposure to infectious disease is controlled.

Occupational exposure to nanoparticles is difficult to control. Careful evaluation should be made to identify the potential sources of exposure and to isolate them from workers using ventilation hoods, frequent air exchanges, and having sufficient quantities of make-up air in buildings. Isolation of the source of the nanoparticle is the best option. Particulate air filters on respirators can control a portion of nanoparticles in the air even though the pore size of the respirator is larger than the nanoparticle due to the multiple layers the particle must go through. Occupational exposure to adverse indoor air quality is best controlled by eliminating the source of the pollution (e.g., cleaning air-conditioning filters, making sure there is no moisture in the system that can grow mold, etc.) followed by balancing of the system by an experienced HVAC professional to ensure sufficient air exchanges and intake of fresh air.

Employee Substance Abuse

SIGNS AND SYMPTOMS OF SUBSTANCE ABUSE

Frontline supervisors and managers should be trained in the signs and symptoms of **substance abuse** in the workplace. This is especially important for safety-sensitive work functions such as forklift drivers and machine operators. Signs of substance abuse include red eyes, slurring words, odor of alcohol on the breath, dilated pupils, erratic behavior, mood swings, poor performance, and excessive absenteeism and lateness. Due to the legal issues regarding handling substance abuse issues, it is important that supervisors be trained in

Copyright © Mometrix Media. You have been licensed one copy of this document for personal use only. Any other reproduction or redistribution is strictly prohibited. All rights reserved.
This content is provided for test preparation purposes only and does not imply an endorsement by Mometrix of any particular political, scientific, or religious point of view.

recognizing the signs and symptoms and that more than one supervisor or manager assess the situation before action is taken. Drug and alcohol testing policies should be established in conjunction with the human resources department in advance to ensure a worker's rights are not violated and that the safety of the workforce is maintained when cases of substance abuse are detected.

LEGAL CONSIDERATIONS REGARDING SUBSTANCE ABUSE

Employers have a responsibility to provide a safe workplace, including a workplace free from potential safety hazards caused by employees who may be under the influence of illegal drugs or alcohol. However, this must be balanced by respect for individual rights. There are several **legal considerations** governing substance abuse on the job:

- Drivers of commercial vehicles are mandated to participate in *drug and alcohol testing programs* by 49 CFR Part 40. The results of a positive drug or alcohol test follow them from job to job.
- Occupational Safety and Health Administration (OSHA) has an anti-retaliation rule that prevents post-accident drug and alcohol testing unless there is some indication that the accident involved being under the influence.
- The Americans with Disabilities Act protects employees with *disabilities* from discrimination on the job. To the extent that an addiction is considered a disability, an employee is protected from termination due to addiction-related medical treatment.

DRUG TESTING

Applicants can be drug tested as a **condition of employment**, but the process and selection must be applied to all applicants without prejudice. With recent changes in drug laws, the topics of drug testing and the related results are being revisited.

Federal law allows periodic testing of **safety-sensitive positions**, such as bus drivers, and when there is **reasonable suspicion** of an employee being under the influence. Caution must be exercised in reasonable suspicion cases in that supervisors should be trained to identify signs of drug or alcohol use. Management must also consider underlying medical conditions that can cause altered behavior (such as a diabetic episode or stroke) that can mimic substance abuse.

The Occupational Safety and Health Administration (OSHA) has cautioned against mandatory drug testing following occupational accidents because they may dissuade employees from seeking medical assistance. Employers should establish criteria that is rigorously adhered to when determining the need for a post-accident drug test.

Epidemiology

Epidemiology is the population-level study of human health and factors that impact it. Examples of topics epidemiologists may study include infectious diseases, occupational exposures and their impact on human health outcomes, causative factors of cancer, and development and control of chronic diseases such as diabetes. Epidemiologists seek to design controlled experiments to determine causative factors of disease and then design interventions or public health communication campaigns to decrease disease prevalence. It is important to understand that epidemiologists study health and disease on a population level; therefore, associations or causations that epidemiology discovers apply, on average, over an entire population but do not predict an individual's chance of developing a certain outcome.

Occupational Exposure Limits

THRESHOLD LIMIT VALUES (TLV)

The American Conference of Governmental Industrial Hygienists, Inc (ACGIH) has developed guidelines, called Threshold Limit Values, some of which have been adopted by OSHA, that estimate the limit that a worker may

Copyright © Mometrix Media. You have been licensed one copy of this document for personal use only. Any other reproduction or redistribution is strictly prohibited. All rights reserved.
This content is provided for test preparation purposes only and does not imply an endorsement by Mometrix of any particular political, scientific, or religious point of view.

be exposed to a substance during a standard, 40-hour, workweek without experiencing undesirable effects. The guidelines are based on inhalation data obtained from scientific journal articles. The two most common units are mg/m³ and parts per million (ppm). The formula for converting between the two units is: $ppm = \frac{\frac{mg}{m^3} \times 24.45}{MW}$ where MW refers to the molecular weight of the substance. The units of MW are g/mol. Care needs to be taken in interpreting reported TLV values. Some values are averaged over a typical 40-hour work week (TWA), some are taken as 15 min (STEL) snapshots, four times a day. The ceiling TLV is the maximum exposure at any time for any duration.

Given the following assumptions about a mixture of liquids, the formula below can be used to estimate a threshold limit value for the mixture (TLV$_m$): 1) The mass fractions of each substance (f_i) in the liquid form are the same as in the vapor that is formed above the liquid mixture. 2) The toxic effects of the components are additive, not synergistic.

$$TLV_m = \frac{1}{\Sigma \frac{f_i}{TLV_i}} \qquad TLV_m = \frac{1}{\frac{f_1}{TLV_1} + \frac{f_2}{TLV_2} + \frac{f_n}{TLV_n}}$$

Where TLV$_i$ is the threshold limit value for component i and f$_i$ = (mass i)/Σ(all masses).

PERMISSIBLE EXPOSURE LIMITS (PEL)

The major distinction between permissible exposure limits and threshold limit values is tat TLV's are guidelines set by an organization, while PEL's are regulations set by OSHA. They are both valuable in ensuring a safe workplace, but PEL's have the power of legal enforcement behind them. The PEL is measured and reported as a time weighted average (TWA). The OHS Act (General Duty Clause) was enacted in 1970 and requires employers to provide a safe working environment, which includes ensuring toxins are maintained below the PEL (or other guideline if OSHA has not determined a PEL for the substance) determined for the chemical.

BIOLOGICAL EXPOSURE INDICES (BEI)

Biological exposure indices are also guidelines developed by ACGIH and are similar to TLV's, but reference the level of chemical found in a specimen sample from a person exposed to a substance at the TLV. The BEI may be measured via a determinant or metabolite found in a specimen such as blood or urine. For example, the BEI for benzene could be measured by directly measuring the benzene in a sample of exhaled air or by measuring the level of phenol (alcohol of benzene) in a urine sample. Safety determinations using BEI values are best determined via repetitive measurements and differing timeframes of exposure. Timing is especially important when measuring metabolites since metabolic processes differ between chemicals as well as between individuals.

IMMEDIATELY DANGEROUS TO LIFE AND HEALTH (IDLH)

IDLH stands for Immediately Dangerous to Life and Health. This term is used by the National Institute of Occupational Safety and Health to indicate the concentration of a substance that poses an acute and immediate danger to human life. Examples of IDLH situations are benzene exposure at 500 ppm, ammonia exposure at 300 ppm, and hydrogen sulfide exposure at 100 ppm.

ACTION LEVEL (AL)

An organization must regularly test for the level of regulated substances to determine the existing exposure level. If the level of a substance is at or above the action level, determined by OSHA to be half of the PEL, the employer must take action to monitor the health of employees, frequently measure the current exposure levels, and lower the level of the hazardous material. If the situation does not improve or gets worse, including the monitored substance reaching or exceeding the PEL, further action is required. In the interest of full compliance, the safety professional should regularly monitor both the exposure levels of any regulated

Copyright © Mometrix Media. You have been licensed one copy of this document for personal use only. Any other reproduction or redistribution is strictly prohibited. All rights reserved.
This content is provided for test preparation purposes only and does not imply an endorsement by Mometrix of any particular political, scientific, or religious point of view.

substances known to exist in the workplace, keep current with the action levels of those substances, and maintain clear and proper documentation of all organizational actions regarding safety.

Chapter Quiz

Ready to see how well you retained what you just read? Scan the QR code to go directly to the chapter quiz interface for this study guide. If you're using a computer, simply visit the bonus page at **mometrix.com/bonus948/csp** and click the Chapter Quizzes link.

Copyright © Mometrix Media. You have been licensed one copy of this document for personal use only. Any other reproduction or redistribution is strictly prohibited. All rights reserved. This content is provided for test preparation purposes only and does not imply an endorsement by Mometrix of any particular political, scientific, or religious point of view.

Environmental Management Systems

Transform passive reading into active learning! After immersing yourself in this chapter, put your comprehension to the test by taking a quiz. The insights you gained will stay with you longer this way. Scan the QR code to go directly to the chapter quiz interface for this study guide. If you're using a computer, simply visit the bonus page at **mometrix.com/bonus948/csp** and click the Chapter Quizzes link.

Environmental Protection and Pollution Prevention

REDUCING AIR POLLUTION IN THE WORKPLACE

The best methods of reducing air pollution in the workplace are to prevent contaminants from entering the air in the first place. Materials should be handled in designated areas with ventilation control that eliminates dusts from entering the work area and vent through a baghouse that filters the air before discharging it into the atmosphere. Volatile chemicals that are vented through a baghouse must be passed through a carbon absorption or other control system to capture pollutants. For sweeping up dusty materials, misting with a fine spray of water prior to sweeping can provide effective dust control. If possible, design and install pneumatic conveyance of dusty solids that need to be transferred.

REDUCING WATER POLLUTION IN THE WORKPLACE

There are several best management practices to prevent pollution of storm water runoff. All materials that can potentially contaminate storm water should be stored inside or covered. Frequent vacuuming and sweeping of outdoor areas is necessary to remove dirt that may contaminate storm water and become suspended solids or may contribute to the metal content of the storm water. When it is not raining, cover the storm drains to prevent contaminants and debris from entering them. Isolate the storm drain system from receiving any runoff from washing vehicles or wastewater from industrial processes. The industrial process water should either be discharged to the sanitary sewer under permit or should be collected and hauled off site by a contractor. Runoff that may be contaminated with sediments and solids should be directed if possible, to a collection basin or settling pond; longer residence times in a settling pond will allow contaminants to settle to the bottom. Once the water has been tested, it can be released to the storm drain system as rainwater runoff.

REDUCING SOIL POLLUTION IN THE WORKPLACE

Prevention of soil pollution from industrial activities requires proper construction and management of facilities. All hazardous materials should be stored indoors; if this is not possible, they should be stored on a concrete surface with a berm around them and covered from rainfall. Loading docks should be kept in good repair so that no cracks for oils and transmission fluids that may leak from delivery trucks can migrate through the concrete. Any delivery trucks that leak oil in the loading dock should be notified that a repair is needed and the spilled material immediately cleaned up using dry, absorbent material. Fueling stations need spill containment to contain small drips of gasoline or diesel. Other potential sources of soil pollution that should be evaluated include windblown dust, contaminated dust that could be carried out of a processing facility on forklift tires, and any sources of storm water pollution that are deposited on soil.

CONTAINMENT AS POLLUTION PREVENTION

Secondary containment is important for any liquid hazardous materials both in storage and in use. Secondary containment pallets made of polymer material are commonly used to provide an easy method to both provide containment for drums and containers and to move them easily. These can be purchased to contain standard 55-gallon drums. Hazardous material and waste storage areas can be constructed as containment areas with a concrete berm around the perimeter and a ramp to provide access in and out of the area, either with a pallet

215

Copyright © Mometrix Media. You have been licensed one copy of this document for personal use only. Any other reproduction or redistribution is strictly prohibited. All rights reserved.
This content is provided for test preparation purposes only and does not imply an endorsement by Mometrix of any particular political, scientific, or religious point of view.

jack or forklift. Common best practice is to coat the interior of the concrete berm storage area with a chemical and oil-resistant epoxy coating so that if chemicals are spilled, they do not soak into the concrete and potentially migrate to the soil below. Portable secondary containment or spill catch basins should be used when servicing forklifts and vehicles or in areas where fuel is dispensed to catch drips and minor spills that can, over time, become a major source of pollution.

SOIL VAPOR INTRUSION

Vapor intrusion is the migration of volatile chemicals into a building, typically from contaminated soil. Chemicals can migrate laterally from contaminated sites or vertically from contaminated groundwater, broken sewer lines, or contaminated soil. Common chemicals associated with vapor intrusion include **volatile organic compounds (VOCs), semi-volatile chemicals (SVOCs), polychlorinated biphenyls (PCBs),** and **pesticides**. Vapors can accumulate inside a structure, which could lead to acute and chronic exposures of hazardous chemicals or the potential for an explosion.

Vapors enter a structure through cracks or gaps in the construction, with some chemicals even able to pass through concrete. Intrusion can be mitigated by sealing cracks and seams in the structure that contact the soil. For new construction or elevated foundation construction, vapor barriers, passive vents, or an electric blower can be installed to prevent the vapors from entering the structure.

POLLUTION PREVENTION

The Environmental Protection Agency defines **pollution prevention (P2)** as any practice to reduce, eliminate, or prevent pollution during the production process.

Pollution prevention is the process of evaluating every step of production to reduce waste, from selecting environmentally conscious raw materials to using more recyclable materials for the end-of-life fate of the product. Pollution prevention even assesses the energy efficiency of equipment to cut down on air pollution. P2 seeks to incorporate less hazardous chemicals to reduce the volume and types of hazardous waste requiring management. Such a program seeks to reduce the overall **financial** and **environmental** costs of any production process. The efforts of any P2 program can benefit a corporation by making it leaner, reducing its financial exposure for pollution, and providing a competitive advantage in the "green" economy.

Hazardous Material Migration

Hazardous wastes and chemical substances can migrate and disperse through air, water, and soil. The extent of migration in any media depends on several factors, such as whether the chemical is soluble in the media, whether it binds to other substances in the media, and whether there is any appreciable degradation of the chemical in the environment. In air, chemicals that are most likely to migrate are those that are volatile or are extremely fine particulate matter. Heavier particulate matter will tend to fall to the surface as dust rather than migrate on wind currents (dispersion) to more distant locations. Materials spilled in the soil can migrate down through the soil by filtering through the interstices (air pockets) in the soil or be carried by percolating groundwater (hydrodynamic dispersion). Some substances will not migrate as readily through soil; for example, soil particles are often negatively charged, and they attract positively charged ions that slow their migration. Uncharged organic chemicals, such as gasoline or diesel compounds, will not be as affected by the ionic properties of the soil and will tend to migrate through the soil more readily.

Sustainability

Although there are various definitions of "sustainability," it is generally recognized to refer to the use of resources in such a way as to ensure resources continue to be available indefinitely for generations to come. As such, three pillars can be considered as follows:

Copyright © Mometrix Media. You have been licensed one copy of this document for personal use only. Any other reproduction or redistribution is strictly prohibited. All rights reserved. This content is provided for test preparation purposes only and does not imply an endorsement by Mometrix of any particular political, scientific, or religious point of view.

Limit use of natural resources to what can be replaced—for example, using energy from renewable sources such as solar or wind energy is more sustainable than using petroleum-derived energy. Recycling falls under this principle as recycling preserves natural resources.

Minimize creation of waste—this is a principle of sustainability because creating waste uses up natural resources and the energy used to produce and transport the goods and takes these resources out of circulation for future generations.

Create systems that leave clean air and water for future generations—this principle seeks to leave our natural environment as clean as possible so that human life can continue to be well supported and productive.

Waste Water Treatment

REGULATORY PROGRAMS GOVERNING STORM WATER

Although there is a **US Environmental Protection Agency (EPA) Multi-sector General Industrial Stormwater Permit**, most states are responsible for implementing their own versions of the requirements. There are common provisions of these permits. Companies must identify the potential pollutants from their activities that may impact storm water runoff, must identify discharge locations, and must develop a **storm water pollution prevention plan (SWPPP)**. **Best management practices (BMPs)** must be implemented to control and prevent pollutants from entering storm water runoff. Regular inspections of the facility for BMP implementation and effectiveness must be conducted, along with sampling of storm water runoff to determine whether the pollutant levels in the runoff comply with EPA benchmark values. Deficiencies must be corrected with appropriate documentation. Annual reports must be filed that include the inspection and monitoring results.

INDUSTRIAL WASTEWATER PERMITTING

Industrial operations that produce wastewater and discharge the water to the sanitary sewer (publicly owned treatment works [POTW]) must obtain a **wastewater discharge permit**. Industries that are in certain standard industrial codes must meet **US EPA categorical treatment standards** for pollutants in their wastewater. Companies that are not covered under a categorical treatment standard must comply with their local **POTW wastewater discharge limits**. These vary depending on the locale and how strict the POTW needs to be with its influent quality to meet its National Pollutant Discharge Elimination System (NPDES) permit limits. Typically, limits are imposed for metals (such as arsenic, lead, cadmium, chromium, iron, copper, nickel, zinc, etc.), biological oxygen demand (BOD), chemical oxygen demand (COD), oil and grease, pH, and total suspended solids.

US EPA BASIC REQUIREMENTS FOR DRINKING WATER SYSTEMS

The US EPA governs the regulation of drinking water systems and sets **Maximum Contaminant Levels (MCLs)** for primary health standards. States are authorized to implement these regulations. Public water systems are required to provide water that meets all MCLs and that meets the secondary drinking water standards. The secondary standards are elements that affect taste or odor but do not pose a health risk. Drinking water systems must regularly test for the presence of bacteria (coliforms) according to their system size and report the result to their state agency. Repeat sampling and corrective actions are required for positive coliform results. In addition, the system must compile a consumer confidence report for its customers annually that provides information on the testing results from the year.

CONTROLS TO PREVENT STORM WATER POLLUTION

Engineering controls for controlling storm water pollution are designed to prevent pollutants from entering storm water runoff. For example, berms can be installed around storage areas to capture runoff that may potentially be contaminated. It can then be tested and released if it is uncontaminated or treated if necessary. Filter socks and drain inserts can be installed that can filter out and trap pollutants. The filters can be stocked with pollutant-specific media to filter out specific pollutants (e.g., zeolites for dissolved metals, activated

Copyright © Mometrix Media. You have been licensed one copy of this document for personal use only. Any other reproduction or redistribution is strictly prohibited. All rights reserved.
This content is provided for test preparation purposes only and does not imply an endorsement by Mometrix of any particular political, scientific, or religious point of view.

carbon for oil and grease, etc.). A roof can be constructed over exposed materials to prevent storm water from impacting materials stored outdoors.

Chapter Quiz

Ready to see how well you retained what you just read? Scan the QR code to go directly to the chapter quiz interface for this study guide. If you're using a computer, simply visit the bonus page at **mometrix.com/bonus948/csp** and click the Chapter Quizzes link.

Copyright © Mometrix Media. You have been licensed one copy of this document for personal use only. Any other reproduction or redistribution is strictly prohibited. All rights reserved.
This content is provided for test preparation purposes only and does not imply an endorsement by Mometrix of any particular political, scientific, or religious point of view.

Training and Education

Transform passive reading into active learning! After immersing yourself in this chapter, put your comprehension to the test by taking a quiz. The insights you gained will stay with you longer this way. Scan the QR code to go directly to the chapter quiz interface for this study guide. If you're using a computer, simply visit the bonus page at **mometrix.com/bonus948/csp** and click the Chapter Quizzes link.

TRAINING DELIVERY METHODS

CLASSROOM TRAINING

Classroom training is often used for safety training, but it has its pros and cons. On the **positive side**, it offers a chance for workers to dedicate their attention to the task without distractions and allows for questions to be asked to clarify concepts. Some types of information are best presented in a classroom; for example, hazard communication and toxicology of chemical exposures are best presented in a classroom setting. On the **negative side**, it can be difficult to make the training class lively and engaging and the participants may get sleepy. It may not be interactive enough for people who do their best learning by doing and not by listening to another person give a presentation.

ON-THE-JOB TRAINING

On-the-job training refers to training given outside of the classroom setting, in the work area. It is usually for teaching the actual mechanics of a production job; however, it is also a great opportunity to present **risk and hazard information** in a real-world setting. A positive reason to do on-the-job training is to provide an opportunity for **interaction and hands-on training**. This can help solidify the concepts and make the training more relevant. A negative aspect of doing on-the-job training is that it is not well-suited to providing information about **academic concepts** such as chemical exposures or hearing conservation. It is also not a good method for large groups or noisy work areas.

ONLINE TRAINING

Online, web-based training classes are useful because they are available any time and do not require scheduling a physical space or trainer. They can be very **cost-effective** and can be tailored to the specific topic to be delivered. Programs purchased from a training program vendor can also keep track of the **training records**. They can also have built-in **competency assessments**. On the negative side, they provide little **interaction** and may be difficult for some people to pay attention to. They do not provide an opportunity for the student to ask questions and get **clarification** on concepts that are not understood. Some people may not be familiar with how to use a computer, depending on literacy levels and background.

TRAINING DELIVERY MEDIUMS AND TECHNOLOGIES

Safety training can be difficult and tedious, but it is critical for worker health. Classroom training is beneficial because content can be tailored to the audience and work environment. It also allows for personal interaction and hands-on training activities that enhance learning. The disadvantages include the difficulty of scheduling a class that can accommodate everybody who needs to take the class. Usually, multiple times and locations must be offered. Online training classes are an attractive option because they can be completed whenever the individual has the time. However, they tend to be generic and not tailored to the audience or specific work environment. Sitting in front of a computer terminal is often boring and it is more difficult for employees to understand and retain information delivered this way.

CHOOSING APPROPRIATE TRAINING

A variety of training techniques should be used to teach and reinforce concepts. The best training programs use a combination of all three methods. Traditional classroom lecture-style training is useful when the topic is

Copyright © Mometrix Media. You have been licensed one copy of this document for personal use only. Any other reproduction or redistribution is strictly prohibited. All rights reserved.
This content is provided for test preparation purposes only and does not imply an endorsement by Mometrix of any particular political, scientific, or religious point of view.

academic in nature. For example, it can be helpful to explain lockout/tagout regulations and procedures in a classroom setting. Demonstration training is best when the topic involves physical manipulation of an object. An example of demonstration training is teaching the use of a respirator, how to disassemble and maintain it. On-the-job training refers to training in specific tasks and occurs in the actual work environment. Written reference material and job aids should be available to reinforce the proper performance of each task. In the example of lockout/tagout above, on-the-job training should be conducted with each piece of equipment to show employees where the lockout points are and to demonstrate proper isolation of the energy source.

Training, Qualification, and Competency Requirements

TRAINING PLANS

A **training plan** is a formal document that guides the planning and execution of a training program. By codifying elements, such as goals, audience, learning outcomes, content, time allotment, and exercises, the training can be consistent between sessions and between facilitators.

- The **goals** in a training plan should delineate the organizational outcomes the training is trying to support.
- A training plan also outlines the training **objectives**—the skills or knowledge that an attendee should possess after the training is complete.
- The **audience** needs to be identified so that those who need the training receive the information.
- The core of the training plan is the **content**—the information that will be delivered and how it will be conveyed. It should contain the materials necessary to conduct the course, the training outline, and a description of any exercises. The content outline should include the time allotted for each section to keep the facilitator on track.
- Finally, the training plan should outline an **assessment** for the attendees and provide a **feedback** mechanism to improve future courses.

ANDRAGOGY

Andragogy is the concept of adult learning. The theory is based on the fact that adults learn differently than children. It has been found that the design and presentation of information to children are not effective at teaching adults.

Unlike children, adult learners tend to be **self-directed**, meaning they guide their own learning based on their interests and questions. Adults **associate** new learning with past experiences and generally have a desire to use new information **immediately** because a delay in applying information can lead to a reduction in retention. Adult learners are **internally motivated** and are more eager to learn when provided with new roles or responsibilities. Adults need to understand the **purpose** of the learning as well as any potential **benefit**. By understanding the needs and abilities of an adult learner, health and safety training programs can be designed to be more effective, resulting in better retention.

Adults learn in different ways, called **modalities**. Most people will have a preferred modality to which they respond and retain information the best. The recognized modalities are:

- **Visual**: Retains information best by seeing; respond to flip charts, diagrams, and visual presentations
- **Aural**: Prefer to hear the information; respond best to oral presentations
- **Print**: Learn best by writing information down; such learners will take notes and benefit from exercises where they fill in blanks
- **Tactile**: Must do an activity to remember information
- **Interactive**: Prefer to discuss new information in small groups or question-and-answer periods
- **Kinesthetic**: Retain best through training exercises or physical activities

Copyright © Mometrix Media. You have been licensed one copy of this document for personal use only. Any other reproduction or redistribution is strictly prohibited. All rights reserved.
This content is provided for test preparation purposes only and does not imply an endorsement by Mometrix of any particular political, scientific, or religious point of view.

If the trainer understands the different modalities of adult learning information, they can design health and safety trainings to achieve maximum effectiveness.

TRAINING MODALITIES

Training modality refers to the method used to conduct a training program and the way material is presented. Common modalities include:

- **Instructor-based learning** is the traditional form of training, wherein a facilitator guides the learning in person.
- **E-learning**, also known as web-based training, is the presentation of information using online platforms.
- **Virtual learning** is a combination of instructor-led training and a web-based platform.
- **Micro-learning** is the presentation of information in small units, typically in the form of short videos, presentations, or articles.
- **Social learning** is leveraging peer groups or internal experts to convey information. This can also take the form of shadowing.
- **Gamification** is where learning is presented under the guise of games or competitions.

NEEDS ASSESSMENTS

A **needs assessment** is a structured process where an organization evaluates its discrepancies and determines how best to address them. The discrepancies identified are the differences between current and desired states. The process starts by identifying the **scope** of the assessment. Next, **data** is collected to determine the current state of the organization. Finally, an **action plan** is developed to close the gaps.

In the health and safety field, needs assessments are typically geared toward identifying training deficiencies. An evaluation of the work is conducted to identify existing and potential hazards. The applicable standards and regulations are located. From those documents, the required training topics are extracted and the impacted employees are put through training, thereby closing the gap.

QUALIFICATION AND COMPETENCY

The Occupational Safety and Health Administration (OSHA) uses the terms "**qualified**" and "**competent**" to refer to those tasked with conducting inspection or audits.

OSHA describes a **competent person** as one who is capable of the task being asked of them and is given the authority to carry it out. Competency is ability and knowledge that can be obtained by experience, skill, or training. Competent persons have the authority to identify hazards and take immediate corrective action to mitigate them.

A **qualified person** is one who, per OSHA, possesses a degree, a certificate, has professional certification, or has other externally validated knowledge. This extensive knowledge and training have provided them with the ability to solve problems in a particular domain. However, they may not necessarily possess the ability to recognize hazards, nor have the authority to mitigate them.

Thus, a qualified person may be responsible for designing a scaffold system for a job while a competent person can remove it from use if it does not pass their inspection.

METHODS OF ASSESSING COMPETENCY

Competency, or possessing sufficient knowledge or skill, should be assessed after training has been conducted to determine whether the knowledge was transferred effectively. Competency can be assessed by way of written exams, self-assessments, feedback, or a skills test.

Copyright © Mometrix Media. You have been licensed one copy of this document for personal use only. Any other reproduction or redistribution is strictly prohibited. All rights reserved.
This content is provided for test preparation purposes only and does not imply an endorsement by Mometrix of any particular political, scientific, or religious point of view.

- **Exam**: A written evaluation of the knowledge retention of an employee. Useful and inexpensive, but suffer in that they only evaluate knowledge, not ability.
- **Self-assessment**: Individual evaluates their own abilities. The success of this method both relies on and suffers from the honesty and objectivity of the individual.
- **Feedback**: Another individual, such as a supervisor, evaluates the effectiveness of the employee's abilities. Whereas the feedback can be objective, it is sensitive to any bias of the evaluator.
- **Skills test**: The employee demonstrates their understanding and abilities using real-world equipment and scenarios. Skills tests may be a truer test of an employee's knowledge and ability. They can be expensive if test equipment must be purchased for these evaluations, or can be disruptive if they occur in actual production areas.

Determining the Effectiveness of Training Programs

COMPETENCY-BASED TRAINING

Competency-based training (CBT) is a method of safety training that requires employees to **demonstrate** their ability to perform the skills conveyed during training. Instead of only verifying that an individual has received the information (typically evaluated using a written test), this method relies on performance-based assessments that allow the employee to demonstrate their **understanding** and application of the knowledge. For example, instead of having an employee complete a written exam on the steps needed to check a respirator prior to use, the evaluator would give the employee a respirator and observe them conducting the checks while donning the respirator.

Learning is the process of acquiring new information and retaining it for future use. This learning may be used to develop skills and abilities, but is primarily used for non-specific and unexpected situations.

Training is the process of acquiring new skills for a specific scenario. The goal is to provide the learner with the expectation of how a task is to be performed so that it can be individually performed in the future.

ASSESSING THE EFFECTIVENESS OF TRAINING

The goal of any training program is to **modify behavior**. Whether the intent is to stop an unsafe behavior or to instill a safe behavior, change is the desired outcome. In order to determine whether training would be appropriate, the safety professional would conduct a **needs assessment**. If training is determined to be a potential method of behavior modification, then the safety professional would either conduct or coordinate the training.

In order to determine the effectiveness of the training, the safety professional would have to compare the state of the organization after the training to its state before the training. Such evaluations could include examining injury or near miss data, or by observing behavior to determine if the training was effective at modifying behavior.

A **competency assessment** is a method to evaluate the ability of an employee to execute the skills for a given task. The assessment can be a **checklist** that denotes the desired skills or **performance objectives** an employee should be able to achieve in order to conduct the job effectively. The employee is **observed or tested** to determine their competency for each skill on the checklist. Such an assessment provides opportunities for employee coaching as well as identifying areas of competency.

Effective Presentation Techniques

TRAINING PRESENTATIONS

Effective presentations use a variety of tools to achieve the best learning outcomes. Presenters will usually use slides to convey the bulk of the information. When preparing slideshow presentations, it is important to ensure

Copyright © Mometrix Media. You have been licensed one copy of this document for personal use only. Any other reproduction or redistribution is strictly prohibited. All rights reserved.
This content is provided for test preparation purposes only and does not imply an endorsement by Mometrix of any particular political, scientific, or religious point of view.

that the slides are not too wordy, and use a variety of graphics and pictures to add interest for the participants. In addition to slideshow presentations, demonstrations and hands-on tools are also important to effectively convey the information in an engaging way that enables learning. For example, have participants practice taking apart and putting together their respirator, or practice putting earplugs in correctly rather than illustrating it for them.

A well-designed training presentation will first present an overview of the course content and will present the learning objectives of the course. The reason for the course will be stated, and participants will have an idea of how they will benefit from the course content. The course should be organized in a logical fashion, building knowledge as the course progresses. The instructor should build in short breaks at least every hour to give participants a chance to stand up and move around—this helps to combat boredom and refocus attention. The visual aids or PowerPoint presentation should also use a variety of slide types and varied content to keep the attention of the participants. For example, photographs and other visual aids should be incorporated into the presentation rather than using exclusively text. When text is used, it should be in a large font so that it is legible from a distance. Summary information and brief, informal quizzes should be presented frequently to provide feedback and opportunities to gauge whether the participants are assimilating the material.

GENERAL PRESENTATION ADVICE
PREPARING FOR A PRESENTATION

Before giving a presentation, one must understand that preparation is vital to effective communication. One should have all the information ready, including notes and documentation, and practice several times (the more practiced, the more confident the presenter will feel, and the better the presentation will serve as a vehicle for communication). Information that answers all of the following questions is useful to keep in mind:

- Who: audience, number of people, job positions, and their relationship to the presentation topic
- What: key points and vital information
- When: time and place, how long the presentation will last, and how many times it will be offered
- Where: location, equipment needed, and accommodations to seat people
- Why: reason for presentation, purpose, and result desired

OUTLINES

The outline for a presentation is used to develop its content. This process has three steps—introduction, body, and conclusion.

- The **introduction** of a presentation tells the audience what the speaker will be talking about. It needs to grab their attention and get them involved. It should also give the main points of the speech.
- The **body** of the presentation is the information being shared. There are different ways to structure the body. It can be done chronologically, by topic, by importance, or by contrasting pros and cons, to name a few.
- The **conclusion** is usually the part of the speech that the audience remembers best, so it is important not to rush through it. A speaker should use this as an opportunity to sum up the main points of the presentation and give the listeners a good overall memory.

Copyright © Mometrix Media. You have been licensed one copy of this document for personal use only. Any other reproduction or redistribution is strictly prohibited. All rights reserved.
This content is provided for test preparation purposes only and does not imply an endorsement by Mometrix of any particular political, scientific, or religious point of view.

TYPES OF OUTLINES

Outlines can help speakers prepare for a presentation and remind them of specific points when presenting. They are usually typed and kept as short as possible—just long enough for the speaker to remember each important point. Three common types of outlines are topical, phrase, and sentence.

- A topical outline lists a few nouns for each point. This outline requires the most memory by the speaker.
- A phrase outline is longer than a topical, but it is still kept as short as possible. A little more information is used to help the speaker.
- A sentence outline includes complete sentences that are important for each point. This has the most information of any outline but can be more complex and cumbersome.

VISUAL & AUDIO AIDS

In order to help the audience both understand and remember the message better, some visual aids can be used, including the following:

- Handouts: Be sure to keep the information simple and readable. Have a date and title printed on it, and use bullet points, underlining, and bold fonts where helpful for emphasis and clarity.
- Video: Using video clips can be an effective way to illustrate points.
- Computer graphics: These can be used to show images related to the presentation. Remember to use simple graphics with limited information per image, and be sure the lighting in the room is conducive to good viewing (consider dimming the lights near the screen, but avoid too much darkness, which will make the audience sleepy).

Various computer programs can be helpful in preparing for a presentation. For example, a content outline can be created and visual aids can be assembled, along with other multimedia such as video clips or sound bytes.

SLIDE LAYOUT

Effective techniques that will help in creating a good slide layout can ensure a polished presentation:

- Select a good layout that is appropriate for the content being presented.
- Find illustrations that will help with content. Use them sparingly so the audience is not overwhelmed or confused.
- Choose text carefully—find fonts and colors that make the information easy to read.
- Do not have too many words on a slide. It will be tempting to just read the words instead of presenting the information, and the audience will be distracted by trying to read everything.
- Do not have too many sound effects or video clips, as this may distract the audience.

IMPROVING DELIVERY & EFFECTIVENESS

Planning and creating a presentation are important, but delivery is key if a presentation is to be effective. Memorize only the crucial parts of the presentation, like the beginning and ending, to keep the body of the presentation fluid and dynamic. Become an expert at the topic, and learn more than is needed to help with taking questions. Practice the speech many times with focus on consistent timing without rushing; speak at a normal rate, and don't try to fit in more material than is possible in the allotted time. Engage the audience by encouraging them to ask questions. If the audience is large, repeat the question so everyone can have context for the answer given. If your audience speaks another language, enunciate carefully. Face the audience as much as possible, and make eye contact with various members throughout the presentation to establish rapport and

Copyright © Mometrix Media. You have been licensed one copy of this document for personal use only. Any other reproduction or redistribution is strictly prohibited. All rights reserved. This content is provided for test preparation purposes only and does not imply an endorsement by Mometrix of any particular political, scientific, or religious point of view.

connection. Avoid fillers like "you know," or "uh," or the audience will be distracted from the message being presented.

Chapter Quiz

Ready to see how well you retained what you just read? Scan the QR code to go directly to the chapter quiz interface for this study guide. If you're using a computer, simply visit the bonus page at **mometrix.com/bonus948/csp** and click the Chapter Quizzes link.

Copyright © Mometrix Media. You have been licensed one copy of this document for personal use only. Any other reproduction or redistribution is strictly prohibited. All rights reserved. This content is provided for test preparation purposes only and does not imply an endorsement by Mometrix of any particular political, scientific, or religious point of view.

Law and Ethics

Transform passive reading into active learning! After immersing yourself in this chapter, put your comprehension to the test by taking a quiz. The insights you gained will stay with you longer this way. Scan the QR code to go directly to the chapter quiz interface for this study guide. If you're using a computer, simply visit the bonus page at **mometrix.com/bonus948/csp** and click the Chapter Quizzes link.

Legal Issues

LEGAL TERMINOLOGY

A "tort" is a wrongful act that takes place outside of a contract that causes injury. The injury can be an actual injury, such as an injury sustained in a car accident, or it can be an economic injury such as an action that causes one to lose business. The tort can be either intentional or accidental; tort cases make up a substantial portion of legal cases. "Negligence" is a legal term that means a failure to exercise the same care that a reasonable person would do. Negligence is assumed to be accidental, and whether it is accidental or not does not remove liability for damages if one is found to be negligent. To prove negligence, one must show that the negligence caused damages. A "contract" is a legal document that can be oral or in writing; however, oral contracts are difficult to prove or enforce. A contract is an agreement between two or more entities with specific terms and a promise to do something. A written contract is legally binding.

CIVIL AND CRIMINAL LAW

Criminal law refers to wrongs or violations against the government, whereas civil law refers to disputes between private parties. A civil dispute can be between individuals or corporations. Criminal violations result in either incarceration, payment of a fine to the government, or (rarely) execution. In contrast, civil violations never result in incarceration. Civil penalties do include punitive fines if it can be shown there was malicious intent, gross negligence, or willful disregard of the rights of others. Civil disputes include contract disputes or disputes about property infringement. Criminal violations are familiar from popular media sources, such as assault, murder, and theft. There are two classifications of criminal violations: felonies and misdemeanors. Felonies are more serious offenses and result in incarceration of more than one year; misdemeanors are less serious and result in incarceration periods of less than one year. A key concept in criminal law is that one cannot be tried twice for the same crime.

DISABILITY LAW

The key law regarding the treatment of persons with disabilities in employment and public spaces is the Americans with Disabilities Act and its amendments. This federal civil rights law makes it illegal to discriminate against a person based on disabilities either in employment or in public accommodations such as restrooms and building access. Under the law a "covered entity" is an organization that must comply with the law, such as employers, labor organizations, or businesses. The "essential job functions" are the fundamental duties of a job or the core activities and responsibilities. An "accommodation" is an adjustment in the work environment or equipment provided to enable a person with a disability to be able to perform the essential job functions. Employers are required to make these accommodations if they do not pose an "undue burden," which takes into consideration the cost of accommodation and the resulting impact on the organization making the accommodation.

Copyright © Mometrix Media. You have been licensed one copy of this document for personal use only. Any other reproduction or redistribution is strictly prohibited. All rights reserved. This content is provided for test preparation purposes only and does not imply an endorsement by Mometrix of any particular political, scientific, or religious point of view.

Protection of Confidential Information

EMPLOYER'S RESPONSIBILITY FOR PROTECTING EMPLOYEE PRIVACY

Employee privacy refers to the extent to which an employer has access to an employee's information regarding their personal lives. Before and during employment, an employer will have access to a variety of personal information. **Personnel files** will contain social security numbers, bank account numbers, names of family members, medical information, and disciplinary actions.

The employee has a certain degree of trust that the employer will keep that information confidential. Limiting access to personal information, securing the information, and destroying the information when no longer needed should be codified in written policies.

Physical files should be kept in locked or limited access rooms or in locked file cabinets to limit access to the files. Policies should clearly state who has access to files and under what circumstances they can access and view the information.

Data stored electronically can be protected with passwords, secure servers, stand-alone servers, encrypted files, and file deletion protocols. Secure lines or physical drives should be used to transmit private information to reduce the chance the information is compromised.

PERSONALLY IDENTIFIABLE INFORMATION

Personally identifiable information (PII) is any information that directly or indirectly identifies an individual. The Department of Labor identifies two classes of PII: direct and indirect.

Direct PII includes name, address, social security number, telephone number, or email address. Indirect PII is a combination of data that, when used together, can identify an individual. **Indirect PII** includes such data as gender, race, birth date, geographic indicators, or other descriptors.

The loss or exposure of PII by an employer can result in identify theft, fraud, and even financial loss for an employee in extreme cases. Thus, it is the responsibility of the employer to properly maintain all PII in a confidential manner. An employer should take reasonable measures, such as firewalls, secure servers, and securing physical files to protect the PII they retain.

TRADE SECRETS

A **trade secret**, as defined by the United States Patent Office, is any intellectual property or information belonging to an entity. This information can include formulas, patterns, devices, techniques, or processes. This information is not generally known outside of the company, is typically a product of the organization's own efforts, and gives the company a competitive advantage in the marketplace. The information must be reasonably kept from the public and must have intrinsic economic value to be legally classified as a trade secret.

As **trade secrets** provide advantages over competitors, the organization should take efforts to keep the information internal. In order to be protected, trade secrets within an organization need to first be identified. Documents relating to the identified information need to be designated as **confidential** and treated accordingly, such as being secured and stored in limited access areas. Any trade secret information stored on an electronic medium must be secured from unauthorized external and internal access. Employees who handle or are aware of the guarded information should be asked to sign confidentiality and **non-disclosure agreements**. Trade secrets should be disclosed only to a limited number of employees. Training on how to handle the information and maintain confidentiality should be given to those employees. Finally, any outsourcing to contractors must include confidentiality agreements and processes to protect the information.

Copyright © Mometrix Media. You have been licensed one copy of this document for personal use only. Any other reproduction or redistribution is strictly prohibited. All rights reserved. This content is provided for test preparation purposes only and does not imply an endorsement by Mometrix of any particular political, scientific, or religious point of view.

GENERAL DATA PROTECTION REGULATION

The **General Data Protection Regulation (GDPR)** is a law promulgated by the European Union which standardizes data protection laws. The intent of the regulation is to provide individuals more control over how their direct and indirect **personal identifying information (PII)** is used. PII includes name, address, username, IP address, and cookie identifiers. Other guidelines address sensitive information such as race, religion, and sexual orientation.

The GDPR operates under seven principles:

- Lawfulness, fairness, and transparency
- Purpose limitation
- Data minimization
- Accuracy
- Storage limitation
- Integrity and confidentiality (security)
- Accountability

Under GDPR, an entity can be a controller or processor. A **controller** decides how or why personal data should be processed. A **processor** works with data that is provided by the controller. For example, a coffee roasting company hires a payroll company to process timesheets and manage payroll. The payroll company stores the employees' social security numbers and wage data on its servers. In this example, the roasting company is the controller and the payroll company is the processor.

Standards Development Processes

International standards are developed in many different areas; a well-known standard for environmental management is ISO14001 developed by the International Standards Organization, and for health and safety in the workplace is OHSAS 18001 developed by the British Standards Institute. However, there are also other organizations that produce standards. The development process for all is similar. First, the standard must meet a need in the marketplace that is beneficial to businesses and customers. Technical subject matter experts in the field of the standard meet and draft the written language of the standard. The standard is developed through global expert opinion and is written to apply to a broad range of industries. The standards are developed through a multi-stakeholder process through consensus by the subject matter experts. There are also opportunities for comment by the broader public before the standards are finalized.

Ethical Professional Practice

ETHICS

Ethics can be defined as the standards of what is right and wrong. As a set of **moral principles**, ethics guide the decisions that a person makes in an effort to benefit both individuals and society. The standards are often set forth by an organization as a **code of ethics**.

A code of ethics is a **written** document that lists the principles of conduct expected for the members of the body. Those principles guide decision-making, establish expectations for behavior, and act as a standard of practice for the members. For example, the code of ethics for the Board of Certified Safety Professionals lists eight principles that it requires of certified members to promulgate the integrity, honor, and prestige of the profession.

ETHICAL PRACTICES IN AUDITING

An **audit** is a systematic examination of an organization's adherence to policies, standards, rules, and laws. Thus, in an audit, the adherence to ethics is critical to provide the client with an **objective assessment** of the compliance of their organization. An auditor should never use subjective criteria, should only arrive at

Copyright © Mometrix Media. You have been licensed one copy of this document for personal use only. Any other reproduction or redistribution is strictly prohibited. All rights reserved. This content is provided for test preparation purposes only and does not imply an endorsement by Mometrix of any particular political, scientific, or religious point of view.

conclusions that can be supported with evidence, and should never adjust the results to appease the client or for personal gain. Additionally, the auditor must maintain appropriate confidentiality, shall avoid any information that could distort findings, shall avoid imparting their own biases, and should only work within their scope of knowledge.

ETHICAL PRACTICES IN RECORDKEEPING

Organizations will maintain a variety of records, including personnel files, medical records, legal documents, and financial records. Thus, record keeping for an organization must be done ethically.

The **integrity** of these files is paramount in maintaining the truthfulness of the information contained within. Records must be as accurate and complete as possible for their intended use. Those responsible for records must maintain the security of the records to prevent tampering or manipulation of the information they contain. Records should be secure from unauthorized access or disclosure and should only be released to those legally allowed to have them. Records should only be maintained for the requisite time period and be properly destroyed when no longer needed.

ETHICAL PRACTICES IN SAMPLING

Sampling is the practice of taking measurements from discrete areas as representative of the whole.

For sampling, the individual conducting the sample must act ethically in order to achieve truthful results. This means that sample location, sample collection frequency, sampling duration, the number of samples, and sample amount must be determined without bias or interference. Samples must avoid focusing on known areas of contamination or known "clean" areas. Proper sample collection and preservation techniques should also be followed to ensure the integrity of the results. Finally, the person conducting the sampling must be familiar with the equipment, sampling method, and the limitations of both to ensure reliable results are obtained.

ETHICAL PRACTICES IN STANDARDS WRITING

Ethics have an important place in the writing of technical standards. **Technical standards** will guide both individuals and organizations and may require expending resources to follow, including significant financial investment. In some cases, standards may be referenced by governmental bodies and carry the power of law. Therefore, those charged with writing the documents have a duty to be ethical in the development and writing of those documents. Authors must ensure that the references used are **reliable** and that salient research was based on good science and done in a professional, unbiased manner.

Ethics can come into play with something as simple as formatting—the location of information can impact how it is perceived by the reader. The type and design of graphs and plots must not be intentionally misleading.

Relationship Between Labor and Management

A positive relationship between management and workers will have a positive impact on workplace safety. This results from the key aspects that comprise a positive relationship between labor and management. Open communication lines mean that workers can voice concerns without fear of reprisal or retaliation. This results in building trust that diminishes the likelihood of non-work-related aches and pains being attributed to workplace injury. In workplaces with a positive relationship between labor and management, employees perceive that their contribution to the overall effort of the organization matters and that they have some control over how their work is executed. Paradoxically, research has shown that actual injury rates in union workplaces is higher than it is in nonunion shops. This phenomenon has not been explained well; it may be because of the buffer or intervening effect of the union stewards between the actual workers and management.

Copyright © Mometrix Media. You have been licensed one copy of this document for personal use only. Any other reproduction or redistribution is strictly prohibited. All rights reserved.
This content is provided for test preparation purposes only and does not imply an endorsement by Mometrix of any particular political, scientific, or religious point of view.

BCSP Code of Ethics

The Board of Certified Safety Professionals (BCSP) has established a code of ethics and professional conduct that must be followed by individuals who are awarded certificates by this organization. The first two standards of this code promote the need for certificate holders to support and promote integrity, esteem, and influence of the safety occupation. The code prioritizes human safety and health as the top concern in any scenario. Additional focus should also be given to environmental safety and the protection of property. Each of these priorities can be promoted by safety professionals in warning people of hazards and risks. These standards also include the promotion of honest and fair behavior toward all individuals and organizations and the avoidance of any behavior that would dishonor the esteem or reputation of the safety profession.

Specifically, Standard 1 focuses on the primary responsibility of a certified safety professional (CSP) to protect the safety and health of humans. A specific component of this responsibility is the need to notify appropriate personnel, management, and agencies regarding hazardous or potentially hazardous situations. An example might be a scenario in which a CSP is analyzing company records of employee exposures to potentially hazardous materials on a consultant basis. The CSP discovers a calculation mistake in transferring readings from a personal monitor into a formula that calculates the daily exposure rate. This mistake has resulted in underestimating the exposure rate by as much as 50%. The CSP immediately notes these findings in an urgent communication to the company. He then follows up with the company on correcting the calculation errors immediately for present and future employees and determining actions taken for employees that might already have received hazardous levels of exposure.

Standard 2 specifically deals with the CSP's character. The CSP should "be honest, fair, and impartial; act with responsibility and integrity..." The CSP has to balance the interests of all involved parties, and represent the profession in all business dealings.

Standard 3 focuses on appropriate public statements and contact. This standard notes that honesty and objectivity are required in all communications and statements. Certified safety professionals (CSP) should only make statements related to areas or situations about which they have direct expertise.

Standard 4 of this code focuses on the professional status and actions of CSP's. A CSP should only engage in projects or activities for which they are highly qualified in terms of knowledge, training, and experience. Additionally, ongoing education and professional advancement activities should be pursued by all CSP's to maintain and improve knowledge and skill level as well as to maintain certification. The Board of Certified Safety Professionals supports annual conferences that enable CSP's to receive valuable training and education while accumulating required points to keep their certification current.

Standard 5 focuses on integrity and honesty in the presentation of professional qualifications. This includes areas such as education, degrees, certification, experience, and achievements. Not only must CSP's be careful to clearly and honestly state all qualifications, but any exaggeration or misrepresentation by omission must also be avoided. When applying for jobs, providing references, or testifying in court, a CSP must not lie about their employment history, professional relationships, or professional qualifications and experience. A CSP with knowledge about violations of this standard should report the information to the Board of Certified Safety Professionals.

Standard 6 specifies that the CSP should avoid all conflicts of interest in order to maintain the integrity of their profession.

Standard 7 focuses on avoiding discrimination and bias. It is specifically noted that CSP's must not discriminate or demonstrate bias based on gender, age, race, ethnicity, country of origin, sexual orientation, or disability. These areas are also regulated by local, state, and federal agencies enforcing Civil Right and other related anti-discrimination legislation.

Copyright © Mometrix Media. You have been licensed one copy of this document for personal use only. Any other reproduction or redistribution is strictly prohibited. All rights reserved.
This content is provided for test preparation purposes only and does not imply an endorsement by Mometrix of any particular political, scientific, or religious point of view.

Standard 8 of this code promotes the need for CSP's to be involved in community and civic events and use their professional qualifications to promote safety within their own community. Examples of this include instructing public safety personnel in handling hazardous materials, teaching public safety classes in areas of fire prevention, home safety, and accident prevention. CSP's can work cooperatively with organizations and agencies already working in the community such as the Red Cross, fire departments, and police departments.

The impartiality principle of the Board of Certified Safety Professionals (BCSP) Code of Ethics holds that:

A certified safety professional (CSP) should adhere to the impartiality principle in all interactions and engage the advice and support of supervisors in determining appropriate actions. One area of concern is to avoid conflicts of interest or promoting oneself beyond actual expertise or competence. For example, if asked to testify in a lawsuit that revolves around an incident involving a former employee of a company affiliated with the CSP's employer, the CSP should defer to avoid conflict of interest. Another example would be a CSP who is asked to testify to the appropriateness of safety procedures related to radioactive materials. Although the CSP received general instruction in this area in a course, they have no direct experience. They should decline to avoid presenting themselves as an expert in that area.

The Code of Ethics and Professional Conduct for certified safety professionals (CSP) notes that the primary responsibility of a safety professional is to safeguard the health and safety of humans as well as providing for the safety of the environment and property. In a typical construction site, numerous organizations, individuals, and entities are working jointly to complete the project. Ultimately, each organization or company bears responsibility for making sure its workers are well trained and have a safe work environment. A main function in ensuring a safe worksite is to include safety stipulations in the contracts of all involved individuals or organizations.

A CSP must earn at least 25 points every five-year period, based on continuing education and professional development in order to retain their certificate.

Workers' Compensation

GOALS

Workers' compensation is an employer-provided insurance program that provides medical coverage for employee injuries. The goals of such a program are to provide medical care for employees and to protect the employee and the employer from the cost and time related to litigation. Exact provisions vary by state.

Employees who are injured on the job are provided medical care, at no cost, for the injury or illness. Prompt medical care has been shown effective at returning employees back to work quickly. The program operates under the **no-fault principle** in that the employee does not have to prove negligence on the part of the employer in exchange for benefits. In turn, the employer provides medical care without admitting fault for the injury.

EMPLOYEE BENEFITS

The intent of the program is to return employees to full duty as quickly as possible.

Workers' compensation programs provide **medical treatment** for occupational injuries or illnesses. The goal is to reduce the recovery time for injured employees. In extreme cases where an employee may not fully recover, workers' compensation may provide vocational rehabilitation or training for a new career.

Workers' compensation is designed to keep injured employees off public assistance programs by providing some means of **compensation** if they are unable to work. Individual states determine the exact benefit.

The employee saves costs of **litigation** by eliminating the need to legally prove fault of the employer in order to provide medical coverage and lost wages.

Copyright © Mometrix Media. You have been licensed one copy of this document for personal use only. Any other reproduction or redistribution is strictly prohibited. All rights reserved. This content is provided for test preparation purposes only and does not imply an endorsement by Mometrix of any particular political, scientific, or religious point of view.

EMPLOYER BENEFITS

Under a **workers' compensation** program, the employer bears the cost of the insurance to provide medical coverage for occupational injuries. In exchange for the cost, the program provides the following benefits to the employer:

Medical treatment and rehabilitation for occupational injuries is provided to injured employees. Thus, an employee who may not otherwise have medical coverage can be treated for an occupational injury to facilitate their return to work.

The company pays a fixed rate for the year's coverage in the form of a premium. This provides **fiscal protections** if an employer has a year with an unusually high number of injuries. Also, if employees seek legal assistance with their claim, awards and attorney fees are typically set by state statutes.

Under the **no-fault principle**, the employer does not accept responsibility for the injury but does agree to pay for care. This reduces **litigation costs** related to determining which party is responsible for treatment costs.

Chapter Quiz

Ready to see how well you retained what you just read? Scan the QR code to go directly to the chapter quiz interface for this study guide. If you're using a computer, simply visit the bonus page at **mometrix.com/bonus948/csp** and click the Chapter Quizzes link.

Copyright © Mometrix Media. You have been licensed one copy of this document for personal use only. Any other reproduction or redistribution is strictly prohibited. All rights reserved.
This content is provided for test preparation purposes only and does not imply an endorsement by Mometrix of any particular political, scientific, or religious point of view.

CSP Practice Test #1

Want to take this practice test in an online interactive format?
Check out the bonus page, which includes interactive practice questions and much more: **mometrix.com/bonus948/csp**

1. Within the realm of statistics, which of the following is TRUE with regard to the fundamental counting principle?

    a. When the principle is applied for a given sample, the standard deviation is always equal to the variance.
    b. The order or position of an occurrence always affects the overall probabilistic outcome of an entire event.
    c. The number of possible permutations is always greater than the possible number of combinations.
    d. The number of possible permutations is always less than the possible number of combinations.

2. Which of the following sets of colors is associated with the NFPA 704 Diamond System for the labeling of hazardous materials?

    a. Magenta, green, black, gold
    b. Blue, green, orange, white
    c. Red, yellow, green, black
    d. Yellow, blue, red, white

3. A company is developing a new pharmaceutical product to help counteract the effects of mercury poisoning. Before it comes to market, however, the company must first seek approval by which of the following US government agencies?

    a. US Department of Health and Human Services (DHHS)
    b. US National Institute for Drug Abuse (NIDA)
    c. US Consumer Product Safety Commission (CPSC)
    d. US Food and Drug Administration (FDA)

4. Which of the following is NOT typically categorized as a "class" of hazard within an industrial or process setting?

    a. First-responder conveyance
    b. Falling of loads
    c. Handling of materials
    d. Materials being in motion

5. If an injured worker wishes to file litigation against a company he or she feels is responsible for his or her maladies, which of the following attorneys should he or she most likely consult?

    a. Compensatory tort
    b. Criminal
    c. Civil
    d. OSHA attorney-general delegate

Copyright © Mometrix Media. You have been licensed one copy of this document for personal use only. Any other reproduction or redistribution is strictly prohibited. All rights reserved.
This content is provided for test preparation purposes only and does not imply an endorsement by Mometrix of any particular political, scientific, or religious point of view.

6. What are the two different categories of workers' compensation laws?

a. Antecedent and post-factual
b. Compulsory and elective
c. Standard and closure
d. Transitional and disability

7. Which of the following is NOT typically regarded as a primary safety hazard associated with the use of powered vehicles in a work area?

a. Potential carbon monoxide overexposure
b. Exceeding load limits
c. Blind spots
d. Operator physical overexertion

8. What is the conventional definition of a blasting agent?

a. A material that demonstrates adequate stability in a stand-alone condition yet possesses enough exothermic potential to prompt an explosion when initiated
b. A material, such as TNT, designed to detonate upon a threshold catalyst
c. A material designed to explode upon mechanical impact
d. Any solid or liquid substance that will easily ignite above standard temperature and pressure (STP) conditions

9. Which of the following is NOT a type of conveyor mechanism that is primarily used for transporting bulk products or materials within an industrial setting?

a. Belts
b. Buckets
c. Winches
d. Rollers

10. If a very large construction company experiences 369 work-related deaths, worldwide, over a recent 10-year span, about what number of them would likely be attributable to falls?

a. 30
b. 80
c. 150
d. 210

11. What device is commonly used in industrial settings to measure potentially hazardous noise levels?

a. A microphone
b. A noise dosimeter
c. An audiometer
d. A gain-differential inductance meter

12. Which of the following is NOT a typical injury or illness-related metric that is regularly tracked by federal agencies?

a. Frequency of work-related retaliation events
b. Frequency of work-related deaths
c. Frequency of job transfers
d. Frequency of restricted duty

Copyright © Mometrix Media. You have been licensed one copy of this document for personal use only. Any other reproduction or redistribution is strictly prohibited. All rights reserved.
This content is provided for test preparation purposes only and does not imply an endorsement by Mometrix of any particular political, scientific, or religious point of view.

13. Which of the following terms is typically NOT associated with the domain of gas or vapor sampling?

   a. Colorimetry
   b. Chromatograph
   c. Centrifugal separation
   d. Grab sample

14. Which of the following is NOT inclusive of the OSHA Classification System for Occupational Illnesses and Conditions?

   a. Respiratory-related disorders or conditions
   b. Radiation-related disorders or conditions
   c. Skin-related disorders or conditions
   d. Blunt trauma-related disorders or conditions

15. US citizen employees who live and work in the United States have a legal right to _____ certain records under their name.

   a. inspect
   b. replace
   c. purge
   d. transfer

16. A CSP and an industrial hygienist determine that the intensity of a certain physical parameter or phenomenon within a work area measures two footlamberts. Which of the following is being measured?

   a. Gamma radiation
   b. Ultraviolet radiation
   c. Microwaves
   d. Visible light

17. To counteract high-pressure environments (e.g., that seen during deep underwater diving), which of the following tactics is typically implemented to counteract the potential effects of nitrogen narcosis?

   a. Replacing nitrogen with inert surrogate gases, such as helium
   b. Increasing supplied-air oxygen levels by 0.5 percent for every 10 ft of depth
   c. Requiring an ascension rate of at least 10 ft per min
   d. Limiting underwater excursions to less than 1 hr for depths greater than 50 ft

18. Per the US Clean Air Act, which of the following outdoor concentration readings would be considered a violation of National Ambient Air Quality Standards (NAAQS)?

   a. 0.5 ppm of carbon monoxide over an 8-hr period
   b. 0.05 ppm of ozone over an 8-hr period
   c. 1.0 μg/m^3 of lead over a 3-month period
   d. 10 ppb of sulfur dioxide over a 1-hr period

19. Which of the following functional-notation representations would depict a discount factor for a present dollar value given a future value at a 3 percent annual interest rate over 7 years?

   a. (F|P, 7, 3%)
   b. (P|F, 3%, 7)
   c. (P|F, 7, 3%)
   d. (F|P, 3%, 7)

Copyright © Mometrix Media. You have been licensed one copy of this document for personal use only. Any other reproduction or redistribution is strictly prohibited. All rights reserved.
This content is provided for test preparation purposes only and does not imply an endorsement by Mometrix of any particular political, scientific, or religious point of view.

20. What is a typical three-step process that should always be employed in industrial settings if there has been a hazardous material(s) spill?

   a. Inspection, notification, cleanup
   b. Isolation, mitigation, remediation
   c. Evacuation, notification, remediation
   d. Safety, containment, notification

21. Acquired data from two distinct and separate variables is known as which of the following?

   a. Bimodal data
   b. Bivariate data
   c. Tandem-statistical corollaries
   d. Quadratic-bipolar data

22. In this data set (3, 7, 9, 12, 26, 32, 45, 58), which of the following is the mode?

   a. 19
   b. 24
   c. None
   d. 0

23. If the illustration shown here represents a standard normal distribution, approximately what percent of the total area below the curve is comprised of [(−2sd < x < −sd) + (0 < x < sd)]?

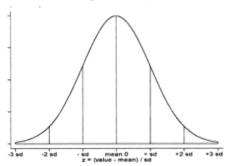

   a. 44 percent
   b. 48 percent
   c. 52 percent
   d. 56 percent

24. Which of the following US federal agencies is responsible for distributing statistical information pertaining to job-related injuries and illnesses?

   a. US Occupational Safety and Health Administration
   b. US Department of Health and Human Services
   c. US Bureau of Labor Statistics
   d. US National Institute of Occupational Safety and Health

25. An ex-employee is looking to pursue legal action against his or her company for alleged wrongdoing. The company, in turn, is planning on defending itself based upon the fellow-servant rule. Which of the following grievance subject areas is the employee pursuing legal action for?

   a. Wrongful termination
   b. On-the-job injury
   c. Racial discrimination
   d. Sexual harassment

Copyright © Mometrix Media. You have been licensed one copy of this document for personal use only. Any other reproduction or redistribution is strictly prohibited. All rights reserved.
This content is provided for test preparation purposes only and does not imply an endorsement by Mometrix of any particular political, scientific, or religious point of view.

26. Which agency or organization is typically responsible for setting the rate premiums that employers will pay for workers' compensation insurance?

    a. US Department of Commerce
    b. US Department of Labor
    c. National Council on Compensation Insurance
    d. National Commission on Banking and Insurance Fiscal Regulation

27. Sound octaves are conventionally characterized by _____ with sequential octaves normally differing by a factor of _____.

    a. wavelength, 10
    b. pitch, 100
    c. frequency, 2
    d. tone, 10

28. If a pregnant employee is concerned about her child being exposed to potential teratogenic sources, which of the following should she avoid?

    a. Microwave radiation
    b. PCBs
    c. Coffee
    d. Acetic acid

29. Which of the following is typically NOT a potential mode of particulate contamination?

    a. Aerosols
    b. Gases
    c. Mists
    d. Fumes

30. Which of the following is usually NOT regarded as a hazard typically related to the use of high-pressure receptacles and containers?

    a. Pressures exceeding design safety levels
    b. Higher fire risks due to enhanced oxygen levels in certain containers
    c. Container failure due to corrosion
    d. Use of containers without always venting excess buildup

31. A monitoring system should be employed in tandem with a(n) _____ system to alert workforces of potentially hazardous conditions being at hand.

    a. warning
    b. emergency response
    c. shutdown
    d. actuator

32. Which of the following is NOT a typical telltale sign that a chemical reaction may be ensuing as the result of a spill?

    a. Emission of smoke or vapor
    b. Evaporation or sublimation
    c. Bubble formation
    d. Unusual odors

Copyright © Mometrix Media. You have been licensed one copy of this document for personal use only. Any other reproduction or redistribution is strictly prohibited. All rights reserved.
This content is provided for test preparation purposes only and does not imply an endorsement by Mometrix of any particular political, scientific, or religious point of view.

33. A new car costs $12,000. It costs $400 per year for gas and $600 for maintenance for the first year. Each subsequent year, maintenance costs $25 more than it did the previous year. The car is expected to last eight years. After eight years, the dealership will pay $2,000 for it. What is the life-cycle cost of owning the car?

   a. $10,000
   b. $12,000
   c. $17,525
   d. $18,700

34. Which of the following graphical tools is typically regarded as the MOST useful for clearly illustrating data groups that may fall within a particular value range?

   a. Histogram
   b. Bar graph
   c. Stem-and-leaf plot
   d. Box-and-whisker plot

35. Which of the following statistical parameters is NOT utilized if one wishes to calculate a measure of dispersion for a given data set?

   a. Variance
   b. Standard deviation
   c. Range
   d. Median

36. What is the approximate standard deviation (σ) for the following "entire population" data set?

      (2, 7, 11, 24, 44, 62, 79, 81, 105, 120, 139, 162)

   a. 39
   b. 52
   c. 54
   d. 70

37. Which of the following is NOT a typical shape or characterization of a frequency curve?

   a. Multimodal
   b. Skewed
   c. J-shaped
   d. Step functional

38. If a population of 100,000 people incurred an "LD50" exposure to radiation or chemicals, approximately how many acute deaths in that population would be expected?

   a. 0
   b. 2,000
   c. 50,000
   d. 100,000

39. Which of the following is a detailed and systematic process to evaluate potential risks associated with the design and operation of a multifaceted, complex technology?

   a. Probabilistic risk assessment
   b. Failure modes and effects analysis
   c. Hazards assessment
   d. Documented safety analysis

Copyright © Mometrix Media. You have been licensed one copy of this document for personal use only. Any other reproduction or redistribution is strictly prohibited. All rights reserved.
This content is provided for test preparation purposes only and does not imply an endorsement by Mometrix of any particular political, scientific, or religious point of view.

40. A group of individuals meets within an organization to discuss several potential tools that may be used for assessing a wide range of workplace system hazards. One of the individuals, in particular, insists that the best tool to employ for such a purpose is a "simultaneous, timed-events plotting analysis" and has successfully utilized them throughout his or her career. What is the MOST likely area of expertise of this individual?

   a. Root-cause analysis
   b. Probabilistic risk assessment
   c. Industrial engineering
   d. Safety engineering

41. Within the specific quality assurance domains of audits and inspections, what does the acronym CAQ typically stand for?

   a. Certification of Absolute Qualification
   b. Condition Adverse to Quality
   c. Codified Audit Query
   d. Correction to Annotated Quantity

42. An individual who is employed by the US Department of Defense has recently been granted a "secret" level security clearance. Per US NISPOM protocols, which of the following document cover color combinations would the employee be allowed to access?

   a. Brown, orange, red
   b. Orange, amber, green
   c. Red, green, blue
   d. Blue, gray, green

43. A craft employee who was not paying attention while working with a circular saw lost two fingers in an accident. Corporate Health and Safety Management reported the accident to OSHA approximately 40 hours after the incident. According to OSHA 29 CFR 1904.39, the company is

   a. in violation of the allowable reporting time frame.
   b. in compliance with the allowable reporting time frame.
   c. in the probation zone of the allowable reporting time frame.
   d. not required to file an OSHA report but is instead required to file with the US Department of Labor.

44. In a total workforce of 200 people (who each work 2,000 hours over a calendar year), if there are 10 total cases of missed workdays, restricted duty, or transfer due to work-related injuries over that calendar year, what is the resulting DART rate?

   a. 10
   b. 5
   c. 20
   d. 2

45. A bar graph most closely resembles which of the following illustrative tools?

   a. A box-and-whiskers graph
   b. A stem-and-leaf plot
   c. A histogram
   d. A rectangular-regression plot

Copyright © Mometrix Media. You have been licensed one copy of this document for personal use only. Any other reproduction or redistribution is strictly prohibited. All rights reserved.
This content is provided for test preparation purposes only and does not imply an endorsement by Mometrix of any particular political, scientific, or religious point of view.

46. A job hazard analysis is performed for an upcoming task that is to take place within a very high radiation area. What type of instrumentation would be most appropriate for use by health physicists (or rad-techs) for determining actual radiation levels of the area before workers enter to perform their assigned task?

    a. A teletector

    b. An explosimeter

    c. A multichannel analyzer

    d. A thermoluminescent dosimeter (TLD)

47. A "fishbone diagram" is also known as which of the following?

    a. A failure modes and effects analysis

    b. An event tree study

    c. A hazard and operability study

    d. A cause-and-effect analysis

48. The 50th percentile value of a normal distribution is also always denoted as which of the following?

    a. Mean

    b. Median

    c. Mode

    d. The bisecting point

49. Which of the following audit-finding classifications is usually considered the most serious?

    a. Conditions adverse to quality

    b. Corrective action issue

    c. Near miss

    d. Tier-1 infraction

50. Per OSHA directive, VPP Merit-status employers are expected to commit to the pursuance of star status within a period of how many years?

    a. 1

    b. 2

    c. 3

    d. 4

51. A waste storage receptacle containing sulfuric acid from used batteries should have which of the following waste code designation numbers?

    a. D-001

    b. D-002

    c. D-003

    d. D-004

52. Which of the following should be regularly implemented or reviewed in coordination with preliminary task walk-downs and pre-job briefings prior to the commencement of activities?

    a. Job safety analysis (JSA)

    b. Task self-assessment (TSA)

    c. Probabilistic risk assessment (PRA)

    d. Hazard and operability study (HAZOP)

Copyright © Mometrix Media. You have been licensed one copy of this document for personal use only. Any other reproduction or redistribution is strictly prohibited. All rights reserved.
This content is provided for test preparation purposes only and does not imply an endorsement by Mometrix of any particular political, scientific, or religious point of view.

53. Which of the following is NOT an established component of NIOSH's lifting equation?

a. Lifting index (LI)
b. Recommended weight limit (RWL)
c. Leverage stability coefficient (LSC)
d. Load constant (LC)

54. A floor surface that has a moderate slip potential has a coefficient of friction approaching which of the following values?

a. −0.8
b. −0.5
c. 0.4
d. 0.8

55. In the following Cartesian data-point set, which of the following points would be considered an anomaly compared to the others? [(0.5, 1.4), (2, 6), (4, 11.8), (7, 20), (9, 22), (12, 37), (15, 45.8), (17, 50)]

a. (9, 22)
b. (0.5, 1.4)
c. (15, 45.8)
d. None

56. Which of the following is a TRUE statement with regard to root-cause analyses (RCAs)?

a. There can only be one tangible underlying root cause outcome for any given RCA.
b. An RCA is only performed after an event has occurred.
c. Historical RCAs should not be utilized for predicting possible events before they occur.
d. Incident management processes and RCAs are normally integrated and implemented in tandem.

57. If a calculated statistical variance for a sample of data values is found to be approximately 2.76, what is the associated standard deviation value correlated to that variance?

a. 1.66
b. 7.62
c. 1.38
d. 5.52

58. A masonry construction company regularly employs the use of a powder that is comprised of 5 percent silica. What would be its calculated PEL (in ppm) when in use?

a. 2.76 ppm
b. 1.99 ppm
c. 1.41 ppm
d. 0.83 ppm

59. Xylene is being generated within a work area per the following contributory parameters:

V = 100,000 ft³, Q' = 2,000 cfm, and G = 3 cfm, whereby V is the volume of the work area; Q' is the air flow rate in the work area divided by a design distribution constant; and G is the contaminant generation rate. How much time will elapse before the xylene concentration in the work area reaches 150 ppm?

a. 5.27 min
b. 7.64 min
c. 10.29 min
d. 13.88 min

Copyright © Mometrix Media. You have been licensed one copy of this document for personal use only. Any other reproduction or redistribution is strictly prohibited. All rights reserved. This content is provided for test preparation purposes only and does not imply an endorsement by Mometrix of any particular political, scientific, or religious point of view.

60. For a worker deployed outdoors with a solar load, what is the calculated wet-bulb temperature if the globe temperature is 92°F, the dry-bulb temperature is 85°F, and the wet-bulb globe temperature index is 89°F?

a. 87.7°F
b. 88.7°F
c. 89.7°F
d. 91.2°F

61. Given the following set of data, what is the calculated correlation coefficient between the two variables x and y?

	x	y
	3	2
	5	4
	8	6
	11	9
	14	13
	16	15
Total	57	49
Average	9.5	8.2

a. 1.000
b. 0.995
c. 0.990
d. 0.985

62. If the partial-pressure of Gas_x = 12 atm, Gas_y = 28 atm, and Gas_z = 50 atm, what is the total calculated pressure of the mixture of Gases x, y, and z?

a. 30 atm
b. 50 atm
c. 90 atm
d. None of the above

63. A steel wire is measured to have an electrical resistivity of 20 ohm-m. What is the associated conductivity of this wire?

a. 0.05 siemens-m^{-1}
b. 20 siemens-m^{-1}
c. 1.0 siemens-m^{-1}
d. 0 siemens-m^{-1}

64. A company's tool and die fabrication process requires a certain mold to be consistently manufactured at a 3.25-in thickness. Seven random mold samples were collected and found to have the following thickness measurements (in inches): 3.21, 3.28, 3.32, 3.36, 3.25, 3.29, and 3.22. What is the calculated "t" value for the collected samples?

a. 1.356
b. 1.279
c. 1.183
d. 1.095

Copyright © Mometrix Media. You have been licensed one copy of this document for personal use only. Any other reproduction or redistribution is strictly prohibited. All rights reserved.
This content is provided for test preparation purposes only and does not imply an endorsement by Mometrix of any particular political, scientific, or religious point of view.

65. If a system (X) has two (and only two) codependent subsystems (y and z) required for its operation, with one having a 0.0001 failure rate and the other having a 0.001 failure rate, what is the overall probability of failure for the entire system (X)?

   a. 0.001
   b. 0.0001
   c. 0.0011
   d. 0.00055

66. If the pH of a sulfuric acid solution used in an industrial setting must be below 1.5 to burn through worker PPE, what must the minimum associated hydrogen-ion concentration of that acid be to reach such a pH?

   a. 1.27
   b. 0.76
   c. 4.48
   d. 0.032

67. A safety training examination given to 50 students showed a mean score of 74.3 percent, with a standard deviation of 6.9. Only one student scored exactly an 80 percent on the exam. If a normal distribution is assumed, how many students received a higher score than this one student?

Z	0.00	0.01	0.02	0.03	0.04	0.05	0.06	0.07	0.08	0.09
0.7	0.7580	0:7611	0.7642	0.7673	0.7704	0.7734	0.7764	0.7794	0.7823	0.7852
0.8	0.7881	0.7910	0.7939	0.7967	0.7995	0.8023	0.8051	0.8078	0.8106	0.8133
0.9	0.8159	0.8186	0.8212	0.8238	0.8264	0.8289	0.8315	0.8340	0.8365	0.8389

   a. 8
   b. 10
   c. 12
   d. 14

68. What is the calculated numerical difference (i.e., delta) between the upper-control limit (UCL) and lower-control limit (LCL) for an accident control-chart distribution with the following statistical parameters?

   Mean = 6.50
   Standard deviation (σ) = 0.75
   Number of allowable standard deviations from the mean (z) = 3

   a. 4.5
   b. 2.25
   c. 1.5
   d. 1.125

69. In this right triangle, the tangent (TAN) of angle <BAC is equal to which of the following?

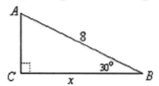

   a. $(0.50 \div 1.414)$
   b. $x \div 8$
   c. $[(8)^{1/2}] \div x$
   d. $(6.93 \div 4)$

Copyright © Mometrix Media. You have been licensed one copy of this document for personal use only. Any other reproduction or redistribution is strictly prohibited. All rights reserved.
This content is provided for test preparation purposes only and does not imply an endorsement by Mometrix of any particular political, scientific, or religious point of view.

Mometrix

70. Which of the following would have a larger "failure-per-hr" rate: a car engine component operating for 10,000 hours with an established reliability of 0.998 or an aircraft component operating for 20,000 hours with an established reliability of 0.997?

    a. The car engine component would have a larger rate.
    b. The aircraft component would have a larger rate.
    c. The failure-per-hr rates would be identical.
    d. It is not possible to determine from the information provided.

71. The following series of force equations characterizes a static hoist apparatus used in the workplace for a given task:

$$2x_1 + x_2 - 4x_3 = 6 \text{ N}$$
$$5y_1 = 3.5 \text{ N}$$
$$x_3 = 2y_1$$

What is the calculated force of x_2 given that $x_1 \neq 0$?

    a. 2.250 newtons
    b. 5.167 newtons
    c. 14.429 newtons
    d. cannot be determined from the information provided

72. If over a 5-year span, a large chemical processing company sees a total of 425 worker accidents or injuries across the United States, according to H. W. Heinrich, approximately how many of these accidents would likely be the result of direct actions of individuals?

    a. 190
    b. 265
    c. 325
    d. 375

73. What is an endeavor to uncover and reduce hazards that may be at hand for product or system users as well as to those who are accountable for their maintenance conventionally known as?

    a. Preliminary hazard analysis
    b. Occupational health hazard assessment
    c. Documented safety analysis
    d. Technical safety requirement evaluation

74. In a fault-tree sequence, Events A, B, and C have estimated probabilities (frequencies) of occurrence equal to 0.1, 0.01, and 0.005, respectively. For a resulting system failure to occur (Event D), Events A and B or Events A and C must transpire. According to the fault-tree's analysis, what is the approximate overall probability that Event D may occur?

    a. 0.0015
    b. 0.0000050
    c. 0.0010
    d. 0.1150

Copyright © Mometrix Media. You have been licensed one copy of this document for personal use only. Any other reproduction or redistribution is strictly prohibited. All rights reserved.
This content is provided for test preparation purposes only and does not imply an endorsement by Mometrix of any particular political, scientific, or religious point of view.

75. A vehicle is moving along at a steady speed of 50 m/s. The driver then notices a pedestrian up ahead and cautiously elects to slow down at a rate of –6 m/s. He or she continues the deceleration for 100 m until the pedestrian completely moves out of the thoroughfare, at which point he or she begins to accelerate again. What is the vehicle's speed at the point where the driver begins to accelerate again?

    a. 30 m/s
    b. 32 m/s
    c. 34 m/s
    d. 36 m/s

76. A plaintiff has sued a company regarding a wrongful injury he or she allegedly incurred from the use of one of its products. During subsequent legal proceedings, the following took place: (1) it was conclusively demonstrated that the product was indeed defective; (2) it was conclusively demonstrated that the product was defective upon departure of the defendant's stewardship; and (3) it was suggested but not conclusively demonstrated that the defect was responsible for the plaintiff's injury. As such, which of the following determinations would likely result from the proceedings?

    a. The defendant is found responsible for consumer fraud.
    b. The defendant is found responsible for obligatory culpability.
    c. The defendant is found responsible for strict liability.
    d. None of the above will occur.

77. Per Mining Safety and Health Administration (MSHA) protocol, what is the calculated severity measure (SM) rate for a mining operation that had five lost workdays and 125,000 hours worked over a given calendar year?

    a. 8
    b. 12
    c. 5
    d. 1.2

78. If two separate containers are being simultaneously filled with a chemical at a rate of 2.5 gal/min, with one container being cylindrically shaped with a diameter of 12 in and a height of 24 in, whereas the other is box shaped with dimensions of 16 in × 9 in × 30 in, which one will have overflowed after exactly 4 min of filling?

    a. The cylinder container
    b. The box container
    c. Neither
    d. Both

79. The following list is comprised of hazard scores associated with each of the noted categories within a given work area, on a scale from 1 to 10, where 1 depicts a minimal hazard and 10 depicts a maximal hazard:

Hazard	Score
Chemical containment	4
Noise	3
Open floor plans / tripping	8
Lighting	1
Electrical	6
Fire suppression	2
Ergonomics	9
Machinery pinch points	7

Copyright © Mometrix Media. You have been licensed one copy of this document for personal use only. Any other reproduction or redistribution is strictly prohibited. All rights reserved.
This content is provided for test preparation purposes only and does not imply an endorsement by Mometrix of any particular political, scientific, or religious point of view.

From this data, which of the following can likely be surmised as a TRUE statement?

 a. The measured 8-hr average ambient noise level in the work area is likely in the range of 90 to 95 dBA.
 b. There are several partially exposed gears, pulleys, and/or belts in the work area that are in need of more robust guarding.
 c. The average ambient lighting level in the subject work area is approximately 2 foot-candles.
 d. Most fire extinguishers in the work area are of the incorrect type and are past due for inspection.

80. The half-life of the isotope Cobalt-60 is approximately 5.3 years. If the measured dose rate from a subject point source at time = t_0 is 2,000 mrem/hr at a distance of 9 ft, approximately how long may one be exposed at a distance of 4 ft at time = t_0 + 16 years without exceeding the 10 CFR 20 annual occupational dose limit of 5 rem/year?

 a. 1 hr
 b. 2 hrs
 c. 3 hrs
 d. 4 hrs

81. Which of the following is larger: the measured area between the function $f(x) = 2x^3 + x^2 - 5$ and the x-axis between the points $x_1 = 0$ and $x_2 = 3$ or the area of a circle with a circumference equal to 25. Note: both the function and the circle are plotted in the same Cartesian coordinate system.

 a. The function is larger.
 b. The circle is larger.
 c. Both areas are approximately the same in value.
 d. it is not possible to determine which area is larger from the information provided.

82. Which of the following constitutes an example of an involuntary risk scenario?

 a. Driving a car
 b. Eating 3-month-old eggs
 c. Breathing in secondhand smoke
 d. Living on a golf course

83. A worker was exposed to a hazardous chemical for 4 hrs per day over a 3-day period. One month later, the individual was diagnosed with a liver condition that has historically been shown to manifest as a result of exposure to this chemical. Which of the following characterizations hence most accurately depicts the type of exposure and health effects that were incurred by the subject worker for this particular case?

 a. Chronic exposure and localized health effects
 b. Acute exposure and systemic health effects
 c. Chronic exposure and systemic health effects
 d. Acute exposure and localized health effects

84. In a horizontally oriented fire system (i.e., no elevation throughout the system), water flows through a 4-in pipe. The measured head loss in a 500-ft section of the system is 20 ft. The pressure at Point A is 30 psi, and the velocity at point A is 8 ft/s. If the velocity at Point B is 10 ft/s, what is the pressure at Point B?

 a. 16.8 psi
 b. 19.3 psi
 c. 21.1 psi
 d. 24.7 psi

Copyright © Mometrix Media. You have been licensed one copy of this document for personal use only. Any other reproduction or redistribution is strictly prohibited. All rights reserved. This content is provided for test preparation purposes only and does not imply an endorsement by Mometrix of any particular political, scientific, or religious point of view.

85. If a 170-lb worker falls off of a 20-ft-high scaffold, what would his approximate speed (in mph) be at ground impact?

    a. 25 mph
    b. 31 mph
    c. 21 mph
    d. 16 mph

86. A parameter that is conventionally used to measure the quantity of time that an unprotected worker may remain in an area that has been infiltrated by a known amount of hazardous or toxic gas (or fumes) without suffering any adverse health effects is known as an emergency exposure limit (EEL). Most EELs fall into which of the following time-unit ranges?

    a. S to min
    b. Min to hrs
    c. Hrs to days
    d. Days to weeks

87. Which of the following isotopes is both radiologically and chemically hazardous to human health?

    a. Lead-208
    b. Argon-40
    c. Mercury-202
    d. Plutonium-239

88. The following is a compendium of noise-level measurements within an assessed work area over a two-week time span. From the provided data, which of the following conclusions should be drawn?

Measurement Day	Number of Hours Measured	Measurement Range	Measurement Average
1 of 10	6.75	74-81 dBA	77 dBA
2 of 10	8	67-79 dBA	71 dBA
3 of 10	3	86-88 dBA	87 dBA
4 of 10	8	71-92 dBA	79 dBA
5 of 10	7	81-85 dBA	84 dBA
6 of 10	3.5	77-80 dBA	78 dBA
7 of 10	8	58-72 dBA	67 dBA
8 of 10	6.5	66-70 dBA	69 dBA
9 of 10	2.25	89-94 dBA	93 dBA
10 of 10	7.5	75-83 dBA	78 dBA

    a. The work area should be designated as a hazardous noise area as per OSHA 1910.95, with mandatory hearing protection PPE always worn.
    b. The work area should be designated as a hazardous noise area as per OSHA 1910.95, with hearing protection PPE recommended.
    c. The work area meets the minimum TWA threshold levels of a part-time hazardous noise area as per OSHA 1910.95; thus, hearing protection PPE is mandatory for at least 4 hrs per workday.
    d. The work area does not meet the minimum TWA threshold levels of a hazardous noise area as per OSHA 1910.95, and thus, hearing protection PPE is not mandatory; however, it should be recommended.

Copyright © Mometrix Media. You have been licensed one copy of this document for personal use only. Any other reproduction or redistribution is strictly prohibited. All rights reserved.
This content is provided for test preparation purposes only and does not imply an endorsement by Mometrix of any particular political, scientific, or religious point of view.

89. An industrial worker was recently occupationally diagnosed with the respiratory disease *Siderosis*. Which of the following industries is this worker most likely employed in?

a. Asbestos remediation
b. Steelworking
c. Woodworking
d. Masonry

90. How many ppm of air contaminants theoretically make their way all the way through a three-stage filter bank with individual respective efficiencies of 90 percent, 95 percent, and 99 percent?

a. 50 ppm
b. 500 ppm
c. 5 ppm
d. 53,333 ppm

91. If a gas at a pressure of 5 psia occupies a volume of 100 cm³ at a temperature of 20°K, what will the resultant pressure be if the temperature is increased to 30°K at a volume of 150 cm³?

a. 2.5 psia
b. 5 psia
c. 7.5 psia
d. 10 psia

92. During a flight in a non-pressurized aircraft, a pilot begins to feel a bit confused, is breathing more rapidly, and has a notably higher resting pulse rate. At what altitude range (above sea level) is the aircraft likely flying?

a. 5,000 to 10,000 ft
b. 10,000 to 15,000 ft
c. 15,000 to 20,000 ft
d. Greater than 20,000 ft

93. If the inhalation dose conversion factor for isotope "X" is 1 rem per curie, and a facility that processes this isotope releases 2.22×10^{13} becquerels of it per year, what is the resulting annual inhalation dose to a downwind receptor who has a breathing rate of 18.31 in³ per s and is subjected to an atmospheric concentration dispersion coefficient of 1×10^{-7} s per cm³?

a. 18 mrem
b. 600 rem
c. 600 mrem
d. 18 rem

94. If a work area has dimensions of 10 m × 10 m × 3 m, what is the shortest amount of time it could potentially take for the entire supply of air in the room to (hypothetically) be completely exchanged via an air-exchanger HVAC system that operates at a rate of 80 cfm?

a. 1.6 hrs
b. 2.2 hrs
c. 2.9 hrs
d. 3.4 hrs

Copyright © Mometrix Media. You have been licensed one copy of this document for personal use only. Any other reproduction or redistribution is strictly prohibited. All rights reserved.
This content is provided for test preparation purposes only and does not imply an endorsement by Mometrix of any particular political, scientific, or religious point of view.

95. A 48-hr radon survey was conducted in a work area that measured radon concentrations every 2 hrs. Given the survey results (in Ci/L) provided in this table, which of the following conclusions should be drawn in regard to whether EPA action levels have been exceeded, and if they have been exceeded, which of the following measures should be taken?

Time	Concentration (Ci/L)
1600 (Day 1)	1.2×10^{-12}
1800 (Day 1)	9.3×10^{-13}
2000 (Day 1)	1.8×10^{-12}
2200 (Day 1)	2.7×10^{-12}
0000 (Day 1)	4.3×10^{-12}
0200 (Day 1)	3.8×10^{-12}
0400 (Day 1)	1.9×10^{-12}
0600 (Day 1)	1.3×10^{-12}
0800 (Day 1)	8.8×10^{-13}
1000 (Day 1)	8.1×10^{-13}
1200 (Day 1)	1.1×10^{-12}
1400 (Day 1)	1.4×10^{-12}
1600 (Day 2)	1.3×10^{-12}
1800 (Day 2)	9.9×10^{-13}
2000 (Day 2)	1.5×10^{-12}
2200 (Day 2)	1.1×10^{-12}
0000 (Day 2)	1.6×10^{-12}
0200 (Day 2)	9.5×10^{-13}
0400 (Day 2)	1.3×10^{-12}
0600 (Day 2)	8.5×10^{-13}
0800 (Day 2)	1.0×10^{-12}
1000 (Day 2)	1.2×10^{-12}
1200 (Day 2)	1.3×10^{-12}
1400 (Day 2)	9.6×10^{-13}

a. No category of action level has been exceeded, and no actions are recommended.
b. The 2 pCi/L threshold is exceeded, and a moderate degree of remedial action should be considered.
c. The 4 pCi/L threshold is exceeded, and a major degree of remedial action should be taken.
d. The average threshold level far exceeds EPA-recommended standards, and respiratory protection should be used by workers.

96. What is the conventionally established definition for upper flammable limit (UFL) or upper explosive limit (UEL) for a gas?

a. The maximum amount of heat (energy) one mole of gas is able to liberate associated with a unit change in temperature equal to 1°K
b. The highest temperature at which a flammable gas is able to undergo detonation
c. The highest pressure at which a gas is able to undergo an equilibrium phase change
d. The highest concentration of gas (or vapor) relative to air at which a material is able to ignite

Copyright © Mometrix Media. You have been licensed one copy of this document for personal use only. Any other reproduction or redistribution is strictly prohibited. All rights reserved.
This content is provided for test preparation purposes only and does not imply an endorsement by Mometrix of any particular political, scientific, or religious point of view.

97. Steve and Mary both work on an assembly line. Steve, who primarily works near one unguarded pulley and three partially guarded belts, never tucks in his shirt and always wears a loose-hanging bracelet. Mary, in contrast, who works near 18 fully guarded axles and six fully guarded gears, always wears a long, dangling necklace to work, and has long hair. From a generic risk perspective, who is seemingly more likely to be involved in a "caught-in-a-machine"-related incident?

   a. Steve
   b. Mary
   c. Both Steve and Mary
   d. Not enough information

98. Which of the following current or voltage combinations would MOST likely result in fatality?

   a. 1 amp/1 volt
   b. 0.5 amp/10 volts
   c. 0.15 amp/100 volts
   d. 0.001 amp/1,000 volts

99. Glassification and ceramification are two modes of immobilization used in the disposition of hazardous, mixed, and nuclear wastes. A waste management company has 10 metric tons (MT) of waste (bulk ρ = 4.8 g/cm^3) that it is required to dispose of (by mandate) using either or both of these technologies. Cost-benefit analyses show that glassification costs $1,000 per cubic ft of waste processed, and ceramification costs about $5,000 per cubic ft of waste processed. Which of the following provides an accurate depiction of the total projected cost estimate for disposing of the waste in equal (i.e., 50/50) quantities (by weight) using both technologies?

   a. $164,392
   b. $220,716
   c. $237,941
   d. $261,855

100. What are the pressure and associated Reynolds number (Re) range for a pipe with a 6-in radius and a laminar flow rate of 1,000 gpm?

   a. 0.269 psi / Re < 2,000
   b. 0.172 psi / Re > 4,000
   c. 0.054 psi / Re < 2,000
   d. 0.028 psi / Re > 4,000

101. A company physician recommends that an overweight employee implement a weight-loss plan to lose 52 lb. If the employee has been regularly eating 5,000 calories per day and exhibits an equilibrium caloric intake level of 2,500 daily calories (the caloric daily intake whereby weight remains stable), by what percentage must he or she decrease his or her daily caloric intake to lose the target weight over 1 year's time, assuming that he or she burns 2,500 calories per day through normal metabolism and exercise over that year, and that 1 ounce of fat is equivalent to 200 calories?

   a. 59.1 percent
   b. 58.2 percent
   c. 57.4 percent
   d. 56.3 percent

Copyright © Mometrix Media. You have been licensed one copy of this document for personal use only. Any other reproduction or redistribution is strictly prohibited. All rights reserved.
This content is provided for test preparation purposes only and does not imply an endorsement by Mometrix of any particular political, scientific, or religious point of view.

102. In a given industrial setting, an oscilloscope is employed for accurately calibrating electronic equipment. From the associated display provided, which of the following characterizations is correct?

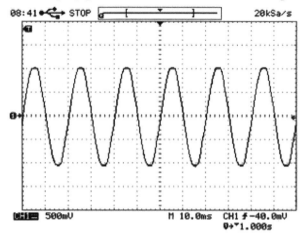

a. Sine wave, amplitude = 4 units, period = 12 units
b. Cosine wave, amplitude = 2 units, period = 6 units
c. Sine wave, amplitude = 2 units, period = 2 units
d. Cosine wave, amplitude = 4 units, period = 1 unit

103. A 5-m diameter aperture circular antenna emits 1-cm wavelength microwaves at a power level equal to 50 W. What is the associated power density level at a distance of 10 m from the antenna?

a. 4.69 mW/cm²
b. 804 mW/cm²
c. 9,817 mW/cm²
d. 12,205 mW/cm²

104. What is the calculated head of a fluid moving inside of a pipe with a constant flow rate of 4 ft/s?

a. 0.25 ft
b. 0.625 ft
c. 1.5 ft
d. 2 ft

105. A 10 micro-curie calibration source of X-isotope emits a single 2.5 MeV gamma ray 100 percent of the time when the isotope undergoes decay. What is the estimated dose rate from this source at a straight-line distance away of 1 ft?

a. 0.000025 rem/hr
b. 0.00015 rem/hr
c. 0.0075 rem/hr
d. 0.010 rem/hr

106. What would be the calculated amount of heat released via a standard reaction between 92 g of pure sodium and 0.072 L of water if approximately 185 kJ/mole is normally released in such a reaction?

a. 1,388 kJ
b. 1,110 kJ
c. 740 kJ
d. 370 kJ

Copyright © Mometrix Media. You have been licensed one copy of this document for personal use only. Any other reproduction or redistribution is strictly prohibited. All rights reserved.
This content is provided for test preparation purposes only and does not imply an endorsement by Mometrix of any particular political, scientific, or religious point of view.

107. Which of these severity ratings would MOST aptly categorize the following conditions after a facility accident event: (1) considerable, but not totally irreparable, damage to equipment or systems; (2) two killed workers and 14 injured workers in a workforce of 200; (3) operational status or capabilities likely delayed for months; (4) roughly $5 million in property damage; and (5) quantities of chemical releases to the environment which exceed EPA NESHAP limits by 40 to 50 percent?

    a. Critical
    b. Catastrophic
    c. Acute severe
    d. Beyond design basis

108. A CSP is attempting to identify an unlabeled chemical within a work area and through a process of elimination has narrowed it down to four separate possibilities, with one by far being the most likely. He or she only has the chemical's Safety Data Sheet's "Exposure Controls/Personal Protection" section summary (as shown) available for guidance.

> Engineering Controls:
> Provide robust exhaust ventilation or other engineering controls to keep airborne vapor concentrations below their respective threshold limit value. Ensure that eyewash stations and safety showers are near workstation locations.
> Personal Protection:
> Gloves, boots, face shield, full suit, vapor respirator—be sure to use an approved or certified respirator or equivalent thereof.
> Personal Protection in Case of a Large Spill:
> Gloves, boots, face shield, full suit, vapor respirator—a self-contained breathing apparatus should be used to avoid inhalation. Suggested protective clothing might not be sufficient against this liquid material; it is recommended a specialist be consulted before handling this product.
> Exposure Limits:
> TWA: 0.025 from ACGIH (TLV) [US] SKIN TWA: 0.05 CEIL: 0.1 (mg/m3) from OSHA (PEL) [US].
> Inhalation TWA: 0.025 (mg/m3) [UK]. Local authorities should be contacted as appropriate for permissible exposure limits.

From the information provided, which of the following four candidates determined by the CSP is most likely the unidentified material in question?

    a. Methyl ethyl ketone
    b. Ammonia
    c. Mercury
    d. Acetone

109. A specialized vacuum process is run on a container with dimensions of 10 ft × 8 ft × 6 ft (LxWxH) to simultaneously filter out oxygen while returning the remaing gases back into the container. Assuming the O_2 levels were at 21% before beginning suction and the vacuum's O_2 extraction rate is constant at 63 cm^3/s, how long until the container would be defined as an oxygen-deficient environment per OSHA requirements for confined spaces? 2.54 cm = 1 in.

    a. 53.94 min
    b. 48.72 min
    c. 66.11 min
    d. 11.33 min

Copyright © Mometrix Media. You have been licensed one copy of this document for personal use only. Any other reproduction or redistribution is strictly prohibited. All rights reserved.
This content is provided for test preparation purposes only and does not imply an endorsement by Mometrix of any particular political, scientific, or religious point of view.

110. Using the quadratic equation, for the expression $3x^2 + 4x - 5 = 0$, the solutions for "x" would be which of the following?

    a. −0.80, 1.55
    b. 0.64, −1.24
    c. −0.47, −1.27
    d. 0.79, −2.12

111. Salt (sodium chloride) has a molecular weight equal to 58.44 g. How many molecules would there be in a sample of salt that weighs approximately 14.61 g?

    a. 3.012×10^{23}
    b. 1.506×10^{23}
    c. 6.023×10^{23}
    d. 2.409×10^{24}

112. Which of the following series of seven elements can only exist as diatoms (dual-atoms) in nature when they are standing alone? In addition, which of these has the highest level of electronegativity (EN) in the entire periodic table?

    a. Hydrogen, helium, argon, nitrogen, oxygen, iodine, bromine—iodine has highest EN.
    b. Hydrogen, nitrogen, oxygen, iodine, bromine, chlorine, fluorine—fluorine has highest EN.
    c. Oxygen, helium, nitrogen, argon, radon, iodine, chlorine—chlorine has highest EN.
    d. Lithium, boron, magnesium, phosphorous, fluorine, chlorine, xenon—phosphorous has highest EN.

113. An employee is exposed to carbon monoxide (CO) concentrations of 100 ppm for 1 hr, 500 ppm for 2 hrs, and 750 ppm for 15 min. What is the resulting time-weighted-average (TWA) of these exposures?

    a. 152 ppm
    b. 288 ppm
    c. 396 ppm
    d. 450 ppm

114. If an 8-hr PEL for a hazardous respirable dust is 20 mg/m³, what is the associated PEL for an employee working a 10-hr shift?

    a. 24 mg/m³
    b. 20 mg/m³
    c. 16 mg/m³
    d. 12 mg/m³

115. A liquid mixture contains 50 percent methyl alcohol, 35 percent methyl ethyl ketone, and 15 percent acetone. The respective lower flammability limits of the individual chemicals are 1.5 percent, 1.1 percent, and 0.75 percent. What is the overall lower flammability limit (LFL) for the entire mixture?

    a. 0.79 percent
    b. 1.25 percent
    c. 0.96 percent
    d. 1.17 percent

116. What is the calculated approximate recommended weight limit (RWL) in pounds that has a load constant equal to 51 lb; a horizontal multiplier equal to 0.75; a vertical multiplier equal to 0.90; a distance multiplier equal to 0.87; an asymmetric multiplier equal to 0.85; a frequency multiplier equal to 0.45; a coupling multiplier equal to 0.95; and a transitional multiplier equal to 0.70?

    a. 24 lb
    b. 8 lb
    c. 37 lb
    d. 11 lb

Copyright © Mometrix Media. You have been licensed one copy of this document for personal use only. Any other reproduction or redistribution is strictly prohibited. All rights reserved.
This content is provided for test preparation purposes only and does not imply an endorsement by Mometrix of any particular political, scientific, or religious point of view.

117. Which of the following two noise scenarios yields a higher noise level at a distance of 30 ft?

Scenario 1: a 100 dB noise that is heard 3 ft away from its source
Scenario 2: a 120 dB noise that is heard 1 ft away from its source

a. Scenario 1
b. Scenario 2
c. Both
d. Cannot be determined from the information provided

118. What are the equivalent polar-coordinates of the Cartesian-plotted point (6, 4)?

a. (8.27, 39.4°)
b. (7.21, 33.7°)
c. (8.27, 50.6°)
d. (7.21, 56.3°)

119. What is the minimum required air sampling volume for a gas that has an LOQ (range) of 5.2–65.7 micrograms and a target concentration of 880 ppm?

a. 0.031 L
b. 0.016 L
c. 0.0047 L
d. 0.0024 L

120. Per OSHA 29 CFR 1910.95, which of the following noise exposure scenarios is beyond specified limits required of the standard?

a. 1 hr at 100 dBA
b. 30 min at 115 dBA
c. 4 hrs at 90 dBA
d. 2 hrs at 95 dBA

121. An industrial organization is in the process of acquiring a new Class-III biological safety cabinet, which is the highest safety classification level available. The following is a list of technical specifications sent by a candidate cabinet vendor. The resident CSP, safety manager, and industrial hygienist all note one major flaw or omission in the specification list.

Technical Specification Summary for Acme Corporation—Level III BioCab—Model # 2A6535001CM
Arm-length rubber gloves
Provides excellent physical protection to workforce
ASTM-rated at 90 percent negative pressure and 95 percent gas-tight efficiency
Sealed front panel
Air drawn into cabinet through HEPA filtration system
Dimensions: 80 in × 48 in × 36 in
Double-welded steel frame and casing
ASTM-rated lead-glass windows
Double-gasket O-ring seal design at outlets
Inflow velocity 150 fpm

Which of the following likely denotes the apparent inadequacy?

a. 90 percent negative pressure and 95 percent gas tight efficiency ratings
b. Arm-length rubber gloves
c. The 150 fpm inflow velocity
d. Lead-glass windows

Copyright © Mometrix Media. You have been licensed one copy of this document for personal use only. Any other reproduction or redistribution is strictly prohibited. All rights reserved.
This content is provided for test preparation purposes only and does not imply an endorsement by Mometrix of any particular political, scientific, or religious point of view.

122. Per the information provided, which of the following substances would have the highest heat of combustion in these case scenarios?

a. 4,600 cal emitted by the combustion of one mole of Na-23
b. 908 cal emitted by the combustion of 0.1 lb of helium
c. 257 cal emitted by the combustion of 1 g of hydrogen
d. 10 kilocalories emitted by the combustion of 2.5 moles of sulfuric acid

123. What is the simplified solution of the following?

$(i^4 + 2i^3 - 5i^2 - 4i - 1)^2$

a. $36i + 8$
b. $-60i - 11$
c. $-48i + 20$
d. $12i$

124. According to NFPA criteria, which of the following combustible liquid classes strictly exhibits flash points that are ≥200°F?

a. Class IA
b. Class IC
c. Class II
d. Class IIIB

125. What is the calculated wind-chill temperature for an air temperature of 20°F and a wind speed of 15 mph?

a. 12.4°F
b. 6.2°F
c. 3.1°F
d. 1.5°F

126. What is the kinetic energy of a 9,000-lb forklift moving at a speed of 5 mph?

a. 40.6 kJ
b. 20.3 kJ
c. 10.2 kJ
d. 5.1 kJ

127. If a company borrows $1 million to start a business, how much will the entire loan actually cost the business over a repayment period of 10 years if the lender charges a 4 percent interest rate compounded monthly?

a. $1,363,298
b. $1,490,833
c. $1,622,916
d. $1,804,552

128. According to US Bureau of Labor statistics, what accident category normally accounts (by far) for the highest fatality rates across all industries (approximately 40 percent)?

a. Falls
b. Electrocutions
c. Contact with equipment or objects
d. Transportation-related incidents

Copyright © Mometrix Media. You have been licensed one copy of this document for personal use only. Any other reproduction or redistribution is strictly prohibited. All rights reserved.
This content is provided for test preparation purposes only and does not imply an endorsement by Mometrix of any particular political, scientific, or religious point of view.

129. The three fundamental categories of risk management (process) controls are _____, _____, and _____.

    a. physical, educational, avoidance
    b. visual, procedural, mitigative
    c. sensory, tactile, reflexive
    d. precursory, process, serial

130. The density of Material-X is equal to approximately 3.5 g/ml. What is the specific gravity of Material-X?

    a. 0.70
    b. 1.75
    c. 3.5
    d. Cannot be determined from the information provided

131. What are human cycles that are believed to affect behavior every 25 to 30 days and can influence facets such as intellect, logic, emotions, strength, and stamina known as?

    a. Human performance variants
    b. Biometrics
    c. Biorhythms
    d. Autonomic frequency parametrics

132. Block-and-tackle equipment and devices are regularly used in industrial settings for lifting heavy loads. An empirical formula of $F = W \div x$ is typically employed for depicting the relationship between the vertical force (F) required to lift the weight (W) of the load. The "x" in the formula, however, is supposed to represent which of the following?

    a. The gravitational acceleration constant
    b. The number of times the connected chain or rope passes between the two ends
    c. The static equilibrium constant accounting for all three dimensions (x, y, and z)
    d. None of the above

133. Which of the following pairs of computer software systems often work best in tandem for optimally improving safety and minimizing hazards in the workplace?

    a. Database management systems and computer-aided-design systems
    b. DART and CAIRS database systems
    c. JOBHAZ and ARCJOB safety assessment models
    d. Failure modes and effects analysis models and probabilistic risk assessment models

134. The two primary standards of the BSCP Code of Ethics and Conduct mandate that certified professionals of all levels uphold which of the following?

    a. The steadfastness, diligence, and responsibility of a safety professional
    b. The esteem, integrity, and influence of the safety profession
    c. The traceability, transparency, and quality of the safety profession
    d. The education, training, and ongoing qualification of a safety professional

Copyright © Mometrix Media. You have been licensed one copy of this document for personal use only. Any other reproduction or redistribution is strictly prohibited. All rights reserved.
This content is provided for test preparation purposes only and does not imply an endorsement by Mometrix of any particular political, scientific, or religious point of view.

135. A company vehicle's odometer is broken. The fleet manager knows that the vehicle's tires (which are rated for 40,000 miles) have never been changed and is feeling uneasy about the safety level of their present tread wear. The vehicle's computer, however, does have extractable data on how many rotations the driveshaft has made since the vehicle was purchased new by the company 3 years ago. From this data, a calculation of tire mileage was hence deemed attainable. Given the following information from the onboard computer as well as the vehicle's published technical specifications, approximately how many miles have the subject tires been driven?

- 92,518,000 driveshaft rotations
- 3.6 driveshaft rotations = 1 complete tire rotation (straight-line driving)
- 30-in diameter tires

   a. 35,498 miles
   b. 38,229 miles
   c. 41,062 miles
   d. 44,370 miles

136. A CSP has been reviewing various safety-incident metrics that track the last 4 years of performance at his or her organization. He or she was able to curve fit each of the 4 years' rates into approximate representative functions (as a function of time), as per the following:

Year 1: $f(t) = t^2 + 4t + 3$
Year 2: $f(t) = 2t^2 - 6t + 1$
Year 3: $f(t) = 3t^3 + 2t - 5$
Year 4: $f(t) = 2t^3 - t^2 + 4t + 6$

Given management's perception that the workforce seems to be more accident prone in the summertime than at any other time during the year, the CSP was asked to assess the rate of change (of the functions) at the midpoint of each year (i.e., t = 6) and compare them for each of the 4 years. Which year was ultimately determined to have the greatest rate of (incident) change at t = 6?

   a. Year 1
   b. Year 2
   c. Year 3
   d. Year 4

137. What is the power in an alternating current circuit where the voltage is 75 V, the impedance is 10 ohms, and the sine of the phase angle is 0.643?

   a. 269 watts
   b. 362 watts
   c. 431 watts
   d. 472 watts

Copyright © Mometrix Media. You have been licensed one copy of this document for personal use only. Any other reproduction or redistribution is strictly prohibited. All rights reserved.
This content is provided for test preparation purposes only and does not imply an endorsement by Mometrix of any particular political, scientific, or religious point of view.

138. The safety manager for an organization has recently revamped his company's entire occupational safety program. The table provides a brief description of each vital program element addressed in the new program. Which of the following key facets, however, seems to be omitted from the summary?

Program Tenet Number	Tenet
1	Hazard Identification
2	Work Control
3	Procedural Compliance/Document Control
4	Emergency Response
5	Incentives
6	Training/Requalification

    a. Personal protective equipment (PPE)
    b. Organizational hierarchical framework
    c. Spill mitigation and remediation
    d. Safety engineering

139. An injured employee goes onto short-term disability for a period of 3 months at full compensation of his or her regular earned wage. At the end of the 3 months, he or she then moves into a long-term disability plan for a period of 5½ months that pays 2/3 of his or her regular earned wage, after which time he or she then returns to work as a 0.75 FTE for the remainder of the year. If the employee's regular earned wage is $50,000 per year, how much income would he or she have made over that year?

    a. $42,361
    b. $27,778
    c. $34,192
    d. $38,716

140. Which government agency should be immediately notified (first) in the event of any accidental release of hazardous materials during their transportation?

    a. US Federal Emergency Management Agency (FEMA)
    b. US Department of Transportation (DOT)
    c. US National Transportation Safety Board (NTSB)
    d. US Department of Homeland Security (DHS)

141. What are the five typical elements commonly associated with a robust risk management program?

    a. Query, measure, bin, correct, and reference
    b. Categorize, characterize, calculate, correlate, and correct
    c. Identification, assessment, mitigation, financing, and administration
    d. Identification, evaluation, enhancement, training, and feedback

142. An organization's CSP has conferred with a resident industrial hygienist, and it was determined that a work area may potentially be contaminated with lead dust concentration levels that are likely well in excess of established action levels. Which of the following types of respiratory PPE should be (most appropriately) recommended for workers that are to occupy this area during their assigned tasks?

    a. Dust mask
    b. Full-face respirator
    c. SCUBA
    d. Loose-fitting powered air purifying respirator (PAPR)

Copyright © Mometrix Media. You have been licensed one copy of this document for personal use only. Any other reproduction or redistribution is strictly prohibited. All rights reserved.
This content is provided for test preparation purposes only and does not imply an endorsement by Mometrix of any particular political, scientific, or religious point of view.

143. The technique of energy _____ is regularly implemented by safety engineers to protect people and products from impacts or damage that may result from accidents.

 a. transfer
 b. misdirection
 c. isolation
 d. conversion

144. Techniques such as peer collaboration, case-study deployment, and role-play are commonly used when attempting to effectively train which of the following groups for protocols not specifically laid out in procedural guidance?

 a. Organizational/line management
 b. Craft
 c. Administrative or overhead
 d. Junior or apprentice

145. A subject pressure vessel within a company factory normally operates at 500 psia with a safety variability margin of ±15 percent. During a given shift, a plant worker notes that the vessel pressure gauge is reading 625 psia. Which one of the following actions would hence be MOST appropriate for the worker to undertake after reading the gauge?

 a. Check the gauge again every 15 min to ensure that pressure is not increasing any further.
 b. Immediately shut down the entire pressure vessel system.
 c. Consult with other plant personnel to see if they have likewise recently noticed the elevated pressure reading.
 d. Immediately consult the appropriate system contingency plan or procedure.

146. A major safety hazard for electrical power industry personnel is _____. These hazards usually result in extremely high temperatures over very small time periods, along with extremely high-pressure waves. In addition, airborne shrapnel also typically manifests from such an event.

 a. electric arcs
 b. megavoltage discharge transfers
 c. high-current impedance offset events
 d. high-energy electrocutive detonations

147. What is an individual who is hired for the specific purpose of impartially investigating worker issues or concerns and then suggesting associated resolutions to directorial boards known as?

 a. A mediator
 b. An arbitrator
 c. An ombudsman
 d. A freelance forward observer

148. Which of the following is NOT a commonly implemented conflict resolution method utilized in industry?

 a. Adjudicative resolution
 b. Consensual dispute resolution
 c. Contractual correspondent resolution
 d. Legislative resolution

Copyright © Mometrix Media. You have been licensed one copy of this document for personal use only. Any other reproduction or redistribution is strictly prohibited. All rights reserved.
This content is provided for test preparation purposes only and does not imply an endorsement by Mometrix of any particular political, scientific, or religious point of view.

149. A chemical tank within an industrial processing facility has a large, highly visible warning label located approximately 1 ft away from the tank, is clearly and legibly marked with large, red-colored, English print, and presents clear and straightforward guidance. The facility employs both native English-speaking and Spanish-speaking personnel. Which of the following potential shortcomings regarding the label should be of the MOST concern?

   a. There is only a single warning label.
   b. The label is not bilingual.
   c. The label is not actually affixed to the tank.
   d. The label is in red print and not black print.

150. Which of the following product life-cycle phases usually concludes with the decision to move forward with a product's development?

   a. The prototype-reconnaissance phase
   b. The conceptual phase
   c. The development-evaluation phase
   d. The cost-benefit analysis phase

151. An employee who has been working in outdoor cold temperatures for his or her entire shift approaches a resident CSP and on-call shift nurse before he or she heads home with complaints of face numbness and drooping, tingling in the arms and legs, difficulty speaking, difficulty walking, and an apparent sudden absence of lucidity. What is the employee most likely experiencing, and what is the most appropriate response for the CSP and nurse to immediately undertake in this scenario?

   a. Bell's Palsy—recommend the employee schedule a physician consult.
   b. Stroke—seek immediate medical attention (dial 911).
   c. Cold exposure symptoms—provide shelter, blanket, and warm beverage.
   d. Not possible to definitively determine from information provided—seek immediate medical attention (dial 911).

152. When undergoing an external audit, what is usually the MOST important aspect to an auditor regarding an employee's knowledge of a specific company procedural document?

   a. The employee acknowledges he or she is aware that the actual procedure exists.
   b. The employee is aware of the procedure and knows where to quickly access it for reference.
   c. The employee maintains a certain degree of knowledge of the procedure from memory.
   d. The employee is able to follow the procedure to the letter, from memory, if an emergency situation should arise and the document is ultimately not accessible for reference.

153. Which of the following is NOT a typical mode in which heat is transferred between a human and the surrounding environment?

   a. Evaporation
   b. RF-pulse emission
   c. Conduction
   d. Radiation

154. Which of the following documents is implemented across a wide array of industries for directing the production of procedural guidance within the realm of system safety?

   a. MIL-STD-882B
   b. ANSI 404.9A
   c. ASTM 972.1-C
   d. OSHA 1929.14 Regulatory Guide 4A

Copyright © Mometrix Media. You have been licensed one copy of this document for personal use only. Any other reproduction or redistribution is strictly prohibited. All rights reserved.
This content is provided for test preparation purposes only and does not imply an endorsement by Mometrix of any particular political, scientific, or religious point of view.

155. What is typically NOT considered a key function of an air ventilation system?

a. Removal of carbon dioxide buildups
b. Enhancement of oxygen levels
c. Removal of odors
d. Elimination of toxins

156. A CSP is performing a walk-through of a heavily trafficked work area looking for potential tripping hazards. Along the way he or she notices various items deposited throughout the work area, including several tools, various refuse articles (rags, empty cans, etc.), and pieces of lumber of various sizes. Which of the following would be the first course of action for the CSP to undertake in response to these observations?

a. Emplace "tripping hazard" warning signs around the area(s) in question.
b. Report the infractions to the health and safety manager.
c. Recommend remedial safety training for responsible staff members.
d. Notify the responsible work parties in the area to remove, relocate and/or properly store the articles in question.

157. What are calculations and assessments that evaluate company loss-rate records for establishing worker compensation rates conventionally known as?

a. Actuarial baselines
b. Risk-equivalence correlators
c. Experience modifiers
d. Premium performance metrics

158. A system safety engineering and design team is ready to emplace a new product concept into the production phase for rendering a prototype or beta version of the subject product. They have paid meticulous detail to facets such as proper implementation, maintenance, hygiene, and safeguards. Which of the following, however, is also a critical area that the team likewise needs to devote considerable attention?

a. Capital costs
b. Utilization schedules
c. Product lifetimes
d. Ergonomics

159. During which of the following stages of the development process for a facility should the most emphasis be placed on quality assurance and quality control?

a. Construction and modification
b. Design
c. Procurement
d. Planning

160. In the realm of safety-basis evaluation, a design-basis accident typically has a frequency (probability) of occurrence in the range of 10^{-6} to 10^{-4} per year. If the consequences of such an accident are calculated to potentially result in 100 to 300 deaths, what is the overall potential range of risk for such an accident?

a. 0.001 to 0.003 per year
b. 0.0003 to 0.01 per year
c. 0.0001 to 0.03 per year
d. 10^{-6} to 10^{-4} per year

Copyright © Mometrix Media. You have been licensed one copy of this document for personal use only. Any other reproduction or redistribution is strictly prohibited. All rights reserved.
This content is provided for test preparation purposes only and does not imply an endorsement by Mometrix of any particular political, scientific, or religious point of view.

161. Bob and Bill are both workers in a loud processing area of a factory. Bob has partial hearing loss and also speaks with a lisp, while Bill's hearing is unimpaired. On nearly a daily basis, Bob and Bill have miscommunications. Which of the following is the MOST likely reason for why these miscommunications occur so frequently?

a. Bob's partial deafness and lisp
b. Bill poor listening skills
c. Ongoing background noise in the work area
d. All of the above

162. A yellow warning sign that shows a downward arrow intersecting with a worker's hardhat is likely depicting which of the following?

a. Potential for falling objects
b. Extreme danger of an electrocution event to the head
c. Extreme danger of falling
d. The need for total awareness of one's immediate surroundings

163. The _____ states that an organization will undergo fiscal hardship if it generates or disseminates a hazardous product and then ultimately neglects to resolve the underlying issue(s).

a. Trans-liability axiom
b. Negligence responsivity clause
c. Law of safety progress
d. Statute of culpability and stewardship

164. Americium-beryllium (Am-Be) neutron sources, and the like, are often used in nuclear reactors and other systems to provide initial quantities of neutrons to help foster an eventual chain reaction that leads to a state of criticality. What is the most accurate description of how an Am-Be source (which can be a significantly hazardous neutron radiation source) generates its neutrons?

a. Through a (γ, n) nuclear reaction
b. Through an (α, n) nuclear reaction
c. Through a (β, n) nuclear reaction
d. Through a (n, n) nuclear reaction

165. Who is usually responsible for taking roll calls during a shelter in place or a building evacuation?

a. Emergency response team manager
b. Emergency coordinator
c. Office warden
d. Office manager

166. A significant acid leak is detected in a chemical processing plant, a type that has never been experienced before during the 40-year operating history of the plant. Which of the following types of procedure categories should be immediately available and consulted for dealing with this most unusual emergency?

a. Transient event procedure
b. Special safety procedure
c. Beyond-design-basis procedure
d. High-risk event response procedure

Copyright © Mometrix Media. You have been licensed one copy of this document for personal use only. Any other reproduction or redistribution is strictly prohibited. All rights reserved.
This content is provided for test preparation purposes only and does not imply an endorsement by Mometrix of any particular political, scientific, or religious point of view.

167. According to Frederick Herzberg's theory of behavior, a worker's desired extrinsic outcomes typically include which of the following?

a. Status, promotion, and power
b. Networking and affiliating
c. Job security, income, and safe and comfortable working conditions
d. Personal recognition, praise, and respect

168. Approximately how much more often do workers who have habitual alcohol or drug problems actually miss work (i.e., incur lost days)?

a. 15 times more often
b. 10 times more often
c. 5 times more often
d. 3 times more often

169. What is a goniometer typically used for within the realm of ergonomics?

a. Measuring average distance between vertebrae while seated
b. Three-dimensionally measuring a full range of motion during a work activity
c. Measuring the actual speed at which an object is lifted
d. Measuring angles associated with human joints (e.g., knees, elbows, wrists, and ankles)

170. A worker is required to undergo annual medical monitoring for his or her assigned position. During the physical, his or her blood pressure is found to be 171/79, with a resting pulse rate of 103. From these results, it is possible the attending physician may come to which of the following preliminary sets of conclusions?

a. High diastolic
b. Low systolic
c. Possible tachycardia
d. Both a & c

171. Which of the following is typically NOT employed to create resistant forces within an apparatus?

a. Springs
b. Inertia
c. Modular strain
d. Viscous damping

172. _____ sickness can be significantly mitigated by preventing overexposure to high-pressure environments and by carefully and steadily employing rates of _____.

a. Bends/nitrogen
b. Decompression/decompression
c. Hypoxia/oxygen
d. High-altitude/pressurization

173. Which of the following would be appropriately categorized as a continuous control mechanism?

a. Computer mouse
b. Light switch
c. Buttons
d. Computer keyboard

Copyright © Mometrix Media. You have been licensed one copy of this document for personal use only. Any other reproduction or redistribution is strictly prohibited. All rights reserved.
This content is provided for test preparation purposes only and does not imply an endorsement by Mometrix of any particular political, scientific, or religious point of view.

174. Within the realm of system design, the integration of multiple elements with overlapping functions that permit the continuous, normal (ongoing) operation of a given product in the case of one (or more) elemental failure(s) is known as which of the following?

   a. Parallel architecture
   b. Functional interdependency
   c. Cross-reliability
   d. Redundancy

175. A state-of-the-art facility employs a system that automatically powers down all major electrical components if the ambient temperature within the facility exceeds a certain predetermined threshold level. This type of system is conventionally known as which of the following?

   a. A lockout thermal regulator system
   b. A fail-safe system
   c. A thermostatic power modulator system
   d. A passive autoregulation system

176. The robustness of hazardous waste shipping containers and casks has been thoroughly tested over the years primarily at which of the following US installations?

   a. US national laboratories
   b. US military bases
   c. US proving grounds
   d. None of the above

177. Which two federal agencies are primarily responsible for regulating the placement, storage, and amounts of combustible materials within industrial settings?

   a. ASTM and NFPA
   b. FEMA and DHS
   c. NFPA and OSHA
   d. OSHA and NIOSH

178. A static analysis determination is made for a piece of piping within an industrial facility. The following is ultimately concluded from the determination:

   The overall compression force on the pipe is about 50 N.
   According to laser-optic results, the pipe has not contracted (or altogether moved) by any discernible amount.

What conclusion can be drawn from this information?

   a. The associated torsional force on the pipe should be equal to $50N \div 2\pi$.
   b. The pipe's outward directional forces should be equal to about 50 N.
   c. The shear force on the pipe should be equal to about 100 N.
   d. The pipe's elastic modulus can be calculated by multiplying 50 N by the length of the pipe.

179. A negative safety margin value is theoretically correlated with which of the following?

   a. A high risk of failure
   b. A low risk of failure
   c. A 100 percent probability of failure
   d. A 0 percent probability of failure

Copyright © Mometrix Media. You have been licensed one copy of this document for personal use only. Any other reproduction or redistribution is strictly prohibited. All rights reserved.
This content is provided for test preparation purposes only and does not imply an endorsement by Mometrix of any particular political, scientific, or religious point of view.

180. How many OSHA regional offices are presently in existence across the United States?

a. 4
b. 10
c. 22
d. 50

181. Which of the following is TRUE with regard to large-quantity hazardous waste generators (LQGs)?

a. There is no designated limit of the quantity of HAZMAT that is allowed to be stored at a specific time.
b. LQGs are defined by the generation of >1 lb of acute HAZMAT per month.
c. LQGs typically have an allowed maximum storage time of 1 year or less for most wastes.
d. They are conditionally exempt from most EPA reporting requirements.

182. In a fault-tree analysis, what does the term or gate "XOR" represent?

a. An output event occurs if some input events occur.
b. An output event occurs if all input events occur.
c. An output event occurs if exactly one input event occurs.
d. An output event occurs if all input events occur in a specific sequence.

183. David is a CSP who works for a rural county located in a southeastern US state. He receives a telephone call from a locally well-known family farming operation that has an ongoing agricultural cooperative agreement with the county. On the call he is told that there has been a tractor accident injuring one of the farmhands and that he should immediately come out to the property to investigate. Upon arrival at the scene, David learns that the injured farmhand is actually the son of the farm's owner. After verifying that the victim has received necessary acute medical care, which organization or agency should be notified of the incident?

a. The US Department of Agriculture
b. OSHA
c. The local police department
d. No organization unless required by local statute or agreement

184. Per OSHA's 29 CFR 1910.147, *Control of Hazardous Energy,* a hot tap is defined as which of the following?

a. The emplacement of a lockout mechanism on an energy-isolating device
b. A maintenance or servicing procedure that entails pressurized welding operations for installing connections or other support equipment
c. A prominent warning device or system
d. An access point via which an electrocution event is of high risk

185. Which of the following scenarios would be categorized as a privacy case on an OSHA 300 form, whereby the employee's name is not ultimately recorded on the form?

a. An injury caused by an intentional destructive act (e.g., system sabotage)
b. An injury resulting from professional incompetence
c. An injury to the gonads
d. An injury resulting from alcohol or drug abuse

186. Most portable fire extinguishers must be hydrostatically tested once every how many years?

a. 2
b. 5
c. 7
d. 10

Copyright © Mometrix Media. You have been licensed one copy of this document for personal use only. Any other reproduction or redistribution is strictly prohibited. All rights reserved.
This content is provided for test preparation purposes only and does not imply an endorsement by Mometrix of any particular political, scientific, or religious point of view.

187. A qualitative fit test for a respirator is conventionally defined by which of the following actions?

a. Assessing the suitability of a respirator by measuring the amount of leakage into the device
b. A respiratory or pulmonary physical examination
c. Comparing blood-oxygen levels between times of respirator wear and normal breathing
d. A pass-or-fail evaluation to assess the level of fit adequacy based on a wearer's response to a testing agent

188. A turtle suit is a form of PPE that is often worn to protect against the hazards of which of the following?

a. Neutron radiation
b. Pinch points
c. High-pressure water blasting
d. Tunneling

189. An employee working in a chemical manufacturing facility is regularly subjected to several potential hazards during the daily work routine, namely of which include the following: hydrochloric acid, hydrofluoric acid, nitric acid, regular machinery noise in excess of 125 dB (unprotected), and falling objects. Which of the following PPE regimes should be regularly prescribed or required for this employee?

a. Apron, full-face respirator, earmuffs, neoprene gloves, and hard hat (that can accommodate earmuffs)
b. Coveralls, half-face respirator, earplugs and earmuffs, nitrile gloves, and hard hat (that can accommodate earmuffs)
c. Apron, safety goggles, earplugs, PVC gloves, and hard hat
d. Coveralls, safety goggles, earplugs and earmuffs, butyl rubber gloves, and hard hat (that can accommodate earmuffs)

190. What is a typical setting that a ground-fault circuit interrupter (GFCI) is normally set to to adequately protect workers from electrocution scenarios?

a. 0.05 mA
b. 0.5 mA
c. 5 mA
d. 50 mA

191. Which of the following scenarios would be categorized as exempt from workers' compensation coverage?

a. An individual employed for 60 consecutive workdays within an employer's private home
b. An individual performing services in return for monetary compensation provided by a religious organization
c. A gardener
d. An individual who elects not to be covered

192. According to Abraham Maslow's hierarchy of needs, personal facets such as creativity, problem solving, morality, spontaneity, and lack of prejudice all fall under which human need?

a. Esteem
b. Self-actualization
c. Love and belonging
d. Enhancement of superego

Copyright © Mometrix Media. You have been licensed one copy of this document for personal use only. Any other reproduction or redistribution is strictly prohibited. All rights reserved.
This content is provided for test preparation purposes only and does not imply an endorsement by Mometrix of any particular political, scientific, or religious point of view.

193. Which of the following leadership personalities typically permits employees to contribute to decision-making processes and affords subordinates a considerable degree of latitude in carrying out their tasks?

    a. Permissive autocrat
    b. Directive democrat
    c. Permissive democrat
    d. Directive autocrat

194. The _____ Theory of Accident Causation asserts that accidents can, in large, be caused or prevented by the manner in which situational characteristics interplay with predispositional characteristics.

    a. Human Factors
    b. Chaos
    c. Domino
    d. Epidemiological

195. The multilinear events sequencing (MES) method uses a(n) _____ to illustrate the sequence of events or occurrences that contributed to or was the direct cause of an event.

    a. flow chart
    b. iterative algorithm
    c. time line
    d. hierarchy

196. Retention rate efficiencies vary greatly in humans depending upon what mode of teaching or training is employed for a set of material. Which of the following delivery or training methods typically results in the highest retention efficiency rates?

    a. Discussion groups
    b. Demonstrations
    c. Teaching others
    d. Audiovisual

197. An extremely dangerous shortcut that is all too often taken with pneumatic nail guns and hammers is which of the following?

    a. Using two machines at the same (i.e., one in each hand)
    b. Electrically overloading to attain a faster punch rate
    c. Deliberately disabling safety catches
    d. Taping down triggers to get automatic repeated action

198. Which of the following storage configurations is considered allowable for oxygen cylinders within the workplace? A separation distance from fuel gas cylinders (or combustible materials) by a minimum distance of _____ ft, or by a noncombustible barrier at least _____ ft in height that has a fire-resistance rating of at least _____ hrs.

    a. 20, 5, 0.5
    b. 18 4, 1.5
    c. 14, 3, 1
    d. 12, 2, 1

Copyright © Mometrix Media. You have been licensed one copy of this document for personal use only. Any other reproduction or redistribution is strictly prohibited. All rights reserved.
This content is provided for test preparation purposes only and does not imply an endorsement by Mometrix of any particular political, scientific, or religious point of view.

199. For a worker to be permissibly located on a moving (mobile) scaffold that has a base of 4 ft, what is the minimum required height for that scaffold?

    a. 6 ft
    b. 8 ft
    c. 10 ft
    d. 12 ft

200. A hard hat's safety zone is defined as the space or clearance between the hat's shell and its suspension. What is a typical minimum recommended measurement for this space or clearance?

    a. 0.5 in
    b. 0.75 in
    c. 1 in
    d. 1.5 in

Copyright © Mometrix Media. You have been licensed one copy of this document for personal use only. Any other reproduction or redistribution is strictly prohibited. All rights reserved.
This content is provided for test preparation purposes only and does not imply an endorsement by Mometrix of any particular political, scientific, or religious point of view.

Answer Key and Explanations for Test #1

1. B: The fundamental counting principle essentially applies to circumstances where the order (or position) of an initial event occurrence ultimately influences the overall probabilistic outcome of an entire event scenario. In essence, the principle maintains that if a first event has "a" possible outcomes, and after that outcome has transpired, a subsequent event then has "b" possible outcomes, then there are resultantly (a × b) potential ways the outcomes can occur in that prescribed order.

2. D: The four colors of the NFPA 704 Diamond System are yellow (right side of the diamond, depicting instability level), blue (left side of the diamond, depicting health hazard level), red (top side of the diamond, depicting fire hazard level), and white (bottom side of the diamond, depicting special hazard levels for oxidizers and water reactions). Numbers from 0 to 4 are provided in each segment depicting the level of hazard (0 = lowest and 4 = highest).

3. D: The US FDA is responsible for protecting the public at large from potential hazards associated with the use of all pharmaceutical products as well as sold foodstuffs, organics, cosmetics, or any other products available for curative applications.

4. A: Within an industrial or process setting, there are three principal hazard modes that a worker may be subjected to: falling of loads, handling of materials, and materials being in motion. Examples of dangers within these categories may include facets such as forklift accidents, toxic exposures, and pinch points, respectively.

5. C: The majority of laws that involve worker safety and health fall under the purview of civil law. The Occupational Safety and Health Act of 1970 is the chief civil law that is in use today for protecting worker safety and health and is regularly enforced by the Occupational Safety and Health Administration. Hence, injured workers should normally seek counsel from civil attorneys.

6. B: Workers' compensation laws are typically categorized into two separate designations: compulsory-related laws and elective-related laws. Compulsory laws require that employers adhere to all facets of the laws, otherwise they may be subjected to legal consequences; elective laws, conversely, provide employers the option of participation.

7. D: Primary safety hazards associated with the use of powered vehicles (e.g., backhoes, bulldozers, etc.) in a work area may include inadvertent exceedance of load limits, potential carbon monoxide overexposure(s), blind spots impeding operator visibility, power source malfunctions, flammable fuels, and operator error due to poor training, inexperience, mental fatigue, or incompetence. Operator physical overexertion is typically not expected because the balance of required actions usually does not go beyond the manipulation of powered controls within a climate-regulated cab.

8. A: The conventional definition of a blasting agent is a material that demonstrates adequate stability in a stand-alone condition yet possesses enough exothermic potential to prompt an explosion when initiated. OSHA 1910.109 defines it as any material or mixture, consisting of a fuel and oxidizer, intended for blasting. A very commonly used blasting agent is ammonium-nitrate fuel oil (ANFO).

9. C: There are several types of conveyor mechanisms regularly implemented within industrial settings for transporting bulk products and materials; these include belts, buckets, rollers, and chains. The primary hazards associated with these devices are usually pinch points, snags, and falling materials.

10. C: Over recent years, fall-related deaths in construction have been accounting for approximately 40 percent of all fatalities in that industry, which is by far the number one cause. According to OSHA statistics, out of 4,251 worker fatalities in private industry for CY 2014, 874 (20.5 percent) were in construction, with falls

Copyright © Mometrix Media. You have been licensed one copy of this document for personal use only. Any other reproduction or redistribution is strictly prohibited. All rights reserved. This content is provided for test preparation purposes only and does not imply an endorsement by Mometrix of any particular political, scientific, or religious point of view.

accounting for 349 out of the 874 total deaths (39.9 percent). Hence, in the case of 369 construction-related deaths, roughly 150 of them would likely be related to fall incidents.

11. B: A noise dosimeter is a commonly used device for measuring potentially hazardous noise levels in industrial settings. It is usually employed in a manner that continuously processes noise levels throughout the duration of a work shift (in a particular work area) and then provides an equivalent cumulative quantity at the end of that shift, depicting what a worker's total noise exposure would be in that area.

12. A: Federal safety-regulating agencies, such as OSHA, normally track a host of metrics related to worker injuries and illnesses. Such metrics typically include frequencies of work-related deaths, job transfers, and restricted duty.

13. C: A variety of terminologies and technologies are regularly employed within the domain of gas or vapor sampling (for contaminants); these include colorimetry, chromatographs, and grab samples. Centrifugal separation, on the other hand, is strictly used within the realm of particulate sampling.

14. D: The OSHA Classification System for Occupational Illnesses and Conditions includes several categorical facets, including respiratory- and lung-related disorders or conditions, radiation-related disorders or conditions, skin-related disorders or conditions, toxic-related disorders or conditions, and repetitive-motion or ergonomic-related disorders or conditions.

15. A: US citizen employees who live and work in the United States have a legal right to inspect certain records under their name.

16. D: There are several units that are regularly employed for characterizing or expressing visible-light intensity levels, including footlamberts, foot-candles, and lumens.

17. A: To counteract high-pressure environments (e.g., that seen during deep underwater diving), replacing nitrogen with inert surrogate gases, such as helium, is a conventionally implemented strategy for counteracting the potential effects of nitrogen narcosis.

18. C: Per NAAQS protocol (40 CFR 50), the maximum allowable criteria pollutant concentration for lead (Pb) is 0.15 $\mu g/m^3$ over a 3-month period.

19. B: A discount factor for a present dollar value given a future value at a 3 percent annual interest rate over a 7-year period would have an associated functional-notation representation of (P|F, 3%, 7).

20. D: A typical three-step process that should always be employed in industrial settings in the event of a verified hazardous material(s) spill is (1) safety, (2) containment or isolation, and (3) notification.

21. B: Acquired data from two distinct and separate variables is known as bivariate data (e.g., x and y). Bivariate data can be displayed through a variety of illustrative and graphical tools, including comparative tables, scatter plots, bar charts, and linear regression best fits.

22. C: For the data set (3, 7, 9, 12, 26, 32, 45, 58), there is no mode. The mode is defined as the data value (or values) that occur(s) the most number of times relative to the rest of the values in a statistical sample or population. Because each (and all) of the subject values only occurs once in the subject data set, there is no mode.

Copyright © Mometrix Media. You have been licensed one copy of this document for personal use only. Any other reproduction or redistribution is strictly prohibited. All rights reserved.
This content is provided for test preparation purposes only and does not imply an endorsement by Mometrix of any particular political, scientific, or religious point of view.

23. B: For a standard normal distribution, approximately 48 percent of the total area below the curve would correlate to the adding of the segments in the ranges of (−2sd < x < −sd) and (0 < x < sd).

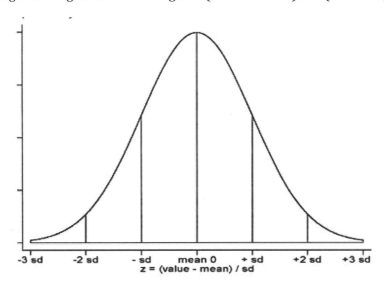

This is derived via the following per the 68-95-99.7 rule: The range of (−2sd < x < −sd) would equate to an area allocation of ½(95%-68%) = 13.5%, and the range of (0 < x < sd) would equate to an area allocation of ½(68%) = 34%. Hence, 34% + 13.5% = 47.5% ≈ 48%.

24. C: The US Bureau of Labor Statistics is ultimately charged with and responsible for distributing statistical information pertaining to job-related injuries or illnesses. Other agencies, however, such as the US Occupational Safety and Health Administration and the US National Institute of Occupational Safety and Health often cite or reference such published statistics in support of their missions, campaigns, outreach, and enforcement initiatives.

25. B: The fellow-servant rule is an often-utilized defense posture corporate entities implement against on-the-job injury claims filed by employees. Dependent upon the situation and extent of litigation, however, other legal defense approaches such as contributory negligence and assumption of risk may also potentially be utilized by employers who endeavor to protect their corporate interests against such claims.

26. C: The National Council on Compensation Insurance is responsible for setting general rate premiums that employers will pay for workers' compensation insurance. Some employers, however, may choose to institute their own private plans or programs with independent funding mechanisms.

27. C: Sound octaves are conventionally characterized by frequency with sequential octaves normally differing by a factor of two. Hence, an octave may exist at a frequency of 100 Hz, with the octave directly below it existing at 50 Hz and the one directly above it existing at 200 Hz.

28. B: A teratogen is best defined as an agent, material, or chemical that can cause deformities or birth defects in unborn embryos or fetuses. Substances such as alcohol, tobacco, psychoactive drugs, various diseases, and an array of potential environmental contributors (including numerous hypothetical workplace chemicals (e.g., PCBs and ionizing radiation) can all be potential teratogens.

29. B: Particulate contamination can come in a variety of forms, including aerosols, mists, fumes, and smoke. Gases are an altogether different state of matter than particulates and hence do not fall under the subject category as a potential form thereof. As such, there is an entirely separate category of contaminants (contamination) that is strictly associated with gases.

Copyright © Mometrix Media. You have been licensed one copy of this document for personal use only. Any other reproduction or redistribution is strictly prohibited. All rights reserved.
This content is provided for test preparation purposes only and does not imply an endorsement by Mometrix of any particular political, scientific, or religious point of view.

30. D: There are several potential hazards that are conventionally tied to the normal use of high-pressure receptacles and containers in the workplace; these may include: pressures exceeding design safety levels, elevated fire risks due to enhanced oxygen levels in certain containers, and possible container failure or rupture due to corrosion buildup.

31. A: A monitoring system should always be employed in tandem with a warning system to alert workforces of hazardous conditions potentially at hand.

32. B: Quite often, hazardous material spills can ultimately result in an ensuing dangerous chemical reaction. Typical observable characteristics of such reactions may include the emission of smoke and/or vapors, bubbling, unusual odors, or the generation or buildup of heat.

33. D: Life-cycle cost is the total cost of a system or component over its entire lifespan. To calculate it, we subtract the total savings from the total costs. In this problem, the life-cycle cost can be calculated by summing the costs and subtracting the dealership's payment, as follows:

$$\text{Life-cycle cost} = \$12{,}000 + (\$400 \times 8) + \sum_{n=0}^{7}(\$600 + \$25 \times n) - \$2{,}000 = \$18{,}700$$

34. C: A stem-and-leaf plot is typically regarded as one of the most useful graphical aids for clearly illustrating data groups that fall within particular value ranges.

35. D: A number of statistical parameters may be potentially utilized if one wishes to calculate a measure of dispersion for a given data set. These may include: variance, standard deviation, and range.

36. B: The standard deviation ("σ") for the whole population data set (2, 7, 11, 24, 44, 62, 79, 81, 105, 120, 139, 162) is calculated per:

$$\sigma = \sqrt{\frac{\sum(x - \bar{x})^2}{N}}$$

This equates to:

σ = [(4579 + 3927 + 3442 + 2085 + 659 + 59 + 87 + 128 + 1248 + 2533 + 4807 + 8525) ÷ 12]$^{0.5}$ ≈ 52.

37. D: There are several characteristic shapes of frequency curves that exist in the realm of statistics. These include multimodal, (left- or right-) skewed, j-shaped, U-shaped, and symmetrical (such as a Gaussian normal distribution).

38. C: "LD50" is conventionally defined as a radiological or chemical dose quantity whereby 50 percent of an exposed population would be expected to acutely (rapidly) die as a result of the subject exposure. Thus, if a population of 100,000 people incurred an LD50 exposure, approximately 50,000 resulting acute fatalities would be expected in that population.

39. A: A probabilistic risk assessment (PRA) is a detailed and systematic process to evaluate potential risks associated with the design and operation of a multifaceted, complex technology. A chemical plant or a new transportation system, for example, would both undergo PRAs during its conceptual design stage.

40. D: Simultaneous timed-events plotting analyses are routinely used by safety engineers for assessing potential workplace system hazards. Such analyses typically assess events through a time-sequence viewpoint.

41. B: Within the specific quality assurance domains of audits and inspections, the acronym CAQ is defined as Condition Adverse to Quality. It usually depicts or categorizes conditions of a serious nature and are typically given high priority (and resources) for prompt corrective action.

Copyright © Mometrix Media. You have been licensed one copy of this document for personal use only. Any other reproduction or redistribution is strictly prohibited. All rights reserved.
This content is provided for test preparation purposes only and does not imply an endorsement by Mometrix of any particular political, scientific, or religious point of view.

42. C: Per the US National Industrial Security Program Operating Manual (NISPOM) security classification protocols, document cover letter and label colors that indicate top secret, secret, confidential, and unclassified are orange, red, blue, and green, respectively.

43. A: Injury information resulting from an accident event should be reported by corporate health and safety management personnel as soon as possible after an occurrence. Specific OSHA protocol (per 29 CFR 1904.39) mandates, however, that any work-related deaths must *be* reported within 8 hrs. Furthermore, any work-related amputations, in-patient hospitalizations, or loss(es) of an eye must be reported within 24 hrs.

44. B: In a total workforce of 200 people (who each work 2,000 hrs over a calendar year), if there are 10 total cases of missed workdays, restricted duty, or transfer due to work-related injuries over that calendar year, the calculated resulting DART rate is 5. This is derived via the following:

[DART = (X/Y) × 200,000], whereby X = the total number of injuries or illnesses with missed workdays or restricted duty and Y = the total number of hrs worked by all employees = (10/400,000) × 200,000 = 5.

45. C: A bar graph most closely resembles a histogram. Both types of illustrative tools use rectangular bars to certain rising (or extending) axis values for depicting a certain measured quantity or value. A histogram is essentially a specific type of bar graph that displays a numerical data (probability) distribution for a continuous variable.

46. A: A teletector would be most suitable for use by health physicists (or radiological technicians) for determining actual radiation levels within a very high radiation area before workers would enter to perform an assigned task.

47. D: A "fishbone diagram" is also known as a cause-and-effect analysis. Its primary function is to provide a visual representation of the numerous potential causes behind a specific problem or effect. It is often especially useful for scenarios in which there is very little existing data in support of an evaluation or assessment.

48. B: The 50th percentile value of a normal distribution is also always denoted as the median. In a normal (e.g., Gaussian) distribution, 50 percent of the subject values will be above the median (50th percentile) value, and 50 percent will be below this value.

49. A: Conditions adverse to quality are usually considered the most serious of all audit-finding classifications. Other types of findings from audits that fall into categories of lesser severity include: conditions not adverse to quality, observations, and opportunities for improvement. All categories would normally be entered, addressed, and closed out via the use of a robust corrective action program database.

50. C: Per OSHA directive, VPP Merit-status employers are expected to commit to the pursuance of star status within a period of 3 years.

51. B: Per 40 CFR 261, corrosivity (code #D002) is a designated hazardous waste material characteristic to which the US Environmental Protection Agency extends an ordinal waste code value; strong corrosives (e.g., acids) would be categorized under this designation. The other coded characteristics under 40 CFR 261 include: ignitability (code #D001), reactivity (code #D003), and toxicity (codes #D004—#D043).

52. A: Job safety analyses (JSAs) should be regularly implemented or reviewed in coordination with preliminary task walk-downs and pre-job briefings, prior to the commencement of activities.

53. C: Lifting indexes (LIs), recommended weight limits (RWLs), and load constants (LCs) are established components of NIOSH's lifting equation. In addition, the equation specifically takes into account factors and parameters such as: object locations relative to the lifter, object locations relative to the floor, vertical moving distances, degrees of lifter twisting, frequencies or durations of lifting, and gripping forces.

Copyright © Mometrix Media. You have been licensed one copy of this document for personal use only. Any other reproduction or redistribution is strictly prohibited. All rights reserved.
This content is provided for test preparation purposes only and does not imply an endorsement by Mometrix of any particular political, scientific, or religious point of view.

54. C: A floor surface with a moderate slip potential has a coefficient of friction value of around 0.4. This means that the surface's traction is considered acceptably marginal and that a reasonable chance of a slip-related accident occurring on such a surface exists under normal conditions.

55. A: In the following Cartesian data-point set: [(0.5, 1.4), (2, 6), (4, 11.8), (7, 20), (9, 22), (12, 37),

(15, 45.8), (17, 50)], the point (9, 22) would be considered an anomaly compared to all of the others. This can be demonstrated by plotting all of the subject values via a scatter plot and noting that all of the other points essentially construct a straight line. The point (9, 22) falls well outside of this line, however, hence denoting it as an anomaly with respect to the rest of the data set.

56. B: With regard to root-cause analyses (RCAs), they are only performed for an event after the event has occurred. Furthermore, there can hypothetically be several tangible underlying root-cause outcomes for any given RCA. Moreover, historical RCAs may (should) be utilized for predicting possible events before they occur. It should also be noted that incident management processes and RCAs should not normally be integrated and implemented in tandem.

57. A: If a calculated statistical variance for a sample of data values is found to be approximately 2.76, the associated standard deviation value correlated to that variance is 1.66—SD = $(Variance)^{0.5}$.

58. B: A powder that is comprised of 5 percent silica would have a calculated PEL of 4.88 mg/m³ per the following derivation found in OSHA 29 CFR 1910.1000, Table Z-3:

$$PEL_{sil} = (10 \text{ mg/m}^3)/(\text{silica-\%} + 2) = 10/(0.05 + 2) = 4.88 \text{ mg/m}^3$$

To then convert into units of ppm from mg/m³, the following formula is employed:

$$ppm = [(4.88 \text{ mg/m}^3)(24.45)] \div [\text{molecular weight of silica (SiO}_2)]$$

$$= [119.3] \div [60] = 1.99 \text{ ppm}$$

59. A: Xylene being generated within a work area per V = 100,000 ft³, Q′ = 2,000 cfm, and G = 3 cfm—whereby V is the volume of the work area, Q′ is the air flow rate in the work area divided by a design distribution constant, and G is the contaminant generation rate—will reach a concentration (C) of 150 ppm within the work area in approximately 5.27 min. This is calculated per the following:

T (time required) = {[-V/Q′] × [ln((G-Q′C) ÷ G)]}

= {[-50] × [ln((3-0.3) ÷ 3)]}

= {[-50] × [-0.1054]} = 5.27 min

60. B: Under normal conditions (indoor or outdoor) with no solar load, a wet-bulb temperature (T_w) is typically calculated via the following equation:

$$T_w = \frac{WBGT - 0.3T_g}{0.7}$$

where *WBGT* is the wet-bulb globe temperature index and T_g is the globe temperature. However, in the case where there is a solar load, the equation is modified slightly to include a component from the dry-bulb temperature (T_d). Hence the adjusted equation now becomes:

$$T_w = \frac{WBGT - 0.2T_g - 0.1T_d}{0.7}$$

For the specific case provided, the calculated T_w is determined to be 88.7 °F:

Copyright © Mometrix Media. You have been licensed one copy of this document for personal use only. Any other reproduction or redistribution is strictly prohibited. All rights reserved.
This content is provided for test preparation purposes only and does not imply an endorsement by Mometrix of any particular political, scientific, or religious point of view.

$$T_w = \frac{89 - 0.2 * 92 - 0.1 * 85}{0.7} = \frac{62.1}{0.7} = 88.7\ °F$$

61. B: Given the following set of data, the calculated correlation coefficient (CC) between the two variables x and y is determined as follows:

	x	y
	3	2
	5	4
	8	6
	11	9
	14	13
	16	15
Total	57	49
Average	9.5	8.2

The fundamental equation that is used for calculating CC is:

CC = [N∑(xy) – (∑x)(∑y)] ÷ {[N∑(x²) – (∑x)²][N∑(y²) – (∑y)²]}^{1/2}

Hence, the values for xy, x², and y² must now be calculated and added to the table:

	x	y	xy	x²	y²
	3	2	6	9	4
	5	4	20	25	16
	8	6	48	64	36
	11	9	99	121	81
	14	13	182	196	169
	16	15	240	256	225
Total	57	49	595	671	531
Average	9.5	8.2	99.2	111.8	88.5

Via deployment of the subject equation, we attain:

CC = [(6)(595) – (57)(49)] ÷ {[(6)(671) – (57)²][(6)(531) – (49)²]} ^{1/2}

[777] ÷ {[777][785]} ^{½}

777 ÷ 781 = 0.995

62. C: Total unit pressure for a mixture or combination of gases within a single container is equal to the sum of the partial pressures of the constituent gases contained within. Thus, for the subject case of Gas_x = 12 atm, Gas_y = 28 atm, and Gas_z = 50 atm, the total calculated pressure for the three-gas mixture is determined via the following:

P Gas_{total} = ∑ (P Gas_x + P Gas_y + P Gas_z) = 12 atm + 28 atm + 50 atm = 90 atm

63. A: Conductivity is the measured degree to which a material conducts electricity and is the direct inverse (reciprocal) of resistivity. Hence, a steel wire that is measured to have an electrical resistivity of 20 ohm-m has an associated conductivity of 0.05 siemens-m⁻¹.

Copyright © Mometrix Media. You have been licensed one copy of this document for personal use only. Any other reproduction or redistribution is strictly prohibited. All rights reserved.
This content is provided for test preparation purposes only and does not imply an endorsement by Mometrix of any particular political, scientific, or religious point of view.

64. C: The t-value test is often utilized for determining the extent of difference(s) between the means of statistical samples. For the example case of a company's fabrication process requiring a certain mold to be consistently manufactured at a 3.25-in thickness, given seven random mold samples of 3.21, 3.28, 3.32, 3.36, 3.25, 3.29, and 3.22 in, the calculated "t" value for those samples is determined as follows:

T = {[(sample mean) – (desired target value)] ÷ [sample standard deviation]} × [Number of samples – 1]$^{1/2}$
T = {[(3.276) – (3.250)] ÷ [0.0538]} × [7 – 1]$^{1/2}$
= {0.483} × 2.449
= 1.183

65. C: If a system (X) has two (and only two) codependent subsystems (y and z) required for its operation, with one having a 0.0001 failure rate and the other having a 0.001 failure rate, the overall probability of failure for the entire system X is equal to the sum of the two subsystem failure rates, given that failure of system X will occur if failure occurs in either of the two subsystems.

$X_{failure} = y_{failure} + z_{failure}$ = 0.0001 + 0.001 = 0.0011

66. D: If the pH of a sulfuric acid solution used in an industrial setting must be below 1.5 to burn through worker PPE, the minimum associated hydrogen-ion (H^+) concentration of that acid must be 0.032 to reach the threshold of such a pH. This is calculated via the following: pH = –log[H^+], whereby [H^+] = hydrogen-ion concentration. Hence, 1.5 = –log[0.032].

67. B: For an examination given to 50 students showing a mean score of 74.3 percent, with a standard deviation of 6.9 and exactly one student scoring an 80 percent, if a standard distribution is assumed, the number of students scoring higher than this one student (i.e., > 80 percent) can be calculated via determining the statistical Z-score of the exam results.

Z = (X^2 – μ) ÷ σ, whereby X^2 is the singular result (chi-square value) to be assessed around, μ is the mean, and σ is the standard deviation. Thus, (80-74.3) ÷ 6.9 = 0.826 = Z.

The provided normal distribution-Z table extract is then employed for determining what percent of students scored above 80 percent on the exam:

Z	0.00	0.01	0.02	0.03	0.04	0.05	0.06	0.07	0.08	0.09
0.7	0.7580	0.7611	0.7642	0.7673	0.7704	0.7734	0.7764	0.7794	0.7823	0.7852
0.8	0.7881	0.7910	*0.7939*	*0.7967*	0.7995	0.8023	0.8051	0.8078	0.8106	0.8133
0.9	0.8159	0.8186	0.8212	0.8238	0.8264	0.8289	0.8315	0.8340	0.8365	0.8389

The Z value of 0.826 is located in the subject table as shown. It must be interpolated between the 0.82 value of 0.7939 and the 0.83 value of 0.7967. It is resultantly determined to be 0.7956. This means that 79.56 percent of the students scored 80 percent or lower, and therefore 20.44 percent of students scored above that mark: 0.2044(50 students) ≈ 10 students.

68. A: The numerical difference (i.e., absolute value or delta) between an upper-control limit (UCL) and a lower-control limit (LCL) for an accident control-chart distribution can always be calculated by 2 × (the number of standard deviations [z]) × (the distribution's standard deviation value [σ]). This is demonstrated via the following calculation:

UCL = mean + zσ

LCL = mean – zσ

UCL – LCL = (mean + zσ) – (mean – zσ) = zσ – (-zσ) = zσ + zσ = 2(zσ). Hence, for the subject case stated in this problem, we attain: 2(3)(0.75) = 4.5.

Copyright © Mometrix Media. You have been licensed one copy of this document for personal use only. Any other reproduction or redistribution is strictly prohibited. All rights reserved.
This content is provided for test preparation purposes only and does not imply an endorsement by Mometrix of any particular political, scientific, or religious point of view.

69. D: In the right triangle shown, the tangent (TAN) of angle <BAC is equal to (6.93 ÷ 4), or $3^{1/2}$, or 1.73.

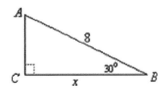

This is derived via the fact that for a 30-60-90 triangle, the respective segment unit lengths (in increasing order) are 1, $3^{1/2}$, and 2. Thus, in the figure, because the hypotenuse is equal to 8, segment AC must be equal to 4, and x must be equal to $(4)(3^{1/2})$. From this, it is now possible to arithmetically determine the tangent of <BAC as $[(4)(3^{1/2}) \div (4)] = [6.93 \div 4] = 3^{1/2} \approx 1.73$. With a calculator, alternatively, this may simply be processed as TAN 60°; however, the user must be able to preliminarily infer that <BAC is in fact 60 degrees from the axiom that all interior angles of a triangle always aggregate to a total of 180 degrees because the value of <BAC is not provided in the diagram.

70. A: A car engine component operating for 10,000 hrs with an established reliability of 0.998 would have a higher failure-per-hr rate than an aircraft component operating for 20,000 hrs with an established reliability of 0.997. This quantitatively determined via the following:

Reliability(t) = $e^{-\lambda t}$, whereby λ is the number of failures per hr and t is the operating time.

Car Engine Case:

$0.998 = e^{-\lambda(10,000 \text{ hrs})}$

$\ln 0.998 = \ln \left(e^{-\lambda(10,000 \text{ hrs})}\right)$

$-0.0020 = (-\lambda)(10,000 \text{ hrs})$

$\lambda = 2 \times 10^{-7}$ failures per hr (or 1 failure every 5,000,000 hrs)

Aircraft Component Case:

$0.997 = e^{-\lambda(20,000 \text{ hrs})}$

$\ln 0.997 = \ln \left(e^{-\lambda(20,000 \text{ hrs})}\right)$

$-0.0030 = (-\lambda)(20,000 \text{ hrs})$

$\lambda = 1.5 \times 10^{-7}$ failures per hr (or 1 failure every 6,666,666 hrs)

This scenario is demonstrative of the concept that just because a component has an overall higher reliability than another component does not necessarily mean that its failure rate is always lower. The amount of time in which reliability is measured is pivotal for accurately defining the relative context of a component's true reliability value.

71. D: Within the realm of statics and mechanics, a structure is considered statically indeterminate if the number of forces (variables) exceeds the number of available equilibrium equations. In this working example, there are four separate forces placed upon the static hoist, and yet there are only three independent equilibrium equations depicting the relationships of these forces; the object's condition is hence considered to be statically indeterminate because the equations cannot be solved to render a single definitive value attributable to each force variable.

Copyright © Mometrix Media. You have been licensed one copy of this document for personal use only. Any other reproduction or redistribution is strictly prohibited. All rights reserved.
This content is provided for test preparation purposes only and does not imply an endorsement by Mometrix of any particular political, scientific, or religious point of view.

72. D: According to H. W. Heinrich, out of every 100 accidents, approximately 88 of them, on average, are the result of direct (erroneous) actions of individuals. Moreover, approximately 10 of them are usually attributable to unsafe conditions, and two of them are typically characterized as unavoidable. Hence, for the case example, out of 425 incidents, approximately 375 would be attributable to the direct actions of individuals.

73. B: An endeavor to uncover and reduce hazards that may be at hand for product or system users, as well as to those who are accountable for their maintenance, is conventionally known as an Occupational Health Hazard Assessment. Such assessments also usually attempt to evaluate ways to reduce risks or impacts resulting from such hazards if an associated undesirable event was to subsequently unfold.

74. A: In a fault-tree sequence, Events A, B, and C have estimated probabilities (frequencies) of occurrence equal to 0.1, 0.01, and 0.005, respectively. For a resulting system failure to occur (Event D), Events A and B or Events A and C must transpire. According to the fault-tree's analysis, the approximate overall probability that Event D may occur is equal to 0.00105. This is derived via the statistical approach of an "OR" (-gate) scenario being followed through the fault-tree to spawn the aforementioned system failure (Event D). Mathematically, this is attained per the following:

Probability of Event D (system failure) = { [($P_A \times P_B$) + ($P_A \times P_C$)] − [($P_A \times P_B$) × ($P_A \times P_C$)] }

= { [0.001 + 0.0005] − [0.0000005] }

$\approx$ 0.0015

75. D: For a vehicle moving along at a steady speed of 50 m/s followed by a deceleration rate of −6 m/s for 100 m, to determine the speed of the vehicle when the vehicle began to accelerate again (after the 100 m slowdown), the following calculation is employed:

$v^2 = v_o^2 + 2ad$, where v is the speed at the point of reacceleration; v_o is the initial speed of the vehicle; a is the acceleration; and d is the change in position between the two speed measurements.

$v^2 = (50 \text{ m/s})^2 + 2(-6 \text{ m/s})(100 \text{ m})$

= (2500) + (−1200)

= $(1300)^{1/2}$

$\approx$ 36 m/s

76. D: For a plaintiff to prove strict liability, he or she must convincingly demonstrate three fundamental evidentiary levels regarding an allegedly defective product: (1) that the product was indeed defective; (2) that the product was defective upon departure of the defendant's stewardship; and (3) that the defect resulted in direct injury to the plaintiff. A consumer-fraud finding would not be applicable to the situation either because it was not demonstrated that the defendant was intentionally selling a defective product. Obligatory culpability is not a finding that could result from this court proceeding.

77. A: For work principally conducted in mines, the US Mine Safety and Health Administration (MSHA) typically employs a measurement parameter known as a severity measure (SM) that is used for assessing levels of worker injury and/or loss. The formula for calculating SM over a calendar year is the following: SM = [(number of lost workdays)(200,000)] ÷ [total number of employee hrs worked]. Thus, in this specific case, SM = [(5)(200,000)] ÷ [125,000] = 8.

78. C: If two separate containers are being simultaneously filled with a chemical at a rate of 2.5 gal/min, with one container being cylindrically shaped with a diameter of 12 in and a height of 24 in, whereas the other is

Copyright © Mometrix Media. You have been licensed one copy of this document for personal use only. Any other reproduction or redistribution is strictly prohibited. All rights reserved.
This content is provided for test preparation purposes only and does not imply an endorsement by Mometrix of any particular political, scientific, or religious point of view.

box shaped with dimensions of 16 in × 9 in × 30 in, neither one will have yet overflowed after exactly 4 min of filling. This is determined via the following:

- Available filling capacity (volume) of cylinder = $\pi r^2 h$ = 2,714 in³ = 11.75 gal
- Available filling capacity (volume) of box = l × w × h = 4,320 in³ = 18.70 gal

If the fill rate is 2.5 gal/min, after 4 min only 10 gal would have been filled in both containers. The cylindrical container would still have a 1.75 gal spare capacity at this point, and the box container would still have an 8.70 gal spare capacity.

79. B: From the following list comprised of hazard scores associated with each of the noted categories within a given work area, on a scale from 1 to 10, where 1 depicts a minimal hazard and 10 depicts a maximal hazard, it can likely be ascertained that a considerable portion of gears, pulleys, and/or belts in the work area are in need of more robust guarding (regarding the provided score of 7 for pinch point hazards).

Hazard	Score
Chemical containment	4
Noise	3
Open floor plans / tripping	**8**
Lighting	1
Electrical	6
Fire suppression	2
Ergonomics	9
Machinery pinch-points	7

80. D: Given that the half-life of the isotope Cobalt-60 (Co-60) is approximately 5.3 year, after 16 years, a given sample would have undergone a decay equivalent to approximately 3 half-lives and would thus be reduced by a factor of 7/8 (87.5 percent, i.e., only 1/8 of the original sample's activity—and hence, corresponding dose rate—measured at time t_0 would remain at time = 16 years). So, if the original dose rate (@ t_0) was 2,000 mrem/hr at 9 ft from the source, the dose rate (@t = 16 years) will equal approximately 0.125(2,000) = 250 mrem/hr at that same 9-ft distance.

Gamma-ray point-source (e.g., Co-60) intensities (and hence, corresponding dose rates) change proportionally with the square of distance (d^2). As such, the change in dose rate between a 9-ft and 4-ft distance is calculated as follows:

Dose rate @ 4 ft = [Dose rate @ 9 ft × (9^2 / 4^2)] = (250 mrem/hr) × (5.0625) ≈ 1,266 mrem/hr

= 1.266 rem/hr

Hence, for 10 CFR 20's annual occupational dose limit of 5 rem not to be exceeded, an individual cannot be exposed for more than approximately 4 hrs at a location of 4 ft from this source.

81. B: The measured area between the function f(x) = $2x^3 + x^2 - 5$ and the x-axis, between the points x_1 = 0 and x_2 = 3, is determined via the integration of the subject function and assessed at the point limits of x = 0 and x = 3. Hence, the (definite) integral of the subject function is $2x^4/4 + x^3/3 - 5x$; upon plugging in the point limits of x = 0 and x =3, we obtain a resulting area (under the curve to the x-axis) of:

$[2(3)^4/4 + 3^3/3 - 5(3) - 2(0)^4/4 + 0^3/3 - 5(0)]$ = [40.5 + 9 – 15] = 34.5

Copyright © Mometrix Media. You have been licensed one copy of this document for personal use only. Any other reproduction or redistribution is strictly prohibited. All rights reserved.
This content is provided for test preparation purposes only and does not imply an endorsement by Mometrix of any particular political, scientific, or religious point of view.

In the case of the circle, if the circumference is 25, then the associated area of the subject circle is derived via: C = π2r = 25; r is thus determined to be 3.98. Then, we are now able to derive the circle's area via: A = πr² = π(15.84) = 49.8.

Area of circle (49.8) > Area under function (34.5)

82. C: Breathing secondhand smoke is an example of an involuntary risk scenario. Such a scenario usually encompasses a situation in which a person is at risk due to a lack of understanding the extent of a given risk or is unknowingly subjected to higher risks that are only known to the entities that are responsible for the presence of an associated hazard at the onset. In contrast, examples of voluntary risks include driving a car, smoking cigarettes, scuba diving, and skydiving.

83. B: A worker who was exposed to a hazardous chemical for 4 hrs per day over a 3-day period, and a month later was subsequently diagnosed with a liver condition that has historically been shown to manifest as a result of exposure to this chemical, is an example of an acute exposure followed by systemic health effects. Acute exposures are typically categorized as those that occur over a very short to short period of time (i.e., a few s to a few days); chronic exposures occur for much longer periods (i.e., weeks to years). Moreover, systemic effects typically manifest in bodily organs or systems that can have long-lasting, serious impacts, whereas localized effects are typically less serious and more temporary in nature (e.g., eye irritation, skin burns, or mucus membrane inflammation).

84. C: For a horizontally oriented fire system (i.e., no elevation throughout the system), water flows through a 4-in pipe. The measured head loss in a 500-ft section of the system is 20 ft. The residual pressure at Point A is 30 psi, and the velocity at point A is 8 ft/s. If the velocity at Point B is 10 ft/s, the pressure at Point B may be determined via the following equation:

$v_a^2/2g + p_a/w + z_a = v_b^2/2g + p_b/w + z_b + h_{ab}$, whereby v_a is the velocity at point a; g is the gravitational acceleration constant; p_a is the pressure at point a; w is the water density (62.4 lb/ft³); z_a is the elevation at point a; v_b is the velocity at point b; p_b is the pressure at point b; z_b is the elevation at point b; and h_{ab} is the piezometric head (equivalent to the sum of elevation-z and head between points a and b)

Hence, employing $v_a^2/2g + p_a/w + z_a = v_b^2/2g + p_b/w + z_b + h_{ab}$, this particular problem is to solve for p_b.

$[8^2/2(32.2)] + [30/62.4](144 \text{ in}^2/\text{ft}^2) + 0 = [10^2/2(32.2)] + [p_b/62.4] + 0 + 20$

$0.994 + 69.2 = 1.553 + [p_b/62.4] + 20$

$70.2 = 21.553 + [p_b/62.4]$

$48.6 = [p_b/62.4]$

$3{,}036 \text{ lb/ft}^2 = 21.1 \text{ lb/in}^2$

85. A: A worker (who weighs 170 lb or any other weight for that matter) who falls off a 20-ft-high scaffold will impact the ground at approximately 25 mph (ignoring any losses due to air friction) and would thus be expected to sustain potentially serious injuries. This resulting impact speed is calculated via the following:

Velocity at Impact = $[(2) × (g) × (\text{height})]^{1/2} = [(2)(32.2 \text{ ft/s}^2)(20 \text{ ft}) x]^{1/2} \approx 35 \text{ ft/s}$

$= (35 \text{ ft/s})(\text{mi}/5{,}280 \text{ ft})(3600 \text{ s/hr}) = 24.5 \text{ mph} \approx 25 \text{ mph}$

86. B: A parameter that is conventionally used to measure the quantity of time that a worker may remain in an area that has been infiltrated by a known amount of hazardous/toxic gas (or fumes) without suffering any adverse health effects is known as an emergency exposure limit (EEL). As the nomenclature indicates, this value is typically employed in emergency situations when retrieval of immobilized personnel or the

Copyright © Mometrix Media. You have been licensed one copy of this document for personal use only. Any other reproduction or redistribution is strictly prohibited. All rights reserved.
This content is provided for test preparation purposes only and does not imply an endorsement by Mometrix of any particular political, scientific, or religious point of view.

stabilization of facilities is required. Most recommended EEL values typically fall in the min to hrs range, with 8 hrs usually seen as a conventional ceiling. There are potential situations, however, where if concentration and toxicity levels are high enough, only a time frame in the seconds range can hence be tolerated.

87. D: Plutonium-239 is both radiologically and chemically hazardous. All plutonium isotopes essentially maintain a chemical toxicity similar to that of lead and are extremely hazardous radiologically (especially when inhaled) due to their very highly energetic alpha particle emissions. In contrast, although lead-208 and mercury-202 are both chemically hazardous, they are also both radiologically stable and therefore do not pose a radiation hazard. Argon-40 is a radioactive isotope; however, it is not considered a chemical hazard.

88. D: Per the work-area noise-level measurements provided (assessed over a two-week time span), a CSP, ASP, or IH should conclude that the area does not meet the minimum TWA threshold levels of a hazardous noise area as per OSHA 1910.95 (i.e., an 8-hr TWA greater than 85 dBA); thus, hearing protection PPE is not mandatory. However, it should be nevertheless recommended due to average levels being close to this threshold, with occasional exceedances at hand.

Measurement Day	Number of Hours Measured	Measurement Range	Measurement Average
1 of 10	6.75	74-81 dBA	77 dBA
2 of 10	8	67-79 dBA	71 dBA
3 of 10	3	86-88 dBA	87 dBA
4 of 10	8	71-92 dBA	79 dBA
5 of 10	7	81-85 dBA	84 dBA
6 of 10	3.5	77-80 dBA	78 dBA
7 of 10	8	58-72 dBA	67 dBA
8 of 10	6.5	66-70 dBA	69 dBA
9 of 10	2.25	89-94 dBA	93 dBA
10 of 10	7.5	75-83 dBA	78 dBA

89. B: The respiratory disease *Siderosis* is known to be caused by exposure to iron oxide (rust) dust. Working in a steel mill (given that iron is the major component of steel) thus entails higher risks of contracting *Siderosis*. In contrast, asbestosis is caused by overexposure to asbestos fibers.

90. A: An air-contaminant concentration of approximately 50 ppm is expected to result in following air-filtration through a three-stage filter bank with individual respective efficiencies (ε_x) of 90 percent, 95 percent, and 99 percent. This is calculated via the following:

Post-filtration contamination = $[(1 - \varepsilon_1)(1 - \varepsilon_2)(1 - \varepsilon_3)] = [(0.10)(0.05)(0.01)] = 0.000050 = 50$ ppm

91. B: If a gas at a pressure of 5 psia occupies a volume of 100 cm³ at a temperature of 20°K, the resultant pressure of the gas will remain at 5 psia if the temperature is increased to 30°K at a volume of 150 cm³. The pressure remains constant in this case because both the temperature and volume increased proportionally by the same quantity (50 percent). This principle is illustrative of Charles' Gas Law.

92. B: At altitudes of about 10,000 ft above sea level, lower concentrations of oxygen in the atmosphere can begin to have noticeable physiological effects on humans (i.e., hypoxia), symptoms of which may include confusion, tachycardia, skin color changes, shortness of breath, and sweating. Over 15,000 ft, symptoms can become acutely serious with blood oxygen saturation levels dropping to near 80 percent. At over 20,000 ft, consciousness will shortly be lost.

93. A: If the inhalation dose conversion factor (DCFᵢ) for isotope "X" is 1 rem per curie (Ci), and a facility that processes this isotope releases 2.22×10^{13} becquerels (Bq, 600 curies) of it per year, a resulting annual inhalation dose of approximately 18 mrem is expected for a downwind receptor who has a breathing rate of

Copyright © Mometrix Media. You have been licensed one copy of this document for personal use only. Any other reproduction or redistribution is strictly prohibited. All rights reserved.
This content is provided for test preparation purposes only and does not imply an endorsement by Mometrix of any particular political, scientific, or religious point of view.

18.31 in^3 (300 cm^3) per s and is subjected to an atmospheric concentration dispersion coefficient (X/Q) of 1 × 10^{-7} s per cm^3. This resultant dose is calculated via the following:

Inhalation Dose ≈ (Source Term)(BR)(DCF)(X/Q)

= (2.22×10^{13} Bq)(1 Ci/3.7×10^{10} Bq)(18.31 in^3/s)(16.39 cm^3/in^3)(1000 millirem/Ci)(1×10^{-7} s/cm^3)

= 18 mrem

94. B: If a work area has dimensions of 10 m × 10 m × 3 m, the shortest amount of time it could potentially take for the entire supply of air in the room to (hypothetically) be completely exchanged via an air-exchanger HVAC system that operates at a rate of 80 cfm would be approximately 2.2 hours. This is calculated via the following:

Total air exchange time = (300 m^3)(1 min/80 ft^3)(35.31 ft^3/m^3) = 132.4 min = 2.2 hours

95. A: Radon, a naturally occurring gas that results from the radioactive decay of radium in earthen soils, is primarily an alpha radiation source. If inhaled, radon's energetic alpha particles (and progeny) are very hazardous to lung tissues and can result in significantly increased risks or incidences of lung cancer. The US Environmental Protection Agency recommends a radon concentration awareness action level at 2 pCi/L and a mitigation action level at 4 pCi/L.

For the case example of a 24-hr radon survey conducted in a work area that measured radon concentrations every hour on the hour, the following may be concluded from the provided information:

Time	Concentration (Ci/L)
1600 (Day 1)	1.2×10^{-12}
1800 (Day 1)	9.3×10^{-13}
2000 (Day 1)	1.8×10^{-12}
2200 (Day 1)	2.7×10^{-12}
0000 (Day 1)	4.3×10^{-12}
0200 (Day 1)	3.8×10^{-12}
0400 (Day 1)	1.9×10^{-12}
0600 (Day 1)	1.3×10^{-12}
0800 (Day 1)	8.8×10^{-13}
1000 (Day 1)	8.1×10^{-13}
1200 (Day 1)	1.1×10^{-12}
1400 (Day 1)	1.4×10^{-12}
1600 (Day 2)	1.3×10^{-12}
1800 (Day 2)	9.9×10^{-13}
2000 (Day 2)	1.5×10^{-12}
2200 (Day 2)	2.5×10^{-12}
0000 (Day 2)	3.9×10^{-12}
0200 (Day 2)	3.5×10^{-12}
0400 (Day 2)	1.3×10^{-12}
0600 (Day 2)	8.5×10^{-13}
0800 (Day 2)	1.0×10^{-12}
1000 (Day 2)	1.2×10^{-12}
1200 (Day 2)	1.3×10^{-12}
1400 (Day 2)	9.6×10^{-13}

The average (mean) measured concentration for the 24-hr sampling period is found equal to approximately 1.77×10^{-12} Ci/L, which equates to 1.77 picocuries/L (pCi/L); therefore, no EPA categorical action level (i.e., 2 pCi/L or 4 pCi/L) has been exceeded, and thus no remedial action is recommended. Given the temporary,

Copyright © Mometrix Media. You have been licensed one copy of this document for personal use only. Any other reproduction or redistribution is strictly prohibited. All rights reserved.
This content is provided for test preparation purposes only and does not imply an endorsement by Mometrix of any particular political, scientific, or religious point of view.

clustered, and consistent nature of the elevated readings (noted in bold) at 2200, 0000, and 0200 on both Days 1 and 2, it is very likely that these are due to nighttime atmospheric inversion layer events, which keep the radon more suppressed at ground levels.

96. D: The conventionally established definition for upper flammable limit (UFL) or upper explosive limit (UEL) for a gas is the highest concentration of gas (or vapor) relative to air at which such a gaseous material is able to ignite.

97. A: Steve and Mary both work on an assembly line with varying degrees of machine-guarding adequacy. Steve, who primarily works near pulleys and belts, never tucks in his shirt and always wears a loose-hanging bracelet. Mary, in contrast, who primarily works near axles and gears, has long, loose-flowing hair and always wears a long, dangling necklace. Via the provided information, because all of the machinery Mary works near is fully guarded (i.e., essentially fully enclosed), it is extremely unlikely for either her necklace or hair to get caught in any of the machinery. Although Steve works near much fewer potential pinch points (four versus 24 for Mary), they are either unguarded or only partially guarded, therefore creating a realistic potential for Steve to be involved in a "caught-in-a-machine"-related incident. Although other potential contributory variables such as lengths of shifts, part-time versus full-time status, and precise work locations or functions relative to pinch point angles and configurations are not known, it can be concluded from the information provided that Steve is at a definitively higher risk due to all of Mary's local potential pinch points being fully guarded.

98. C: Current is the standard electrical parameter (not voltage) that potential electrocution deaths to humans are measured by. In relative terms, it does not require considerable quantities of current to adversely impact biological functions. Current levels in the range of 0.1 to 0.2 amperes (amps) are typically denoted as the death range in which fatalities will most likely occur. Ironically, at currents greater 0.2 amps, although breathing may temporarily stop and burns may occur, the heart will often clamp itself shut during the period of exposure. A clamping condition such as this actually protects the heart from entering into ventricular fibrillation, with a person's chances for resulting survival usually being quite optimistic following the event.

99. B: Glassification and ceramification are two modes of immobilization used in the disposition of hazardous, mixed, and nuclear wastes. Such waste materials are usually industrially amalgamated in tandem with stable glass or ceramic matrices to prevent the leaching of such materials into the surrounding environment.

For the case of a waste management company required to dispose of 10 MT of waste using either or both of these subject technologies, the cost of a 50-50 allocation (by weight) endeavor is calculated via the following:

Cost to glassify 5 MT of waste with a bulk density (ρ) = 4.8 g/cm³ and at \$1,000/ft³:

(5MT)(1000kg/MT)(cm³/4.8g)(1000g/kg)(\$1000/ft³)(ft³/28,317cm³) = \$36,786

Cost to ceramify 5 MT of waste with a bulk density (ρ) = 4.8 g/cm³ and at \$5,000/ft³:

(5MT)(1000kg/MT)(cm³/4.8g)(1000g/kg)(\$5000/ft³)(ft³/28,317cm³) = \$183,930

Total cost estimate = \$220,716

100. C: Given that the pipe's flow is definitively characterized as laminar, by definition, the Reynolds number (Re) must be less than 2,000. To calculate the pressure for such a pipe with a 6-in radius and a laminar flow rate of 1,000 gpm, the following formula is employed:

$P = Q^2/891d^4$, where Q is the laminar flow rate and d is the pipe diameter

$P = (1000 \text{ gpm})^2 / (891)(12 \text{ in})^4$

$P = 0.054$ psi

Copyright © Mometrix Media. You have been licensed one copy of this document for personal use only. Any other reproduction or redistribution is strictly prohibited. All rights reserved.
This content is provided for test preparation purposes only and does not imply an endorsement by Mometrix of any particular political, scientific, or religious point of view.

101. A: A company physician recommends that an overweight employee implement a weight-loss plan to lose 52 lb. If the employee has been up to that point in time regularly eating 5,000 calories per day and exhibits an equilibrium caloric intake level of 2,500 daily calories (the caloric daily intake whereby weight remains stable), the percentage he or she must decrease daily caloric intake to lose the target weight over 1 years' time (assuming that he or she regularly burns the equilibrium-level 2,500 calories per day through normal metabolism and exercise over that year, and that 1 ounce of fat is equivalent to 200 calories) is determined via the following:

To lose 52 lb over a year is equivalent to an average of 1 lb per week. To lose 1 lb per week through caloric cutbacks alone, a total of 457 less net calories must be consumed per day. This is derived per the following:

[(–200 cal/oz)(16 oz/lb)(1 lb/wk)(1 wk/7 days)] = –457 cal/day

Given that the worker's equilibrium intake level is 2,500 calories, he or she must therefore take in no greater than 2,043 calories (i.e., 2,500 – 457) on an average daily basis to meet the weight-loss goal within a year's time.

This is a 59.1 percent reduction in daily caloric intake from the present level of 5,000 calories/day.

102. C: Oscilloscopes are normally utilized within industrial settings for assessing electronic output signals and associated parameters. Each block on the provided oscilloscope display represents one unit. The signal's amplitude is defined as the number of units from the x-axis to the peak of the waves (2), and the period is defined as the number of units covered (x-directionally) from the start of a wave cycle through its completion (2). The signal shape is symmetrically sinusoidal (i.e., a sine wave) given that it starts and ends at a functional (y) value equal to zero on the x-axis, has maxima and minima at the $\pi/2$ and $3\pi/2$ points, and is symmetrically bisected by the x-axis.

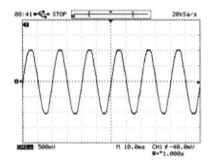

103. C: Microwave power density from an antenna or similar RF-type source may be calculated at any discrete distance via the use of the following formula: $W = AP/\lambda^2 r^2$, whereby W = power density, A = the effective area of the antenna, P = the antenna's power, λ = wavelength distance, and r = distance from the antenna.

$W = \{ [\pi(250 \text{ cm})^2] \times [50,000 \text{ mW}] \div [(1 \text{ cm})^2 \times (1,000 \text{ cm})^2] \} = 9,817 \text{ mW/cm}^2$

104. A: Head of a fluid moving through a pipe is calculated via the following: $h_v = v^2/2g$, where v = fluid velocity and g = gravitational acceleration constant (32.2 ft/s^2). Thus, for this subject case,

$h_v = [(16 \text{ ft}^2/\text{s}^2) \div 2(32.2 \text{ ft/s}^2)] = 0.25 \text{ ft.}$

105. B: Approximate exposure or dose rates from gamma sources at a distance of 1 ft can be calculated per the formula D = 6CEN, where C = the number of curies of the source, E = the energy of the emitted gamma ray (in MeV), and N = the percent of time the subject gamma ray is emitted when a disintegration occurs. Thus, for a 10 micro-curie source with a single 2.5 MeV gamma ray that is emitted 100 percent of the time, the estimated resulting dose rate (in rem/hr) at 1 ft is calculated to be 0.00015.

Copyright © Mometrix Media. You have been licensed one copy of this document for personal use only. Any other reproduction or redistribution is strictly prohibited. All rights reserved.
This content is provided for test preparation purposes only and does not imply an endorsement by Mometrix of any particular political, scientific, or religious point of view.

D = 6CEN = 6(10x10^{-6} Curies)(2.5 MeV)(1.0) = 0.00015 rem/hr

106. C: Alkali metals, such as sodium, lithium, and potassium typically react strongly (and often violently) when exposed to water. Soluble alkaline hydroxides and hydrogen gas are normally produced in these highly exothermic reactions. From a safety perspective in the workplace, it is always vital to keep these metals dry and isolated and away from any potential water or moisture sources. In the subject case, the calculated amount of heat released via a standard reaction between 92 g of pure sodium and 0.072 L of water, if approximately 185 kJ/mole is normally released in such a reaction, is determined as follows:

$2Na + 2H_2O \rightarrow 2NaOH + H_2$, with an associated heat release of 370 kJ (i.e., 2 moles × 185 kJ/mole)

2 moles of sodium = 46 g and 92 g = 4 moles

2 moles of water = 36 g and 72 g = 4 moles

Because 0.072 L = 72 ml and the density of water is 1 g/ml, there are therefore 72 g of water (i.e., 4 moles) for the case of this reaction.

Hence, because there are 4 moles of each substance involved in the reaction, the resultant quantity of heat released is 4 moles × 185 kJ/mole = 740 kJ.

107. A: In risk-assessment space, a severity-rating of critical is typically associated with the following conditional scenarios: (1) major damage to equipment or systems; (2) permanent partial impairment or temporary total impairment to workforces (likely includes injuries and/or fatalities); (3) appreciably disabled operational capabilities; (4) a major degree of overall property damage; and/or (5) high degrees of environmental releases or impacts.

108. C: A chemical's (Material) Safety Data Sheet (SDS) is virtually always produced and supplied by the chemical manufacturer. Moreover, there are numerous SDS databases and resources available via the Internet for locating a particular SDS, especially for generic-type materials. For this subject case, a CSP is attempting to identify an unlabeled chemical within a work area per with information he or she has analyzed in the chemical's SDS's "Exposure Controls/Personal Protection" section, including the following:

Engineering Controls

Provide robust exhaust ventilation or other engineering controls to keep airborne vapor concentrations below their respective threshold limit value. Ensure that eyewash stations and safety showers are near workstation locations.

Personal Protection

Gloves, boots, face shield, full suit, and vapor respirator—be sure to use an approved or certified respirator or equivalent thereof.

Personal Protection in Case of a Large Spill

Gloves, boots, face shield, full suit, and vapor respirator—a self-contained breathing apparatus should be used to avoid inhalation. Suggested protective clothing might not be sufficient against this liquid material; it is recommended a specialist be consulted before handling this product.

Exposure Limits

TWA: 0.025 from ACGIH (TLV) [US] SKIN TWA: 0.05 CEIL: 0.1 (mg/m3) from OSHA (PEL) [US]. Inhalation TWA: 0.025 (mg/m3) [UK]. Local authorities should be contacted as appropriate for permissible exposure limits.

Copyright © Mometrix Media. You have been licensed one copy of this document for personal use only. Any other reproduction or redistribution is strictly prohibited. All rights reserved. This content is provided for test preparation purposes only and does not imply an endorsement by Mometrix of any particular political, scientific, or religious point of view.

It can be resultantly determined (through the process of elimination from the provided information) that the unidentified material in question is most likely mercury, particularly in light of the very conservative TWAs and PEL presented. In addition, MEK, acetone, and ammonia would typically not mandate the rigorous levels of PPE controls that are recommended.

109. A: Per OSHA's 29 CFR 1910.146, *confined space entry,* a permit-required confined space, means that the space may exhibit the potential for engulfing an entrant. In addition, the space may contain an oxygen-depleted or hazardous atmosphere or may present an internal configuration such that a worker could become trapped or asphyxiated by inwardly converging walls or by a floor that slopes downward and tapers into a smaller cross-section.

For the case of a rectangular-shaped confined space with associated dimensions of 10 ft × 8 ft × 6 ft (i.e., 480 ft^3), the amount of time it will contain enough breathable oxygen for OSHA thresholds (i.e., 19.5 percent) if the total oxygen volume is decreasing at a rate of 63 cm^3/s is determined as follows:

480 ft^3 = 13,592,086.36 cm^3
(13,592,086.36 cm^3 free-air in room)(0.21 O_2 content) = 2,854,338.14 cm^3 O_2
(13,592,086.36 cm^3 free-air in room)(0.195 O_2 content) = 2,650,456.84 cm^3 O_2
2,854,338.14 cm^3 – 2,650,456.84 cm^3 = 203,881.3 cm^3

Divide the difference of volumes at both oxygen concentrations by the suction rate of the vacuum to find the time needed. 203,881.3 cm^3 ÷ 63 cm^3/s = 3,236.21 s = 53.94 min.

110. D: The quadratic equation is used for solving second-order expressions (in the form of $ax^2 + bx + c$) that cannot be directly factored. The formula is as follows:

$$x = \frac{-b \pm \sqrt{b^2 - 4ac}}{2a}$$

Hence, solving for the expression $3x^2 + 4x – 5 = 0$, the derived solutions for "x" would be as follows:

x = 0.79 and x = –2.12

111. B: Salt (sodium chloride) has a molecular weight equal to 58.44 g. By definition, this means that 1 mole of salt = 58.44 g = 6.023×10^{23} molecules. Consequently, in 14.61 g of salt, there would be ¼ (6.023×10^{23} molecules), or 1.506×10^{23} molecules.

112. B: The series of seven elements that can only exist as diatoms (dual-atoms) in nature when they are standing alone are: hydrogen (H_2), nitrogen (N_2), oxygen (O_2), iodine (I_2), bromine (Br_2), chlorine (Cl_2), and fluorine (F_2). One will note that these are all gasses at standard temperature and pressure. Moreover, fluorine has the highest level of electronegativity in the entire periodic table, which means that it has the highest tendency of any atom to attract a bonding pair of electrons. In the frequently used Pauling scale, which measures electronegativity, fluorine has an assigned value of 4.0, which is higher than any other element in the periodic table.

113. C: Time-weighted-average (TWA) exposures to a singular chemical are calculated per the following:

$[(aC_1 + bC_2 +... xC_z) \div (\sum \text{exposure times})]$

Thus, an employee who is exposed to carbon monoxide (CO) concentrations of 100 ppm for 1 hr, 500 ppm for 2 hrs, and 750 ppm for 15 min, receives a TWA exposure of 396 ppm.

{ [(1 hr)(100 ppm) + (2 hr)(500 ppm) + (0.25 hr)(750 ppm)] ÷ [3.25 hr] } = 396 ppm

Copyright © Mometrix Media. You have been licensed one copy of this document for personal use only. Any other reproduction or redistribution is strictly prohibited. All rights reserved. This content is provided for test preparation purposes only and does not imply an endorsement by Mometrix of any particular political, scientific, or religious point of view.

114. C: If an 8-hr PEL for a hazardous respirable dust is 20 mg/m³, the associated PEL for an employee working a 10-hr shift is equal to 16 mg/m³. This is derived via solving the following equation for 10-hr extended shifts:

(8 hr PEL value)(8 hrs) = (x)(10 hrs)

(20 mg/m³)(8 hrs) = 10x

x = 16 mg/m³

115. D: To calculate an aggregate lower flammability limit (LFL) for a chemical mixture, the following formula is applied:

$LFL_m = 1 / [(f_1/LFL_1 + f_2/LFL_2 + ... f_n/LFL_n)]$; where f = fraction of the mixture

Hence, a liquid mixture containing 50 percent methyl alcohol, 35 percent methyl ethyl ketone, and 15 percent acetone, with respective lower flammability limits of 1.5 percent, 1.1 percent, and 0.75 percent results in an overall (aggregate) LFL for the entire mixture of 1.17 percent.

$LFL_m = 1 / [(0.50/1.5 + 0.35/1.1 + 0.15/0.75)] = 1/0.8513 \approx 1.17\%$

116. D: The calculated approximate recommended weight limit (RWL) in pounds that has a load constant (LC) equal to 51 lb; a horizontal multiplier (HM) equal to 0.75; a vertical multiplier (VM) equal to 0.90; a distance multiplier (DM) equal to 0.87; an asymmetric multiplier (AM) equal to 0.85; a frequency multiplier (FM) equal to 0.45; and a coupling multiplier (CM) equal to 0.95 is determined to be 11 lb. (Note: there is no such parameter as a transitional multiplier.")

Hence, the result is derived via the following calculation:

RWL = LC × HM × VM × DM × AM × FM × CM = (51 lb) × (0.75) × (0.90) × (0.87) × (0.85) × (0.45) × (0.95) ≈ 11 lb

117. B: To determine which noise would be louder at a distance of 30 ft from its source, the following formula is employed:

$dB_2 = dB_1 - |20\log(d_1/d_2)|$

For case #1, a 100 dB noise is heard 3 ft away from its source:

$dB_2 = 100 - |20\log(3/30)|$
$dB_2 = 80$ dB @ 30 ft

For case #2, a 120 dB noise is heard 1 ft away from its source:

$dB_2 = 120 - |20\log(1/30)|$
$dB_2 = 90.4$ dB @ 30 ft

Thus, at a distance of 30 ft, the 120 dB noise at 1 ft is louder than the 100 dB noise at 3 ft. In addition, hearing protection would be required at this distance for an 8-hr TWA due to it exceeding hazardous noise level thresholds.

118. B: The equivalent polar-coordinate (r, θ) of the Cartesian-plotted point (6, 4) is calculated as follows:

The point (6, 4) is plotted in the Cartesian system, with "r" connecting the point (0, 0) to (6, 4). This "r" in essence, is the hypotenuse of the resulting created triangle; thus, the Pythagorean Theorem may be employed to find the value of "r." It is 7.21.

Copyright © Mometrix Media. You have been licensed one copy of this document for personal use only. Any other reproduction or redistribution is strictly prohibited. All rights reserved.
This content is provided for test preparation purposes only and does not imply an endorsement by Mometrix of any particular political, scientific, or religious point of view.

The value of θ is the newly created angle (which completed the triangle) between the x-axis and "r." Through simple trigonometric application, the angle can be calculated. For example, sin θ = 4 ÷ 7.21 = 0.555. Arcsin 0.555 = 33.7°.

119. D: Minimum required air sampling volume for a gas is determined via the following equation:

V_{min} = (1000 L/m³ × LOQ) / C_t, whereby LOQ = limit of quantification (range) [in mg], and C_t = contaminant target concentration [in mg/m³]. (Note: 2.42 mg/m³ = 1 ppm.)

Hence, for a gas that has an LOQ (range) of 5.2 – 65.7 micrograms and a target concentration of 880 ppm, the minimum required sampling volume is derived as follows:

V_{min} = (1000 L/m³ × 0.0052 mg) / 2,130 mg/m³ = 0.0024 L

120. B: Per OSHA 29 CFR 1910.95, 30 min of continual exposure at a 115 dBA noise level is twice the specified limit (of 15 min) required by the standard. Thirty min of continual exposure is, however, permitted at a level of 110 dBA or less.

121. A: A Class-III biological safety cabinet is the highest degree of protection available within the biological safety classification system. Given the case example of an industrial organization being in the process of acquiring a new Class-III biological safety cabinet, with the following comprising a list of technical specifications provided by a candidate cabinet vendor, one major flaw or omission is noted.

- Technical Specification Summary for Acme Corporation—Level III BioCab—Model # 2A6535001CM
- Arm-length rubber gloves
- Provides excellent physical protection to workforce
- ASTM-rated at 90 percent negative-pressure and 95 percent gas-tight efficiency
- Sealed front panel
- Air drawn into cabinet through HEPA filtration system
- Dimensions: 80" × 48" × 36"
- Double-welded steel frame and casing
- ASTM-rated lead-glass windows
- Double-gasket O-ring seal design at outlets
- Inflow velocity 150 fpm

The cabinet should be 100 percent negatively pressurized and have a 100 percent gas-tight efficiency rating.

122. C: Within the realm of thermodynamics, the term heat of combustion (hoc) is conventionally defined as the amount of heat (in cal) emitted by the combustion of 1 g of a substance. For the four generic-example scenarios provided to assess which has the highest associated hypothetical hoc, individual evaluations must be performed to ascertain which has the highest cal count per unit g.

Case 1—4,600 cal emitted by the combustion of one mole of Na-23:

      1 mole of Na-23 = 23 g; 4,600 cal/23 g combustion = 200 cal/g

Case 2—908 cal emitted by the combustion of 0.1 lb of helium:

      0.1 lb of helium = 45.4 g of helium; 908 cal/45.4 g = 20 cal/g

Case 3—257 cal emitted by the combustion of 1 g of hydrogen = 257 cal/g

Case 4—10 kilocalories emitted by the combustion of 2.5 moles of sulfuric acid:

      2.5 moles of sulfuric acid = 2.5 moles H_2SO_4; 1 mole of H_2SO_4 = 98 g; 2.5 moles = 245 g;

Copyright © Mometrix Media. You have been licensed one copy of this document for personal use only. Any other reproduction or redistribution is strictly prohibited. All rights reserved. This content is provided for test preparation purposes only and does not imply an endorsement by Mometrix of any particular political, scientific, or religious point of view.

10,000 cal/245 g $\approx$ 41 cal/g

So, Case 3 (1 g of hydrogen) is determined to be the highest for this example problem.

123. B: The solution to the expression $(i^4 + 2i^3 - 5i^2 - 4i - 1)^2$ is determined as follows:

(Imaginary) value *(i)* = $(-1)^{1/2}$

$[((-1)^{1/2})^4 + 2((-1)^{1/2})^3 - 5((-1)^{1/2})^2 - 4((-1)^{1/2}) - 1]^2 = [(1) + 2(-i) - 5(-1) - 4i - 1]^2$

$= [1 - 2i + 5 - 4i - 1]^2 = [5 - 6i]^2 = (5 - 6i)(5 - 6i) = 25 - 60i + 36i^2 = 25 - 60i + 36(-1)$

$= -60i - 11.$

124. D: According to NFPA criteria, Class IIIB combustible liquid classes strictly exhibit flash points that are in exceedance of 200°F. A substance's flash point is defined as the minimum temperature at which it gives off a vapor in sufficient concentration to form an ignitable mixture with the air near the material's surface. As such, this class is considered the safest of all potential categories due its susceptibility to ignition being the most minimal.

125. B: Wind-chill (factor) temperature is calculated per the following formula:

WC (°F) = $35.74 + 0.6215T - 35.75(V^{0.16}) + 0.4275T(V^{0.16})$

Hence, for the case of an air temperature (T) equal to 20°F and a wind speed (V) of 15 mph, the associated wind-chill temperature is found to be 6.2°F.

WC = $35.74 + 0.6215(20) - 35.75(15^{0.16}) + 0.4275(20)(15^{0.16})$

WC = $35.74 + 12.43 - 55.14 + 13.19$

WC = $6.22 \approx 6.2$

126. C: Kinetic energy (in joules [J]) is calculated per the formula KE = $1/2mv^2$, where m = mass (in kg) and v = velocity (in m/s). Thus, the kinetic energy of a 9,000 lb forklift moving at a speed of 5 mph is calculated via the following:

KE = $1/2mv^2$ = { 0.5(9000 lb)(0.454 kg/lb)[(5 mph)(1609 m/mile)(0.000278 hr/s)]^2 }

KE = 10,219 kg-m^2/s^2 = 10,219 joules = 10.2 kJ

127. B: If a company borrows $1 million to start a business, the entire loan will cost the business $1,490,833 over a repayment period of 10 years if the lender charges a 4 percent interest rate compounded monthly. This is calculated via the formula F = P(1 + i/n)^{nt}, whereby F = loan future value, P = initial loan amount, i = the interest rate, n = number of times per year the interest is compounded, and t = the number of years loan is being repaid.

F = P(1 + i/n)^{nt} = $1,000,000(1 + 0.04/12)$^{(12)(10)}$

F = $1,000,000(1.490833) = $1,490,833

128. D: According to US Bureau of Labor statistics, transportation-related incidents normally account for the highest fatality rates across all industries (approximately 40 percent). The second-highest is contact with objects or equipment at about a 20 percent incidence rate.

Copyright © Mometrix Media. You have been licensed one copy of this document for personal use only. Any other reproduction or redistribution is strictly prohibited. All rights reserved.
This content is provided for test preparation purposes only and does not imply an endorsement by Mometrix of any particular political, scientific, or religious point of view.

129. A: The three fundamental categories of risk management (process) controls are physical, educational, and avoidance. Examples of physical controls are guarding, barriers, and signage; examples of educational controls are knowledge, training, and skills; and examples of avoidance controls are the initiation of programs or incentives by management in support of hazard-aversion reinforcement goals.

130. C: A material's specific gravity (SG) is defined as the ratio of that material's density to that of the density of water and is particularly important when addressing issues resulting from chemical spills. In general, if an SG is < 1, the material will float, and if it is > 1, it will sink. Thus, if the density of Material-X is equal to approximately 3.5 g/cm³ (or 3.5 g/ml), then the SG of that material is calculated as ($Density_x$ ÷ $Density_{H2O}$) = (3.5 g/cm³ ÷ 1.0 g/cm³) = 3.5.

131. C: Human cycles that are believed to affect behavior every 25 to 30 days and can influence facets such as intellect, logic, emotions, strength, and stamina are known as biorhythms. In the workplace (as in everyday life), it is important to recognize that employees will likely have varying degrees of acuity and focus due to these cycles; thus, associated variances in human performance metrics should resultantly be expected.

132. B: Block-and-tackle equipment and devices are regularly used in industrial settings for lifting heavy loads. As such, the generic formula of F = W ÷ x is typically utilized for depicting the relationship between the vertical force (F) and the weight (W) of the lifted load. The "x" in the formula conventionally represents the number of times the connected chain or rope passes between the load end and the anchored end of the block-and-tackle system.

133. A: Database management systems and computer-aided-design (CAD) systems often work best in tandem for optimally improving safety and minimizing hazards in the workplace.

134. B: The two primary standards of the BSCP Code of Ethics and Conduct mandate that certified professionals of all levels uphold the esteem, integrity, and influence of the safety profession.

135. B: Given the following information from the vehicle's onboard computer as well as the vehicle's published technical specifications, the approximate number of miles the tires have been driven can be calculated as follows:

- 92,518,000 driveshaft rotations
- 3.6 driveshaft (DS) rotations = 1 complete tire rotation (straight-line driving)
- 30-in diameter (15-in radius [r]) tires

Tire mileage = (2rπ/tire rotation)(1 ft/12 in)(1 mile/5,280 ft)(1 tire rotation/3.6 DS rotations)(92,518,000 DS rotations) = 38,229 mile

Although the 40,000-mile limit has not yet been officially reached, good safety management practices would mandate that the tires be changed at this point in time. This is all the more substantiated by the visual inspection performed by the fleet manager.

136. C: For the CSP to assess the rate of change (of the functions) at the midpoint of each year (i.e., t = 6), the slopes of the functions must be calculated for each of the functions at the point t = 6. This is accomplished by taking the derivative of each function and then plugging in the value of 6 for "t," globally.

Year 1: $f(t) = t^2 + 4t + 3$: Derivative = 2t + 4; @ t = 6, the slope = 2(6) + 4 = 16

Year 2: $f(t) = 2t^2 - 6t + 1$: Derivative = 4t – 6; @ t = 6, the slope = 4(6) – 6 = 18

Year 3: $f(t) = 3t^3 + 2t - 5$: Derivative = $9t^2$ + 2; @ t = 6, the slope = $9(6)^2$ + 2 = 326

Year 4: $f(t) = 2t^3 - t^2 + 4t + 6$: Derivative = $6t^2$ – 2t + 4, the slope = $6(6)^2$ – 2(6) + 4 = 216 – 12 + 4 = 208

Copyright © Mometrix Media. You have been licensed one copy of this document for personal use only. Any other reproduction or redistribution is strictly prohibited. All rights reserved.
This content is provided for test preparation purposes only and does not imply an endorsement by Mometrix of any particular political, scientific, or religious point of view.

Thus, the function for Year 3 is determined to have the highest slope (i.e., rate of change) at time point t = 6.

137. C: The power (P) in an alternating current circuit where the voltage is 75 V, the impedance (R) is 10 ohms, and the sine of the phase angle (Φ) is 0.643, is calculated via the following:

arcsin 0.643 = 40°

$P = [(V^2)(\cos \Phi)] \div [R] = [(5,625)(0.766)] \div [10] = 431$ watts

138. A: A robust occupational safety program should include, at a minimum, the seven following key categories or tenets: hazard identification, work control, procedural compliance and document control, emergency response protocol, training, incentive programs (e.g., VPP), and proper use and deployment of personal protective equipment (PPE).

139. D: For the case of a $50,000 per annum injured employee going on short-term disability for a period of 3 months at full compensation, followed by long-term disability for a period of 5½ months that pays two-thirds of his regular wage, and then returning to work as a 0.75 full-time-equivalent (FTE) for the remainder of the year, the employee would have resultantly made $38,716 in equivalent income over that year. This is calculated via the following:

{[(0.25 yr)($50,000/yr)] + [(0.4583 yr)($50,000/yr)(0.6667)] + [(1-0.25-0.4583 yr)($50,000/yr)(0.75)]} =

{[$12,500] + [$15,277] + [$10,939]} = $38,716

140. B: The US Department of Transportation (USDOT) should be immediately notified (first) in the event of any accidental release of hazardous materials during transportation. This includes, but is not limited to, any chemical, radiological, or biohazardous media.

141. D: The five prototypical elements commonly associated with a robust risk management program cycle are (1) identification, (2) evaluation, (3) enhancement, (4) training, and (5) feedback. These elements are generally implemented as stand-alone items within the risk management cycle; however, there can often be numerous overlaps and interdependencies among them depending on the precise construct of the subject program at hand.

142. B: A full-face respirator is most appropriate while working in an area with high lead dust concentration levels, which are likely in exceedance of established action levels. Although a half-face respirator in many cases may also be adequately suitable from a respiratory-protection standpoint, utilizing a full-face system provides protection to the eyes.

143. C: The technique of energy isolation is regularly implemented by safety engineers to protect people and products from impacts or damage that may result from accidents. Prime examples include car bumpers, crumple zones, and hard hats.

144. A: Techniques such as peer collaboration, case-study deployment, and role-play are commonly used when attempting to effectively train supervisors and upper management on protocols not specifically laid out in procedural guidance.

145. D: If a plant employee notes that a subject pressure-vessel pressure gauge is reading 625 psia, when it normally operates at 500 psia with a safety variability margin of ±15 percent, the MOST appropriate action for the worker to undertake after reading the gauge is to immediately notify the shift supervisor of the situation and consult the appropriate system contingency plan or procedure on how to appropriately respond to the transient (anomalous) reading.

Copyright © Mometrix Media. You have been licensed one copy of this document for personal use only. Any other reproduction or redistribution is strictly prohibited. All rights reserved. This content is provided for test preparation purposes only and does not imply an endorsement by Mometrix of any particular political, scientific, or religious point of view.

146. A: Electric arcs are a major safety hazard for electrical power industry personnel. These hazards usually result in extremely high temperatures over very small time periods, along with extremely high pressure waves. In addition, airborne shrapnel also typically manifests from such an event. Workers who survive such events are typically the victims of severe burns.

147. C: An individual who is hired for the specific purpose of impartially investigating worker issues or concerns and then suggesting associated resolutions to directorial boards is known as an ombudsman. Such individuals are typically independent contractors or freelancers to the subject organization and have no direct affiliation or history (i.e., subjectivity) with its workforce or management personnel.

148. C: Commonly implemented conflict resolution methods utilized in industry include adjudicative resolution, consensual dispute resolution, and legislative resolution. These methods can employ the use of negotiators, arbitrators, and possibly the court system.

149. B: A chemical tank within an industrial processing facility that has a large, highly visible warning label located approximately 1 ft away from the tank, and is clearly and legibly marked with large, red-colored English print and a clear and straightforward message, is a suitable warning system for such a container. However, given the fact that the facility employs both native English-speaking and Spanish-speaking personnel, the label should be posted in both English and Spanish.

150. C: The development-evaluation phase of the product life cycle usually concludes with the decision of whether (or not) to move forward with a product's development.

151. D: From the information provided, it is not possible to definitively determine with certainty what the subject employee may be experiencing. He or she may possibly just be experiencing temporary muscular or nerve tightness and numbness (and other possible symptoms) that often accompany exposure to cold, or he or she may in fact be possibly experiencing the onset of a stroke. The most appropriate response for the CSP and nurse to undertake in this scenario is to dial 911 for a medical emergency in case it is indeed the latter scenario (given the litany of associated keynote symptoms) and to provide shelter and warmth to the worker until the medical team arrives for its evaluation.

152. B: When undergoing an external audit, the MOST important aspect to an auditor regarding an employee's knowledge of a specific company procedural document is usually whether the employee

is aware of the procedure's existence and knows where and how to quickly access it for reference. Auditors usually do not require employees to memorize any parts of procedures, and in fact, many consider such an endeavor a liability given the increased likelihood of an error or noncompliance when attempting to work from memory, as opposed to having a live or written copy available to follow in a step-by-step fashion.

153. B: Heat is transferred between a human and the surrounding environment through means of:

(1) evaporation, (2) conduction, (3) radiation, and (4) convection. Heat is always transferred from higher temperatures to lower temperatures. Too much heat dissipation can result in cold stress-related conditions, and not enough dissipation can result in heat stress-related conditions.

154. A: MIL-STD-882B is regularly implemented across a wide array of industries for directing the production of procedural guidance within the realm of system safety.

155. B: Air ventilation systems are usually responsible for a variety of functions within the workplace. They facilitate the removal of carbon dioxide (CO_2) buildups, they remove odors, and they regularly eliminate toxins especially through the use of built-in filtration units. They do not, however, directly increase the concentration of indoor oxygen levels (it is accurate to assert, however, that they may indirectly increase oxygen levels via their CO_2 removal capability).

Copyright © Mometrix Media. You have been licensed one copy of this document for personal use only. Any other reproduction or redistribution is strictly prohibited. All rights reserved.
This content is provided for test preparation purposes only and does not imply an endorsement by Mometrix of any particular political, scientific, or religious point of view.

156. D: Tools, refuse articles (rags, empty cans, etc.), and lumber can all be significant tripping hazards depending on the size, weight, balance, and frictional coefficients of the item(s). In addition, uneven floor or ground surfaces, open file drawers, and electrical cables are also regularly responsible for tripping incidents in the workplace. The most appropriate course(s) of action for the CSP would be to immediately notify the responsible work parties in the area to remove, relocate, and/or properly store the articles in question. The CSP should also then notify the area manager in regard to these safety infractions and also recommend remedial safety training for responsible staff members.

157. C: Calculations and assessments performed by insurance companies that evaluate company loss-rate records for establishing worker compensation rates are conventionally known as experience modifiers.

158. D: On behalf of the user and to protect against liabilities, system safety designs normally allocate considerable detail to vital product facets such as proper-use protocols, maintenance, hygiene, safeguards, and ergonomics.

159. A: The construction or modification phase during a facility development process should place considerable emphasis on quality assurance and quality control. Any significant lapse in these areas at this final stage of the process could potentially result in severe consequences.

160. C: In the realm of safety-basis evaluation, a design-basis accident that has a frequency (probability) of occurrence in the range of 10^{-6} to 10^{-4} per year and potential associated consequences in the range of 100 to 300 deaths will have a resulting overall risk range of 0.0001 to 0.03 deaths per year. This is derived given that risk = probability × consequences that an associated range would result from grouping the lowest probability and consequence combination for the low end, and that the highest probability and consequence combination for the high end.

Low end of risk range = 10^{-6} × 100 fatalities = 0.0001

High end of risk range = 10^{-4} × 300 fatalities = 0.03

161. D: Given that Bob and Bill both work in a loud processing area, Bob has partial hearing loss and also speaks with a lisp, and Bill's hearing is unimpaired, it is likely that the frequent miscommunications are due to Bob's deafness, Bob's not speaking clearly, and/or the ongoing loud background noise in the work area. Indeed, the communication issues may be predominately tied to one, two, or possibly all three of these factors; however, there may potentially be even other factors at play that may not be regularly accounted for (e.g., Bill may not have good listening skills or is always preoccupied or Bob and/or Bill may not be good body language communicators, etc.). In summary, there are too many potential causal variables in this case (several more of which may be unknown) to be able to render a firm determination as to the predominant (i.e., most likely) reason why there is so much miscommunication between these two individuals.

162. A: A yellow warning sign that shows a downward arrow intersecting with a worker's hard hat is likely depicting a potential (danger) for falling objects. If the sign were red colored, it would be representing a very high danger of falling objects.

163. C: The law of safety progress states that an organization will undergo fiscal hardship if it generates or disseminates a hazardous product and then ultimately neglects to resolve the underlying issue(s) that is/are causing the hazard.

164. B: Americium-beryllium (Am-Be) neutron sources, and the like, are often used in nuclear reactors and other systems to provide initial quantities of neutrons to help foster an eventual chain reaction that leads to a state of criticality. The most accurate description of how an Am-Be source generates its neutrons is via the employment of an (α, n) nuclear reaction. Americium is a prolific alpha-emitting radionuclide, and beryllium is very susceptible to absorption of such particles (i.e., it has a high alpha cross-section). When an alpha particle

Copyright © Mometrix Media. You have been licensed one copy of this document for personal use only. Any other reproduction or redistribution is strictly prohibited. All rights reserved.
This content is provided for test preparation purposes only and does not imply an endorsement by Mometrix of any particular political, scientific, or religious point of view.

is absorbed by a beryllium atom, the beryllium undergoes a nuclear reaction in which its nucleus moves into a higher energy state and resultantly expels a neutron to regain stability.

165. C: The office warden is usually responsible for taking roll calls during a shelter in place or a building evacuation. These roll calls help to ensure that all employees are accounted for during an emergency situation.

166. B: If a rare event is at hand, such as a significant acid leak in a chemical processing plant, a special safety procedure that covers this type of event should be made immediately available and ultimately implemented for dealing with this type of transient or anomalous scenario.

167. C: According to Frederick Herzberg's theory of behavior, a worker's desired extrinsic outcomes typically include facets such as job security, income, and safe and comfortable working conditions.

168. A: According to statistical measures, workers who have habitual alcohol or drug problems miss work (i.e., incur lost days) approximately 15 times more often than those who do not have such problems. This statistic is especially compounded for those cases in which workers come to work in conditions not fit for duty and must subsequently leave the premises.

169. D: A goniometer is typically utilized within the realm of ergonomics for measuring angles associated with human joints (e.g., knees, elbows, wrists, and ankles).

170. D: A blood pressure reading of 171/79 along with a resting pulse rate of 103 would likely be inferred by an attending physician as a high systolic (hypertension) reading, a normal diastolic reading, and possible tachycardia (rapid pulse).

171. C: There are numerous mechanisms and/or design configurations that can be employed within system components and machinery to create desired resistant forces that serve a functional purpose. Such mechanisms and configurations may include springs, inertia, and viscous damping.

172. B: Decompression sickness can be significantly mitigated by preventing overexposure to high-pressure environments and carefully and steadily employing rates of decompression.

173. A: A computer mouse or joystick is categorized as a continuous control mechanism. Light switches, buttons, and computer keyboards, although control mechanisms, are not of the continuous variety.

174. D: Within the realm of system design, the integration of multiple elements with overlapping functions that permit the continuous normal (ongoing) operation of a given product in the case of one (or more) elemental failure(s) is known as redundancy.

175. B: A system that automatically powers down all major electrical components if the ambient temperature within the facility exceeds a certain predetermined threshold level (due to fire) is an example of a fail-safe system.

176. A: The robustness of hazardous waste shipping containers and casks has been thoroughly tested over the years, primarily at US national laboratories such as Sandia National Laboratory and Los Alamos National Laboratory. Evaluation modes have included thermal (high temperature), high impact, and drop testing.

177. C: The two federal agencies that are primarily responsible for regulating the placement, storage, and amounts of combustible materials within industrial settings are the NFPA and OSHA.

178. B: A static analysis determination is made for a piece of piping that renders the following results:

The overall compression force on the pipe ≈ 50 N.

According to laser-optic results, the pipe has not contracted (or altogether moved) by any discernible amount.

Copyright © Mometrix Media. You have been licensed one copy of this document for personal use only. Any other reproduction or redistribution is strictly prohibited. All rights reserved.
This content is provided for test preparation purposes only and does not imply an endorsement by Mometrix of any particular political, scientific, or religious point of view.

Then a conclusion can be drawn that the pipe's outward directional force should (also) be equal to about 50 N given that the pipe has had no record of discernible movement. This conclusion is in accordance with Newton's Third Law as well as the statics-based fact that the sum of the forces in all directions must be equal to zero if there is no movement by a subject object.

179. A: A negative safety margin value is theoretically correlated with a high risk of failure. A failure would hypothetically be expected to occur before a system or component reaches its predetermined design limit or load.

180. B: There are 10 individual OSHA regional offices presently in existence across the United States. They are located in Boston, MA; New York City, NY; Philadelphia, PA; Atlanta, GA; Chicago, IL; Dallas, TX; Kansas City, MO; Denver, CO; San Francisco, CA; and Seattle, WA.

181. A: There are several unique characteristics regarding regulation criteria of large-quantity hazardous waste generators (LQGs). These include no designated limit of the quantity of HAZMAT that is allowed to be stored at a specific time; the generation of > 1 kg of acute HAZMAT per month; an allowed maximum storage time of 90 days or less for most wastes; and a generation rate of > 1,000 kg per month for ordinary waste classifications.

182. C: In a fault-tree analysis, the term or gate "XOR" represents a condition whereby an output event occurs if exactly one input event occurs. Other terms or gates used in fault-tree analyses include: "AND," "OR," "Inhibit," "Voting-OR," and "Priority-AND."

183. D: Given that farming family injuries do not officially fall under the jurisdiction or auspices of OSHA, it is not necessary for any regulatory agency to be notified. David, may, however, follow any local county protocols for logging or tracking the incident if the associated agricultural cooperative agreement so requires it. Otherwise, no notifications should be made to any organization.

184. B: Per OSHA's 29 CFR 1910.147, *Control of Hazardous Energy*, a hot tap is defined as a maintenance or servicing procedure that entails pressurized welding operations for installing connections or other support equipment.

185. C: An injury to the gonads would be categorized as a privacy case on an OSHA 300 form whereby the employee's name is not ultimately recorded. Other scenarios that could qualify as privacy cases include a mental illness or condition, an injury or illness resulting from a sexual assault, HIV, TB, hepatitis, and potentially contaminated needle-stick injuries.

186. B: Most portable fire extinguishers must be hydrostatically tested once every 5 years. There are certain types of extinguishers (e.g., dry chemical or steel shell, halon, and dry powder), however, that need only be hydrostatically tested once every 12 years.

187. D: A qualitative fit test for a respirator is conventionally defined by a pass-or-fail evaluation to assess the level of fit adequacy based on a wearer's response to a testing agent. In contrast, a quantitative fit test is typically defined as an assessment to determine the suitability of a respirator by measuring the amount of leakage into the device.

188. C: A turtle suit (or a water-armor protective suit) is a form of PPE that is often worn to protect against the hazards of high-pressure water blasting. The suit adequately protects the legs, arms, and chest from glancing water blows for pressures up to 40,000 psi.

189. D: An employee who is regularly subjected to several potential hazards, including strong inorganic acids (e.g., hydrochloric, hydrofluoric, or nitric), excessively loud noise (e.g., > 125 dB, unprotected), and falling objects should be required to adhere to the following PPE regimen in the performance of his or her regular

Copyright © Mometrix Media. You have been licensed one copy of this document for personal use only. Any other reproduction or redistribution is strictly prohibited. All rights reserved.
This content is provided for test preparation purposes only and does not imply an endorsement by Mometrix of any particular political, scientific, or religious point of view.

daily activities: coveralls, safety goggles, earplugs and earmuffs, butyl rubber gloves, and a standard hard hat that can accommodate earmuffs.

Coveralls should be worn at all times to help protect from acid splashes to the torso or limbs; safety goggles should be worn at all times to protect the eyes from acid splashes; and earplugs and earmuffs should be worn due to double protection being required to lower noise levels down to below 8-hr TWA hazardous thresholds. According to ANSI guidance, gloves made of butyl rubber are usually best suited for protecting workers from strong, inorganic acids (e.g., hydrochloric, hydrofluoric, and nitric); and a hard hat (which can accommodate earmuffs worn inside) should always be worn to protect the head against falling objects.

190. C: Ground-fault circuit interrupters (GFCIs) are normally set at about 5 mA to adequately protect workers from electrocution scenarios. The GFCI works by detecting potential leakage current (a ground fault) in a circuit and then ultimately switches off the current in the circuit. This leakage detection is usually via an exposed person who is just beginning to be shocked; once the threshold of 5 mA leakage (loss) is attained, the GFCI switches off the circuit's current in entirety.

191. D: There are several case scenarios that could be categorized as exempt from workers' compensation coverage. These may include such instances as an individual who purposefully elect not to be covered; an individual employed for fewer than 20 consecutive workdays within an employer's private home; an individual performing services in return for nonmonetary compensation (e.g., aid or sustenance) provided by a religious organization or charity; or any person directly employed in agriculture.

192. B: According to Abraham Maslow's Hierarchy of Needs, personal facets such as creativity, problem solving, morality, spontaneity, and lack of prejudice all fall under the human need of self-actualization.

193. C: A permissive democrat-type leadership personality typically permits employees to contribute to decision-making processes and affords subordinates a considerable degree of latitude in carrying out their tasks. Other types of leadership personalities include permissive autocrat (semi-liberal style), directive democrat (semi-liberal style), and directive autocrat (prototypical micromanagement style).

194. D: The Epidemiological Theory of Accident Causation asserts that accidents can, in large part, be caused or prevented by the manner in which situational characteristics interplay with predispositional characteristics. Situational characteristics essentially depict the current state of affairs that workers are engaged in at a particular juncture, whereas predispositional characteristics are those that essentially depict the emotional states and moods of their colleagues.

195. C: The multilinear events sequencing (MES) method usually employs a time line to illustrate the sequence of events or occurrences that contributed to or was the direct cause of an event.

196. C: Retention rate efficiencies vary greatly in humans depending upon what mode of teaching or training is employed for a set of material. Studies have repeatedly shown that teaching or instructing others typically results in the highest material retention efficiency rates by a considerable margin. Employing discussion groups, utilizing demonstrations, and audiovisual training methods have also shown to be effective tools for yielding high retention but not as high as that attained through the teaching or training of others.

197. D: An extremely dangerous shortcut that is all too often taken with pneumatic nail guns and hammers is the taping or fastening down of triggers and switches to attain automatic (effortless), repeated actuation of such tools. Numerous puncture accidents have occurred, particularly in the construction industry, due to this hazardous tactic.

198. A: Per 1910.253(b)(4)(iii), oxygen cylinders in storage shall be separated from fuel gas cylinders (or combustible materials) by a minimum distance of 20 ft or by a noncombustible barrier at least 5 ft in height that has a fire-resistance rating of at least one half-hour.

Copyright © Mometrix Media. You have been licensed one copy of this document for personal use only. Any other reproduction or redistribution is strictly prohibited. All rights reserved.
This content is provided for test preparation purposes only and does not imply an endorsement by Mometrix of any particular political, scientific, or religious point of view.

199. B: For a worker to be permissibly located on a moving (mobile) scaffold that has a base width of 4 ft, the minimum required height for that scaffold must be at least 8 ft. OSHA requires at least a 2:1 height-to-base ratio for mobile scaffolds.

200. C: A hard hat's safety zone is defined as the space or clearance between the hat's shell and its suspension. The typical minimum recommended measurement for this space or clearance is 1 in. Many hard hat manufacturers, however, recommend a space of 1.25 in for additional safety margin.

Copyright © Mometrix Media. You have been licensed one copy of this document for personal use only. Any other reproduction or redistribution is strictly prohibited. All rights reserved. This content is provided for test preparation purposes only and does not imply an endorsement by Mometrix of any particular political, scientific, or religious point of view.

CSP Practice Test #2

To take this additional CSP practice test, visit our bonus page:
mometrix.com/bonus948/csp

Copyright © Mometrix Media. You have been licensed one copy of this document for personal use only. Any other reproduction or redistribution is strictly prohibited. All rights reserved.
This content is provided for test preparation purposes only and does not imply an endorsement by Mometrix of any particular political, scientific, or religious point of view.

How to Overcome Test Anxiety

Just the thought of taking a test is enough to make most people a little nervous. A test is an important event that can have a long-term impact on your future, so it's important to take it seriously and it's natural to feel anxious about performing well. But just because anxiety is normal, that doesn't mean that it's helpful in test taking, or that you should simply accept it as part of your life. Anxiety can have a variety of effects. These effects can be mild, like making you feel slightly nervous, or severe, like blocking your ability to focus or remember even a simple detail.

If you experience test anxiety—whether severe or mild—it's important to know how to beat it. To discover this, first you need to understand what causes test anxiety.

Causes of Test Anxiety

While we often think of anxiety as an uncontrollable emotional state, it can actually be caused by simple, practical things. One of the most common causes of test anxiety is that a person does not feel adequately prepared for their test. This feeling can be the result of many different issues such as poor study habits or lack of organization, but the most common culprit is time management. Starting to study too late, failing to organize your study time to cover all of the material, or being distracted while you study will mean that you're not well prepared for the test. This may lead to cramming the night before, which will cause you to be physically and mentally exhausted for the test. Poor time management also contributes to feelings of stress, fear, and hopelessness as you realize you are not well prepared but don't know what to do about it.

Other times, test anxiety is not related to your preparation for the test but comes from unresolved fear. This may be a past failure on a test, or poor performance on tests in general. It may come from comparing yourself to others who seem to be performing better or from the stress of living up to expectations. Anxiety may be driven by fears of the future—how failure on this test would affect your educational and career goals. These fears are often completely irrational, but they can still negatively impact your test performance.

Elements of Test Anxiety

As mentioned earlier, test anxiety is considered to be an emotional state, but it has physical and mental components as well. Sometimes you may not even realize that you are suffering from test anxiety until you notice the physical symptoms. These can include trembling hands, rapid heartbeat, sweating, nausea, and tense muscles. Extreme anxiety may lead to fainting or vomiting. Obviously, any of these symptoms can have a negative impact on testing. It is important to recognize them as soon as they begin to occur so that you can address the problem before it damages your performance.

The mental components of test anxiety include trouble focusing and inability to remember learned information. During a test, your mind is on high alert, which can help you recall information and stay focused for an extended period of time. However, anxiety interferes with your mind's natural processes, causing you to blank out, even on the questions you know well. The strain of testing during anxiety makes it difficult to stay focused, especially on a test that may take several hours. Extreme anxiety can take a huge mental toll, making it difficult not only to recall test information but even to understand the test questions or pull your thoughts together.

Copyright © Mometrix Media. You have been licensed one copy of this document for personal use only. Any other reproduction or redistribution is strictly prohibited. All rights reserved. This content is provided for test preparation purposes only and does not imply an endorsement by Mometrix of any particular political, scientific, or religious point of view.

Effects of Test Anxiety

Test anxiety is like a disease—if left untreated, it will get progressively worse. Anxiety leads to poor performance, and this reinforces the feelings of fear and failure, which in turn lead to poor performances on subsequent tests. It can grow from a mild nervousness to a crippling condition. If allowed to progress, test anxiety can have a big impact on your schooling, and consequently on your future.

Test anxiety can spread to other parts of your life. Anxiety on tests can become anxiety in any stressful situation, and blanking on a test can turn into panicking in a job situation. But fortunately, you don't have to let anxiety rule your testing and determine your grades. There are a number of relatively simple steps you can take to move past anxiety and function normally on a test and in the rest of life.

Physical Steps for Beating Test Anxiety

While test anxiety is a serious problem, the good news is that it can be overcome. It doesn't have to control your ability to think and remember information. While it may take time, you can begin taking steps today to beat anxiety.

Just as your first hint that you may be struggling with anxiety comes from the physical symptoms, the first step to treating it is also physical. Rest is crucial for having a clear, strong mind. If you are tired, it is much easier to give in to anxiety. But if you establish good sleep habits, your body and mind will be ready to perform optimally, without the strain of exhaustion. Additionally, sleeping well helps you to retain information better, so you're more likely to recall the answers when you see the test questions.

Getting good sleep means more than going to bed on time. It's important to allow your brain time to relax. Take study breaks from time to time so it doesn't get overworked, and don't study right before bed. Take time to rest your mind before trying to rest your body, or you may find it difficult to fall asleep.

Along with sleep, other aspects of physical health are important in preparing for a test. Good nutrition is vital for good brain function. Sugary foods and drinks may give a burst of energy but this burst is followed by a crash, both physically and emotionally. Instead, fuel your body with protein and vitamin-rich foods.

Also, drink plenty of water. Dehydration can lead to headaches and exhaustion, especially if your brain is already under stress from the rigors of the test. Particularly if your test is a long one, drink water during the breaks. And if possible, take an energy-boosting snack to eat between sections.

Along with sleep and diet, a third important part of physical health is exercise. Maintaining a steady workout schedule is helpful, but even taking 5-minute study breaks to walk can help get your blood pumping faster and clear your head. Exercise also releases endorphins, which contribute to a positive feeling and can help combat test anxiety.

When you nurture your physical health, you are also contributing to your mental health. If your body is healthy, your mind is much more likely to be healthy as well. So take time to rest, nourish your body with healthy food and water, and get moving as much as possible. Taking these physical steps will make you stronger and more able to take the mental steps necessary to overcome test anxiety.

Copyright © Mometrix Media. You have been licensed one copy of this document for personal use only. Any other reproduction or redistribution is strictly prohibited. All rights reserved. This content is provided for test preparation purposes only and does not imply an endorsement by Mometrix of any particular political, scientific, or religious point of view.

Mental Steps for Beating Test Anxiety

Working on the mental side of test anxiety can be more challenging, but as with the physical side, there are clear steps you can take to overcome it. As mentioned earlier, test anxiety often stems from lack of preparation, so the obvious solution is to prepare for the test. Effective studying may be the most important weapon you have for beating test anxiety, but you can and should employ several other mental tools to combat fear.

First, boost your confidence by reminding yourself of past success—tests or projects that you aced. If you're putting as much effort into preparing for this test as you did for those, there's no reason you should expect to fail here. Work hard to prepare; then trust your preparation.

Second, surround yourself with encouraging people. It can be helpful to find a study group, but be sure that the people you're around will encourage a positive attitude. If you spend time with others who are anxious or cynical, this will only contribute to your own anxiety. Look for others who are motivated to study hard from a desire to succeed, not from a fear of failure.

Third, reward yourself. A test is physically and mentally tiring, even without anxiety, and it can be helpful to have something to look forward to. Plan an activity following the test, regardless of the outcome, such as going to a movie or getting ice cream.

When you are taking the test, if you find yourself beginning to feel anxious, remind yourself that you know the material. Visualize successfully completing the test. Then take a few deep, relaxing breaths and return to it. Work through the questions carefully but with confidence, knowing that you are capable of succeeding.

Developing a healthy mental approach to test taking will also aid in other areas of life. Test anxiety affects more than just the actual test—it can be damaging to your mental health and even contribute to depression. It's important to beat test anxiety before it becomes a problem for more than testing.

Study Strategy

Being prepared for the test is necessary to combat anxiety, but what does being prepared look like? You may study for hours on end and still not feel prepared. What you need is a strategy for test prep. The next few pages outline our recommended steps to help you plan out and conquer the challenge of preparation.

STEP 1: SCOPE OUT THE TEST

Learn everything you can about the format (multiple choice, essay, etc.) and what will be on the test. Gather any study materials, course outlines, or sample exams that may be available. Not only will this help you to prepare, but knowing what to expect can help to alleviate test anxiety.

STEP 2: MAP OUT THE MATERIAL

Look through the textbook or study guide and make note of how many chapters or sections it has. Then divide these over the time you have. For example, if a book has 15 chapters and you have five days to study, you need to cover three chapters each day. Even better, if you have the time, leave an extra day at the end for overall review after you have gone through the material in depth.

If time is limited, you may need to prioritize the material. Look through it and make note of which sections you think you already have a good grasp on, and which need review. While you are studying, skim quickly through the familiar sections and take more time on the challenging parts. Write out your plan so you don't get lost as you go. Having a written plan also helps you feel more in control of the study, so anxiety is less likely to arise from feeling overwhelmed at the amount to cover.

Copyright © Mometrix Media. You have been licensed one copy of this document for personal use only. Any other reproduction or redistribution is strictly prohibited. All rights reserved.
This content is provided for test preparation purposes only and does not imply an endorsement by Mometrix of any particular political, scientific, or religious point of view.

STEP 3: GATHER YOUR TOOLS

Decide what study method works best for you. Do you prefer to highlight in the book as you study and then go back over the highlighted portions? Or do you type out notes of the important information? Or is it helpful to make flashcards that you can carry with you? Assemble the pens, index cards, highlighters, post-it notes, and any other materials you may need so you won't be distracted by getting up to find things while you study.

If you're having a hard time retaining the information or organizing your notes, experiment with different methods. For example, try color-coding by subject with colored pens, highlighters, or post-it notes. If you learn better by hearing, try recording yourself reading your notes so you can listen while in the car, working out, or simply sitting at your desk. Ask a friend to quiz you from your flashcards, or try teaching someone the material to solidify it in your mind.

STEP 4: CREATE YOUR ENVIRONMENT

It's important to avoid distractions while you study. This includes both the obvious distractions like visitors and the subtle distractions like an uncomfortable chair (or a too-comfortable couch that makes you want to fall asleep). Set up the best study environment possible: good lighting and a comfortable work area. If background music helps you focus, you may want to turn it on, but otherwise keep the room quiet. If you are using a computer to take notes, be sure you don't have any other windows open, especially applications like social media, games, or anything else that could distract you. Silence your phone and turn off notifications. Be sure to keep water close by so you stay hydrated while you study (but avoid unhealthy drinks and snacks).

Also, take into account the best time of day to study. Are you freshest first thing in the morning? Try to set aside some time then to work through the material. Is your mind clearer in the afternoon or evening? Schedule your study session then. Another method is to study at the same time of day that you will take the test, so that your brain gets used to working on the material at that time and will be ready to focus at test time.

STEP 5: STUDY!

Once you have done all the study preparation, it's time to settle into the actual studying. Sit down, take a few moments to settle your mind so you can focus, and begin to follow your study plan. Don't give in to distractions or let yourself procrastinate. This is your time to prepare so you'll be ready to fearlessly approach the test. Make the most of the time and stay focused.

Of course, you don't want to burn out. If you study too long you may find that you're not retaining the information very well. Take regular study breaks. For example, taking five minutes out of every hour to walk briskly, breathing deeply and swinging your arms, can help your mind stay fresh.

As you get to the end of each chapter or section, it's a good idea to do a quick review. Remind yourself of what you learned and work on any difficult parts. When you feel that you've mastered the material, move on to the next part. At the end of your study session, briefly skim through your notes again.

But while review is helpful, cramming last minute is NOT. If at all possible, work ahead so that you won't need to fit all your study into the last day. Cramming overloads your brain with more information than it can process and retain, and your tired mind may struggle to recall even previously learned information when it is overwhelmed with last-minute study. Also, the urgent nature of cramming and the stress placed on your brain contribute to anxiety. You'll be more likely to go to the test feeling unprepared and having trouble thinking clearly.

So don't cram, and don't stay up late before the test, even just to review your notes at a leisurely pace. Your brain needs rest more than it needs to go over the information again. In fact, plan to finish your studies by noon or early afternoon the day before the test. Give your brain the rest of the day to relax or focus on other things, and get a good night's sleep. Then you will be fresh for the test and better able to recall what you've studied.

Copyright © Mometrix Media. You have been licensed one copy of this document for personal use only. Any other reproduction or redistribution is strictly prohibited. All rights reserved.
This content is provided for test preparation purposes only and does not imply an endorsement by Mometrix of any particular political, scientific, or religious point of view.

STEP 6: TAKE A PRACTICE TEST

Many courses offer sample tests, either online or in the study materials. This is an excellent resource to check whether you have mastered the material, as well as to prepare for the test format and environment.

Check the test format ahead of time: the number of questions, the type (multiple choice, free response, etc.), and the time limit. Then create a plan for working through them. For example, if you have 30 minutes to take a 60-question test, your limit is 30 seconds per question. Spend less time on the questions you know well so that you can take more time on the difficult ones.

If you have time to take several practice tests, take the first one open book, with no time limit. Work through the questions at your own pace and make sure you fully understand them. Gradually work up to taking a test under test conditions: sit at a desk with all study materials put away and set a timer. Pace yourself to make sure you finish the test with time to spare and go back to check your answers if you have time.

After each test, check your answers. On the questions you missed, be sure you understand why you missed them. Did you misread the question (tests can use tricky wording)? Did you forget the information? Or was it something you hadn't learned? Go back and study any shaky areas that the practice tests reveal.

Taking these tests not only helps with your grade, but also aids in combating test anxiety. If you're already used to the test conditions, you're less likely to worry about it, and working through tests until you're scoring well gives you a confidence boost. Go through the practice tests until you feel comfortable, and then you can go into the test knowing that you're ready for it.

Test Tips

On test day, you should be confident, knowing that you've prepared well and are ready to answer the questions. But aside from preparation, there are several test day strategies you can employ to maximize your performance.

First, as stated before, get a good night's sleep the night before the test (and for several nights before that, if possible). Go into the test with a fresh, alert mind rather than staying up late to study.

Try not to change too much about your normal routine on the day of the test. It's important to eat a nutritious breakfast, but if you normally don't eat breakfast at all, consider eating just a protein bar. If you're a coffee drinker, go ahead and have your normal coffee. Just make sure you time it so that the caffeine doesn't wear off right in the middle of your test. Avoid sugary beverages, and drink enough water to stay hydrated but not so much that you need a restroom break 10 minutes into the test. If your test isn't first thing in the morning, consider going for a walk or doing a light workout before the test to get your blood flowing.

Allow yourself enough time to get ready, and leave for the test with plenty of time to spare so you won't have the anxiety of scrambling to arrive in time. Another reason to be early is to select a good seat. It's helpful to sit away from doors and windows, which can be distracting. Find a good seat, get out your supplies, and settle your mind before the test begins.

When the test begins, start by going over the instructions carefully, even if you already know what to expect. Make sure you avoid any careless mistakes by following the directions.

Then begin working through the questions, pacing yourself as you've practiced. If you're not sure on an answer, don't spend too much time on it, and don't let it shake your confidence. Either skip it and come back later, or eliminate as many wrong answers as possible and guess among the remaining ones. Don't dwell on these questions as you continue—put them out of your mind and focus on what lies ahead.

Copyright © Mometrix Media. You have been licensed one copy of this document for personal use only. Any other reproduction or redistribution is strictly prohibited. All rights reserved.
This content is provided for test preparation purposes only and does not imply an endorsement by Mometrix of any particular political, scientific, or religious point of view.

Be sure to read all of the answer choices, even if you're sure the first one is the right answer. Sometimes you'll find a better one if you keep reading. But don't second-guess yourself if you do immediately know the answer. Your gut instinct is usually right. Don't let test anxiety rob you of the information you know.

If you have time at the end of the test (and if the test format allows), go back and review your answers. Be cautious about changing any, since your first instinct tends to be correct, but make sure you didn't misread any of the questions or accidentally mark the wrong answer choice. Look over any you skipped and make an educated guess.

At the end, leave the test feeling confident. You've done your best, so don't waste time worrying about your performance or wishing you could change anything. Instead, celebrate the successful completion of this test. And finally, use this test to learn how to deal with anxiety even better next time.

> **Review Video: Test Anxiety**
> Visit mometrix.com/academy and enter code: 100340

Important Qualification

Not all anxiety is created equal. If your test anxiety is causing major issues in your life beyond the classroom or testing center, or if you are experiencing troubling physical symptoms related to your anxiety, it may be a sign of a serious physiological or psychological condition. If this sounds like your situation, we strongly encourage you to seek professional help.

Copyright © Mometrix Media. You have been licensed one copy of this document for personal use only. Any other reproduction or redistribution is strictly prohibited. All rights reserved.
This content is provided for test preparation purposes only and does not imply an endorsement by Mometrix of any particular political, scientific, or religious point of view.

Additional Bonus Material

Due to our efforts to try to keep this book to a manageable length, we've created a link that will give you access to all of your additional bonus material:

mometrix.com/bonus948/csp

Copyright © Mometrix Media. You have been licensed one copy of this document for personal use only. Any other reproduction or redistribution is strictly prohibited. All rights reserved. This content is provided for test preparation purposes only and does not imply an endorsement by Mometrix of any particular political, scientific, or religious point of view.